Science for the Empire

Science for the Empire

Scientific Nationalism in Modern Japan

HIROMI MIZUNO

Stanford University Press
Stanford, California

Stanford University Press
Stanford, California

Printed in the United States of America on acid-free, archival-quality
paper

Library of Congress Cataloging-in-Publication Data

Mizuno, Hiromi, 1969–
  Science for the empire : scientific nationalism in modern Japan /
Hiromi Mizuno.
    p. cm.
  Includes bibliographical references and index.
  ISBN 978-0-8047-7656-1 (cloth : alk. paper)
  1. Science and state—Japan—History—20th century.
  2. Imperialism and science—Japan—History—20th century.
  3. Nationalism and science—Japan—History—20th century.
  4. Religion and science—Japan—History—20th century.   5. Japan—
Politics and government—1926–1945.   I. Title.
  Q127.J3M596 2009
  509.52'0904—dc22
                                        2008024570

Typeset by Bruce Lundquist in 10/12.5 Bembo

To my mother, whose wisdom and
strength inspired me
Mizuno Michiyo (1938–2007)

Contents

Acknowledgments

The production of this book was, like that of any book, a long journey. It is impossible to list all the people who helped me along the way. My foremost appreciation goes to Miriam Silverberg, Herman Ooms, Sharon Traweek, and Sandra Harding, who nurtured me at UCLA. Many thanks to those who read various versions of the manuscript: James Bartholomew, Ellen Gerdts, Laura Hein, Chris Isett, Christine Marran, M. J. Maynes, Grace Ryu, J. B. Shank, Ann Waltner, and Thomas Wolf. Much appreciation to Jennifer Robertson, Ōyodo Shōichi, Koyasu Nobukuni, Miyagi Kimiko, and Matsumoto Miwao for supporting and discussing my work. Special appreciation to Akiko and Hiroshi Miwa, Marcus Thiebaux, and my friends in Japan for various support, copyeditor Cynthia Lindlof, and Muriel Bell and Carolyn Brown at Stanford University Press for making the publication possible. I also offer acknowledgments to the UCLA graduate school and the University of Minnesota for research support. This book would not have existed without my family: Michiyo and Takashi Mizuno, Courtney Aldrich, and my beautiful children, Kumi and Kai, who were born and have grown along with this book. To all these and many other colleagues and friends, the credit and the indebtedness; to myself alone, the faults.

Minneapolis
June 10, 2008

Note on Transliteration

Japanese names appear in Japanese order, with family name first. Japanese names of works in English, however, follow the order given in the publication. Macrons have been omitted from common names, such as Tokyo.

Science for the Empire

Introduction

ON TWO HOT, STEAMY DAYS in July 1942, inspired by Japan's attack on Pearl Harbor, a small group of Japanese intellectuals gathered for a symposium titled "Overcoming Modernity." They discussed the Renaissance, democracy, individualism, and Americanization, among other things. One topic, however, troubled them most: science.

In the words of the main organizer, the symposium, organized as a "Conference of Intellectual Collaboration," was held to deal with a problem that had been "tormenting Japanese intellectuals"—the problem of how to reconcile "Japanese blood and Western intellect."[1] Most of the thirteen participants were literary writers and scholars associated with the Japan Romantic School and the Kyoto school of philosophy, both popular during wartime for elaborating upon spiritualism, aestheticism, and a criticism of reason and objectivity. The symposium did not reach any conclusions about how to overcome modernity, let alone what overcoming modernity meant; but they had things to say about classical Japanese poetry, traditional Japanese music, spiritualism, and gods.

When it came to science, however, evasion and silence prevailed. The symposium's discomfort with the topic of science was clear from the beginning. The first day of the symposium began with a discussion of the Renaissance as the essence of Western modernity. Eventually, a Kyoto Imperial University historian, Suzuki Shigetaka, intervened in this conversation, stating that "when we discuss overcoming modernity, it necessarily includes the problem of how to solve the question of science. We have been saying that overcoming modernity means overcoming the Renaissance, and it is rightly so. . . . [B]ut apart from that, there is a question of science. I think that makes overcoming modernity more difficult and complicated."[2] Suzuki's problematization of the relationship between science and modernity was not pursued further, as the other participants moved on to discuss the relationships among science, magic, and religion in premodern Europe. Although the topic of science continued to come up during the symposium, each time the discussion digressed toward spiritualism and mysticism. When pressed to say something as the only scientist participating, physicist Kikuchi Masashi, who had been silent until then, apologetically stated: "I do feel science needs to be overcome, but I have no idea how."[3]

The uneasiness surrounding the topic of science in fact characterizes the modernity of Imperial Japan (1868–1945), whose history was in part shaped by two potentially opposing aspirations: to be recognized by the West as a modern, civilized nation, as the Western powers were, and to celebrate the nation's particularity to build a national identity. The symposium could not deal with the topic of science, but not because most participants were not scientists. Rather, it was extremely difficult to conceive of a modern yet non-Western science. Not only was modern science introduced to Japan as Western science but more to the point, despite its Western origin, modern science gained legitimacy and authority on account of its supposed universality. Universally verifiable and applicable, modern scientific knowledge made local cultural logics irrelevant. For non-Western nations whose modern national identities were constructed around local cultural logics and mythologies, incorporating modern science into those logics and mythologies posed a problem, even a threat. For Imperial Japan, imperial mythology constituted the absolute core of its national identity and was thus something that could not be made irrelevant by modern science.

Imperial ideology was based on the Shinto creation mythology, according to which Japanese emperors were understood to be the direct descendants of the sun goddess Amaterasu. Low-ranking samurai who overthrew the Tokugawa shogunate (1603–1868) legitimized their new Meiji government (1868–1912) by bringing the emperor to the center stage of national politics, from which the imperial family and aristocracy had been excluded since the fourteenth century. To solidify the authority of the state as well as to instill a sense of national community, the Meiji government elaborated an imperial ideology that emphasized the distinctiveness of the Japanese nation; unlike other nations that had experienced dynastic changes, Japan was a unique nation ruled through the continuing, single line of the divine emperors for more than two thousand years. According to this ideology, Japan was founded in 660 BCE by a great-grandson of Amaterasu, Emperor Jinmu. Although there was (and still is) no evidence of Jinmu's existence beyond an appearance in an eighth-century chronicle, *Nihongi*, the Meiji government officially assigned Jinmu's inauguration day (February 11 of the Gregorian calendar) to be the national foundation day—one of the first national holidays created in Japan. Declared the unique essence of the Japanese national polity (*kokutai*), imperial mythology and authority were incorporated into the constitution (constitutional monarchy) and various laws, taught in schools, and used to justify Japanese colonization of Asia as well as the mobilization of the empire for World War II.[4]

While mythologizing the emperor and the nation, Meiji Japan also promoted a modern economy, industry, and science and technology to survive in the capitalist and colonial competitions of the nineteenth and twentieth centuries. After two hundred years of national seclusion,[5] Japan had lagged behind in military technology and industrialization, which forced the nation to accept unequal commercial treaties imposed by the United States and other Western nations in the 1850s. Meiji leaders were well aware that to maintain the independence of the nation and to rid itself of the humiliating unequal treaties, Japan needed to catch up with Western science and technology.

In Meiji Japan, modern science and imperial mythology did not, by and large, appear incompatible with each other because they were neatly dichotomized as "Western science and technology" and "Eastern ethics."[6] Under the national imperative of "Western science and technology, and Eastern ethics," Meiji leaders hired teachers and technicians from the West, sent students to Europe and the United States, and bought patents from Western countries to acquire the latest knowledge in science and technology. At the same time, they placed a high value on Confucian ethics, which emphasized the filial duty of imperial subjects: obedience both to the nation's father, the emperor, and to the male heads of households. By 1912, when Emperor Meiji died and his son's succession began a new era (the Taishō period, 1912–26), Japan had surfaced as the modern power of the East. Not only had it avoided being colonized by the West but it also had defeated China and Russia in two major wars and acquired Taiwan and Korea as colonies. Imperial authority as well as Confucian-based civic education and laws were firmly established. The simultaneous promotion of Eastern ethics and Western science and technology had worked well.

By the time the wars with China (1937–45) and the United States (1941–45) began, however, this dichotomous characterization no longer existed in Japan. Increasingly oppressive imperial ideology and anti-Western wartime policies led to the banning of many things identified as Western, such as dance halls, hair permanents, political parties, and labor unions, but science was not identified as Western any longer. Nor was it suppressed. In fact, to win modern wars, the state promoted science at an unprecedented level. The state-sponsored Cultural Awards, first announced in 1937, were awarded to more natural scientists than artists and writers under the wartime government. The 1941 state education reform expanded science curriculums of the elementary and middle schools, and the government even launched the Special Science Education Program (*tokubetsu kagaku gumi*) with carefully chosen "scientific genius" children.[7] Things related to science and technology gained popularity among ordinary Japanese as well; in 1942, for example, an increasing popularity and scholarly interest in the history of science led to the establishment of the Japanese Society of the History of Science (*Nihon kagakushi gakkai*), the first and largest of its kind in Japan. In fact, throughout the wartime years, "Scientific Japan" (*kagaku Nihon*) and "Do science" (*kagaku suru*) were popular slogans that embellished both official and nonofficial publications. All these promotions and the popularity of science occurred at a seemingly contradictory moment when imperial mythology and romantic spiritualism were exalted to the extreme.

How did the wartime promotion of science embrace both the rationality that denied mythology and the nationalism that promoted mythology? What kind of science were the Japanese expected to "do"? What did the "scientific" part of "scientific Japan" mean? In other words, how did science promoters and the wartime state "overcome" science, the question that troubled the Overcoming Modernity symposium participants?

These are the central questions this book addresses. The answers this book provides reveal highly complicated and contested discourses of what science was, what Japan was, and what Japanese modernity was. This book is as much a history of the discourse of science as it is a history of nationalism and modernity in interwar and wartime Japan. Scholars have examined Imperial Japan's nationalism and its ideological mobilization of mythology, such as how the imperial ideology was established and disseminated, how traditions were "invented," and how cultural particularism was elaborated by the state and intellectuals. How nationalism mobilized science and how, in turn, the promotion of science mobilized nationalism, however, are new questions. As nationalism and science are two major aspects of modernity, it makes sense to ask how the two worked together in modern Japan.[8]

The discourse of science this book explores is complex and contested because what counted as scientific differed, depending on who spoke of it and for what political purpose. Labeling something "scientific" is not a mere definitional practice but also political and ideological. I am problematizing the word *scientific* here, because a goal of this book is to find what was regarded or claimed to be scientific by Japanese intellectuals and policymakers at the time rather than to judge whether or what part of Imperial Japan was *really* rational or scientific.[9] This book sees science as a dynamic site where its definition and political power are continually contested. The aim of this book is to dissect the politics of the scientific (*kagakuteki*)—that is, what "science" meant—in interwar (1920–36) and wartime (1937–45) Japan.[10] As Pierre Bourdieu argues, science is "a social field of forces, struggles, and relationships that is defined at every moment by the relations of power among the protagonists."[11]

The specific protagonists examined in this book are (1) Japanese technology-bureaucrats (*gijutsu kanryō*), whom I call "technocrats"; (2) Marxist intellectuals who discussed the definition of science extensively; and (3) popular science writers, who developed new genres of popular science (*tsūzoku kagagku*) journalism. These groups of Japanese policymakers and intellectuals had competing definitions of science, yet all ended up contributing to the wartime cry for a scientific Japan. The book traces their attempts to define and promote science in the interwar and wartime years and their differing yet equally complicated trajectory toward the wartime collaborative promotion of science. These policymakers and intellectuals were not the only promoters of science during these decades; however, they were among the most vocal and influential advocates of a scientific Japan.[12] The definition of science was central to all three groups in their own struggles. Although their competing visions for a scientific Japan were all eventually incorporated into the wartime mobilization of science and technology, their politics of the "scientific" were initially developed for entirely different missions and political views. To show how dynamics and challenges specific to technocrats, Marxists, and popular science writers shaped their definitions of science and trajectory to the wartime promotion of science, the following chapters are organized along each group's politics of the "scientific." Part 1 focuses on technology-bureaucrats, or technocrats; Part 2, on Marxists; and Part 3, on popular science promoters.

Some terms emerge in this book as more significant than others, and I should explain how those terms are translated before I introduce the book's protagonists in detail. *Kagaku gijutsu*, a phrase central to Japanese technocratic politics, is translated as "science-technology" in this book. This somewhat awkward translation is due to the lack of any appropriate phrase in the English vocabulary. The Japanese phrase now commonly refers to the general fields of science and technology, with an occasional emphasis on technological aspects of science. When technocrats coined it in 1939, however, it meant something different, as my discussion in Chapter 2 will make clear. I avoid English words such as *technoscience* and *techno-science*, whose connotations do not apply to *kagaku gijutsu* as it was coined in wartime Japan.[13]

Minzoku, which will be discussed in Part 2, is another difficult Japanese word to translate. Although often translated as "the nation," "a people," "*Volk*," "ethnicity," or "civic," *minzoku* in fact has been used to refer to any of these things by different individuals at different times. No single English word covers such historically and contextually diverse meanings. Rather than mechanistically applying a single English word to it, therefore, I find it more appropriate to translate it according to its intended meaning in that specific discourse while making clear the trace of my own interpretation of the word and its context at each translation. The same is true for *kokumin*, which is commonly translated as "the nation." In my view, *kokumin* could and should be translated variously depending on the context, such as "a nation," "the people," or "civic"; accordingly, *kokumin shugi* can mean such different—albeit potentially overlapping at times—things as "nationalism" and "populism." My contextual approach occasionally results in cumbersome English renderings, such as "national people's school" for *kokumin gakkō*, but I believe it provides a more precise understanding of discourses. This approach is true to the book's methodology to ground discourse in specific contexts and politics.

Part 1 (Chapters 1 and 2) examines how Japanese technocrats defined science in relation to their struggles and politics. The key phrase in Part 1 is "science-technology," or *kagaku gijutsu*, previously mentioned as the phrase the technocrats coined for the promotion of their vision of a scientific Japan and of their own political power. "Science-technology" originated in a technocratic movement in early twentieth-century Japan that aimed to raise the status of engineers, to redefine science, and ultimately to realize their vision of a scientific empire. This book focuses on the most important players of the technocratic movement: Japan's first engineers' trade union, the Kōjin Club (*kōjin kurabu*), and its leader, Miyamoto Takenosuke, a civil engineer in the Ministry of Home Affairs.

The Kōjin Club was established in 1920 by Miyamoto and his engineer friends to raise the status of engineers in Japan and to gain decision-making power in the government over policies related to science and technology. Although most of these technology-bureaucrats were elite engineers, they were the minority in a government dominated by graduates with law degrees (law-bureaucrats, or *hōka kanryō*) and constantly had to struggle for equal status and access to power within the bureaucracy. In this book, as "technology-bureaucrat" is an awkward literal translation of *gijutsu kanryō*, "technocrats" is used more frequently in its place, except when the discussion is concerned with law-bureaucrats, for which there exists no adequate translation in the English vocabulary. Chapter 1, which covers the early stages of the movement (1920–32), examines how the Kōjin Club developed trade unionism and class consciousness in the midst of "Taishō democracy" and how its failure to unite engineers based on class politics led the organization and Miyamoto to become nationalist technocrats. Chapter 2 follows the Kōjin Club and Miyamoto up to the wartime years, when the technocratic movement culminated in the promotion of science-technology, which defined science as subservient to wartime technology, while eliminating social sciences from the category. With this new definition of science, the technocrats put forth the vision of the New Order for Science-Technology. To technocrats, science had little to do with universality and critical thinking; rather, a scientific Japan, in their minds, could only be realized when technocrats planned and managed science-technology specifically developed to utilize natural resources in Asia. The technocrats are discussed first among the three groups of the protagonists because of their proximity to policy-making power and the resulting effect that their promotion of science-technology had on Marxists and popular science writers.

Japanese Marxists, discussed in Part 2 (Chapters 3, 4, and 5), developed their politics of the scientific for an entirely different purpose from that of the technocrats. Marxists in Imperial Japan were part of a small minority who vocally challenged imperial ideology and later the military government and its war-making efforts, identifying and criticizing them as "unscientific," "feudalistic," and "fascistic." Promoting what they regarded as scientific was, thus, a central part of Marxist politics toward their vision of a modern, scientific Japan. This book focuses on three Marxist intellectuals who developed a definition of science for this politics: Tosaka Jun, a philosopher and relentless critic of capitalism, fascism, and irrationalism; Ogura Kinnosuke, a historian and mathematician who pioneered the field of the history of science in Japan; and Saigusa Hiroto, a historian and philosopher who established the field of the history of Japanese science and technology. All three were founding members of Yuibutsuron Kenkyūkai, or the Study Group of Materialism (hereafter Yuiken, as the group was called). I identify what I call the "Yuiken project," the group's critique of Japan through the politics of the scientific, by closely analyzing writings by Tosaka, Ogura, and Saigusa inside and outside *Yuibutsuron kenkyū*, Yuiken's monthly publication (1932–38).

Chapter 3 discusses Ogura Kinnosuke's critique of Japanese science in the 1920s and his radical historicization and class analysis of mathematics that his encounter with Marxism in 1929 inspired. Ogura believed that Japan was not as modern as the West because feudalistic remnants hindered the development of the true scientific spirit in Japan. His intellectual engagement with Marxism since 1929 further led him to identify what he saw as the "deformed" Japanese science as the reflection of the unique, "semifeudalistic" Japanese modernity. In his view, promoting the right kind of science—proletarian science, or practical science for the masses—was therefore the crucial step toward a truly modern, scientific Japan.

Chapter 4 examines the Yuiken politics of the "scientific" explored in *Yuibutsuron kenkyū* from 1932 to 1938. The goals of the Yuiken project in the early 1930s were to identify the class nature of science, critique Japan's incomplete modernity, and establish proletarian science in Japan. Critical of "bourgeois science" in the capitalist world, Yuiken Marxists analyzed science as part of the superstructure of society and historicized science to reveal its relationship to the changing economic base. For Ogura, Tosaka, and their Yuiken colleagues, to be "scientific" meant to hold the critical, rational, and universal view espoused by Marxism. The chapter maps out the terrain of the politics of the scientific according to Yuiken leader Tosaka's charting of three political currents in mid-1930s Japan: liberalism, Marxism, and Japanism (*Nihon shugi*), which Tosaka defined as the Japanese version of fascism. Yuiken Marxists believed that Marxism was the only truly scientific theory among them, but as my mapping of the politics of the scientific in 1932 and 1936 illustrates, each of the three political currents claimed the supremacy of its own definition of science. These maps demonstrate the highly contested nature of the discourse of the scientific.

After the war with China began in 1937, the Yuiken intellectuals shifted the target of their criticism from bourgeois science to fascism. They criticized what they saw as the unscientific way the fascist wartime government mythologized the nation and assigned irrationalism as the tradition of the Japanese *minzoku*. The goal of the Yuiken project in the late 1930s was to prove that Japan had a scientific tradition. Chapter 5 looks at this effort, focusing on Saigusa Hiroto's endeavor to carry out the Yuiken project after its dissolution in 1938 by writing a history of science in Japan. Saigusa found the critical, rational, and universal spirit manifested in the Japanese past, the Edo period (1603–1868), and asserted the scientific tradition of Japan in the face of fascism's mythologization of the national past. However, as the state itself began to actively promote the vision of a scientific Japan in the early 1940s, Saigusa's rendering of Confucian intellectuals as modern, scientific thinkers came to be used to celebrate Japan's scientific superiority and to justify its colonization of Asia. The Yuiken Marxists' politics of the scientific, in other words, ironically became part of the wartime celebratory discourse of a "scientific" Japan and empire.

Part 3 (Chapter 6) examines how science was presented and promoted by the media of popular science culture from the 1920s to 1945. It focuses on two popular science magazines, *Children's Science* (*Kodomo no kagaku*) and *Science Illustrated* (*Kagaku gahō*). The genre of popular science magazines emerged in the early 1920s at the intersection of the rapidly developing commercial mass media and the "liberal education movement" (*jiyū kyōiku undō*) that swept Taishō Japan. Harada Mitsuo, the editor, began the pioneering science magazines as a more effective pedagogical alternative to the rigid school science education established by the Ministry of Education. Only through genuine excitement, Harada and liberal education reformers believed, could children be motivated to learn science.

The key term in Part 3 is "wonder." Harada's definition of science and approach to the scientific were different from those of technocrats and Yuiken

Marxists. To him, to be scientific meant to experience and appreciate the wonder of nature. In the pages of these magazines, science was packed and packaged for sale as wonder-filled knowledge that the enlightened nation needed to have. His magazines emphasized the wondrous and spectacular aspects of nature by using the latest visual print technology, and the various acts of seeing and doing were incorporated into the magazines' pages to elicit the sense of wonder. His approach succeeded in creating an active, intimate community of young scientists in the Japanese Empire in the 1920s and 1930s.

These techniques to get children excited about science—the act of sensing the wonder, seeing, and doing—were later utilized by the wartime government to get them excited about wartime science and technology. Moreover, in such efforts as the 1941 science education reform by the Ministry of Education to create the scientific imperial subject, the appreciation of the wonder of nature came to be emphasized specifically as a uniquely Japanese trait. When paper shortages and censorship forced most popular magazines to cease publishing or reduce their pages drastically, the science magazines received support from the wartime government as part of science mobilization. Writers of science fiction, a genre first developed in the popular science magazines, also played an important role in fascinating Japanese children with wondrous, undefeatable Japanese military science-technology. My analysis demonstrates that the sense of wonder, together with the liberal education movement, although initially developed as a critique of the state curriculum, was co-opted by the wartime state for the education of imperial subjects. It turned out that the nature of science and the sense of wonder were highly malleable; science could be easily encouraged either for peace or for war, and the sense of wonder as either universal or Japanese, depending on the current of the time.

The technocrats, Marxist intellectuals, and popular writers in this book represent different segments of society, which allows for the weaving of policy-making history, intellectual history, and cultural history into a history of science, nationalism, and modernity in Japan. I approach this history by incorporating discursive, biographical, and institutional aspects.

Although these protagonists have attracted relatively little attention from scholars, they were influential and visible figures in Japan whose significance lasted into the postwar period. Miyamoto Takenosuke became the vice-minister of the Planning Agency (*kikakuin*) in 1941, an exceptionally high profile for a technocrat. His influence, despite his death during wartime, was central to the post–World War II establishment of the Ministry of Construction and the Science-Technology Agency, the two long-awaited home grounds for technocrats.[14] Ogura Kinnosuke was appointed as the first chair of the Association for Democratic Scientists (*minshushugi kagakusha kyōkai*), the largest organization of natural and social scientists in the immediate post–World War II decade. Saigusa Hiroto is considered one of the most important pioneers of the history of science in Japan; after World War II, he was appointed as the chair of the Society for the History of Science in Japan, established a unique citizens' university (Kamakura Academy) that trained leading historians of technology, and became the chancellor of Yokohama Municipal University. Harada Mitsuo's *Children's Science*, whose publication continues to this day, set the standards for most postwar popular science magazines.[15] Japanese publishers have acknowledged the popularity and significance of wartime Japanese science fiction by publishing the collected works of these writers. Unno Jūza in particular has been awarded this special status, with several "collected works" series published by major publishing houses and most of his works reprinted in various forms.[16]

Besides their visibility and significance, there is one more important reason why these specific figures are discussed in this book: they wrote and published. This book is interested in the discourse of science and nationalism that circulated publicly in Japan, via journals, newspapers, books, museums, policies, and laws, in the increasingly suppressive public sphere of wartime Japan. I do not assume that what was published was a true reflection of what people really thought or agreed about. Rather, a critical discourse analysis, in the words of Norman Fairclough, aims "to map three separate forms of analysis onto one another: analysis of (spoken or written) language texts, analysis of discourse practice (processes of text production, distribution and consumption) and analysis of discursive events as instances of sociocultural practice."[17] In other words, how things are said, expressed, and explained, and how and where discourses are produced and consumed, constitutes a crucial analysis of that society.

Such a critical analysis of discourse is also appropriate for the study of a society, such as wartime Japan, under strong censorship rules. Censorship does not only limit discourse; it also creates it. It creates new language, new rules, new ways of manipulating language and expressing dissidence or collaboration. No matter how repressive censorship becomes, discourse remains a dynamic social and political process.

This is especially relevant for those Japanese Marxists and liberals who continued to publish throughout the wartime years of censorship. Not only does an analysis of discourse allow us to investigate what kind of discourse on science was sanctioned and promoted by the wartime state whose official ideology rested on mythology and cultural uniqueness, but it also demonstrates how those critical of the wartime state used, manipulated, and ended up endorsing the state-sanctioned language and concepts. Rather than simply labeling these Marxists and popular writers collaborationists, this book analyzes how exactly this process took place. It was a complicated process.

Recollecting his own and other intellectuals' experiences during wartime, prominent historian Takeuchi Yoshimi wrote that "[s]ubjectively speaking, it would make more sense to most intellectuals to say that, while continuing to reject and hate the mythology, we became incorporated into the mythology in a doubly and triply warped way."[18] A critical analysis of the discourse of science in interwar and wartime Japan helps us to understand the complex process of this "doubly and triply warped way" of incorporation/participation that was at the same time protest.[19]

Protest can simultaneously be co-optation because the power of ideology does not lie solely in its silencing of the dominated (though I do not dismiss its ability to do so); it also lies in its ability to incorporate the dominated into the system as its active agents. Ideology legitimizes the social and political order while incorporating the dominated as active participants in the process of such ideological construction.[20] Only by being part of the discourse could one participate in changing and challenging the dominant ideology; at the same time, however, participating in discourse as praxis of resistance requires utilizing accepted rules and languages to make one's message comprehensible to the listener or to simply avoid censorship. "Resistance," by way of critically participating in the discourse, could be at the same time incorporation into the dominant ideology.

For the protagonists of this book, the venue for this incorporation/participation was their demand for a scientific Japan. All three groups of science promoters had demanded the construction of a scientific Japan since the 1920s based on their politics of the "scientific." In this regard, they were motivated by what they each identified as unscientific trends in Japan, especially certain practices of the state. For Marxists, it was fascism that defined Japan as uniquely mythological. For technocrats, it was law-bureaucrats, who did not know how to promote science and technology for the nation. For liberal popular science promoters, it was the lack of scientific knowledge among ordinary Japanese that resulted from the state school curriculum. When the state itself actively began to promote science and technology for war in the early 1940s, however, this politics of the scientific was co-opted. By the time the war with the United States began in 1941, these Marxist historians, technocrats, and popular science writers were participating in the construction of the past, future, and utopia of "scientific Japan."

While discussing the intersection of the three protagonist groups at significant moments, Parts 1, 2, and 3 focus on the development of the rich politics of the scientific within each group. The concluding chapter synthesizes the groups' politics of the scientific. It does so by proposing a theory of scientific nationalism. "Scientific nationalism," my coinage, is a kind of nationalism that believes that science and technology are the most urgent and important assets for the integrity, survival, and progress of the nation. The concept helps to make the politics of the scientific in interwar and wartime Japan relevant both to other nations and to present-day Japan.[21] The Japanese government has recently been engaged in vigorous promotion of science-technology, and the discourse of science in this promotion presents a troubling resemblance to that of the wartime science promotion. It is, in my view, important to ponder how science and nationalism mobilized each other under the call for a scientific Japan during wartime and why this specific page of Japanese history has been lost in the nation's memory. I choose to discuss scientific nationalism in the conclusion because the concept of scientific nationalism can only be fully appreciated after understanding the complex and contested nature of the politics of the scientific, and this complexity and contestation of the scientific are what this book aims to demonstrate.

This book begins with the 1920s for a specific reason. There were, of course, promoters of science in Meiji Japan. However, the discourse of science after the 1910s was very different from the previous discourses. It was during the 1910s that, generally speaking, the conception of science as specifically Western disappeared in Japan. As the following chapters demonstrate, science had lost that geographical identification and came to be universalized by the beginning of the 1920s. This was largely due to the level of industrialization Japan had achieved during and after World War I and also to the effect of World War I on the promotion of the domestic production of science in Japan.

World War I is often regarded as a minor war in modern Japanese history. Standard textbooks would explain that Japan, fighting on the side of the Allied powers as a result of the 1902 Anglo-Japanese Alliance, acquired the former German territories of Tsingtao and South Pacific islands (*nanyō*). The significance of World War I, however, goes far beyond the expansion of the Japanese Empire. World War I transformed Japan into a nation of heavy and chemical industries.[22] By the end of the war, the value of industrial production had exceeded that of the agricultural sector in Japan. Whereas light industries such as textiles and spinning had been the engine for Meiji Japan's industrialization, after the 1910s heavy industry became a major source of capital accumulation for the zaibatsu such as Mitsubishi and Mitsui. The growth of these industries was supported by rapidly expanding energy production. With the construction of large-scale hydroelectric power stations—the first was the Inawashiro Hydroelectric Power Station, completed in 1915, which produced the third-largest output of electricity in the world (37,500-kilowatt capacity)—the major source of power shifted from thermoelectric to hydroelectric, marking Japan's transition into the stage of electrification.[23] The latest in science and technology was no longer something that students in the ivory tower learned from Western teachers and textbooks. It was integral to the everyday modernity of Japan.

The rapid heavy industrialization in the 1910s was accompanied by a widening gap between the rich and the poor as well as between the urban and the agrarian areas. Labor and tenant farmer movements had begun to be organized throughout the nation since the early 1910s, and the number of unions increased rapidly and steadily during World War I. The establishment of the Soviet Union in 1917 helped to propel unionism in Japan: the labor conflict reached a prewar peak in numbers in 1919, the first May Day demonstration took place in 1920, and a massive, violent labor strike occupied the Mitsubishi and Kawasaki shipyards in Kobe in 1921. The emergence of the Soviet Union also led to the theoretical development of Marxism among Japanese socialists. Marxism, introduced to Japan in the 1900s as a theory of social movements, came to be clearly distinguished from other theories of socialism, and the Japan Communist Party was founded in 1922 (though banned immediately). Unionism did not appeal only to factory workers and socialists. As we will see in Chapter 1, it appealed to technocrats who wanted to organize engineers across industries as well.

World War I also brought about another change in Japan that is centrally important to this book. The war led to an unprecedented level of the promotion of research and development, or "R&D" as it is now commonly called, in Japan. Japan was one of numerous countries that suffered from the halt of exports from Europe during World War I. The Anglo-French blockade of Germany especially posed a challenge to Japan, which had relied heavily on German supplies of industrial chemicals, pharmaceuticals, and precision instruments.[24] The challenge, however, turned out to be a "blessing from heaven," in the words of renowned Japanese chemist Sakurai Jōji.[25] During World War I, the Japanese government aggressively pursued policies for the promotion of domestic production (*kokusan shōrei*) and invested in building the infrastructure for research and development. The need for the domestic production of science and technology was further amplified as World War I showcased increasingly mechanized and sophisticated technologies and science. It made clear to the Japanese government that an effective promotion and mobilization of science and technology was of vital importance to national defense. The Japanese government sent scientists and military officials to inspect the wartime mobilization of science and technology in Europe and the United States, and in response it issued the War Industry Mobilization Law in 1918 (though it was not implemented until 1937).[26] World War I, in short, demonstrated to Japanese leaders that science and technology were no longer things that could be reliably imported from the West. Japan needed homegrown science and technology. Various efforts were made, therefore, to promote the domestic production of science and research that would support Japan's further industrialization in the decades to come.[27]

To address the immediate problem of material shortages, the Japanese government set up research committees and passed several laws to support domestic production. For example, upon a request by the chemical industry research committee to develop the soda, coal tar, and electrochemical industries, the government promptly passed a law to support the dye- and medical-material-manufacturing industries and guaranteed a newly founded Japan Dye Manufacturing Company (*Nihon senryō seizō kabushiki gaisha*) to cover any economic loss. Likewise, the government swiftly passed the Iron Manufacturing Promotion Law in 1917, based on the iron-manufacturing research committee's report that alerted the government to the shortage of iron and steel. To be sure, these actions did not transform Japanese industry overnight. Once the war was over, for instance, the Japan Dye Manufacturing Company went bankrupt under competition from better German and American products.[28] Nonetheless, World War I pushed the Japanese government to actively initiate the promotion of research and development.

The most notable example of this new interest in research and development is the opening of the Research Institute for Physics and Chemistry (*rikagaku kenkyūsho*; hereafter, the Riken) in April 1917, Japan's first major research facility for the physical sciences, which would later gain an international reputation. The establishment of such an institute was originally proposed in 1903 by scientist Takamine Jōkichi "so that [Japan could] stand among the world powers and keep its place as a first-class nation." Takamine's proposal, however, did not gain adequate governmental support until World War I.[29] A mixed public-private facility, the Riken was administered by the Ministry of Agriculture and Commerce, and its mission was to develop basic and applied sciences in the fields of chemistry and physics for the industrialization of the nation.[30]

Many other changes were made during and immediately after World War I. New research positions and centers were created in universities and by private individuals,[31] and much-needed research grants and awards were newly established.[32] The state also began to actively encourage invention and created the Invention Promotion Fund (*hatsumei shōreihi kōfukin*) in 1917, which provided 30,255 yen (the amount doubled in the following year).[33] The government also passed a new university law in 1918 that upgraded private colleges to universities, despite much opposition from the powerful alumni of Tokyo Imperial University; private universities such as Waseda and Keiō could now utilize the same privileges that the imperial universities had enjoyed to build their science and engineering programs and accommodate a rapidly increasing demand for scientists and engineers.[34] The promotion of research and development continued after the end of World War I. For example, in 1920 the Ministry of Education presented its plan to spend 70 million yen over a ten-year period on the establishment of new research facilities at the imperial universities, the introduction of research professorships, and the completion of Hokkaido Imperial University.

The promotion of domestic production of science and technology reflected the growing recognition that science and technology were "universal." It was understood that anyone, in any culture, could produce modern science and technology. This universalization of things that would have been considered strictly "Western" derivatives in Meiji Japan occurred in many areas of Taishō life. By the 1910s, almost all university teaching, which had been done by European and American professors in foreign languages, was conducted by the first generation of the Japanese faculty who had been trained under them. Western mathematics, which was introduced specifically as "Western mathematics" in place of "Japanese mathematics" under the Meiji education system, was by the 1910s simply called "mathematics" (*sūgaku*). The Japanese modernization process had "caught up" in a temporal sense, such that *modernity* was no longer a synonym for the West but had become part of Japan's everyday life.

These changes in the 1910s—the maturity of industrialization, the promotion of research and development, the universalization of science, and the intensification of class conflicts—created the matrix from which the protagonists of this book emerged. The following pages will demonstrate that promoting science was—and is—never just about science. The discourse of science was at the same time that of the nation, national culture, and modernity.

PART ONE

Technocracy

CHAPTER 1

Toward Technocracy

INTERNATIONALLY, during the 1910s elite engineers began to demand higher status and access to political power. Technocrats (technology-bureaucrats) in Japan, too, responded to the rapid development of heavy industrialization and the rigorous promotion of research and development by organizing themselves to make such demands. Civil engineers in the central government were particularly active in this technocrat movement. They were in charge of the development of the nation's land but had very limited access to policy-making power as a result of the discriminatory Civil Servant Appointment Law (*bunkan nin'yōrei*). The fierce friction between technology-bureaucrats and law-bureaucrats was at the core of the technocracy movement in Japan that would later shape the Japanese Empire's science and technology policies based on the technocratic definition of science, "science-technology." At the center of this technocratic movement was Miyamoto Takenosuke, an engineer in the Civil Engineering Bureau in the Ministry of Home Affairs.[1]

This chapter looks at the early stages of the technocratic movement (1920–32) through Miyamoto and an engineers' organization he founded in 1920, the Kōjin Club, whose objective was to unite engineers and demand access to political power. The trajectory of the Kōjin Club demonstrates how a belief in science and rationality was closely related to class formation and nationalism. As large-scale technological networks were changing Japan's industrial and socioeconomic landscape, the Kōjin Club engineers drew upon the proletarian movement to construct their own class consciousness in their efforts to unite engineers. But they soon abandoned the language and politics of the proletarian movement because they could not translate their engineering background into a unifying class identity. Rather, it was the "scientific" expertise that they realized affirmed their identity as a

group regardless of class. The nation rather than class—industrial rationalization rather than class struggle—provided the language and ideology needed
to transform their cultural capital into political power. Their trial-and-error
search for an engineer's identity led them to develop their technocracy.

Although the term "technocracy" (*tekunokurashii*) was introduced to Japan
only after it became a buzzword in the United States in the early 1930s,[2] the
history of the Kōjin Club demonstrates that Japanese engineers had begun
to develop their own technocracy well before that. "Technocracy" has been
defined in various ways, but it generally entails the rule by experts, technological determinism, and the belief that technological considerations render
politics obsolete.[3] I add to this common definition of technocracy that nationalism is often an important ingredient, at least until a recent global trend
toward regional economic blocs (such as the European Union) rendered
the nation-state less meaningful to technocratic governance.[4] I use "technocrats" interchangeably with elite "technology-bureaucrats" (bureaucrats
in the central government with degrees in engineering, agriculture, forestry,
and other technical and professional fields), and "technocracy" for a specific
vision of governance that these technocrats developed based on their definition of science. As such, Miyamoto and his engineer colleagues' movement
to access political power was both justified and inspired by their concern for
the nation.

Miyamoto and Kōjin Club members also remind us that technocracy,
whether in Japan, the United States, or Europe, was proposed as an alternative to Marxism and thus competed with it to be the better solution to
the economic and labor crises of the early twentieth century. Trust in science, although defined differently by Marxists, played a central role in their
claim to offer better management of society. Like Marxism, technocracy was
critical of the existing capitalist management of society, but unlike Marxism,
which called for the ruling of society by the proletariat made possible by
the "scientific" observation of the history of a society, technocracy called for
management of the nation by engineers with "scientific" expertise.[5] In Parts
1 and 2 of this book, I will demonstrate that the rivalry between technocracy and Marxism did not come only from the competing visions of an ideal
society; it also came from their competing definitions of the "scientific."

Defining Engineers as Creators

The founder and leader of the Kōjin Club, Miyamoto Takenosuke, was an
ambitious and talented man with leadership capability. Miyamoto was born
on Gogo Island, Ehime Prefecture, in 1892 to a once-wealthy merchant
family. The decline of his family's fortune forced him to leave junior high
school and find a job as a sailor when he was fourteen. With the help of his

brother-in-law and a wealthy acquaintance, however, he was later able to enter a private junior high school in Tokyo. A smart, hardworking student, Miyamoto was always at the top of his class; in fact, his grades were so excellent that he was admitted to First Higher School (*daiichi kōtō gakkō*), the most prestigious high school in prewar Japan, without taking the entrance examination. As expected of First Higher School graduates, he went on to Tokyo Imperial University and graduated in 1917 as the "silver watch" student of the Engineering Department (in prewar Japan the top imperial university students received a silver watch from the emperor). The same year, he entered the Bureau of Civil Engineering in the Ministry of Home Affairs. He worked on the nation's two largest river improvement projects, the Tone River project and the Arakawa River project, and proved himself to be a young leader in ferroconcrete construction, a cutting-edge field in engineering. After a state-funded study trip to Europe and the United States (1923–25), he steadily moved up the ladder in the bureaucracy, eventually to the vice-ministerial position, the highest rank that any bureaucrat could attain.

Miyamoto was also a remarkably prolific writer. In addition to numerous technical writings, he published nine books on technology and society written for a general readership and was a regular contributor to the Kōjin Club's monthly publication, *Kōjin*, and other journals. This was highly unusual for engineers, especially for an engineer-bureaucrat. In fact, Miyamoto had once wished to become a writer. During his junior high years, he became attracted to literature, compiled three collections of original works, and seriously considered becoming a literary writer. This was the time in late Meiji Japan when elite youths began to ponder the meaning of life beyond material success—as portrayed well in Natsume Sōseki's *Kokoro* (1914)—and naturalist literature seized the mind of youths like Miyamoto. Only after his brother-in-law persuaded him not to pursue his interest in literature did Miyamoto decide to major in engineering at First Higher School; he came to agree with his brother-in-law that literary life was a decadent, self-indulgent life of "the weak" and "the crippled."[6] Miyamoto, instead, resolved to lead "a manly, splendid life" that was devoted to the improvement of society.[7] He found this "manly, splendid life" in becoming an engineer in the central government.

The "weak," in Miyamoto's mind, not only meant self-indulgent literary writers but also included the poor and the powerless. He was rather sympathetic to the latter but from an elitist perspective. Miyamoto was already greatly interested in labor issues in junior high school and read leftist newspapers such as *Heimin shinbun* and *Yorozu chōhō* to learn about the poor working conditions of destitute workers.[8] He stated in his diary in 1915 that "I have sworn to fight for the human race and help the weak. . . . Oh, how miserable the fate of the weak is. I wish to never forget my responsibilities, to always believe in myself, and to work relentlessly toward my true vocation."[9] Miyamoto was convinced that engineers had a special obligation to solve labor issues because they could mitigate conflicts between laborers and factory owners through technology. He was never interested in joining the labor struggle; he wanted to manage conflicts rather than engage in them. Even though sympathetic to the weak, he differentiated himself from them. As is also clear from his thoughts on literary writers, Miyamoto's elitism led him to look down on the weak and to see himself as their "manly" savior. Historian Ōyodo Shōichi rightly describes him as someone who strove to serve society through the ideal of management (keiseika).[10]

One large hurdle in the way of Miyamoto's ideal of a "manly, splendid" life was the low status of engineers in government offices and in society at large.[11] Considered to be mere technical experts, engineers in public and private offices rarely attained positions powerful enough to direct the nation, companies, and factories. As in the West, where many professional engineers began to demand more power in politics and society in the 1910s, World War I raised the consciousness of elite Japanese engineers and their level of frustration with the status quo. For technology-bureaucrats, this had a concrete meaning. Civil servant engineers were subject to the Civil Servant Appointment Law and the Civil Servant Examination Rule, which together prevented them from attaining high-ranking positions. These positions were reserved for law-bureaucrats, those who studied in the department of law. The Civil Servant Appointment Law stipulated that only those who passed the higher civil servant examinations could be appointed to top positions such as vice-ministers, chiefs of bureaus, and section chiefs.[12] Engineer-bureaucrats were exempted from the examination because it was written specifically for students majoring in law, covering no technical and scientific fields. They were instead hired as bureaucrats through separate appointment. The overwhelming majority of those who passed the examination before 1945 were Tokyo Imperial University law students, with a very small minority of economics majors. Among thousands of students who passed, only a handful were engineering majors ambitious enough to prepare for and pass the exam.[13] This systematically excluded engineer-bureaucrats from the conventional career paths in government offices.

For example, a successful career course for a law-bureaucrat would entail graduating from Tokyo Imperial University, passing the civil servant examination, moving around various sections and bureaus to be trained to be a generalist while climbing the bureaucratic ladder, and ultimately becoming a bureau chief or vice-minister. In contrast, technology-bureaucrats stayed in one section or bureau for their entire careers as specialists, and it took longer for them to be promoted. For engineers and other technical experts, the highest attainable position was "vice-minister for technological affairs" (*gikan*) in a ministry, but even this position was placed under the vice-minister of a ministry, the position held by law-bureaucrats. This system also created a wide gap in salaries between law-bureaucrats and technology-bureaucrats, as much as a difference of ten times at the point of retirement.[14] Some technology-bureaucrats became bureau chiefs and section chiefs, but these were rare cases of individuals who skillfully used their political connections.[15]

Believing that technocrats as a whole deserved to be treated better, technocrats in various ministries began to voice their frustration during World War I. In 1918, leading engineers in industry, the universities, and the central government established Kōseikai, the first political association of engineers, to pressure the government to amend the Civil Servant Appointment Law. In the same year, Furuichi Kōi (1854–1934), a civil engineer and president of Kōgakkai (Japan's first academic association of civil engineers), together with twenty other established civil engineers, submitted a recommendation to the government, requesting the revision of the Civil Servant Appointment Law. The following year, Nōseikai (the association for those with agriculture degrees) and Rinseikai (the association for those with forestry degrees) were established based on Kōseikai's model. Together, the three associations submitted a petition to the prime minister to amend the law. No meaningful response reached them, however. The government's reaction was disheartening to Japan's engineers: though the Civil Servant Appointment Law did go through minor changes, the discriminatory provision against engineers remained. When a group of young technocrats in the Ministry of Agriculture and Commerce proposed the promotion of Matsunami Yoshimi, a renowned forestry expert, to the office of bureau chief, the minister rejected the promotion because appointing a technocrat as head of a bureau would "destroy the bureaucratic order."[16]

It was becoming painfully clear that engineers needed to do something more than occasionally send petitions. Engineers as a whole needed to organize and stand up. Naoki Rintarō, a civil engineer in the Tokyo municipal government, began writing essays in various journals advocating a new type of engineer who was more socially and politically active. His 1918 book, *From an Engineering Life*, is full of inspirational and motivational calls to engineers to raise their consciousness and to work toward the advancement of their social standing as well as that of the nation.[17] Ichinohe Naozō, a former instructor of astronomy at Tokyo Imperial University, succinctly summarized the frustration that Naoki and other engineers endured. In the periodical he edited, *Contemporary Science*, Ichinohe urged engineers to stand up and organize themselves: "Why can't engineers try to unite themselves? Even though there are probably differences among engineers of the public sector and those in the private sector . . . they are all engineers who contribute to the world of engineering. I believe they should form some kind of organization for the advancement of their social position."[18]

Organizing the Kōjin Club was Miyamoto's response to such a call. In October 1920, Miyamoto and eight other engineers gathered in an office in Tokyo and discussed plans to launch Japan's first engineers' trade union, the Kōjin Club. They were all young—in their thirties—and elite engineers with Tokyo Imperial University degrees who were currently or formerly bureaucrats in the central government.[19] Its official establishment with over two hundred members was announced in December 1921.[20] The club made its main objectives the advancement of the status of engineers and the reform of society. Miyamoto wrote the inaugural manifesto, which clearly laid out his technocracy.

The inaugural manifesto was ambitious and radical. Since this manifesto is crucial to understanding the organization's aspirations, its politics, and the direction it would later take, I quote the text at length below. Divided into five articles, the manifesto reads as follows:

(1) Technology is a cultural creation that unites the natural sciences and technique: Technology is creation and an end, not a means; it is absolute, not relative. Culture is not created by technology alone, but human culture in a way has always been [a form of] technological culture. . . .

(2) Engineers are creators: Engineers are not materialists; they should go beyond materialism. It is the responsibility of engineers to actively engage in political economy through the mission of cultural creation. Our activities should not only concern one aspect of society but should embrace the whole of human life.

(3) The position of the engineer is just like the pivot of a pole: We acknowledge that the capitalistic trade union is not a healthy social institution. Capitalists and workers should not be in a master-slave relationship. Capitalists and workers, who share rights and responsibilities, are equal tools in the creation of technological culture. It is the responsibility of engineers to lead capitalists and workers.

(4) The Kōjin Club is the source of the creation of technological culture: Its function and organization should include the whole society. We will establish an academic section to develop technology, a trade union section to train section, and a finance section.

(5) The Kōjin Club uses rational means: It is a worldwide trend that economic movements for class struggle are becoming political movements. The Kōjin Club not only aims to protect the technological class. Considering the vocational responsibility of engineers to advance the level of social life for the human race, we avoid radical, direct actions and strive to realize our ideas by leading a social movement with our delegates to the Diet and by raising the consciousness of the political masses.[21]

This manifesto puts forth three definitions. First, it defines technology and engineers; engineers are creators, and technology is a creation that is the end itself rather than a means. Second, it defines engineers' class identity and location in society; engineers are located between capitalists and workers ("the pivot of a pole") and thus have the responsibility and the capacity to solve labor problems. Third, the manifesto defines what is rational and irrational; engineers have a responsibility to improve society and to use "rational means" for that goal, such as sending delegates to the Diet. It follows that engineers do not consider "radical, direct actions" rational. The radical and innovative character of these definitions becomes clear with a deep contextual and intertextual analysis. I will now discuss the first definition, that of engineers and technology; the second and third points about class, unionism, and political strategies will be examined in the next section.

One of the goals of the Kōjin Club was to raise the status of engineers in the bureaucracy and in society, to launch "a war against so-called law-bureaucrats." Asserting in 1920 that engineers were creators was a bold and ambitious challenge to the bureaucratic hierarchy that viewed engineers as mere technical experts useful for the implementation of projects and policies over which law-bureaucrats and politicians reigned. Moreover, the manifesto declared, engineers were creating not simply technology but in fact a technological culture.

Technology as creation was also drastically different from an earlier view of technology that found expression in the Meiji slogan "Western science and technology, and Eastern ethics." The Meiji government took pains to import the latest knowledge and techniques of science and technology from the West to build industry and a military that could compete with the West. At the same time, the Meiji government strengthened its political authority by incorporating the imperial ideology and Confucian ethics into the 1889 constitution, civil and penal codes, compulsory school education, and military training systems. In this earlier understanding, science was something to be learned and imported from the West to coexist with Eastern ethics. Technology as creation, however, rejected any explicit association with the West. In the same manner in which the vigorous promotion of research and development during and after World War I assumed the universality of science and technology (see this book's Introduction), the Kōjin Club's manifesto asserted the capacity and agency of Japanese engineers as creators of new science and technology rather than as consumers of Western science and technology. Technology, as defined by the Kōjin Club in 1920, was no longer something to be borrowed or imported; it was something to be created by Japanese engineers.

In fact, an attempt to define technology (*gijutsu*) itself was a new endeavor in 1920. According to historian of technology Iida Ken'ichi, the compound word for technology did not gain popular currency until the Taishō period. The compound *gijutsu* (技術) itself had existed in Japan and China for a long time, but it was rarely used. Instead, characters such as 工 (*kō*; craft), 芸 (*gei*; learning), 術 (*jutsu*; art/technique), and 技 (*waza*; performance/technique) were more commonly used for knowledge and work related to technology. The boundaries between learning, art, craft, and technique were a modern product of the late nineteenth century. Thus, whereas scholars have translated Sakuma Shōzan's famous 1854 dictum as "Western science and technology, and Eastern ethics," Sakuma used the compound *geijutsu* (芸術). This compound, which in present-day Japanese denotes "fine art," meant various kinds of artistic and technical skills and learning in nineteenth-century Japan. Meiji dictionaries continued to reflect this overlapping of art and technology.[22]

The blurring of boundaries between art, technology, learning, and science was not a unique Japanese phenomenon. In English, too, these boundaries were not established until the early twentieth century. Jacob Bigelow's *Elements of Technology* (1829) is often regarded as the book that introduced the word *technology* into popular English, but he used it to mean useful arts or accumulated knowledge, something very similar to Sakuma Shōzan's *geijutsu*. Moreover, Bigelow's neologism was largely ignored by the American public until the beginning of the twentieth century. Scholars generally locate the emergence of the contemporary meaning of "technology" in English lexicons in the decades between the 1880s and 1930s.[23] This was the case in Europe as well. One may recall that Karl Marx, who was highly devoted to analyzing the relationship between technology and humans, did not use the word *technology*.

The word *gijutsu* also went through the same transformation in Japan between the 1880s and the 1930s, with the contemporary meaning of "technology" emerging only in the late 1910s and the 1920s. In Japanese, the demarcation of *gijutsu* as technology, separate from art and other learning, began in the 1870s in a small circle of intellectuals and government officials.[24] Although *gijutsu* as technology appeared more frequently in various writings in the 1880s, the common understanding of technology nonetheless remained centered on arts and crafts until much later. Japan's first industrial encyclopedia, *Kōgyō daijiten* (1913), still listed English, German, and French words for "art" in the *gijutsu* entry and defined *gijutsu* as that which "can be understood as synonymous to '*geijutsu* [art].'"[25] By the 1930s, however, the word *technology* had become a familiar term in Japan, and in the mid-1930s the first serious scholarly discussion on the nature of technology—as we understand it now—took place. In 1937, citing the above-mentioned *Kōgyō daijiten*, historian of science Saigusa Hiroto wrote that "it is clear that the concept of technology was still very vague back then [in 1913], though Japan was already beginning to industrialize itself with full force. Today, however, . . . people know what 'technology' is, even though they may not be able to define it exactly."[26] What, then, happened in the late 1910s and the 1920s that established the contemporary meaning of "technology"?

Historian Leo Marx explains in the context of U.S. history that it was the building of large-scale technological systems such as the railroad system that led to the replacement of earlier terms by the contemporary term "technology." By the end of the 1920s, terms such as "the machine" and "mechanical art" no longer adequately described massive networks webbed by collections of machines, devices, and knowledge. The locomotive, the quintessential nineteenth-century symbol of progress in the West as well as Japan, had become part of colossal railroad systems by the early twentieth century. Similarly, telecommunication and power networks, factory systems, and industrial complexes had all developed into large technological networks.[27] World War I played a significant role in this transformation. Just like Japan, Europe and the United States experienced serious shortages in dyestuffs, pharmaceuticals, tungsten, zinc, and other items during the war.[28] Historians Susan Douglas and Thomas Hughes, for example, have shown how during World War I military and corporate control over science and technology replaced the nineteenth-century model of the lone inventor-entrepreneur.[29] The era of machines, in other words, became the era of technological networks. As historian Charles Maier puts it, "The engineer, who was central to the new industrial gospel, appeared not so much a master of machines as a potential manipulator of all industrial relationships."[30] Thus, it is not a mere coincidence that the attempt to articulate technology in a radically new way in Japan came from Miyamoto and his engineer-bureaucrat friends who were in charge of building large national networks of infrastructure. It is also not mere chance that such an attempt took place in 1920, immediately after World War I.

The concept of technology as creation was also radically different from the popular imagery of technology in Taishō Japan. Street-poster collections common to this era show that two kinds of visual representations of technology and humans were dominant. The predominant image is of a female consumer enjoying technology. Advertisement posters—not only for products specifically targeted at women, such as cosmetics and kitchen products, but also for radios, subway lines, and cruise trips—very frequently featured beautiful women next to the product. The other representation is of a male worker raising his fist against factories or machines in posters for labor unions, for May Day demonstrations (which began in 1920 in Japan), and, after the passing of the universal suffrage law in 1925, for proletarian political parties.[31] Absent from this popular visual imagery of technology are the engineers who actually designed, maintained, and developed technology. The Kōjin Club's definition thus placed (male) engineers as the creators vis-à-vis the feminized consumer and the masculinized proletarian.

As clearly declared in the manifesto, the Kōjin members believed that engineers could and should create a new social order, one that would do away with the capitalist-labor conflict. Their reference to the pole as a metaphor explains their vision well. With the engineer (the pivot) bearing the pole, capitalists and workers would sit at either end in perfect balance. Thus, the engineer was understood as creating a nonhierarchical relationship between worker and factory owner that neither owner nor worker could create.

Behind this seemingly humanistic ideal was a strong sense of the engineers' moral superiority, even arrogance, as social elites. A brief comparison with a Marxist definition of technology in Japan will make this point clearer. A dominant Marxist understanding that emerged in the mid-1930s held that technology is a "system of means of production," a definition that still has currency in contemporary Japan.[32] Although technology in this definition is a system of means that serve human production, the Kōjin engineers considered technology as the end itself, whose potential is brought to the fullest by engineers; workers and capitalists were the means to achieve this. Also indicated in the Kōjin Club's definition of technology is that only the degree-certified engineers were capable of assuming the leadership role. In Taishō Japan, this meant the exclusion of women and the majority of men from that category. Until the end of the war, only a small percentage of the Japanese population went to universities, and women were not admitted to imperial universities (except Tohoku Imperial University). The fact that the manifesto considered sending a representative of the club to the Diet itself indicates the social and economic standing of the members that it anticipated. In 1920, five years before the proclamation of universal suffrage for men, only 5.5 percent of the entire population—men who paid more than three yen of tax—were eligible to vote. The Kōjin Club's emphasis on the training of the character and spirit of engineers as future leaders further distanced engineers from workers. The differentiation between engineers and workers was also made on the basis of rationality. The manifesto distinguished engineers' "rational" unionism from laborers' confrontational and "irrational" unionism.

The Proletarianization of Engineers

Uniting and unionizing engineers, however, proved to be more difficult than Miyamoto Takenosuke had expected. The most challenging question the Kōjin Club faced was that of class. The organization grew in size from the starting membership of two hundred to more than five thousand by the mid-1920s by absorbing nonbureaucrat engineers. This was remarkable, since other technocratic organizations ceased to be active or disbanded by the latter half of the 1920s. However, the diversity of member engineers in terms of their political views and socioeconomic backgrounds provoked a fierce debate among members as to whether engineers could be united as a class and where the engineers' union should be located in the political spectrum. The demarcation that the manifesto drew between the engineer and the worker was slowly engulfed by the bourgeoning mass political movements of "Taishō democracy" by workers, minorities, feminists, and leftists.[33] How the Kōjin members reacted to and appropriated the "Taishō democracy" movements for their own purposes is detailed here. We will examine their struggles to establish the engineers' identity in the politically volatile decade of the 1920s through the pages of the organization's monthly publication, *Kōjin*.

One movement of "Taishō democracy" that particularly inspired the Kōjin members was the Leveling Movement, a liberation movement by the social minority who lived in special villages (*tokushu buraku*) and had been discriminated against since the feudal period. They organized the Leveling Society in 1922 to fight against the social and economic discrimination they had historically suffered. The Kōjin members soon began to refer to their own technocratic movement as the "Leveling Movement for engineers." To the Kōjin members, engineers were much the victims of the system as the *buraku* people. Such identification provided a powerful rhetoric with which to raise the engineers' consciousness. The front page of *Kōjin*'s June 1923 issue asked its readers: "Do we, the engineers, want to remain the *tokushu buraku* of society?"[34] If engineers did not want to, *Kōjin* writers insisted, then they had better join the Kōjin Club.

The sense of injustice and the need for leveling inequality were keenly felt especially after the great Kantō earthquake of September 1923, which devastated the Tokyo-Yokohama area. The prospect of radically reshaping Tokyo excited the governor of Tokyo, Gotō Shinpei, as well as civil engineers all over the nation. Both the Kōjin Club and Kōseikai submitted detailed proposals as to what physical improvements new Tokyo should achieve and how to rebuild the city's infrastructure according to such planning. Governor Gotō, with his grandiose vision of transforming Tokyo into another Paris, proposed a large budget for the project, but most politicians and citizens demanded a quick reconstruction rather than a systematic yet slow rebuilding of the city. After much debate and lobbying, both the budget and the scale of city planning were radically reduced. Engineers were as frustrated and disappointed as Governor Gotō. Their proposals were ignored, and those who were assigned to the Tokyo reconstruction project had to deal with pressure to get the job done quickly from politicians and law-bureaucrats who did not care much about engineering perspectives. Naoki Rintarō, who was assigned to be head of the Bureau of Reconstruction, recalled this position as the most difficult job he ever had to perform in his life. The Tokyo reconstruction project left elite engineers extremely frustrated and feeling powerless.

More decisive in fostering rapid membership growth and influencing Kōjin politics were the passage of the universal male suffrage law in 1925 and the resulting development of proletarian party politics. The increasing intensity of Taishō mass movements pushed the reluctant government to broaden the electorate before the situation became too radical (while simultaneously passing the Peace Preservation Law, which suppressed socialism, communism, and anarchism). With the new suffrage law, approximately 21 percent of the population—men older than twenty-five, regardless of income—gained the right to vote, increasing the number of eligible voters fourfold. Subsequently, numerous parties were created in anticipation of the general election of 1928, many of which were proletarian parties organized by leftist activists seeking a legitimate venue for political participation instead of going underground with the Comintern-led, outlawed Japan Communist Party.

Miyamoto had long been interested in the trade unions for intellectual workers that had emerged in the West. His trip to Europe and the United States from 1923 to 1925 strengthened his conviction that trade unionism was the best way to unite engineers and to voice their demands. The main purpose of this seventeen-month study abroad was to collect materials on reinforced concrete, on which he wrote a thesis after his return and earned the Engineering Award and his D.Sc.Engr. from Tokyo Imperial University.[35] But Miyamoto also used this opportunity to learn about trade unionism in the West, especially in England, visiting such organizations as the Fabian Society; the Labor Party; and the Federation of Professional, Technical and Administrative Workers.[36]

Radical engineers were quickly caught up in the fervor of party politics. Although the Kōjin Club's manifesto painstakingly differentiated engineers from laborers, its attempt to seek a broader base of engineers for its movement brought in leftist engineers with proletarian politics. Koike Shirō and Koyama Toshio were among the most vocal Kōjin members who argued for the merger of the engineers' movement with the proletarian movement. Koike had been a close friend of Miyamoto since high school and was his classmate at Tokyo Imperial University. While working for a mining company, however, Koike decided to devote his life to social reforms and moved to Tokyo. Miyamoto and Koike shared an ideal of British-style labor unionism; by 1925 Koike had published a book on the British Labor Party and translated a work by Sidney Webb, the British socialist. Koike continued to write and translate works on class, socialism, and the international Communist movement in the 1920s while he was actively involved in the Kōjin Club.[37] Koyama had been involved in the engineers' movement since his university days. With support from Miyamoto, Koike, Koyama, and other leftist engineers pushed the organization to affiliate with the proletarian movement.

The Kōjin Club also drew closer to the proletarian movement because of the proletarianization of engineers caused by the recession that began immediately after World War I. With the expansion of engineering fields at higher-education facilities during World War I, a larger number of engineers were being produced, but the post–World War I recession limited employment opportunities. For most young engineers, finding a job became very difficult, and even having an engineering degree from imperial universities no longer led to an elite career path. The Kōjin Club's growth meant that its membership no longer represented only elite engineers but also embraced those whose life styles and income were much closer to those of laborers than of elite bureaucrats.

By 1925 a change in the Kōjin's political and ideological direction was clear. *Kōjin*, for example, began to fashion itself as a leftist liberation movement's magazine. The 1925 cover of the journal had in red letters the German phrase "Die Zeitschrift des Vereines" (Club Journal) alongside the title *Kōjin*; the style was clearly taken from a popular leftist magazine, *Kaihō* (Liberation). The shift in Kōjin politics was reflected in a change in the list of invited lecturers as well. In the early 1920s, the club had maintained a strong tie with the Kyōchōkai (Harmonizing Society), the government-sponsored think tank charged with "harmonizing" labor-capital conflicts. Sharing a common goal of "harmonization" as the ideal way to mitigate labor conflicts, the Kōjin Club had regularly invited Kyōchōkai members to its lecture series. By 1926, however, the club was instead inviting more stridently leftist speakers, including renowned socialists such as Abe Isoo and Ōyama Ikuo.[38]

Because the language, symbols, and organizational skills of the proletarian movement proved to be powerful tools for political struggle in the 1920s in Japan, the Kōjin Club appropriated them for its own empowerment. The club's trade unionism was not considered a form of spiritual cultivation any longer. In 1925, the members now declared that "our organization, needless to say, aims to be a trade union based on class consciousness."[39] The Kōjin Club's 1925 agenda included "the organization of an employment agency and a consumer cooperative for engineers," "the opening of engineers' vocational schools," and "the publication of engineering books and pamphlets"—activities that the labor unions pioneered.[40] Contrary to their earlier identification as mediators between the two classes, the Kōjin members now associated themselves with workers and characterized engineers as an oppressed class. The lead article of the May 1925 issue made this declaration:

A social movement is a class movement [*kaikyū undō*]. It is the class movement in which the majority of the ruled, against the minority of the rulers, demand the reform of life [*seikatsu kaizen*] and the establishment of social justice.... Our nation only has a weak sense of class, ... and this is even truer among engineers.... If we do not wake up now, we will never be able to escape from our lot as slaves. . . . We cry out loudly for the unionization of engineers and demand social justice. Come, those who share this resolution. . . . Engineers will not be ruled forever. We envision the day when Japan will establish itself through industry and be ruled by engineers.[41]

This was one of the most radical and explicit statements that the Kōjin Club made regarding the rule of the nation by engineers. It makes a sharp contrast with Kōseikai, whose chair around the same time declared that Kōseikai was not a "so-called political organization" and that it would have nothing to do with political activities.[42]

Uniting engineers according to class politics, however, proved to be extremely difficult. For one thing, it was not exactly clear which class was the "technological class." Engineers were in a precarious position: on the one hand, they were like any other workers who, without ownership of the means of production, were at the bottom of a hierarchy in their own field; on the other hand, those with university degrees and employment in the government and major corporations clearly belonged to the social elite. During the latter half of the 1920s, the Kōjin Club spent much energy debating the precise relationship between engineers and class.

On this question, club members were split between those who regarded engineers as part of the new middle class (*chūkan kaikyū*) and those who argued that they belonged to the proletariat (*musan kaikyū*). To define engineers as the proletariat, leftist members used new language to characterize engineers. For example, Koike argued that there were only two classes in capitalist society and that engineers must therefore belong to the working class as "brain workers."[43] Another member argued that engineers were "proletariat intellectuals," the rearguard of the proletarian movement, whereas laborers and farmers were the vanguard.[44] Part of the problem was that the concept and socioeconomic reality of *musan kaikyū* in Japan was still in the process of being determined in the 1920s. *Musan kaikyū*—literally, "propertyless class"— was very new vocabulary, which began to be used in Japan as a translation of "the proletariat" only after 1919. A key term by the 1920s, it was not always clear to whom it referred. *Shakai undō jiten* (1928), a dictionary of terms related to labor and mass movements, gives a vague, confusing definition of *musan kaikyū* as follows: "Strictly speaking, the modern working class, or factory workers. But it generally includes the propertyless people who earn a living by physical and intellectual work."[45] According to this dictionary, then, engineers were "generally speaking" proletarians, but "strictly speaking" they were not. The Kōjin Club's debate reflected as much a process of creating an identity for engineers as the larger creation of class as a category in Japan.

Ultimately, the Kōjin Club decided to proletarianize engineers by adopting the phrase "brain workers." In 1926, Koike and Koyama were elected to the club's board, and in July of that year, the directors' board voted to rewrite the bylaws of the club to proclaim that "this organization represents engineers as brain workers." The club also adopted a Marxist explanation for the oppressed conditions of engineers, emphasizing the class character of the engineer problem: "It is no longer bureaucrats and businessmen who oppress engineers: engineers are exploited by the economy."[46] After all, Koike explained, the majority of the five thousand engineer members of the club were low-paid employees.[47] With the development of capitalism, engineers "became modern proletarians who sell a commodity called 'technology' in exchange for clothes and food only to barely survive."[48]

The new direction of the organization also politically affiliated the Kōjin Club with a proletarian party. Koike was a member of the left-wing Political Studies Group (*seiji kenkyūkai*) organized in 1923, a group established by Abe Isoo and Yoshino Sakuzō to prepare for the passage of the new suffrage law. The Political Studies Group soon became the Socialist Mass Party (*shakai minshū tō*), a party aligned with the Japan Federation of Labor (*sōdōmei*), which was to the right of the proletarian movement. Through Koike and Koyama, the Kōjin Club officially declared its affiliation with the Socialist Mass Party (hereafter, the SMP) immediately after that party's establishment. The SMP, in return, appointed Koike and Koyama as members of its central committee. In December 1927, *Kōjin* announced the SMP's endorsement of Koike's candidacy in the upcoming election. It was unheard of for an engineering association to be an official supporter of a proletarian party, and the SMP members did not uniformly welcome the Kōjin Club. Some members severely criticized the party for aligning itself with engineers, whom they considered "capitalists' aids."

Within the Kōjin Club, too, the organization's explicit endorsement of a proletarian party caused much tension. Some argued that since engineers belonged to various social and economic classes, they could not be united behind a single social movement. Miyamoto, in contrast, did not see any incongruity between the two categories. He continued to defend trade unionism as the ideal form of the engineers' movement. Although many club members wondered whether engineers constituted a class, Miyamoto believed that occupation and class went hand in hand. "Occupation and class cannot be completely separated," he continued to argue in 1926. "The trade union movement is the most effective and the best movement for us to rationally lead society."[49]

The honeymoon of the SMP and Kōjin Club, however, did not last long. As membership in the Kōjin Club grew to fifty-five hundred in 1926 with its unionism attracting nonelite and leftist young engineers, conservative members became increasingly concerned with the club's politicized activities and direction. Soon after the club's board announced its party affiliation, a member from Osaka complained to the directors: "How dare you lure our members into the short-sighted, vulgar conflict [of party politics] through something like the Socialist Mass Party!" This member found it unacceptable for engineers to "forget the nation and society and to behave selfishly like the ignorant and blind workers."[50] The members of the Sapporo branch also believed that the SMP misrepresented the interest of engineers, and they passed out ballots through *Kōjin*, asking all members to vote on whether the club should support the SMP.[51] Another member argued that Koike Shirō and Koyama Toshio, graduates of the elite universities, were blinding club members to the real problem for engineers, the dominance of law-bureaucrats, by leading them astray into anticapitalist politics.[52] Aside from these political disagreements, there was also a practical concern. One board member warned that although the club's affiliation with the SMP would be an effective way to send an engineer delegate to the Diet, the club lacked sufficient funds to remain involved in party politics.[53] Throughout 1928 and 1929, in every issue of *Kōjin*, vocal members on both sides of pro- and antiparty politics exchanged intense criticisms of each other, alarmed by a sense of crisis. The exchange escalated to unproductive personal attacks, to the point that one member gave up, saying, "[A]fter all, this is a matter of personal ideological differences."[54]

Finally, internal opposition became so strong that the club decided to disassociate itself from the SMP. Koyama and Koike were voted off the board of directors in January 1928, a month before the first general election under the new suffrage law. The new board members immediately removed the phrase "brain workers" from its bylaws, which now stated that the club was "a trade union of engineers" whose aim was to "advance engineers' welfare and to promote the healthy development of technology." In February, the board declared that the club would not support any specific political party. The following year, the club even deleted the term "trade union" from its bylaws because it was "a misleading term that overly emphasizes class consciousness." "The purpose of the club," the bylaws now stated, "is to break down the wrongs of society, to establish the status of engineers, to facilitate the development of industry, and to contribute to the culture of our society and to improve its welfare."[55] After the conservatization of the Kōjin Club in 1929, it lost many members and its dynamism faded. In 1932, a member would send a message of grief that "our organization's situation these days is utterly lamentable for those who know the dynamic activity of the past."[56]

With the decline in membership, it was clear that the Kōjin Club's attempt to mobilize engineers through class consciousness had failed. But this failure was not merely about unionism or party affiliation. Deeper-seated questions remained: What should the identity of engineers be, and how could they be united? Miyamoto, an original advocate and adamant supporter of trade unionism, continued to argue that trade unionism was the most appropriate form to represent and protect engineers' interests. By 1930, however, even he had grown rather pessimistic. He confessed that "in reality it is perhaps impossible to have a trade union with members like ours who come from such diverse backgrounds."[57]

During the latter half of the 1920s, the Kōjin Club's political stance wavered between left and right, struggling to find a mediating middle. At the height of the club's class politics in 1927, some members came to demand radical social change, like Takeda Harumu, who asserted that "politics should be entrusted to the hands of those who are directly engaged in production."[58] Takeda's assertion here came very close to the American technocracy of Howard Scott, which would reach Japan five years later. However, before these radical demands could earn majority support, they stirred grave concern and disgust among conservatives. Miyamoto put it well in 1930 when he said: "Perhaps it is understandable that my attitude has been criticized as 'too mild' from the left and 'too radical' from the right. My dilemma, I think, was at the same time the dilemma of the club."[59] Although the manifesto declared that the organization would find the middle position between the capitalists and the workers, finding such a middle position on the political spectrum was not so easy.

Koyama's essay in 1925 had already identified this difficulty. In hindsight, this article reads like an ironic prophecy, but when written, it was meant to be a story (with a sarcastic touch) designed to urge his fellow rank-and-file engineers to commit to unionism. Santarō, a protagonist in Koyama's essay, becomes an engineer rather accidentally and gets a job in a shipbuilding yard. He works from seven in the morning to nine at night and has to apologize if he ever leaves work at five or takes a Sunday off. He is tired of the stifling real world. One day, shipyard laborers go on strike, but office workers and engineers continue to come in and stamp their time cards for fear of losing their bonuses. Santarō, who learned about engineer unionization in college, becomes disgusted by the apathy of the "middle class" and begins preaching unionism. As he succeeds in union organizing, however, the managers find him annoying and his coworkers and laborers look at him with suspicion. He must have an ulterior motive. Maybe he is going to use the union to run for election. Given the cold shoulder from both above and below, Santarō feels demoralized and sad. At the end of his first five years as a salaried engineer, Santarō "settles his accounts" with his past:

What's gained: wife and children, illness, debt, and vulgar savvy.
What's lost: health, spirit, and innocence.
What's not changed: salary, position, and faith.[60]

In 1925 when this was written, Koyama had Santarō proudly retaining his unchanged "faith" in unionism, despite his awkward "middle" position between workers and bosses. On the Kōjin Club's balance sheet, however, by the 1930s faith had been added to the "what's lost" category.

The French cadre (industrial engineer) union movement, examined in Luc Boltanski's work, shows that this problem of unionizing the "middle" class was neither unique to the Kōjin Club nor to Japan. The class consciousness of the cadre owed its origin to the proletarian movement, as was the case with the Kōjin Club. One cadre unionist explained that "as soon as one class becomes conscious of its existence, as the working class has now done, it forces all the others to do the same. . . . [A]nd the first thing that a reinvigorated class does is to demand its rights and privileges."[61] In unionizing themselves as a class, French cadres faced a dilemma similar to that encountered by the Kōjin Club. Santarō's plight in Koyama's essay is strikingly similar to that described by the French cadre unionist Georges Lamirand, who wrote in 1932: "In every firm, on the day the occupation began, workers' delegates headed straight for the owner's office. . . . The engineer? He was out of the picture. . . . Abandoned by both sides, engineers discovered that they were neither fish [n]or fowl, that they constituted a third party imperil[ed] on two fronts, in the sad position of an iron caught between hammer and anvil."[62]

Like the Kōjin Club unionists, the French cadres were the "middle" class caught between capitalist and proletariat. Also caught between left and right on the political spectrum, as Boltanski explains, the cadres maneuvered to "outflank established positions by creating a new image of the center."[63] Neither right nor left, the French cadres struggled to maintain a politically middle position. The case with the Kōjin Club was similar. Neither capitalists nor laborers, the Kōjin Club's engineers were a new group of technological experts that emerged in industrializing Japan in the 1920s with their diplomas distinguishing them from the other Japanese. Awakened by the proletarian movement, proud of the significance of their expertise, they could ultimately not find an answer to the question of how to reconcile their diplomas, a form of cultural capital, with proletarian politics that divided the world on the basis of economic capital.[64]

From Class to the Nation

The Kōjin Club failed to organize engineers through class politics in the 1920s. In Miyamoto Takenosuke's analysis, engineers had failed to form a strong union because they did not constitute a socioeconomic class. Miyamoto realized that "it is harder to build a solid organization for engineers with various interests than for a camel to enter the tiny hole of a needle. As I have witnessed actual examples of this difficulty, I cannot but sigh for grief over the difficulty in uniting engineers."[65] In my analysis, however, the members' different socioeconomic standings were only one factor in their failure. Another important factor was the club's failure to produce a discourse that would convince engineers that they could and should be united regardless of their socioeconomic differences. A social group, as Pierre Bourdieu has argued, needs to have a language and an ideology to distinguish its members from others, and such language and ideology need to be grounded to some degree in how individuals perceive reality.[66] The ideology and language of proletarian politics were clearly not grounded in the reality that the Kōjin members perceived.

The Kōjin Club's political trajectory reflected the general trend in Japan. By the early 1930s, the era of "Taishō democracy," cosmopolitanism, and proletarian politics was over, and reactionary, promilitary nationalism was on the rise. In 1929, Yamamoto Senji, the former Labor-Farmer Party (*rōnō tō*) activist and birth control promoter, was assassinated by right-wing nationalists. The party cabinet system collapsed in 1932, with the dissolution of the Friend of Constitutional Government Party (*rikken seiyūkai*) cabinet and the succession of the prime minister Okada Keisuke, a navy officer. Many scholars of technocracy, such as Beverly Burris, point to the transcendence of politics as the most important characteristic of technocracy.[67] Japanese technocrats' apostasy and transcendence of politics came from their disappointment in party politics. The corruption of Diet members, sensationally embellishing newspaper headlines in the latter half of the 1920s, disillusioned activist engineers as well as the general Japanese public with party politics. By the end of the 1920s, party politics seemed dysfunctional, unable to provide an effective means for engineers to present their interests. For many engineers, politics no longer appeared "rational." Even Miyamoto came to think that party politics was an "anachronism of the pre-1930 period."[68] The June 1930 issue of *Kōjin* republished the club's founding declaration of 1920, as if it were unmaking the engineer class. In the place of class, the technocrats needed something else with which to start anew the demoralized organization. They found it in "the nation."

One *Kōjin* article, "Patron, Nationalism, and Me," critically described how nationalism had grown to be an effective alternative to class politics during the last few years of the 1920s. Sakata Tokikazu, the author, portrayed the power of nationalism as analogous to the power that a patron bestows on an actress or a geisha. According to the article, the presence of a patron enables the client to act boldly, and many Japanese began to use nationalism to advance their own interests. Sakata explained that magazines such as *Jitsugyō no Nihon* (Business Japan) and *Sokoku* (Homeland) had taken nationalism as their patron because an appeal to it raised sales, and noted that "Marxism is becoming more and more oppressed."[69] This essay was critical of the trend. The author called nationalism a "feudalistic thing" and sarcastically compared nationalism with a geisha patron to emphasize the frivolous and profit-making nature of the recent nationalists.

However, the Kōjin Club was no exception in making nationalism its patron. While a few members such as Sakata criticized this trend, the Kōjin Club was also leaving class politics behind and embracing nationalism as its new focus. Miyamoto as the leader declared that "we retreat from the front-line of class war and enter a new battle by and for engineers."[70] This move, according to him, was based on two realizations:

First, it is impossible for an organization like ours to hope to develop as a trade union as traditionally defined because our organization embraces a diverse member-ship. Second, even if trade unionism is not entirely impossible, we have to make the nation [minzoku] our priority at a time like now when, as the recent international situations show, the conflict between minzoku has become so intense. . . . We have decided to revise our principle: "[T]he Kōjin Club aims to guide national opinions from the technological perspective. . . ." This is a tenkō that should be noted in the history of our organization.[71]

The word tenkō, strictly speaking, refers to the political conversion from communism and/or Marxism to nationalism that many Japanese activists and intellectuals went through in the last years of the 1920s and the early 1930s due to the government's suppression. By the early 1930s, the word was used more generally to refer to a political conversion from class politics to nationalism.[72] Earlier, Miyamoto had argued that occupation and class of engineers could not be separated. By 1934, though, this was no longer his conviction: "I still believe that a trade union is the most rational social and political unit. However, a trade union and a class need to be clearly distin-guished, at least in theory."[73] For him, the new and more important concern now was the survival of the Japanese nation, not a class. As he stated, "I be-came very concerned with issues of nations [minzoku], population, and colo-nization, issues that are opposite of democracy, and I get excited whenever the topic of struggles of nations [minzoku] comes up."[74]

Provoking nationalism was not something new in Kōjin Club discourse. Even as early as 1925, when the proletarian rhetoric embellished Kōjin, the September issue declared:

Legal supremacy, bureaucratic supremacy, capitalist supremacy, and party suprem-acy: all these unpleasant evil practices that deepen domestic conflicts are a crime to the nation because they prevent national efficiency. . . . We engineers will be the vanguard. Now is the time we stand at society's front line under the banner of what we in the Kōjin Club have been advocating for years. When the iron arms of engineers are put into full force, how the nation will flourish. Mighty engi-neers . . . gather under our banner! Unite! Advance! For our homeland, for our homeland.[75]

There is, of course, no inherent reason why proletarian politics and nationalism should be regarded as mutually exclusive ideologies.[76] The difference before and after the 1929 shift of the Kōjin Club is that the nation replaced class completely in its efforts to establish the identity of engineers, its attempts to unite engineers, and its struggle to access political power.

It was the industrial rationalization movement (*sangyō gōrika undō*) that finalized the shift in the Kōjin Club's focus from class to the nation. Industrial rationalization was one of the main policies advocated by the Hamaguchi cabinet (1927–31) to alleviate the impact of the Great Depression on Japan and to prepare for the lifting of the embargo on the export of gold. At this point, Japan was the only nation in the industrialized world that had kept an embargo on gold, originally imposed during World War I. Exchange fluctuations made Japan's foreign trade difficult and kept the balance of trade in the red after 1919. By removing the embargo, the Hamaguchi cabinet hoped to stabilize the exchange rate, improve exports, and energize the domestic economy, which had been in recession since 1927. Industrial rationalization with its premise of efficiency was advocated by men like Ōta Masataka, economist and politician, and Dan Takuma, head of the Mitsui conglomerate. Hamaguchi's "industrial rationalization movement" established the ad hoc Industrial Rationalization Bureau (*rinji sangyō gōri kyoku*) and focused on several measurements: the promotion of capital accumulation through cartels, the consumption of domestic products, standardization, and the harmonization of labor relations through scientific management.[77]

To its advocates, who thought of the movement as the "second industrial revolution," industrial rationalization was not meant to be a mere solution to the immediate problem of the depression.[78] According to *Jiji shinpō* (Current Topics), whose editors were major proponents of the policy,

[industrial rationalization is] not exactly an idea of capitalists or the working class's demand or an invention of socialists. Nor is it exactly the creation of Americans or the realization of the German imagination or the result of British thought. Rather, it is an opportunity of the new times . . . emerging from the chaotic atmosphere made by all those above. . . . Our economy stands at a critical turning point. . . . We are faced with the critical need to completely rationalize industries based on specific Japanese conditions while keeping up with the world standard.[79]

More than a solution to the troubled economy of Japan, it was meant to be a reform of the entire industrial structure for future Japan.

Critics of industrial rationalization worried that Japan would not be able to carry it through. For example, Ishibashi Tanzan, editor of a major economic journal, *Tōyō keizai shinpō* (East Asian Economic News), argued that Japanese industries were not strong enough to launch such a program. Forcing rationalization, like "spinning a machine without lubricant oil," would only increase the unemployment rate.[80] Teruoka Gitō, director of the Research Institute for Science of Labor (*rōdō kagaku kenkyūjo*), was also wary of what it might do to the welfare of workers.[81]

The technocrats in the Kōjin Club, however, strongly supported the industrial rationalization policy and dedicated the May 1930 issue of *Kōjin* to the topic. While aware of a likely increase in unemployment, they argued nonetheless that it had to be carried out for the sake of the nation. After all, one member wrote rather irresponsibly, its effects on employment could only be known after it was carried out.[82] They lamented that proletarian parties were opposed to rationalization only because capitalists initiated it, when the real concern should have been that of the nation, not one segment of society. According to Miyamoto, industrial rationalization meant "taking action under the principle of the *Yamato minzoku*," since its aim was to save the nation, not just one class.[83] Moreover, he argued, proletarian parties had not done anything for Japan's "real" problems, such as overpopulation or lack of natural resources. In their minds, it was not proletarian politics but engineers' expertise that could and should guide Japan's future. "Doesn't the Kōjin Club," Miyamoto clamored, "have a responsibility to establish policies from the perspective of the engineers?"[84] As the concept of class acquired the negative meaning of "selfishness" in the Kōjin Club, the "nation" was now used to argue for the significance of the "engineer's perspective."

By this logic, those who did not have the engineers' perspective were incapable of saving the nation. Kōjin engineers shifted the focus of their adversary energy from economic exploitation back to law-bureaucrats who refused to share decision-making power and thereby wasted engineering expertise. To the engineers, it was utterly lamentable that when the nation required a major reformation of its industry, policies regarding technology and industry were made and carried out by law-bureaucrats who did not know anything about engineering or science.[85] Just as the engineers' movement had compared the social standing of engineers to that of those with *buraku* origin, so did its indignation at the discrimination against the engineers' origin—in this case, the Department of Engineering—remain a main theme of the Kōjin Club.

It seems, however, that this was also a tricky issue because the leading Kōjin members were themselves bureaucrats who worked side by side with law-bureaucrats. One member wrote in 1928 that when the Kōjin Club's Osaka branch was formed, the branch bylaws did not mention a challenge to the dominance of law-bureaucrats. "If it wants to challenge [the law graduates]," he wrote, "it should state so in its bylaws. . . . Of course, engineers have no such courage. We too have a weak spot. If the anti–law graduates agenda becomes an official motto, the club may attract many lower-level engineers but would not be able to keep the elite engineers."[86] Even though it was not always explicit, the Kōjin Club had nonetheless always maintained a critical position against law-bureaucrats and dreamt of the day when engineers could become political leaders like their American hero, Herbert Hoover.[87]

The technocrats' belief in their capacity for managing the nation derived from their claim that they understood what it meant to be "scientific." The January 1931 issue of *Kōjin* declared that "engineers are all scientists. We, who truly understand natural phenomena, can also truly understand social phenomena."[88] To them, it was clear that the engineer's scientific training would necessarily endow him with the capacity to scientifically understand social matters. As we will see in Part 2, Japanese Marxists around this time began to develop their own definition of science, based on their belief that Marxism, or scientific socialism, provided the truly scientific way of understanding society. Although Miyamoto and other Kōjin members endorsed the idea of trade unionism in the 1920s, their unionism came from their positive assessment of the British Labor Party, not Marxism. As for Marxism, Miyamoto had nothing positive to say. He argued that "so-called scientific socialism" was really unscientific, a mere "dogma of a good-hearted socialist who does not know what mathematics is or what science is," and he would "waste no time" reading leftist magazines such as *Kaihō*, *Kaizō* (Reconstruction), or *Gendai* (Contemporary). Even though Miyamoto was at least sympathetic to the "good-heartedness" of socialists who cared about social ills, to him it was engineers, not Marxists, who could provide a scientific way to cure the ills of Japan, as engineers really knew "what mathematics is and what science is."[89]

Other Kōjin members also shared this mistrust in the scientific claim of Marxism. The lead article of *Kōjin*'s January 1926 issue harshly criticized the government for banning the first proletarian party, the Farmer-Labor Party, merely three hours after its establishment in December 1925. The focus of the anonymously written essay was the government's "reactionary" way of dealing with "irrational" thought like communism. Forceful suppression of socialism and communism, this author argued, would only invite people's distrust in the government, just as it did when the police unwarrantedly killed anarchist Ōsugi Sakae in the aftermath of the Kantō earthquake in 1923. Communism was not dangerous but "irrational," the author continued. "Why can't the Japanese government become like the British government" and choose to provide quality education instead of coercion so that people would not accept such an irrational thought?[90] Elsewhere, an elementary school science teacher, Hashimoto Tameji, also argued in 1929 that "it seems that those who sympathize with socialism and communism are those who have not mastered rational thinking.... If there are more elementary teachers who study science and mathematics harder during these hot summer days, these political problems would be simply solved."[91] To Kōjin engineers and intellectuals like Hashimoto, "scientific" education meant the training of the "exact" and "experimental" attitude, which would prevent the spread of "irrational" and "unscientific" Marxism and communism. To technocrats, the scientific understanding of nature and society meant the scientific management of nature (through rational means provided by technology) and society (through industrial rationalization), not by way of class analysis or proletarian science, as advocated by Japanese Marxists.

At the same time, technocrats' pride in being scientific also refused to align with the political right. A member asserted in 1931: "As long as the nationalist and patriotic movement is based on mythologies and anecdotes, it [will] deny science, dry out culture, and prevent the development of the nation [*minzoku*]. We need to criticize old, superficial mythologies or anecdotes in order to raise a new *minzoku* spirit, a new *minzoku* movement."[92]

In the rationalization of the nation, technocrats found the place where they could use their expertise to the fullest extent. In this "scientific" service to the nation, they found the place where they could secure the middle position between "irrational" Marxism and the equally "irrational" extreme right. They believed that they were more "scientific" than believers of scientific socialism because they were trained in science. They believed that they were more useful to the nation than the right-wing nationalists because they could provide science and technology to the nation, instead of nonsense mythologies and anecdotes. To these engineers, they alone—neither left-wing activism nor right-wing romanticism—could create a new Japan, a scientific Japan. After a decades-long search for a unifying identity for engineers, the technocrats finally found a middle position between right and left in the technocratic vision of a scientific Japan.

CHAPTER 2

Technocracy for a Scientific Japan

THIS CHAPTER follows the development of the technocratic movement into the 1930s, when the technocrats became interested in Manchuria and China, and into the war years, 1937–45, when their technocracy finally bore fruit. Natural resources on the continent attracted the Kōjin Club technocrats who were concerned with the lack of natural resources in Japan. They linked Manchuria to their earlier vision of the engineer as the creator of a new culture; to them, resources in Manchuria and China were the materials provided by heaven with which they could engage in "creation"—the creation of new technological culture, a powerful empire, and a scientific Japan. This would lead them to envision their role in creating the scientifically and technologically superior Japanese Empire after Japan entered the war with China in 1937. This chapter examines how Japanese technocracy, which began as a solution to the class problem at home in interwar years, came to define what it meant for the Japanese Empire to be scientific.

The onset of the war with China marked the beginning of the full-fledged state science and technology mobilization for total war. The technocrats' discourse of "technological patriotism" (*gijutsu hōkoku*) is very revealing here because the technocrats, who considered the engineer central to the empire, argued that the technological expert alone could sustain the hierarchy between Japan as a scientific leader and China as its resource provider. It demonstrates that besides the kind of racializing nationalism that emphasized the superiority of the "Japanese spirit" and "blood," wartime Japan also embraced a nationalism that based its claim of Japan's superiority entirely on its advancement of science and technology. As this chapter argues, this division of labor in Asia constituted the core of the technocrats' vision of a new order in Asia, the "New Order for Science-Technology" (*kagaku gijutsu shin taisei*).[1]

The wartime coinage of *kagaku gijutsu*, or "science-technology," by the technocrats was central to the technology-bureaucrats' politics of the "scientific."[2] Science-technology can be summarized as the demand for the independence of technology both at home and internationally. First, it meant the independence of technology from law-bureaucrats in Japan. Science-technology defined science in relation to strategically important fields of technology, while excluding social sciences and basic science that had little direct practical implication. Science-technology also challenged the existing mapping of administrative jurisdiction, which the technocrats viewed as hindering the effective and efficient synthesis of technocratic policies. Second, the independence of technology also meant the independence of Japanese technology from Western patents, researchers, and materials. The technocrats' "anticolonial" sentiment against the West was simultaneously translated into colonial desire. They argued that for Japanese science and technology to be independent of the West, Japan needed to have unrestrained access to the resources of Asia; in return, Japan would provide Asia with the science and technology necessary to protect Asia from Western imperialism. The New Order for Science-Technology was to achieve all these goals for a "scientific Japan." Although the new order movement only partially realized the bureaucratic power that the technocrats had dreamt of having, "science-technology" did become the established phrase of wartime Japan, shaping thinking and the priority of policies related to science and technology. In other words, by asserting "science-technology," the technocrats successfully changed the field of the politics of the "scientific." For such politics, Manchuria and China were indispensable.

The Colonial Landscape of Technocracy

The failure of unionization and the unchanging low status of technocrats in the 1920s proved to the Kōjin Club leaders that the domestic political terrain was no fertile ground for technocracy politics. They turned their attention to a frontier abroad: Manchuria.

Manchuria had been a contested region among Russia, China, and Japan since the mid-Meiji period. Japan stationed the Kwangtung garrison in south Manchuria in 1905 (reorganized in 1919 as the Kwangtung Army) and established the semipublic company, the South Manchurian Railway (*minami Manshū tetsudō gaisha*; hereafter Mantetsu), in 1906 to control the area. Built on the former Russian railway that Japan acquired as a result of the Russo-Japanese War in 1905, Mantetsu developed south Manchuria into a profitable "kingdom" that attracted many Japanese with "an immediate taste of empire."[3] However, with the rise of Chinese nationalism in the late

1920s demanding the unification of China, including Manchuria, tensions surrounding the region became extremely high. As the Nationalist Party in China led by Chiang Kai-shek advanced north and the Manchurian warlord Chang Hsüeh-liang pledged his allegiance to the Nationalist Party, the Kwangtung Army decided to do something. In 1931 it secretly blew up a section of the Mantetsu, blamed the Chinese troops for it, and used the incident as an excuse for a military seizure of Manchuria by Japan. The following year, the Japanese government established a puppet state, Manchukuo. The League of Nations did not acknowledge Manchukuo and instead dispatched an investigation team, the Lytton Commission, to examine who really destroyed the railway. Japan soon withdrew from the League of Nations.[4]

Most Japanese, including Kōjin technocrats, never questioned the nature of the Manchurian Incident. Instead, they quickly joined what Louise Young describes as "war fever," that is, the media hype that created the image of utopian Manchuria.[5] In March 1932, in the midst of the Lytton Commission's investigation, *Kōjin* published a special issue on Manchuria, calling the region "our Mecca, the most fertile place for the salvation of the engineers' world."[6] Kōjin leader Miyamoto Takenosuke saw Manchuria as a virgin land free of law-graduate supremacy where engineers could advance their status and construct a new technological culture. It was in this sense that, to Miyamoto and other technocrats, Manchuria was a "Mecca."

There were, in fact, a few voices among the Kōjin members critical of Japan's invasion of Manchuria. Sakata Tokikazu, for example, criticized that the "so-called Japan-China friendship" (*Nisshi shinzen*) simply meant "the colonization of China," which would only make China angry and the United States and Britain nervous. He worried that such a move by Japan would possibly result in a second world war.[7] Another member wondered whether the occupation of Manchuria would bring any benefit to Japan. After all, this member said, "Japan's enormous investment in Korea only produced many Korean laborers who pushed out our own workers into the life of '*rumpen*' [lumpen; i.e., homeless and jobless]."[8]

However, such voices were rare. The pages of *Kōjin* after March 1932 were saturated with a salute to Japan's colonization of Manchuria. Koike Shirō, who had left the SMP and become a Diet member representing the Kōjin Club, maintained that "freedom of economic activities in Manchuria is indispensable for the survival of our proletarian class" and argued that what needed to be criticized was the monopoly of Manchurian benefits by the Japanese bourgeoisie and military.[9] Even those who found the usual state slogans about Manchuria empty and brazen concluded that "a real, active fusion between Japanese and Manchurians" would make a mutual relationship possible.[10]

Miyamoto was one of the most enthusiastic supporters of the Japanese occupation of Manchuria. He had been interested in China since junior high school and even wished to take an internship in Manchuria when in college, though his visit to China was not realized until May 1931.[11] Miyamoto argued:"All humans should have the freedom and the right to live wherever they wish and to collectively develop natural resources for the welfare of the whole human race."[12] According to him, it was hypocritical for the Western nations to hinder Japan's freedom and right over Asia; after all, even Christ "encouraged profusion and immigration of the human race."[13] Contrary to the popular image of China at the time as antiquated and languid, Miyamoto perceived China as "still so young."[14] This arrogant denial of China's long history of civilization came from his view of China as a place of uncultivated natural resources. Miyamoto argued that it would be best if "Japan and China were to create a heaven of truly mutual prosperity by having Japan provide China with 'organization' and 'technology' and China supply its 'resources.'"[15] Japan, in other words, would discipline and train "young, immature" China, and China would provide resources necessary for the schooling. Such a self-serving logic was a typical rationalization of Japanese colonialism among technocrats, to whom Manchuria was especially attractive because of its natural resources and flexible political system.[16]

Natural resources were in fact the Achilles heel of Japan, whose growing heavy industry relied heavily on imports. Exploring for new resources had become such a desperate concern that it even established a new field of science after the Manchurian Incident, "resource science" (*shigen kagaku*) or "resource chemistry" (*shigen kagaku*). Katō Yogorō, a researcher at the Research Center for Resource Chemistry established in the Tokyo Institute of Technology in 1939, explained that "resource chemistry is a totally new term that probably doesn't exist in any other countries. . . . Before the Manchurian Incident, our country was a so-called country of have-nots. But now, all sorts of new resources are open to us."[17]

The wealth of natural resources and the loose political system resulting from its newness made Manchuria appear to be the most promising place in which to create a new technocratic culture. The word *creation* (*sōsaku*) quickly became the key word in the technocratic discourse of Manchuria (and of the empire later). The technocrats' frequent and symbolic use of the word *creation* reminds us of the 1920 inaugural declaration of the Kōjin Club. It was there that "creation" was first articulated as a mission for engineers. After more than a decade of their unsuccessful movement to raise the engineers' status and consciousness in the metropole (*naichi*), the technocrats found an ideal place for their technocratic creation in Manchuria. When Naoki Rintarō, a senior technocrat in Tokyo (whose writings in the 1910s inspired many young engineers, including Miyamoto), accepted an administrative position in the Road Construction Bureau in Manchuria, he left this message to his fellow engineers: "I devote my life to technology. . . . I am going to Manchuria to do some creation" (*sōsaku o shini iku*).[18] The Kōjin Club technocrats spoke of technology as the end and means of this creation, and natural resources in China were the material for their creation.

Even the name of the organization, Kōjin, acquired a new symbolic meaning from this perspective. Originally, the founding members named their organization Kōjin (literally, a person of technology) to emphasize the person in control of technology. This makes sense, since, as was clearly declared in the inaugural manifesto, the aim of the organization was to empower engineers and to raise their status.[19] Once Manchuria emerged as a place for their creation, Kōjin came to signify a more grandiose and imperialist role of engineers. In the April 1932 issue of *Kōjin*, along with the lead article declaring "Make promptly a technological advancement in developing Manchuria!" appeared a small section that explained the meaning of Kōjin. The anonymous author explained that the upper line of the character 工 (*kō*) signified the universe and nature and that the lower line represented the human world; the central vertical line connecting the two horizontal lines symbolized the engineer, whose "mission is to skillfully unite the universe and human beings!"[20] In other words, the engineer—and not just any engineer, but the Japanese engineer—was the one who could unite China and Japan, or, more specifically, the natural resources in China and the Japanese people.

As was the case with Western imperialism, various research institutions were created in Japanese colonies to provide grounds for such creation at an unprecedented scale as well as funding. Mantetsu research sections are a well-known example of this, housing numerous social and natural scientists to research natural resources, land-distribution systems, and local customs to aid Japanese colonial rule. Many other research institutions were created, often on a scale unthinkable at the metropole, as in the case of the Shanghai Natural Science Research Institute (*Shanhai shizen kagaku kenkyūjo*), founded by the Ministry of Foreign Affairs in April 1931 for studies in physics, chemistry, biology, geology, pathology, bacteriology, and medicine. With a budget of more than 400,000 yen a year, as one scientist described it, "[I]ts research budget is so large, incomparable to any laboratories and classrooms in Japan proper."[21]

But the envy and pride of technocrats was the Continental Science Institute (*tairiku kagakuin*), established in Harbin in March 1935 by the Manchurian government. The institute was like a dream come true for technocrats. It was a powerful science research institution whose director was given a position equivalent to that of a minister. Some researchers were ranked higher and paid more than law-bureaucrat staff.[22] This was unthinkable in the metropole, where engineer-bureaucrats had suffered poor treatment both formally and informally. The City of Tokyo, for example, had such a negative reputation among engineers that it even suffered a shortage of engineers in 1938 in preparing for the (never-realized) Olympics.[23] The Continental Science Institute in Manchuria was also very well funded.[24] Together with Express Train Asia, a state-of-the-art luxury train that ran through Manchuria at the impressive speed of 120 kilometers per hour, the Continental Science Institute symbolized technologically progressive Manchuria.[25]

The Continental Science Institute was in fact intentionally built so as not to duplicate the shortcomings of the metropole, namely, the inefficient use of technical and scientific expertise due to the Civil Servant Appointment Law and the lack of a central administrative unit to oversee the development of science and technology as a whole. The plan for the Continental Science Institute began in 1934 when the vice–director general of Manchuria, Hoshino Naoki, saw a need for a central research institution for industrial development in Manchuria. Upon Hoshino's request, Ōkōchi Masatoshi, director of the Riken, and Fujisawa Takeo, a Natural Resources Agency (shigenkyoku) bureaucrat who was preparing for a science mobilization plan at the time, were invited to Manchuria to draft a plan. It was decided that research institutions would be managed by the new Continental Science Institute instead of the existing ministries because "in naichi ... more than 680 institutions ... are scattered among various ministries, which prevents effective communication, flexibility, and efficiency. Manchuria wants to avoid these shortcomings and wishes to establish something closer to the ideal."[26] The draft was passed easily in the following year, and the Continental Science Institute was founded to manage all research projects related to the development of natural resources in Manchuria. As we will see later, the ease and swiftness of this process contrast sharply with the major obstacle that technocrats faced during wartime when they promoted the creation of a similar institution in Tokyo.

The Continental Science Institute demonstrates how science and technology were viewed as essential for Japan's "harmonious" colonization of Manchuria. The first director, Suzuki Umetarō (1874–1943), an internationally renowned authority on vitamins, stated the following in the institute's mission statement:

Manchuria aims to construct a heavenly land under the mottoes "harmonious coexistence of five ethnicities" [gozoku kyōwa] and "coexistence, co-prosperity" [kyōzon kyōei] under Japan's leadership. However, can this be achieved without taking science seriously? National defense, industry, and all are based on science. Politics and economy cannot ignore science. ... We do not sympathize with the politics and ideals of Russia, but we share with Russians the emphasis on and respect for science. ...

[A]s far as the development of Manchuria goes, many people have presumed that we receive capital and technology from Japan or from other countries if Japan could not provide [them]. Thus, even though Manchuria became an independent nation, [they assume that] its science and technology are not independent. From our perspective, however, Manchuria is like a branch family of Japan. If a branch family continues to rely on the main family and depend on its support, that is not only cowardly but also lamentable, since the branch family should be able to help the main family in such emergency. . . . We must spread science education in Manchuria and promote scientific research so that we no longer will have to borrow science from either Japan or foreign countries.[27]

As in Miyamoto's justification of Japan's dominance over Manchuria, Suzuki's statement emphasized science as the most basic and necessary factor in Japan's successful colonization. The desired independence of Manchuria and its science and technology did not mean Manchuria's total separation from Japan. As if to balance out his favorable reference to the Soviet Union, Suzuki emphasized the complementary relationship between Manchuria and Japan by employing the familial metaphor. According to Suzuki's logic, Manchurian science and technology ought to be strong and independent so that Manchuria could help its "main family," Japan.

The researchers and technocrats perceived Manchuria to be vacant land waiting to be explored and exploited by the Japanese. The Japanese government and the media created this "virgin land" image of Manchuria to promote the migration of Japanese farmers to Manchuria to solidify Japan's occupation of the region as well as to solve the metropole's overpopulation problem. Through this policy alone, more than 350,000 Japanese migrated to the region as farmer-settlers. They, however, faced hostility from Korean and Chinese farmers whose lands had been taken by the Japanese government to make space for the Japanese settlers. Manchuria was not as "open" as the Japanese government had made it appear.[28]

Manchuria was not an open land for engineers either. Like the Japanese farmers who moved to Manchuria, the Kōjin members soon realized that the region was already populated—by Japanese engineers who had moved there some decades ago.[29] A roundtable discussion with members of the Manchurian Technology Association in the May 1932 issue of *Kōjin* made it clear that they had their own sense of mission and pride as pioneer engineers in Manchuria. Among many things they discussed, one message was clear: We, who have already been in Manchuria for twenty years, will do the job; if *naichi* engineers should decide to come to Manchuria, they had better learn the Chinese language and be ready to follow us.[30]

Even in Manchuria, where the technocratic dream of the Continental Science Institute was realized, engineers felt that their expertise was not utilized and appreciated enough. Even researchers at the institute needed to purchase all their research supplies through an office staffed by a "Compendium of Law–type officials who don't even know the names for pipettes."[31]

They were particularly frustrated with businessmen and bureaucrats who came to Manchuria without any scientific background; they did not know how to assess resources in Manchuria and thus could not provide a good blueprint for commercial and governmental enterprises to fully utilize Manchurian resources. They argued that Manchuria was also important because it provided engineers with jobs. The participants of the roundtable discussion were pessimistic about Japanese laborers finding jobs in Manchuria because the Chinese were a cheaper and harder-working labor force than the Japanese (and Koreans were better than Japanese but worse than Chinese). But the prospect for engineers was good. In fact, they assured, the only possible positions that Japanese would be able to fill were those of officers and technical experts.[32]

As the Kōjin technocrats' ambition became greater, and Manchuria and China occupied a larger space in their vision for a scientific Japan, they came to think that the name "Kōjin" was inappropriate. They found out that the compound *kōjin*, which initially appeared so symbolically suited to their organization, meant a "coolie" in Chinese. In 1935 the board of directors voted to replace such a "degrading" name with Nihon Gijutsu Kyōkai (Japan Technology Association; hereafter NGK). Its monthly journal also acquired a new title, *Gijutsu Nihon* (Technology Japan), beginning with the January 1936 issue. This meant more than simply adopting a "respectable" name. As Miyamoto Takenosuke explained, "[W]hen we renamed the Kōjin Club the Japan Technology Association, we also set up a new slogan: to lead the nation through technology. It clearly reveals our *tenkō* from trade unionism to nationalism."[33] In other words, it meant a shift in focus from the interests of engineers to the interests of the nation. It signified a change of direction from a movement for engineers to an engineers' movement for the nation.

However, much to the engineers' frustration, the technocratic movement struggled to grow. The Kōjin Club lost almost four-fifths of its members at the end of the 1920s when it decided not to support any proletarian party, and it never recovered.[34] Desperately seeking to revitalize the organization, the NGK leaders approached younger engineers by setting up a roundtable discussion. The young engineers told the hosts that they had little interest in organizations like the NGK or in issues such as law-bureaucrat supremacy or academic cliques. In fact, many of the invited participants were not even aware of the existence of the NGK.[35] "I am afraid that your 'youth impeachment plan' has failed," one of the young participants wrote to the NGK after the event. "The consciousness of young engineers is very different from that of a generation ago. . . . It is no wonder we all were agape after hearing your anachronistic founding spirit of the NGK."[36] Such a reaction from the younger generation made one older member feel "a sense of resignation."[37]

It was clear that the younger generation of engineers was completely un-interested in defining the social responsibility of engineers or collectively seeking better status and political power.

This declining interest among young engineers in such issues as the status of engineers might be a reflection of a change in the private sector. In the early 1930s, many started noting that engineers were finally being acknowl-edged in the business world. They were referring to the rise of a new kind of enterprise, the so-called newly rising zaibatsu (*shinkō koncherun*) represented by Ayukawa Gisuke's Nissan Zaibatsu, Noguchi Shitagau's Nihon Chisso Zabaitsu, Mori Nobuteru's Mori Zaibatsu (with Nihon Denki Kōgyō, or NEC), Nakano Tomonori's Nihon Sōda Zaibatsu, and Ōkōchi Masatoshi's Riken Zaibatsu, whose founders were, except Mori, all engineers. As his-torian Kawahara Hiroshi points out, there were other notable differences between the old zaibatsu, such as Mitsui and Mitsubishi, and the new ones. The new zaibatsu's management was based on a fresh principle: the new zaibatsu took a form that united companies with technology, whereas the old zaibatsu were organized in a kind of *ie* system, with the zaibatsu family-owned company at the top. Ayukawa, for example, advocated a "publicly owned joint stock company," challenging the old zaibatsu of the family ownership style. More important, the new zaibatsu took advantage of Japan's heavy industrialization, the production of which came to occupy more than half of the total production of the nation by 1935 (a rapid increase from 36 percent in 1929). Whereas the old zaibatsu's investment in heavy industry remained at 31 to 32 percent of their total capital, the new zaibatsu invested 94 percent of their capital in heavy industry.[38] These new zaibatsu became the important apparatus of Japan's colonialism in Manchuria. Ayukawa, for example, made inroads into Manchuria with Manchuria Heavy Industry (*Manshū jūkōgyō*) by making connections with military and political leaders such as Tōjō Hideki, Hoshino Naoki, and Kishi Nobusuke.[39]

Although the situation for engineer leaders in the private sector may have been improving, reality remained too frustrating for technology-bureaucrats. For one thing, the Civil Servant Appointment Law still limited technocrats' access to policy-making power. The Kōjin technocrats dreamt of creating a twin organization of the Continental Science Institute in the metropole, a new institution that would overcome law-bureaucrat supremacy. In their analysis, Japanese science and technology suffered from the lack of expert leadership, coherent planning, and communication among scientists, engi-neers, and their programs. In their vision, there also needed to be a new ad-ministrative unit headed by a technology-bureaucrat with executive power that was independent of various ministries dominated by law-bureaucrats and capable of managing various strategically important fields of science and technology as a whole. Who else could make use of the potential for unexplored resources in China besides technocrats who had technological expertise and knew what rationality and efficiency meant?

With the new name and new slogan of the organization, the technocrats hoped to revitalize their movement and realize the ambition of creating such an executive unit specifically for science and technology policies. Their ambition, however, remained blocked by the unchanging hierarchy within the bureaucracy as well as their own failure to mobilize the younger and wider spectrum of engineers for the cause. As the next section demonstrates, the war with China brought the much-needed momentum to the technocratic movement.

Technological Patriotism and a "Uniquely Japanese" Technology

On July 7, 1937, the Japanese military found one soldier missing from night practice after several gunshots at the Marco Polo Bridge near Beijing. We do not know who shot the gun or where this missing soldier, who was found later, had been. What we know is that this so-called Marco Polo Bridge Incident (*rokōkyō jiken*) was the beginning of Japan's war with China, which lasted until August 1945. It was also the beginning of a new stage in the technocratic movement.

The war brought technocrats a renewed sense of urgency and a formal occasion to bring up the old problem, to improve the "situations where a novice law-bureaucrat in his thirties would become a division chief and command a much senior, renowned engineer without even calling him 'Mister'"[40] Three months after the Marco Polo Bridge Incident, an NGK member sent a letter to the various ministries and the City of Tokyo demanding the fair employment of engineers. In December 1937, the NGK also officially sent a letter to the Konoe cabinet (the first Konoe cabinet, June 1937–January 1939) asking it to employ more engineers in the government and appoint technology-bureaucrats to the heads of the departments and divisions that dealt with technology.[41] The technocrats asserted that technology was crucial to Japan's victory in the war and the development of the continent and that the government really ought to put engineers to better use.

The technocrats made this demand under the motto "technological patriotism" (*gijutsu hōkoku*).[42] The NGK even declared in July 1937 that "only those activities that will rationalize our technological patriotism will be adopted as our activities."[43] The phrase embellished the pages of *Technology Japan* as the journal began to carry significantly more articles and discussions on policies related to China.[44] Technological patriotism in these pages became synonymous with the demand for the breakdown of the law-bureaucrat supremacy because, in the technocrats' minds, they could serve the nation better only if they held higher positions and more power in the government. The intensity of their cry for technological patriotism was such that it made Miyamoto Takenosuke anxious. He worried that their technological patriotism would sound like a selfish ideology for their status aspiration and would not be taken seriously.[45] His concern was understandable, since some members had become extremist in challenging the law-bureaucrat dominance, saying: "Have laws and speeches [as opposed to science and technology] made any contribution to the modern Japanese nation anyway?"[46] Their fervor was received with a hint of sarcasm by one outside observer, renowned science journalist Ishihara Jun, who wondered why the technocrats would want to add more responsibility to their already busy lives.[47] However, it was impossible to separate technocrats' technological patriotism and their status politics. After all, Miyamoto, too, deemed the two goals—technology gaining national significance and technocrats gaining political power—as the same process for the construction of a scientific Japan. The NGK's call for technological patriotism and for the higher status of engineers continued throughout the wartime years, expanding its audience beyond the NGK members, as the journal was yet again renamed as *Gijutsu hyōron* (Technology Critics) in 1939 and began to be sold in regular bookstores.

The discourse of technological patriotism that developed after 1937 embraced a specific historical understanding of Japan's place in the world, based on which it demanded the planned and regulated development of technology. Technocrats tended to hold the historical narrative that the world was transitioning from the capitalist economic system to the new planned or regulated economic system. In this narrative, capitalism was associated with liberalism, a free market, and science, while the new, emerging system was characterized by corporatism, a planned economy, and technology. An NGK member, Matsuoka Hisao, wrote in 1940 that Japan was involved in the process of a transition from "the world order of the British capitalist power to the world order of national [*minzoku*] corporatism." He declared that "the time is now rapidly shifting from that of science to that of technology."[48] According to Matsuoka, the technology of the new era was not just any technology, but "scientific" technology. In the time of scientific technology, it was engineers who "stood up on the front line as the vanguard": "History finally has atoned for the supremacy and transcendentalism of science and its slavelike subjugation of technology. It now demands the political characterization of scientific technology [*kagakuteki gijutsu*]."[49] The engineers would have a new position in the new system. Matsuoka maintained that in a planned economy, capital and labor would be united, and engineers, who had been the sorry victims caught between capital and labor in the liberal capitalist society, would become the leaders of society.[50]

This narrative of a worldwide transition from capitalism to a new system was most explicitly expressed in Ōkōchi Masatoshi's *kagakushugi kōgyō*, or "scientific industry." Ōkōchi, a graduate of the mechanical engineering department of Tokyo Imperial University, advocated what he called "scientific industry" through numerous books, articles, and his journal, *Kagakushugi kōgyō*.[51] Scientific industry was a principle, an approach, and a practice of combining science and technology with industry. It attracted much public attention when Ōkōchi saved the Riken, the research institute established by the state as part of the promotion of domestic research and development during World War I, from the verge of bankruptcy by building up the Riken Zaibatsu in the late 1920s. He argued that an economy based on capitalism should be replaced by an economy based on scientism (*kagakushugi*). Profit was the main driving force in capitalist industry, he maintained, but a new, ideal economy should use science as the basis to achieve high wages and low costs. By "science," Ōkōchi meant an innovative use of technology and the industrialization of results of scientific research. He put this idea into practice when he dealt with the Riken's troubled financial situation; scientific results and intellectual property produced at the Riken research laboratories, which housed some of the nation's most prominent scientists, were industrialized and commercialized by the Riken Zaibatsu, whose profit, in turn, funded research projects at its research institution. This operation brought wealth to the Riken during the 1930s, through the successful sales of various Riken brand products, such as Riken vitamins, a commercial application of the research conducted by a vitamin pioneer and Riken researcher Suzuki Umetarō (who would later become the first director of the Continental Science Institute), as well as the skillful management of spun-off companies like Ricoh that commercialized Riken-patented light-sensitive papers.[52] Ōkōchi's scientific industry and the technocracy advocated by technology-bureaucrats like Matsuoka all emphasized the development of science for the purpose of technological, practical application rather than the pursuit of knowledge per se, as well as the necessity to plan and regulate that process.

Behind the technocrats' emphasis on the significance of the rule of technology in the planned economy lay the changing political and economic structure of Japan. One major problem that plagued the Japanese economy and caused frequent turnovers of the cabinet in the late 1930s was how to manage and expand the budget for defense as demanded by the military. The Depression was at its worst around 1932 in Japan, but by 1936 the Japanese domestic economy had recovered (though the countryside remained poor), and the trade balance had been more or less maintained between 1932 and 1936. But the 1937 budget that the Hirota cabinet (1936–37) prepared was 25 percent larger than that of the previous year, with 40 percent allotted to military expenses, an impossible budget to meet unless a radical measure was taken. Unlike the prior cabinets that attempted to tighten the nation's purse strings and restrict military expenditures, the Hirota cabinet not only accepted the military's financial demands—the army wished to strengthen its navigation power, and the navy planned the construction of megasized battleships, *Yamato* and *Musashi*—but also agreed with the Key Industries Five-Year Plan drawn up by the military that aimed to encourage the rapid growth of the automobile, metal, aluminum, and defense industries in the Manchuria-Japan economic bloc. To create a larger budget, the government declared that a "quasi-wartime economic system" be adopted based on the state regulation of the economy and planned distribution of various materials.[53]

With the outbreak of the war with China, this "quasi-wartime economic system" became the wartime economic system that further emphasized a planned economy and regulated distribution of both material and human resources. The central institution for this wartime system was the Planning Agency, established in October 1937 to manage the economic and industrial development of Japan and northern China and to control the distribution of materials and natural resources. For human resources, the government issued the National Mobilization Law (*kokka sōdōin hō*) in April 1938, which regulated the labor force and employment as well as business activities. The "national spirit" was mobilized, too, under the National Spiritual Mobilization Movement (*kokumin seishin sōdōin undō*), which was initiated by the government in late 1937 but was also supported by various political and civilian organizations on their own initiatives. For example, the proletarian parties and labor unions in late 1937 decided not to engage in labor strikes any longer to show support for the wartime national economy. The Konoe government created a new name for the cause of this total mobilization of the nation in November 1938: the New Order for Greater East Asia (*Daitōa shinchitsujo*).[54] The New Order for Greater East Asia was Japan's colonial vision in which Japan would replace the West as the center of Asia and ultimately the world.

The war also put technocrats into action. For the first time since World War I, technocrats in various fields who had hitherto been organized separately began to get together under technological patriotism. Miyamoto was a central figure in this development. He, together with other NGK leaders, collaborated with technocrats in other ministries, such as Matsumae Shigeyoshi and Kajii Takashi of the Ministry of Communications and Miura Yoshio of the Ministry of Railway, and rapidly expanded the technocracy movement. In June 1937, Miyamoto held the Six Ministries Engineering Conference (Home Affairs, Finance, Agriculture and Forests, Commerce and Industry, Communications, and Railway), with Miyamoto making the opening speech on the mobilization of Japanese technology; the following year saw the Seven Ministries Engineering Conference, with the addition of the newly created Ministry of Welfare. The technocrats also mobilized engineers in the private sector: on November 13, 1937, the NGK and the Inter-Ministries Conference held the National Engineers' Meeting (*zenkoku gijutsusha taikai*). In September 1938, the Industrial Technology Federation (*sangyō gijutsu renmei*) was organized with the Inter-Ministries Conference, the NGK, and two groups of private-sector engineers (the Engineer Leadership Group [*kōseikai*] and the China Technology Federation [*taishi gijutsu renmei*]), declaring that "no national policies should ever fail to be planned from the perspective of modern production technology—the production technology that synthesizes the natural and social sciences—that aim to expand productivity."[55] The problem of recruiting younger engineers that had plagued the NGK for more than a decade finally seemed to have been resolved, for in late 1937 the younger members took over leadership from the older members. "We will finally be able to regain energy," the board of directors sighed with joy.[56]

The war against China not only stirred up technological patriotism but also urged the government to take up the engineers' call. In 1938 the government created the Asia Development Agency (*kōain*) under the Konoe cabinet to establish policies regarding China. Within it the Technology Department was set up along with the Departments of Politics, Economy, and Culture, and Miyamoto Takenosuke was appointed as the first director of the Technology Department. Originally, the Technology Department was going to be a mere consultant division, with its head being simply called the "chief engineer." After much contention by Miyamoto and his colleagues, it was decided that his position would be titled "division head," as used in the other three divisions. However, by the time this decision was made, the draft had already been completed. Miyamoto was assured by the secretary of the prime minister that he would have as much executive power as the other division heads and was asked to take the position without much ado. The Technology Department, in other words, was a full division in practice but not on paper. Miyamoto initially had trouble accepting this. "If I accept this position," he confided to his friend, "some may think, much to my chagrin, that Miyamoto has always talked big but jumps on the position of a chief engineer. But more importantly, if I take up the position, it would mean that we affirm a technology department of such a lowly status." His friend, though, told Miyamoto to take the job because he alone could run this experimental Technology Department successfully; the job, he added, could go to someone suggested by law-bureaucrats who wanted to destroy this opportunity for technocrats.[57] Miyamoto decided to accept the position, and the division was staffed with engineers who had been active in the technocratic movement with Miyamoto. The full-fledged science and technology mobilization by the state had at last begun to fulfill Miyamoto's lifelong wish to participate in central policymaking.[58]

The technocrats' technological patriotism frequently involved discussions of "uniquely Japanese technology" (*Nihonteki gijutsu* or *Nihonteki seikaku no gijutsu*). As I discussed earlier, technocrats argued that nineteenth-century capitalism was based on the principle of free trade, whereas the twentieth-century economy was a bloc economy in which nations constituted a regional economic bloc and the flow of materials, goods, and ideas between blocs would be regulated. Thus, they argued, Japan's bloc of Greater East Asia—Japan, Manchuria, and China (soon to be called the Greater East Asia Co-Prosperity Sphere [*Daitōa kyōeiken*], with the addition of Southeast Asia)—needed to be self-sufficient, and for this purpose, Japanese science and technology needed to be self-sufficient. It followed that Japan needed to develop technology and science that were independent of the West, that is, technology and science unique to Japan.

What exactly was meant by "Japanese" technology? Many discussed it using the empty rhetoric of the merger of Western technology with the Japanese spirit without offering any concrete content. In a 1937 conference of engineers, for example, an engineer in the House of Peers, Yata Yoshiaki, stated: "We need to merge the Japanese spirit that we have embraced since ancient times with the technology that came from modern Europe. We need to create a slogan of a new, patriotic technology, Japanese technology, Japanist [*Nihonshugi teki*] technology." Great applause followed Yata's speech. Yata, however, never explained what constituted the Japanese spirit or how differently such a merger would produce technology.[59]

Katō Yogorō, a researcher at the Research Center for Resource Science, provided the most concrete definition of a uniquely Japanese technology. He argued that in order to utilize East Asian resources, Japan needed to develop its own technology, for different natural environments required different techniques. For example, the Western technique for producing aluminum from bauxite was not suitable for Japan, which did not have bauxite. Japan solved this problem creatively by inventing a new way of using phosphoric acid buried in northern Japan. If Japanese engineers and scientists continued to use such creativity, Katō maintained, "natural resources that had been asleep in East Asia [would] continue to make a debut in the world." According to him, the most important thing was "to creatively develop our research, without depending on Western technology, to explore natural resources unique to East Asia."[60]

As the Asia Development Agency's Technology Department director, Miyamoto defined Japanese technology as "Asia development technology" (*kōa gijutsu*).[61] Similar to Katō's definition, his "Asia development technology" consisted of three characteristics: "progressiveness" (*yakushinsei*), "synthesis" (*sōgōsei*), and "locationality" (*ricchisei*). According to Miyamoto, Japanese technology must be "progressive" because it had to stay ahead of Chinese technology. This condition is "fundamental to the East Asia Co-operative Sphere, which is the union of Chinese resources and Japanese technology."[62] Second, Japanese technology needed to "synthesize" various fields of science and technology to be effective. Finally, Japanese technology, he argued, needed to be sensitive to "locationality" because the technology that had developed in the specific Japanese environment might not be best suited to China: "It is necessary to revise Japanese technology to meet the reality of the continent."[63]

Thus, according to Miyamoto and Katō, "Japanese" technology was made of Chinese resources and the Japanese brain, and the Japanese engineer's responsibility was to maintain this division of labor on which the Japanese Empire rested. This division of labor in Asia ensured that the New Order of what was now the Greater East Asia Co-Prosperity Sphere radically differed from the Kōjin technocrats' identification as the "brain workers" a decade earlier. In the mid-1920s, the Kōjin Club's unionism attempted to position engineers among the proletariat as the "brain workers." In their new vision, engineers were no longer proletarians who happened to hold a specialized degree, nor was their expertise something to be exploited by capitalists. Engineers were now the brain of the empire that fundamentally sustained the technological hierarchy (or "cooperation" in the technocrats' words) of the empire.

Most discussions on technology with Japanese character, however, remained prescriptive rather than descriptive, ideal rather than realistic. Even Miyamoto argued that Japanese technology *should* have the three characteristics just described. Japan, in other words, was characterless, as it were. This was precisely what the technocrats recognized as the problem of Japanese technology. They argued that since modern technology had been so rapidly imported from the West after the Meiji Restoration and had continued to rely on the West, it had not developed into a truly Japanese technology. The technocrats were concerned about the fate of Japan should the supply of materials, information, and technology from abroad be completely cut off in the event of a war against the Western nations. Most Japanese companies continued to spend fortunes buying foreign patents and importing machines while refusing to share technical information with the public so they could protect their profits. Many engineers, scientists, and business leaders recognized that such practices hindered the development of domestic production and consumption of ideas and technology.[64] Japanese reliance on the West was also a psychological issue: in academia the criterion for good scholarship was based on reputation abroad. One scientist wrote in 1940 that "Japanese scientists actually look down on their own country's scientists and do not read their works. If a Japanese work is fortunately noticed by a foreign scientist and praised abroad, then they would finally acknowledge it." He continued to say that Western scientists visiting Japan often commented on the fetishistic collection of Western books and technical journals in libraries. Such conditions, in his words, constituted "the colonial landscape of Japanese academia."[65] The technocratic logic held that to remain the leader of Asia, Japan needed to free itself from these colonized conditions and mentality. The discourse of a uniquely Japanese technology and science was more about lamenting this colonial condition of a characterless Japanese technology and science than it was about celebrating an actual "uniquely Japanese" accomplishment.

One thing was clear, however. The way out of this lamentable condition was to secure resources in Asia to develop a uniquely Japanese technology and science. "Colonized" Japan, in other words, required the colonization of Asia to free itself from Western influence. But as the renowned physicist Nishina Yoshio confessed in 1942, the conditions of science in Japan were far inferior to those of the West, both in terms of the quantity of scientists and the quality of facilities; thus, how "to construct a Japanese science under such conditions is a very difficult question."[66] To the frustrated Nishina, the only answer he could come up with was simply to keep trying harder: "As long as it is developed by the Japanese, then it will be Japanese science."[67] On this point, the technocrats' assertion of a unique Japanese technology was rather tautological. Japanese technology consisted in constructing a new Asia, but before such a "construction," there first had to be Japanese technology. However, to construct Japanese technology and obtain its technological independence from the West, they argued, Japan needed Asian resources. Technocrats never went beyond this tautological circle, leaving the slogans "Japanese technology" and "Japanese science" rather empty. As Tessa Morris-Suzuki has pointed out, both the content and style of the "uniquely Japanese" technology that the technocrats advocated were largely based on Western models rather than truly unique.[68] The technocrats' main concern, after all, was the effective and efficient exploitation of natural resources in Japan's empire. "Japanese" technology was fundamentally about the division of labor between the Japanese brain and Asian materials within the Japanese Empire, rather than the style of technology or science. The logic of technological patriotism emphasized the centrality of technology for the construction and maintenance of the new order. Engineers and scientists were the crucial brain of this new order, and technocrats, they claimed, guided this brain.[69]

As the war against China dragged on, science and technology gained more political significance in the eyes of political leaders. On August 1, 1940, the second Konoe cabinet announced the Outline of Basic National Policies and listed "the radical promotion of science and the rationalization of production" among the most urgent national agendas.[70] The first administration to explicitly make the promotion of science a basic national policy, the Konoe cabinet was hailed by technocrats. Moreover, for the position of minister of education, Konoe Fumimaro appointed physiologist Hashida Kunihiko, a Tokyo Imperial University professor and the principal of a high school. Hashida's appointment became quite a sensation, for he was the first scientist in thirty years (and the second one in its history) to head the Ministry of Education, one of the most law-bureaucrat-dominated ministries.[71] Miyamoto soon was invited to be on the board of a science mobilization committee created in the Planning Agency, where he urged the establishment of a central science research institution similar to the Continental Science Institute in Manchuria. Finally, in 1941 he was appointed as the vice-minister of the Planning Agency. Although he held this position only for a short period due to his early death, the position of the vice-minister, the highest that any bureaucrat—law or technology—could hold, fulfilled his political ambition at last.

As science gained greater presence on the central stage of national and imperial administration, other technocrats carried on and sought to seize this opportunity to realize their final dream—to create a powerful, independent administrative system that unified and controlled research programs that were scattered among various ministries and institutions. They called it the New Order for Science-Technology.

Defining Science for the Empire

The phrase "science-technology" has become such a standard in the Japanese language that the initial politics behind the coinage has been forgotten. Prior to 1940, those who wrote on science and technology conventionally spelled out "science and technology" or "science as well as technology" (*kagaku to gijutsu*, *kagaku narabi ni gijutsu*, or *kagaku oyobi gijutsu*), indicating a clear distinction between the two fields.[72] Technocrats found the distinction unnecessary and provided a new language, the one that would redefine science for them and support their demand for power. Fujisawa Takeo, a leading technology-bureaucrat in the Planning Agency, explained in February 1940:

As we have been talking to many people recently, there is one thing we keep in mind—language. We use "science-technology." We want to create a new term: "science-technology," not "science and technology" (as generally used). This is because if we say "science," it is broad, including human and natural sciences. What is at stake now is not science in such a broad sense, but technological science. By adding "technology," "science-technology" articulates many issues that have been raised regarding so-called scientific technology.[73]

Fujisawa's science-technology limited science to merely technology-related sciences. In the realm of science-technology, social- and humanities-oriented sciences did not exist because they were not directly related to what the nation needed most: production and national defense.

Such a narrow definition of science explicitly challenged various definitions of science that existed at the time. First, it refuted the Marxist definition of science. As we will see in Part 2, Marxism, which was understood to be "scientific socialism" in Japan, dominated the social sciences in the 1920s and early 1930s, making the "scientific study of society" (*shakai kagaku*) synonymous with Marxism. Science-technology was a direct challenge to this strong association between Marxism and the "scientific." Mōri Hideoto, one of the law-bureaucrats who supported technology-bureaucrats, makes this point explicit. He argued in 1940 that the emergence of science-technology signified the triumph of the "Japanese way" of thinking over Marxist science:

If we remained stagnant with science of the nineteenth century, the worldview based on its scientific understanding would necessarily remain materialist and mechanist. . . . In the history of intellectual and political struggle in modern Japan, we engaged in the struggle against Marxist theory. In this struggle, the Japanese nation [*minzoku*] has gained the intellectual victory over the materialist and mechanist worldview. This intellectual struggle of the Japanese *minzoku* was a struggle against the so-called scientific [*iwayuru kagakuteki*].[74]

Mōri continued to argue that Newtonian atomic theory represented the science of the nineteenth-century materialist and mechanist worldview but that it was overcome by a new science of quantum physics based on a new worldview "closer to Eastern philosophy."[75] Although Mōri did not explain why in this essay, it is most likely that he identified the concepts of probability, uncertainty, and relativity that the new physics provided—which indeed challenged Newtonian physics' worldview—as similar to Eastern philosophy. It should be noted that by 1940 the Soviet Communist Party had concluded, after much debate, that quantum physics and the relativity theory were the products of bourgeois idealism and liberalism. Japanese Marxists, as we will see later, did not reach any agreement on this question. Mōri, in contrast, seized the rise of quantum mechanics and used it to legitimate the intelligence of Japanese *minzoku*.

Second, the phrase "science-technology" also challenged the conventional hierarchy that placed science intellectually higher than technology. By limiting the significance of science to the technological fields, it asserted that technology was the purpose of science, not a mere tool for science. Shinohara Takeshi's "Theory on Science-Technology," for example, insisted that science be regarded as part of technology.[76] According to Shinohara, the common view that science existed independent of technology whereas technology relied on science came from the Middle Ages, when God was still the holder of Truth and science meant seeking this Truth: "Science has nothing to do with the medieval metaphysical Truth of Nature or natural laws that is assumed to be so-called purely objective existence."[77] Such naive thinking, Shinohara maintained, was what created a false hierarchy between science and technology. Instead, he argued: "We should make no discrimination between science and technology. . . . [W]e believe we should discard concepts and terms of science that are associated with the Middle Age-ish concept of truth, modern rationalism and positivism . . . and [instead] unify the whole with the concept and term 'technology.'"[78]

Instead of "Middle Age-ish" science, Shinohara argued, science should mean achieving the planned objectives according to social needs. Advocating "technologism" (*gijutsushugi*), Shinohara explained his concept of science:

Scientific research needs to be done in an organized and systematic fashion with a certain plan and control toward a clear objective for social production. Mere preference of individual psychology such as love for knowledge and admiration for truth needs to be absolutely excluded. It is imperative that scientific research be always conducted for practical purposes [*jissen*] and that its results be materialized and industrialized immediately without any delay. . . . Science is not simply a system of scientific laws; it needs to be interpreted as part of a wider activity that creates and applies such laws. Thus, the real issue in science is how to create the most efficient laws and how to apply such laws in a most efficient manner. This is precisely the issue in technology. Science is nothing but a system of technology in our intellectual activity.[79]

In short, from his perspective, the establishment of scientific facts and laws as truth alone meant little to society. Only when these results of scientific inquiries were embodied in practical technology and transformed into economic capital did science bear any significance.

Shinohara's point was further emphasized in the discussion of science-technology by a former Marxist theorist of technology, Aikawa Haruki.[80] Although technology had been regarded as something whose development depended on the advancement of science, he contended, national defense now required that technology should direct science. Wouldn't Japan rather choose Nazi Germany, which expelled Jewish scientists but developed excellent technology, over the United States, which welcomed those scientists but suffered the Depression? Aikawa's rhetorical question was answered with his assertion that it was the mechanized military, not the Nobel Prize, that was crucial for wars: "I believe that this is a new conscience . . . [to think that it is better] to be buried under *tochka* [*tōchika*] of technology for the power and will of culture than to protect a pantheon of science under 'culture without power.'"[81] In the new, reversed hierarchy of science-technology advocated by Fujisawa, Shinohara, and Aikawa, science could serve the nation only through technology.

These discussions of the phrase "science-technology" were so lively that already in January 1940 a journalist had noted that "so-called science-technology brought a new epoch to journalism."[82] By 1942 "science-technology" was in wide use. In 1942 a new journal titled *Science-Technology* (*Kagaku gijutsu*) appeared, declaring its objective to be "the encouragement of science-technology, which is the fundamental source of national power, in order to establish a nation with a high capacity for military defense" (*kokubō kokka*) and "the introduction of German science-technology."[83] The phrase even created a new literary genre: in 1944 an established opinion magazine, *Kaizō*, called for "science-technology literature" from its readers.[84]

It is no wonder that "science-technology" was widely used by 1942, for the phrase was adopted as a new policy of the second Konoe cabinet, the Outline for the Establishment of the New Order for Science-Technology (*kagaku gijutsu shintaisei kakuritsu yōkō*; hereafter Outline). Part of the Konoe cabinet's new order movement, the Outline passed the Diet on May 27, 1941.

The Outline was the triumphant culmination of prewar technocracy. It declared that its purpose was to "establish the Japanese character of science-technology [*kagaku gijutsu no Nihonteki seikaku*] using resources of the Greater East Asia Co-Prosperity Sphere."[85] The Outline introduced its aim as follows:

It is a lamentable fact that the level of our nation's science-technology is generally lower than that of Western nations and that we have relied heavily on those nations. Scientists and technicians have made enormous efforts to overcome this, but considering the present critical international politics and our leadership in the Greater East Asia Co-Prosperity Sphere, it has now become urgent and essential that we prepare for the total mobilization of science-technology, to promote science-technology development, and to establish it with a Japanese character based on raw materials and ecology in the Greater East Asia Co-Prosperity Sphere. . . .

This Outline for the Establishment of a New Order for Science-Technology focuses on the following: to demonstrate the most efficient research—both basic and applied—and its industrial usage; to develop scientific studies of raw materials in the Greater East Asia Co-Prosperity Sphere as well as technologies necessary for total war mobilization; to solidify the basic policies for the encouragement of science-technology in various areas, including the nurturing of the scientific spirit among people; as a more concrete goal, to increase the speed of . . . the development of science-technology; to systematize and control basic applied research and its industrialization in each field; and to quickly establish a central organization that specializes in the studies and administration of science-technology to unite various fields of research, separate from general industrial and educational institutions.[86]

Following this general description, the Outline highlighted three goals: the promotion of science-technology research, the industrialization of such research, and the nurturing of the scientific spirit. More detailed strategies for each goal were also presented. Under "Policies concerning the Encouragement of Science-Technology Research," one finds a list of eight areas through which this goal was to be pursued, such as promoting the "unification of various applied sciences" and the "efficiency of research in those fields"; promoting "industrialization and practical application of research"; securing the funding and materials for the mobilization of research; and rewarding "scientists and engineers who contribute to the development of the nation's science-technology capacity." It is clear that technocrats successfully managed to redefine science with the phrase "science-technology." Science here is understood to be a planned and systematized science for the purpose of industrialization and practical applications, just as Shinohara Takeshi's "Theory on Science-Technology" had argued a few years earlier. These agendas were clearly based on the technocratic claim regarding the reversed hierarchy of technology and science, emphasizing the usage of science only in terms of industrialization and practicality.

The second objective of the Outline, detailed under the section "Policies concerning the Advancement of Technology," makes it even clearer that research in science was expected to cater specifically to the development of technology. Science here meant "basic research of raw materials and of ecology of the Greater East Asia Co-Prosperity Sphere" that would advance "epoch making and progressive goals for technology urgent to the nation." Miyamoto's definition of "Asia development technology" is easily discernible here. The efficient and planned development of such technology was repeatedly emphasized, which was to be promoted through such proposed means as rewards for private corporations, the effective usage of industrial patents, standardization in industry, and the systematic training and distribution of technically capable personnel for the "total war mobilization."

The final section, titled "Policies concerning the Nurturing of the Scientific Spirit," demonstrates the technocrats' belief that the systematic and rational "science-technology" was impossible unless people were also trained to be systematic and rational. This goal was to be met through four means: a complete reform of education to "nurture the scientific spirit of people"; technological training of the younger generation for national defense science (kokubō kagaku) and counterespionage; the expansion of social facilities to promote science-technology; and the improvement of the national physique and the making of the national life (kokumin seikatsu) more scientific (kagakuka).[87] It is clear from this listing that the "scientific spirit" here had little to do with the minds of people but rather with the technical and physical disciplining of people. It echoes Shinohara's point discussed earlier that being "scientific" had little to do with Truth or empiricism but was all about the planning and rationalization of science-technology for the higher productivity of defense and production industries.

To achieve these three goals, the Outline stipulated the establishment of three institutions: the Technology Agency (gijutsuin), an administrative unit to manage science-technology research; the Science-Technology Research Organization (kagaku-gijutsu kenkyū kikan), a research institute to industrialize results of science-technology research; and the Science-Technology Council (*kagaku gijutsu shingikai*), a policy advisory council to promote the scientific spirit and science-technology policies. These institutions were to be directed and staffed with capable technocrats, and their ranks were to be equal to or higher than those of law-bureaucrats.

The Outline, thus, was the blueprint for a scientific empire that technocrats had been dreaming of constructing. It was enthusiastically welcomed by technocrats, engineers, and scientists. This blueprint, however, also encountered just as much resistance from those who did not agree with the kind of science the Outline promoted and the way it was promoted. A look at both criticism of and support for the Outline reveals how the politics of the "scientific" operated in wartime Japan.

The strongest support for the Outline came from engineers' organizations. For example, the All-Japan Board of Associations of Scientists and Engineers (*zen Nihon kagaku gijutsu dantai rengōkai*; hereafter Zenkaigiren, as it was called then), which was founded in August 1940 to unite scientists, engineers, and their associations to promote national goals, published a declaration of support in major daily newspapers immediately after the announcement of the Outline.[88] This declaration of support, signed by its chair, Nagaoka Hantarō, a renowned physicist, presented a long, elaborate reiteration of the Outline. According to Zenkaigiren, Japan's science-technology was inferior because the Japanese had been mimicking and relying on the West so heavily, which meant that once the tie with the West was cut, Japan would be left with nothing. To avoid such misery, it argued, Japan needed to establish "science-technology with Japanese character" (*Nihonteki seikaku*). Zenkaigiren reinforced the Outline's logic, arguing that such science-technology, first, would use the resources that existed in the sphere of Japanese influence; second, it would create physical environments that were suited to the Japanese *minzoku*; third, it would increase the power of the Japanese *minzoku*; and fourth, it would create a new culture from which the Japanese *minzoku* could excel in the world. According to Zenkaigiren, among the plans that the Outline laid out, especially urgent were policies that provided "progressive goals" in scientific research for the Greater East Asia Co-Prosperity Sphere and total war mobilization.[89]

Zenkaigiren's declaration of support makes it clear that scientists and engineers in industries and academia had adopted the logic and language of the technocrats as their own. While some scientists publicly criticized the limited definition of science and slighting of basic (nonapplicable) research by science-technology, the majority of Zenkaigiren members enthusiastically supported the New Order for Science-Technology.[90] They had little direct interest in the conflict between technology-bureaucrats and law-bureaucrats. Whether they actually believed in the technocrats' assertion about the uniquely Japanese technology and science or cared if science-technology institutions should be headed by technology-bureaucrats or law-bureaucrats, they had a great interest in seeing a larger budget for scientific and technological research, creating larger and more science and engineering education programs, and securing materials and resources for their own research. It is possible that by expanding the science-technology programs, they had hoped to avoid losing their students to the war. The majority of students in social sciences and humanities were drafted after 1943; however, those majoring in science, engineering, and medicine were exempt from conscription.[91] What should be noted here is that once the logic and language of science-technology became official, they also became available for opportunists to use for their own purposes.

The greatest opposition to the New Order for Science-Technology came from the existing ministries.[92] After all, should science-technology be regarded as science or technology? Since it was a hybrid of science and technology, the concept of science-technology violated the existing taxonomy in bureaucracy. This was precisely the aim of the technocrats, who wanted to create an institution transcendent of all bureaucratic jurisdictions, but in reality it brought on conflicts with the existing power structure. According to the advocates for science-technology, their movement for the new order for science-technology was analogous to the administrative reorganization that followed the Meiji Restoration. It was "*haihan chiken* of the Showa Restoration."[93]

The most powerful contender in this politics of the scientific was the Ministry of Education. Scientific research activities, as part of higher learning, had been under the jurisdiction of the Ministry of Education, but the ministry instead had laid emphasis on compulsory education since its founding and did not even have a separate department for science research. Only in 1938, when army general Araki Sadao became the minister, did it begin to initiate policies to promote science research, as he had a vested interest in developing science and technology for the war. In August 1938, Araki established the Science Promotion Research Committee (*kagaku shinkō chōsakai*), with forty-three members from various ministries, the military, the Planning Agency, and academia; in March 1939, it added a new budget for science research of 3 million yen, a phenomenal jump from the previous years, when the average budget to facilitate research remained at fifty thousand to sixty thousand yen. The following year, in 1939, the ministry created the Science Section specifically to deal with the funding of science research, which became an independent department in 1942.[94] In short, as technocrats began to gain institutional power after the war with China began, the Ministry of Education, which had been rather negligent in promoting science policies, also embarked on claiming its power over the field of science.

For the Ministry of Education, the technocrats' "science-technology" meant a direct challenge to its authority. "Throughout the draft prepared by the Planning Agency, a new phrase *kagaku gijutsu* is used. . . . The Ministry of Education understands science as consisting of basic research, applied research, and practical research. Science-technology refers to this practical research." Because "pure science, or so-called learning, has been a jurisdiction of the Ministry of Education," it argued, the Planning Agency should be in charge only of technology, not science-technology or science and technology. Even among the NGK members, the administrative jurisdiction affected their views of science-technology. Matsuoka Hisao, a Ministry of Education technocrat, argued in *Gijutsu hyōron* that it was impossible for science and technology to constitute one field: "The bylaws of the Technology Agency uses the phrase [science-technology]. However, in my view, there is scientific technology or science and technology, but no science-technology. . . . I believe science policies should be handled by the Ministry of Education."[95]

Even after the Outline was passed in the Diet, these territorial conflicts prevented the full materialization of the plan.[96] The Science-Technology Research Institute was not realized before the end of the war. Although the Technology Agency was to begin operation by September 1941, this did not happen until January 30, 1942, due to the complicated negotiations with the various ministries, especially those of education, finance, and the military. Moreover, the outline for the Technology Agency, which was originally a grand plan for the radical reformation of the bureaucracy, was heavily compromised and altered by the time the Diet finally passed it in October 1941. The Technology Agency was to take the leadership role in the fields that made up science-technology, but the word *leadership* was erased from the original draft.[97] The number of sections it planned to house was reduced from seven to four. Among the fifteen areas of research that were to be transferred from the existing ministries, only six ended up in the hands of the Technology Agency. Meanwhile, as mentioned earlier, the Ministry of Education created its own Department of Science, going directly against the purpose of the Outline, which was to consolidate science and technology research programs under one leadership.[98] In the end, the Technology Agency was nicknamed the "Air Technology Agency," as it was only able to get hold of the field of aeronautics—which was so new that it was easier for the Technology Agency to claim—among many "urgent technologies" it wanted to promote. The Technology Agency turned out to be more a coordinator of ministries and laboratories than a leader in science-technology fields and industries.[99] The Technology Agency did grow rapidly after the outbreak of the war with the United States, obtaining the largest budget for science and technology. In 1944, its budget more than doubled that of the previous year, prompting its rival, the Ministry of Education, to also increase its budget substantially in 1944.

The Science-Technology Council, established within the cabinet on December 26, 1942, played a more significant role in terms of promoting national and colonial policies related to science and technology. According to the Planning Agency, the Science-Technology Council was going to be the "express train" with which Japan would catch up to Western science-technology. It would be managed with "the [most] absolute sense of responsibility under fervent nationalism and the power of execution as independent as it is allowed." Moreover, the Planning Agency wanted it to be the brain power of the cabinet, finally "making science-technology political."[100] With the prime minister as president and the head director of the Technology Agency as vice president, the council was composed of about two hundred bureaucrats, academicians, and nonacademic intellectuals. The Science-Technology Council covered areas from shipbuilding, chemistry, mining, agriculture, medicine, and hygiene to the development of resources in the South Pacific region. An almanac published by technology-bureaucrats declared the Science-Technology Council to be "the most critical event in our national history of science-technology . . . since it shoulders significant responsibility for examining crucial national policies from the perspective of science-technology as the highest advisory organization of science-technology in our nation."[101] Whereas the main responsibility of the technocrats remained the negotiation and coordination of the various offices and ministries, the Science-Technology Council at least finally realized the technocrats' goal to establish an institution that would transcend administrative barriers and sectionalism to promote science-technology efficiently and systematically.[102]

The interwar movement for technocracy in Japan initially began proposing a new social order in the metropole in which engineers would manage laborers and capitalists to create and maintain a harmonious, mutually beneficial relationship. During the 1930s and wartime years, the technocrats' movement developed and expanded to propose a new order for the Japanese Empire. Claimed to be a harmonious, mutually beneficial order, the New Order for Science-Technology envisioned by technocrats rested on the ceaseless supply of natural resources in the empire exploited to realize the self-sufficiency of Japanese science-technology.

To the technocrats, a "scientific" Japan meant a Japan that would efficiently develop technology necessary to win the war and to maintain the empire, a Japan that would let technological experts manage the national priority and distribution of resources for that goal. Defining "scientific," as seen in their coinage of "science-technology," was a crucial part of their struggle against law-bureaucrats. A "scientific Japan," however, meant different things to different people, as the following chapters will demonstrate with the cases of Japanese Marxists and promoters of popular science culture.

Marxism

CHAPTER 3

*Incomplete Modernity and the
Problem of Japanese Science*

SCIENCE IS NEVER SIMPLY about experiments in a laboratory or new discoveries of phenomena and laws of nature. It is a highly contested social field in which its legitimacy, territoriality, and definition are constantly challenged, negotiated, and asserted by various participants in the discourse of science. World War I opened a new space for the discourse of science in Japan that was shaped and energized by the vigorous promotion of research and development, the rapid and unbalanced heavy industrialization, and the increase in class conflict. Part 1 examined how technocracy emerged as a response to these new developments in Japan and how technocrats defined technology and science. Part 2 looks at another group of Japanese who responded to the same economic and social changes during World War I by developing a completely different discussion on class and science. They were Marxist intellectuals critical of Japanese modernity, capitalism, and science. Their vision of a scientific Japan was different from that of technocrats. In fact, their critique of Japan was initially a challenge to the kind of Japan that the technocrats envisioned.

Ogura Kinnosuke (1885–1962), a focus of this chapter, played a key role in initiating and developing the historical analysis of class and science in the circle of Japanese Marxist intellectuals. Trained as a mathematician in the late Meiji years and active as an education reformer during the Taishō period, he began writing a historical class analysis of science in 1929. His innovative works not only pioneered the field of the history of science in Japan but also established a view that came to be shared by many Japanese intellectuals: that Japan was not scientific enough because of its incomplete modernity. This chapter examines Ogura's transformation from a liberal mathematics education reformer to a Marxist historian of science in the 1920s. Ogura's intellectual path is significant for our discussion of the Marxist politics of the "scientific" as well as our understanding of the intellectual and political developments in post–World War I Japan. He is an illustrative example of many prewar Japanese intellectuals who had not been part of the proletarian movement but were nonetheless greatly influenced by Marxism. To them, the appeal of Marxism lay in its claim of being scientific and universal, especially in assessing the level as well as nature of Japan's modernity.

An analysis of the Marxist politics of the scientific in interwar Japan would have to involve the question of whether to regard social sciences as a field of science. Marxism was introduced to Japan as scientific socialism in the 1900s. By the mid-1920s, Marxism was one of the major currents in the Japanese intellectual milieu, synonymous with "social sciences" (*shakai kagaku*). While the technocrats made it explicit that their science-technology did not include social sciences, the process and reasons for how social sciences came to be viewed as less scientific than natural sciences involved a much more complex history, as this and following chapters demonstrate.

Toward the Marxist Analysis of Science

In 1929, while Kōjin technocrats criticized Marxism as "unscientific" and gave up proletarianizing engineers, Ogura Kinnosuke presented a new Marxist attempt to discuss proletarianism and science in a sensational article in a widely circulated opinion journal, *Shisō* (Thought). Titled "Arithmetic in Class Society: An Analysis of Arithmetic in the Renaissance," this article examined the emergence of modern mathematics during the Renaissance in Europe from the perspective of class struggle. He argued that between the twelfth and sixteenth centuries, two kinds of mathematics competed with each other. The first was the arithmetic of the ruling class, fostered by the medieval church. This mathematics, based on Greek and Roman texts, did not seek mathematical practicality but focused instead on the mystical and religious features of numbers. The second was the new mathematics of the emerging merchant class. It was based on Arabic and Indian mathematics and emphasized the daily and commercial application of numbers. With the development of the commercial economy after the fourteenth century, the new, commercial arithmetic became popular, first in Italy and then in France and Germany. Some progressive universities began teaching the new arithmetic in the fifteenth century, and by the sixteenth century church arithmetic had declined as the power of the elite and the church had dwindled. The newly rising bourgeoisie established their own universities and their mathematics became dominant in society, but the peasants could not develop their own arithmetic because only the merchant class had been liberated by the collapse of feudalism. Ogura concluded that even mathematics, considered to be the most abstract and value-free field of science, reflected the class nature of society: "The class who rules society also rules arithmetic."[1]

What was radical and sensational about this essay was that Ogura applied class analysis to mathematics and, by implication, to the natural sciences at large. He elaborated this thesis further in four more essays that examined arithmetic in France and the United States. Ogura's thesis was so bold and influential that most first-generation historians of science in Japan claimed it to be their career-defining work. Even physicist Ishihara Jun, who never accepted Marxism in his life, listed Ogura's study as one of the most important works in 1929 and hoped to see more studies like it (though Ishihara did not forget to add that he himself believed the natural sciences would have much less of a class character than the social sciences).[2] It is not an overstatement to say that Ogura laid the foundation of the field of the history of science in prewar and postwar Japan. The Marxist politics of the "scientific," as we will see, owed much to Ogura's historical and class analysis of science as well.

Historians of science call Ogura's approach to the history of science the "externalist" approach. According to the standard dictionary of the history of science, "externalism examines science and scientists in their socio-cultural setting ... and claim[s] that social and economic circumstances have affected the rate and the direction of some scientific work," whereas internalists view science "primarily as [an] abstract intellectual enterprise insulated from social, political, and economic circumstances ... and focus on the obviously intellectual aspects of setting and solving problems concerned with the understanding and the control of the natural world."[3] The appeal of the internalist approach, thus, is its presentation of "the continuity, coherence and progressiveness" of science as "an awesome intellectual enterprise."[4]

Ogura published his essays two years before Soviet scholar Boris Hessen (1893–1936) presented his famous thesis on Isaac Newton, a thesis that scholars of science studies conventionally cite as the first externalist approach to the history of science. Whereas Ogura's essay is little acknowledged outside Japanese-language scholarship, the so-called Hessen thesis has been well known as a "paradigm-setting analysis" in the field of the history of science.[5] In 1931, Hessen, a Marxist physicist and the director of the Moscow Institute of Physics, presented "The Social and Economic Roots of Newton's 'Principia'" at the Second International Congress of the History of Science and Technology in London. In it he argued that the newly rising merchant society following the English revolution of the seventeenth century had demanded new technologies of trade, industry, and war and that these social and economic demands were what created an environment for Newton's three laws of physics. Hessen also explained that Newton's religious claim—that his view of creation had affirmed God's

creation—provided a sense of stability that England needed after a generation of political turmoil. According to Hessen, "Newton was the typical
representative of the rising bourgeoisie, and his philosophy embodied the
characteristic features of his class."[6] In other words, Hessen attributed the
emergence of classical physics to economic and political forces rather than
to Newton's genius.[7] This was a sensational reevaluation of Newton, especially to be presented in England, where the scientist had been raised to
the status of national genius. To Hessen's Western audience, his paper was a
bold and stirring interpretation of science from the Marxist perspective.

To the Soviet audience, however, the Hessen thesis was meant to convey
a more complex message. At the time, Hessen was involved in an intense
battle between two factions of Marxist scientists and philosophers in the
Soviet Union, in which the so-called Deborinites and Mechanists debated
whether quantum mechanics and the relativity theory were in accordance
with Marxism.[8] The militant Mechanists regarded quantum physics and
the relativity theory as the science of the bourgeois and imperialist West
and thus harmful to the materialist worldview of the Soviet Union, while
the Deborinites (including Hessen) defended the new physics, resisting the
Mechanists' too-rigid connection between science and ideology. As historian
Loren Graham makes clear, Hessen's paper on Newton was written in such
a way as to allow him to defend the new physics and at the same time avoid
being accused of idealism by the Mechanists back home. Hessen "strongly
emphasized the role of practice in determining theory . . . , obeyed Stalin's
command to stress technology . . . and copiously quoted Marx, Engels, and
Lenin," while showing that even Newton, whose physics Soviet Mechanists
had firmly accepted as materialist and mechanist science, was a product of
the bourgeois society. By pointing out the cognitive value of Newtonian
physics despite its bourgeois and religious contexts, Hessen had hoped—in
vain, as it turned out—he could also defend the new physics.[9]

Ogura's class analysis, while similar to the Hessen thesis, came out of
a completely different political and intellectual context. New physics did
not meet resistance in Japan. The Deborinite-Mechanist debate itself was
not even introduced to Japanese Marxists until several years later. At the
time, Japanese Marxists were involved in their own internal debate between
the Kōza (Lecture) faction and the Rōnō (Labor-Farmer) faction over the
nature of Japanese capitalism and modernity, as I will explain in more detail later. But even this debate was not a context for Ogura's original class
analysis of science, because he did not know much about the debate. In
fact, Ogura was not familiar with Marxism when he wrote the first essay, as
he later confessed.[10] Ogura was one of many prewar Japanese intellectuals
who were distant from the Communist movement and labor struggles but
came nonetheless to be greatly influenced by Marxism. In this sense, Ogura

walked a similar intellectual path to that of Maruyama Masao, one of the most established postwar political scientists in Japan. While acknowledging Marxist influence, however, Maruyama developed a non-Marxist exploration of Japanese modernity. In contrast, Ogura fully incorporated what Marxism offered to him and devoted his energy to class analysis of Japanese modernity throughout the topic of science.

Ogura was the first Japanese to receive his D.Sc. in mathematics without graduating from an imperial university. The lack of an imperial university pedigree exposed him to the arrogance of elitist academicism. In his private life, he struggled with poor health and the lot his family imposed on him, that of succeeding to the family shipping business in Tsuruoka, Yamagata. These experiences probably shaped Ogura's antiauthoritarian stance. Despite his father's disapproval, his mother helped him study chemistry and physics at a private college, Tokyo Institute for Physics and Chemistry (*Tokyo butsuri gakkō*), the only higher education institution at the time where students could major in science besides the imperial universities in Tokyo and Kyoto.[11] He proceeded to study chemistry at Tokyo Imperial University for several months but was forced to go home in 1906 to inherit his family's business. Ogura could not commit to the mercantile world he disliked deeply, however. He studied mathematics during his free time; mathematics, unlike chemistry, did not require access to classroom experiments. Fortunately, Ogura was able to receive guidance from Hayashi Tsuruichi, an established mathematician and later a professor of the newly created Tohoku Imperial University. Through this mentorship, Ogura became a lecturer at Tohoku Imperial University in 1911 and received his D.Sc. in 1916 with a dissertation that examined dynamics from the perspective of differential geometry. Photos of him taken around this time show the young, tall, brilliant man with glasses, whose frail physique reveals his poor health but whose confident look radiates with pride in his academic achievement as well as liberation from his familial restraints.

Ogura's mentor, Hayashi, was an enthusiastic advocate of mathematics education reform and introduced Ogura to new books on mathematics and its pedagogy.[12] Ogura was particularly inspired by Felix Klein's *Elementarmathematik vom höheren Standpunkt* (Elementary Mathematics from an Advanced Standpoint, 1908) and its description of John Perry's education movement. The movement began with a lecture by Perry in England in September 1901 and gained an international reputation through such mathematicians as Felix Klein (Germany), Émile Borel (France), and Eliakim Hastings Moore (United States). Their education reform movement criticized the abstract geometry-centered curriculum dominant at the time and instead advocated the integration of algebra, applied mathematics, experiments, and an understanding of mathematics in relation to other subjects of science.[13] Their critique struck

Exposed + expanded

↳ Promoted new mathematical ideology

a chord with Ogura. The Japanese mathematics curriculum that the Meiji government established also focused on the abstract theory of geometry and on the mechanical memorization of textbooks. While pursuing his career as a mathematician, Ogura began to lecture and publish, promoting the new mathematics education, which he called "practical mathematics" (*jitsuyō sūgaku*).

Ogura's criticism of the Japanese mathematics education in the 1910s and early 1920s can be summarized in two points. First, the Japanese mathematics education was too centered on theoretical mathematics that bore little relation to practical needs of society. He demanded the introduction of "practical mathematics" into the school curriculum and also advocated the use of graphs and statistics. Statistics for Ogura constituted an important connection between mathematics and society because its application would benefit various areas, including the fields of medicine and insurance After returning from a study trip in France in 1922, Ogura regularly lectured on statistics at the Osaka Medical School (*Osaka ika daigaku*) as part of its mathematics curriculum and continued to do so even after he became the director of a research institution in Osaka, the Shiomi Institute for Physics and Chemistry. This was a bold endeavor, since statistics at the time was, as in Europe, a new field considered to be a part of the social sciences, as were finance and labor studies.[14]

Second, Ogura criticized Japanese mathematics education for its inability to achieve what he regarded as the ultimate purpose of education: to nurture the "scientific spirit." He believed that mathematics, more than any other branch of learning, was better suited to provide a foundation for life because it was about "a scientific view, a scientific thought, and a scientific spirit." His definition of the scientific spirit at this point was "the spirit that attempts to determine, based on experiential facts, whether any causal relationship exists between plural facts, and to discover and identify laws governing such relationships."[15] He promoted statistics not only because of its practicality but also because of its capacity to identify causal relationships. Influenced by Henri Bergson's philosophy of life, as were many other Taishō Japanese intellectuals, Ogura considered mathematics not to be a fixed body of knowledge but a way of thinking, a way of life that was always evolving. Moreover, to him the scientific way of thinking was intimately related to modernity, as it is "the unique character of modern civilization." The scientific spirit was born out of "people's struggle to destroy the hoary religion, nation, and ethics" and to attain "freedom of thought."[16] He believed that the promotion of the right kind of mathematics education was crucial for the development of the scientific spirit in Japan and, ultimately, for the achievement of modernity in Japan.

According to Ogura, nurturing of the scientific spirit needed to begin early in one's life. Japanese science education for younger students, thus, did

↳ For ex.

not escape his harsh critique. It was clear to him that the current education system's "formalistic" focus on theories killed students' curiosity about nature. Children, Ogura argued, had a distinctive psychological development pattern: when small, they wonder at nature (*shizen no kyōi*); in youth, their spiritual growth allows them to understand the theoretical aspects of nature; and when mature, they can reflect on nature, which enables them to detach themselves from it. Only when children's curiosity about the wonder of nature and instinct to know were combined would real science be possible.[17] In Ogura's analysis, the entire Japanese science education system, from the elementary school up to the university level, was responsible for the failure to develop the scientific spirit.

Ogura's was one of the earliest discussions of the "scientific spirit" in Japan, a concept that would become popular in the following two decades. However, Ogura was not the first Japanese to talk about it. Already in 1915, physicist Tanakadate Aikitsu had emphasized the significance of the scientific spirit in his speech in the House of Peers to obtain support for the establishment of an aeronautic science institute in Japan. He stated: "It is thought that Western civilization is a material and mechanistic civilization, that is, a physical civilization that lacks spirituality. It is also thought that Eastern civilization is metaphysical, spiritual, characterized with a superior sense of duty and filial piety. . . . I wonder if we can interpret Western and Eastern civilizations in such a simplistic manner. . . . I ask you, is Western civilization really based on such a superficial basis?"[18] To further elaborate this point, Tanakadate gave the example of Galileo as someone who sacrificed himself for his belief in scientific truth. "This spirit," he explained, "seems to me to be the spirit behind the so-called material and mechanistic civilization."[19] And it is this spirit, Tanakadate continued, that Japan needs in order to develop science domestically rather than merely importing technologies from the West. Tanakadate's speech indicates that rather than see the difference between Meiji and Taishō as that of material production versus spiritual cultivation, or science versus culture, we should see Taishō as the time when this distinction itself was being challenged. By the mid-1910s, science had begun to be discussed as part of the spiritual culture.

The scientific spirit, understood by Tanakadate Aikitsu and Ogura Kinnosuke, was something new, a radical departure from the Meiji slogan of "Western science and technology, and Eastern ethics." The dichotomization of Western science and Eastern ethics presumes the lack of spirituality in science. Science (and technology) is assumed to be knowledge, techniques, something that can be superficially learned, copied, and reproduced. Spirituality is reserved for the "East," as if spirituality and science can be completely separated. The concept of the scientific spirit, on the other hand, challenges this dichotomy. Taishō Japan's promotion of research and development during and after World War I destabilized the Meiji dichotomy of "Eastern" ethics and "Western" science and technology by presuming and promoting Japan's own ability to produce new science and technology; that is, science and technology were not simply Western products to be bought and copied any longer. The Kōjin Club's definition of technology as a cultural creation was a technocratic expression of this new view of science and technology that was no longer particularly "Western" but universal. Tanakadate and Ogura, too, both viewed the scientific spirit as something universal. Both believed that this spirit could be, and should be, acquired by Westerners and Japanese alike. To them, the scientific spirit was the spirit of modernity, specific to time but not to place.

Yet, Ogura's concept of scientific spirit was different from that of Tanakadate. It should be noted that Tanakadate's speech was made to support the establishment of a research center as part of the promotion of the domestic production of science and technology. To Ogura, however, the scientific spirit had ultimately little to do with the discovery of scientific theories and new technologies. To him, the scientific spirit was about a way of thinking, a way of life, that characterized modernity. Education was thus important. He believed that the Japanese needed to be exposed to the scientific spirit during childhood and that children needed to learn it through a better mathematics education.

Ogura was not alone in seeing the need to reform science education in Japan. The promotion of domestic science and technology during and after World War I led to the rigorous promotion of science education, and many educators began to advocate a new science education radically different from the existing school curriculum established under the Meiji government. One elementary school educator recalls this time as follows:

> It was around the end of World War I that I became a teacher. The nation was full of loud calls for self-sufficiency, domestic production, and further industrialization. In the field of education, too, practical science education was vigorously promoted. You would not believe the extent of the promotion of the popularization of scientific knowledge and the development of the scientific training. We would even scrutinize materials for the reader and examine how to teach reading in relation to science.[20]

Teachers discussed, advocated, and experimented with new pedagogy, which was often referred to as the "liberal education movement." In 1918 elementary school educators from all over the nation established the Natural Science Education Study Group (*rika kyōiku kenkyūkai*), the first association of its kind in Japan, and began a monthly journal, *Rika kyōiku* (Natural Science Education). Like Ogura, these reformers advocated the incorporation of experiments, visual aids, and children's voluntary participation into classroom teaching. The Taishō government, also galvanized by the power of science and technology in the European War, actively responded to the reformers' demands. In 1919, for example, the Ministry of Education increased the number of hours for natural sciences for both elementary and middle schools. Before this revision, the natural science curriculum began in the fifth grade of elementary school and the fourth year of middle school; the new science curriculum started in the fourth grade of elementary school and the third year of the middle school. The education reformers, however, envisioned a more radical reform. For example, at the first meeting of the Natural Science Education Study Group, an officer from the Ministry of Education stood speechless as participants demanded reasons for why the natural science curriculum could not start in the first grade.[21] In fact, many reformer-educators in private schools had already begun experimenting with teaching natural sciences to younger students, calling it "natural studies."

Besides natural studies, mathematics was another field of science that received much criticism from education reformers. Like the natural science textbook, the mathematics textbooks that the Ministry of Education prepared had remained unchanged since the mid-Meiji period. New mathematics pedagogies such as the one advocated by Perry and Klein were being introduced to Japan through works by those who had studied abroad, including Ogura.[22] Although the state-produced textbooks were not revised until 1931, many schools—especially private schools and girls' schools, which were not as restricted as public schools by state protocols—began to develop their own mathematics curricula. As we will see in Chapter 6, the science education reform movement—both in natural studies and mathematics—continued and culminated in the 1941 Education Edict under the wartime government.

In the mid-1920s, Ogura became ill and was forced to slow down publishing mathematical writings. He decided to use his time of rest to translate Western works on new mathematics. Among the books he translated was Florian Cajori's *History of Elementary Mathematics* (1893),[23] which had a section on the rise of mercantile mathematics. Curious about mercantile mathematics, he ordered from abroad a number of the sixteenth-century British textbooks cited in Cajori's work. Meanwhile, Ogura picked up a book in a department store that would drastically change his life and scholarship. It was a Japanese translation of *Art in Class Society* by a Soviet theorist, Georgi Plekhanov (1856–1918).[24]

Plekhanov's *Art in Class Society* examined the development of aesthetics within the context of social conditions and rejected the assumption that the feeling for beauty was universal and inherent in humans. After reading Plekhanov, Ogura began to wonder whether mathematics could also be understood as part of the superstructure, like art in Plekhanov's work. As soon as Ogura received the sixteenth-century mathematics textbooks he had ordered, he wrote a series of articles, beginning with his famous "Arithmetic in Class Society" published in the September 1929 issue of *Kaizō* (Reconstruction), a

[handwritten margin notes: "How ~ many intellectuals were influenced by Marx ism JP"; "Marxism was big w/ intellectuals"]

leftist monthly opinion journal. The conclusion of this article, that "following the logic in Plekhanov's work on art . . . the class who rules society also rules arithmetic," shocked any reader who had assumed that mathematics was pure science that stood aloof from social relationships.[25]

It may be difficult to understand why Ogura, a specialist in mathematics, would cite a Soviet Marxist work on art so casually, unless we comprehend the status of Marxism among Japanese intellectuals in the 1920s. The extent of Marxist influence among Japanese intellectuals—whether Marxists or not—in prewar and postwar Japan was such that it is probably extremely difficult to find a scholar completely immune to it, at least until the 1980s. It was during the 1920s that Marxism established itself as a "science of society" in academia, constituting a dominant current in social science. The association of science with Marxism had already been made when Marxism was first introduced to Japan in the 1900s as "scientific socialism." Meiji socialists like Sakai Toshihiko and Kōtoku Shūsui welcomed Marxism as a new, scientific theory to guide the Japanese socialist movement that had just begun. One of the earliest Marxist works introduced to Japan was Engels's *From Utopia to Science*, translated in 1906 as *Kūsō kara kagaku e*.[26] By the time *Das Kapital* was translated into Japanese in 1920, "scientific socialism" systematized by Engels constituted the core of Marxism as it was understood in Japan.[27] Upon the establishment of the Soviet Union, Marxism came to be clearly distinguished from Christian socialism and anarchism, and the founding of the Japan Communist Party in 1922 made Marxist-Leninist socialism the mainstream of the leftist camp.[28]

Japan's post–World War I recession contributed to the proliferation of Marxist scholarship, especially in the field of economics. The wartime economic boom, which worked advantageously for factory workers, ended rather abruptly with a recession in 1920. Japan of the 1920s lay before Japanese economists as a patient plagued with a chronic recession and infested with social unrest. World War I brought the rapid development of monopoly capitalism in heavy industry due to the temporary withdrawal of Western products from the international market, but it also disproportionately distressed the agrarian sector. The tenant farmers' and factory workers' dispute reached a prewar peak. The Tokyo earthquake of 1923 further aggravated Japan's sluggish economy, and the 1927 financial crisis pulled the Japanese market into a depression even before the New York stock market collapsed in 1929. "Social problems" (*shakai mondai*) caused by this malady—agrarian poverty and labor issues in particular—were the symptoms of deeper problems of the Japanese economic and political system that awaited the economists' diagnosis and remedy.

As a progressive alternative to the British neoclassical economics and German historical economics that had dominated the field, Marxian economics was mainly introduced to Japan by economists who studied abroad in Germany. It is rather ironic that elite universities like the imperial universities, whose purpose was to produce the nation's leaders and bureaucrats, should send their faculty abroad to learn Marxism, which was soon to be a target of severe state suppression. Germany, however, had been a favorite place for state-funded studies abroad since the Meiji period, and it also had been an international center for the study of economics as well as other fields. A decade earlier, Japanese students came back with the historical economics dominant at the time in Germany. In the 1910s and 1920s, those students with a moral and intellectual interest in Japanese social and economic problems, such as Kawakami Hajime, keenly absorbed the Marxian economics that flourished in their host country, which was also struggling with similar "social problems."

This was also the time economics gained an independent professional identity in Japan. In 1919 Tokyo Imperial University's economics department was separated from the Department of Law, and other imperial and private universities followed suit. The first economics faculty in the nation included such Marxist scholars as Ōuchi Hyōe (Tokyo Imperial University), Gonda Yasunosuke (Tokyo Imperial University), Kushida Tamizō (Tokyo Imperial University), Kawakami Hajime (Kyoto Imperial University), and Ōtsuka Kinnosuke (Hitotsubashi University). They all learned Marxian economics in Germany and brought back a large collection of Marxist works to Japan (Kushida and Ōuchi allegedly competed with David Riazanov, the director of the newly established Marx-Engels Institute in the Soviet Union, in hunting for used Marxist books in Germany). They also invited the Marxist economist Emil Lederer from Heidelberg to teach at Tokyo Imperial University between 1923 and 1927.[29]

By the mid-1920s, Marxian economics constituted a dominant current in social science. In fact, "social science" in interwar Japan meant specifically a scientific study of society based on Marxism. All the volumes, for example, in the series Social Science Collection (*Shakai kagaku sōsho*) published in 1921 were on Marxism.[30] As historian Ishida Takeshi describes, "[S]ocial science was nothing but a synonym for Marxism, rather than a general term for the various fields of the sciences of society."[31]

The establishment of Marxism as a social science also owed much to Fukumoto Kazuo's exploration of Marxism and the so-called Kōza Series (*Nihon shihonshugi hattatsushi kōza*), a collection of studies that examined Japanese capitalism based on Fukumoto's thesis. Fukumoto, after studying Marxism in Germany from 1922 to 1924, wrote numerous articles introducing names unfamiliar to the Japanese at the time—for example, Karl Korsch and Georg Lukács—and developed an understanding of Japan that emphasized the unique characteristics of its capitalism, namely, the coexistence of capitalism and feudalism (i.e., the emperor system and the landlord system) that kept Japan "semifeudalistic" (*han hōkenteki*). The Kōza thesis was a direct challenge to the Rōnō faction, which regarded Japan as already being a bourgeois society. Fukumoto argued that Japanese Marxists needed to first solidify their own theoretical understanding of Marxism and Japanese modernity before forming a united front with the masses for a revolution. When the 1927 Comintern thesis condemned Fukumoto's strategy (while emphasizing that Japan was indeed too backward to have a revolution), Fukumoto lost his influence within the Japan Communist Party. However, the Kōza thesis emphasizing Japan's semifeudalistic, incomplete modernity remained the dominant view of Japanese modernity among Japanese Marxists, as was confirmed in the 1932 thesis of the Comintern. To Japanese Communists, the conflict between the Kōza and Rōnō factions meant not just a different analysis of Japan's past and present but also a different line of actions required for a socialist revolution in Japan's future.

In the eyes of non-Communist or non-Marxist intellectuals, however, the significance of the Kōza series had little to do with the authority of the Comintern or the internal debate among Japanese Communists. Maruyama Masao, a political scientist known for his non-Marxist critique of Japanese modernity, recalled in 1961 how he felt when he first read the Kōza series in the mid-1930s:

> It has been common to explain the influence of the Kōza series as inseparable from the authority of the Communist Party and Comintern . . . but my experience was totally different. The 1932 thesis and all that had nothing to do with me. It was the [series'] *scientific* analysis of Japanese capitalism that opened my blind eyes. I believe there were quite a few people who were influenced by it without having any knowledge of the Communist Party or its members.[32]

For intellectuals like Maruyama and Ogura, the appeal of Marxism presented through the Kōza series lay in its "scientificity" (*kagakusei*)—as claimed by Marxists and perceived by the Japanese audience—of universal, systematic, and critical theory.[33] Even after the demise of the Fukumoto thesis among Japanese Communist members, the Kōza faction's analysis of Japanese capitalism and modernity remained influential among Japanese intellectuals. It continued to constitute the core of Ogura's analysis of Japanese modernity and science even into postwar years.

The characterization of Marxism as "scientific" and the dominance of Marxism in the social sciences explain the accessibility of Marxist scholarship to intellectuals like Ogura whose primary concern had been mathematics rather than the issue of class. Plekhanov's work was especially popular in Japan, as he was one of a few Soviet theorists known to Japanese socialists whose exposure to Marxism had been exclusively to the German theories, at

least until the October Revolution of 1919.[34] Japanese Marxist literary critics and writers such as Nakano Shigeharu and Kurahara Koreto introduced
Plekhanov's theory of art to Japan.[35] The fact that Ogura read Kurahara's
translation of Plekhanov's *Art in Class Society* within several months of its
publication attests to the popularity of Marxism and Plekhanov outside the
Communist intellectual circle. Ogura later recalled the shock he received
from the work: "To kill time during my train trip to Kurashiki where I was
asked to give a lecture, I bought this book at Hankyū Department Store. But
once I opened the book, I was taken aback. Is this what the class nature of
arts means? If [Plekhanov's] theory was right, I knew I had noticed the class
nature in mathematics as well. It was as if vague ideas floating in my head all
of [a] sudden came to have clear shapes."[36]

The impact of Ogura's 1929 essay on Japanese intellectuals was both
immediate and enormous. Ogura's first "Arithmetic in Class Society" attracted much attention from Japanese Marxist historians such as Hani Gorō
(1901–83) and Marxist philosophers such as Tosaka Jun (1900–1945) and
Miki Kiyoshi (1897–1945). Hani, Tosaka, and Miki had just begun to explore new theoretical understandings of Marxism and society after the fall
of the Fukumoto thesis, by publishing a new magazine, *Shinkō kagaku no
hata no motoni* (Under the Banner of the New Science; hereafter *Shinkō
kagaku*), a resurrection of Fukumoto's 1926 journal, *Marukusu shugi no hata
no motoni* (Under the Banner of Marxism), which lasted only four months.
As historian Kevin Doak argues, the use of "new science" in the title instead
of "Marxism" is significant, as it emphasized the ambition of these Marxist
intellectuals to be open to non-Marxism in creating a new science across
disciplines and ideologies.[37] It should also be emphasized that "new science"
was meant to attract non-Marxists as well as to distract the Special Higher
Police (*tokubetsu kōtō keisatsu*, or *tokkō*), a police force established in 1910
specifically to control political groups and thoughts deemed to be a threat
to the state, which had conducted a mass arrest of leftist leaders six months
prior to the first issue (October 1928) of *Shinkō kagaku*.

It was in this intellectual and political environment that Ogura began to
study Marxism. He began ordering Marxist books from abroad and sub-
scribed to *Shinkō kagaku*.[38] Even though his subscription to the journal was
short-lived (the Marxist journal ended its publication with the December
1929 issue), the results of their interaction instantly appeared in Ogura's
scholarship and its impact was long lasting. Shortly after his "Arithmetic
in Class Society," Ogura published four more articles under the same title.
First, in December 1929 came "Arithmetic in Class Society: An Analysis
of Arithmetic in North and South America during the Colonial Period,"
which compared arithmetic textbooks in the areas under British rule and
Spanish rule, while citing Hani's works and articles from *Shinkō kagaku*.

Three more articles, published in the spring and summer of the following year, discussed mathematical education in France from the sixteenth to the nineteenth centuries and examined how the content of mathematical education reflected a shift in political power from the absolutist, elite class to the bourgeoisie. Besides the Arithmetic in Class Society series in *Shisō*, Ogura also published "The Social Nature of Arithmetic" (*Sanjutsu no shakaisei*) in *Kaizō* (September 1929). This article examined the economic conditions of sixteenth-century Britain as reflected in the content of an arithmetic textbook written by a renowned mathematician, Robert Recorde. Ogura explained that "since [an introductory arithmetic textbook] incorporates problems of everyday life, even if the author did not intend to do so, the textbook provides materials for social sciences."[39] Together, all these essays strengthened Ogura's earlier argument: the development of science reflected the development of the political economic structures in society.[40]

Historicizing Science as Ideology

Ogura Kinnosuke's encounter with Marxism changed his scholarship in three major ways. First, he came to deny the separation of the natural and social sciences; instead, he began to argue that the same scientific approach should be applied to the studies of both the natural and the social worlds. This was made most clear when Ogura republished his 1923 essay on mathematics education in 1937. In his note to the reprinted essay, he explained that "back then, I thought of science only as referring to natural science. . . . The scientific spirit, however, does not only belong to natural science."[41] Accordingly, he corrected his earlier writing, adding that one should "please read 'nature and society' where I have written 'nature,' and 'natural and social sciences' where I have written 'natural science.'"[42]

Second, as class became the central feature of Ogura's analysis after 1929, mathematics came to be explicitly identified as an ideology. When Iwanami published a series on ideology in the early 1930s, Ogura contributed a volume titled *The Development of Ideology: Mathematics*, which argued that "like other fields of science, mathematics is, on the fundamental level, determined by the evolutionary stages of productive power, technology, and economy."[43] This work covered a longer time period than his earlier essays, starting with ancient Greece. He also pushed the relationship between mathematics and ideology further. In the thinking of Plato and his successors, Ogura saw the beginning of mathematics as a distinctive field of learning as well as the ideological separation of mathematics as pure learning from its practical uses in commerce. He also regarded eighteenth-century German mathematics, which emphasized pure mathematics over practical mathematics, as an idealist "German ideology." Ogura concluded that in the period of the maturity of capitalism, mathematics developed aloof from practical matters into "mathematics for the sake of mathematics."[44] In contrast to his earlier humanistic idealization of "mathematics for the sake of mathematics,"[45] Ogura now regarded this kind of mathematics as that of the ivory tower.

Third, and most important for our discussion, after 1929 Ogura turned his attention to a historical explanation of the problems with Japanese mathematics he had earlier identified. Ogura came to hold a firm view that the history of science had to be scientific itself. Based on his understanding of Marxism, he defined a scientific history as a history that examined science as part of the superstructure: "The history of science becomes a scientific history of science only when it is sought as the history of the superstructure and examines its relationship to the base economic relations and various ideologies."[46] Based on this new historicism, Ogura began to criticize Japanese science as feudalistic and bureaucratic.

For example, as part of the 1932 Kōza series Lectures on the History of Development of Japanese Capitalism, Ogura wrote a history of mathematics in modern Japan. According to Ogura, while the Meiji government replaced the "feudalistic" *wasan*—Japanese mathematics developed in the Tokugawa period—with the international and more systematic Western mathematics, it also molded this Western mathematics into a bureaucratic discipline monopolized by the imperial universities in which no outsider could participate. Ogura explained that this process was completed as Japanese capitalism was established through the Sino-Japanese War (1894–95) and matured into the imperialist stage through the Russo-Japanese War (1904–5). The bureaucratic academic mathematics focused on theoretical mathematics such as geometry and dismissed practical mathematics, which, to Ogura's dismay, led to the separation of mathematics from society. He concluded that such mathematics was not mathematics for the people but merely "a pretty flower nurtured in the greenhouse called the university." It was something that "needs to be thoroughly criticized."[47]

Although Ogura had never been a part of the Kōza-Rōnō debate itself, the influence of the Kōza interpretation of Japanese capitalism is clear in his characterization of Japanese modernity as an incomplete modernity hindered by feudal remnants. He also used the vocabularies established by the Kōza faction, such as "parasitic landlords" and "semifeudal." For example, Ogura's 1935 writing, "The Historicity of Japanese Mathematics Education," argued that the Meiji Restoration was "basically incomplete as a democratic and bourgeois revolution. It resulted in a Japanese capitalism full of parasitic landlords, commercial loan sharks, and militarism that led to the establishment of the oligarchy-dominated government and the lingering of many semifeudalistic remnants."[48] He directly correlated and connected the problems of mathematics in modern Japan to the characteristics identified by

Kōza-faction Marxists as the unique problems of Japanese capitalism. After 1929 Ogura came to view the problems with Japanese mathematics as the result of the unique, problematic development of Japanese capitalism. The problems he had earlier found in Japanese mathematics were now identified specifically as the problems of Japanese modernity. Through Marxism, Ogura's earlier criticism found a historical explanation of why it became the kind of mathematics that needed to be criticized.

In Ogura's analysis, these problems did not only plague Japanese mathematics. They were the problems of science in Japan. Ogura's critique of Japanese science was concrete and remained unchanged throughout his life. His 1936 essay "The Duty of Natural Scientists" summarized his critique most succinctly. In it, he articulated five major problems. First, because Japan was a late developer in the competitive industrialized world, Japan had focused on importing and mimicking science abroad. This led to the lack of creativity among Japanese scientists. Second, because Japan had lacked its own established scientific tradition, the development of modern science occurred without the participation of the masses. As a result, the ordinary Japanese, especially those in agricultural areas, had no access to science. Third, Japanese science had been heavily slanted toward military science, with the military and capitalists dominating research facilities. This again had resulted in the exclusion of the masses; even libraries were closed to them. Fourth, Japanese natural scientists were bureaucratic and feudalistic. They formed strong cliques along academic lineages and did not engage in productive criticism among themselves in fear of being excluded from their own clique. Fifth, instead of intellectual, critical conversations, they engaged in unproductive cliquish disputes for their own egos and career ambitions. These problems explained why, according to Ogura, Japan was still behind the West in the scientific competition.[49] To Ogura, the problems reflected the serious deformation of science, a clear sign of Japan's incomplete modernity.

In addition to highlighting these problems, Ogura was especially critical of Japanese scientists for their lack of concern for social issues. He was frustrated that they only cared about protecting their research positions and that they were too isolated from society to even be aware of social problems and needs. They confused being patriotic with blindly following orders from the state and their seniors, Ogura lamented. Study social problems! Cleanse factionalism! Promote science education for the masses! Ogura impatiently demanded that natural scientists fulfill their duties.[50]

To Ogura, the lack of interest in society among Japanese scientists meant that they lacked the scientific spirit for critical thinking. They were not truly scientists, for the real scientist "must fiercely exercise the scientific spirit that denies any idol,"[51] as the "scientific spirit respects and promotes the freedom of thought. The modern scientific spirit was born of an attempt to break down and overcome the old, fixed forms of religion, the nation-state, and ethics."[52] Ogura always referred to the scientific spirit as a universal spirit, neither Western nor Japanese. But it is presumable that the "real scientist" in Ogura was his idealized image of scientists of the Enlightenment, since in various places he wrote very favorably about French and British mathematics (France, where Ogura received much intellectual and cultural stimulus, was held especially high in his assessment). Whether or not such a scientist really existed, Ogura's criticism of the "uniquely deformed" Japanese science depended on his conception of an ideal scientist who truly cared more about social needs than about his own career. Marxism offered Ogura a framework in which Japanese problems could be compared to and measured by a universal norm. For Marxist economists, the development of capitalism in the West constituted the universal norm; for Ogura, it was Western science.

The Unique Problem of Japanese Science

The history of *wasan* compared to that of Western mathematics seemed to Ogura to be particularly convincing and convenient evidence for the problems of Japanese science and modernity. *Wasan* was a kind of mathematics that developed during the Tokugawa period (1603–1868). It was a field that developed as an intellectual game rather than for practical uses. Originally based on Chinese mathematics books brought to Japan in the late sixteenth century, *wasan* was developed by Japanese mathematicians to be a highly sophisticated game of algebraic calculation, geometry, and number theory through such formats as *idai* (posing challenging algebraic or geometric problems in books and then having those who solved the problems publish their solutions along with another set of problems) and *sangaku* (beautifully decorated hanging wooden tablets with their geometric problems and solutions under the roof of a shrine or temple). *Wasan* mathematicians studied certain aspects of mathematics deeply—for example, the area of circles, length of circular arcs, volume of intersecting solids, and solutions to indefinite equations and magic squares—but did not attempt to synthesize their solutions into a systematic understanding of geometry or algebra. Although some mathematicians studied selective aspects of astronomy and surveying, *wasan* remained a problem-solving brain exercise and never became a systematic knowledge of nature to be used for practical applications.[53] For this reason, when the Meiji government instituted the new education system, it chose Western mathematics as the modern mathematics to be taught at school in Japan. The introduction of Western mathematics in the school curriculum together with the Confucian ethics classes serves perhaps as the best example of the Meiji slogan "Western science and technology, and

Eastern ethics." *Wasan* rapidly declined and by the 1910s had become a topic of historians' research.

To Ogura, *wasan* was representative of the problems caused by Japan's feudalism. Ogura argued that *wasan* did not develop as a practical science partly because the natural sciences and industrial technology were still immature in Tokugawa Japan, but more important, because of its feudal practice—various guildlike schools of *wasan* would conceal their techniques from one another. In Ogura's eyes, such feudalistic practice continued to haunt Japanese science even after Western mathematics replaced *wasan*. Meiji and Taishō scientists formed factions among themselves just as *wasan* mathematicians had, and their "selfish" factionalist competitions hindered the development of science as a whole.[54]

Ogura, however, was not the first to critically approach the history of *wasan* in Japan. *Japanese Mathematics As Seen from Cultural History* (*Bunkashijō yori mitaru nihon no sūgaku*) by an independent researcher from Hiroshima, Mikami Yoshio (1875–1950), published in 1922, was both the first work that examined the history of *wasan* and the first cultural history of science in Japan.[55] Like Ogura, Mikami was highly critical of the Japanese knowledge-making practice and concerned with the status of Japanese mathematics and modernity. At the same time, Ogura's critical view of *wasan* sharply contrasted with that of Mikami. A comparison between Ogura's and Mikami's history of *wasan* is helpful here because it illuminates Ogura's class analysis more lucidly while also locating his scholarship in a wider intellectual context. Mikami's ahistorical conception of the "Japanese national character" would later be used to celebrate the very Japanese character that Mikami was critical of, as we will see in the following chapter.

Mikami's *Japanese Mathematics* began with his explanation that *wasan* emerged in the late sixteenth century as a reflection of commercialization and urbanization and flourished during the Tokugawa period as these conditions intensified. Mikami then demonstrated that unlike mathematics in the West, *wasan* did not develop as practical knowledge or philosophical thesis: The major questions of *wasan* had less to do with practical concerns and more to do with the intellectual joys of working on challenging problems, such as calculating pi to fifty decimal places; *wasan* was initially most popular among samurai, who did not use mathematical knowledge for their work; and Edo, heart of the samurai culture, rather than the commercial hub Osaka, was the center for *wasan*.[56] This phenomenon completely undermined Mikami's conviction that the Japanese were practical minded: "Mathematics grows apart from its practical usage in any country's history . . . , but we have to ask why the Japanese, who are not theoretical about anything else, developed only mathematics to such a degree beyond practicality."[57] According to Mikami, *wasan* developed during the Tokugawa period mainly as a hobby of samurai and wealthy commoners who had the time and money to indulge in it. However, during the Bunka and Bunsei periods (1804–27), "*wasan* rapidly spread around the nation, and *wasan* practitioners came from all the classes in society as well as various regions of the nation."[58] Its popularity declined, though, once the Meiji government adopted Western mathematics, considered more practical than *wasan*. As a consequence, to Mikami's dismay, mathematics became a field monopolized by an academic elite who had mastered Western mathematics.

To the extent that Mikami attributed the rise of *wasan* to social and economic factors, his work resembles Ogura's analysis of the class origin of modern mathematics. Class, however, is not a significant factor in Mikami's analysis and in fact disappears in the middle of his narrative. He ended up portraying *wasan* as a classless, nationally enjoyed hobby. As to why *wasan* came to be enjoyed across class lines at the beginning of the nineteenth century, Mikami offered no social or economic explanation. Rather, he attributed this phenomenon to the national character: *wasan* attained the status of a nationwide hobby because of the unique character of the Japanese people. According to him, the Japanese enjoyed *wasan* just as elites and commoners alike enjoyed *waka* because it required nothing "intellectual" (*richiteki na mono*).[59] Mikami's work, thus, is as much about the character of the Japanese people as it is about *wasan*.

Mikami understood the Japanese character to be as follows. First, the Japanese were neither logical nor philosophical; rather, they were emotional and technical. His chapter titled "Japanese Logical Thought" actually discussed the *lack* of logical thought of the Japanese. Referring to Japanese music and other kinds of artistic pastimes such as composition of Japanese poetry, he asserted that the Japanese favored arts that appealed to emotion rather than to philosophical or systematic thought.[60] It made sense, then, to Mikami that Westerners and the Chinese were concerned with the philosophical and political implications of mathematics, while the Japanese were not.[61] Second, the Japanese had little respect for knowledge. For example, he found it customary for Tokugawa mathematicians to use the names of others instead of their own as the authors of texts, just as the texts of unknown students were published under the names of their well-known teachers in the Meiji and Taishō periods.[62] In an article published the same year as his *Japanese Mathematics*, Mikami focused on this point. If mathematicians, who "are supposed to be fair," would do such a thing, "there must be a deep-rooted reason for such a deplorable state of Japanese mathematics. I think we can conclude that Japanese in general have a dishonest character and that Japanese mathematicians are a reflection of this."[63]

Ogura acknowledged Mikami's scholarship by citing his works frequently. He also respected Mikami's tireless devotion to research without institutional support or academic acknowledgment. However, he did not agree with Mi-kami's analysis of *wasan*. In contrast to Mikami's characterization of *wasan* as a classless hobby, Ogura viewed *wasan* as a mathematics of the elite, a "mathematics for the exploitation of peasants."[64] The two pioneers in the history of Japanese mathematics never became close associates because of this political and intellectual difference. When Ogura cited Mikami's schol-arship, he emphasized only a selected aspect of Mikami's analysis, namely, unproductive competition and secretiveness among the *wasan* schools, which Ogura called "guilds."[65] Although Ogura did identify a difference between Western and Japanese mathematics, to him the difference lay between West-ern "international, systematic mathematics" and Japanese "feudalistic, guildish mathematics," not the distinction between the Westerners' disposition toward philosophical and logical thinking and the Japanese disposition to pleasure that Mikami highlighted. It was important for Ogura to ground his criti-cism on the social and economic structure rather than on a fixed national trait, because the goal for Ogura was for Japan to overcome its incomplete modernity, to change and modernize itself. Ogura identified the problems of Japanese science so that Japanese scientists could correct them. To Ogura, the scientific spirit was universal, something attainable regardless of nationalities; in fact, the scientific spirit was something that should have come to Japan together with modern science. To Ogura, to view the "feudalistic" traits in modern Japan as an inherent, unchanging character of the Japanese as Mi-kami did would be a denial of the potential progress of Japan toward a real modernity.

It is important to note here that even though Ogura did not agree with Mikami's essentialization of the Japanese people that ignored class differ-ence and power dynamics, the concept of *kokumin* in the early 1920s had progressive, critical force. Mikami's invocation of the concept of people—as *kokumin*—as the main operative of his history writing was in fact a bold challenge to the dominant elitism in academic historiography in Taishō Japan. In Mikami's work, *kokumin* meant "people" as opposed to "the state" or "the elite."

Mikami's choice of cultural history as a methodology was itself a protest against academic elitism.[66] Cultural history as a genre was just emerging in Japan in the early 1920s. In fact, Mikami's work is one of the earliest book-length works titled "cultural history." Called "a history of Taishō de-mocracy" by some, cultural history developed as a challenge to the highly empirical academic historiography of Tokyo Imperial University.[67] Pioneer cultural historians such as Nishida Naojirō refused to see history as a mere chronology of political and war-related events of the political elites and instead attempted to write a history of people and their culture. Sharing this spirit, Mikami declared in the introduction to *Japanese Mathematics* that, rather than write the history of *wasan* through an internal development of problems, solutions, and lineages, "we need to see it from the broad perspective of cultural history and to determine how it was related to the development of social conditions, the national [*kokuminteki*] character, and culture in general."[68] Mikami, in other words, wanted to interpret *wasan* history as a history of people, not of the samurai and wealthy merchants. This desire may have partly come from his own position in the academic world. He was an independent researcher who did not graduate from or teach at an imperial university. As a result, his research suffered greatly, as he had little access to university archives and research funding. Despite his contribution to the history of *wasan* and the introduction of *wasan* to the Western world, Mikami rarely received academic acknowledgment until after World War II.[69] The newly emerging field of cultural history gave him a methodology and framework that allowed him to analyze *wasan* as a "bottom-up" history, and his use of *kokumin* as an antidote to the elite-centrism constituted his critical stance toward the authoritative government and its historiography.

Cultural history that essentialized a national culture without considering the context of class and other power dynamics, however, was problematic. Marxist critic Tokasa Jun predicted in the 1930s that phenomenological cultural history would become an ally of fascism later. Although Tosaka did not discuss Mikami's work, his criticism of phenomenology in fact articulates the problem of Mikami's approach to history. Tosaka argued that phenomenologists look at "a stage on which phenomena appear and disappear, and that stage is called various things, such as consciousness or existence. . . . The problem is that the meaning of phenomena is always only examined at the surface level." Such an approach, Tosaka continued, would not allow one to delve into something deeper that lay behind the observed phenomena.[70] Tosaka warned that liberalism, to which the "philologism" of phenomenology belonged in his analysis, could easily turn into a friend of fascism because it disregarded deeper problems behind phenomena.

By imposing the modern concept of "Japanese national people" onto Tokugawa society and examining phenomena of *wasan* at the "surface level," Mikami's analysis did suffer. Since Mikami characterized *wasan* as an expression of the national character rather than a reflection of specific social and economic conditions, it suffered from being tautological and ahistorical. He characterized *wasan* as an impractical mathematics because it developed as a hobby of the leisure class. But he also explained that *wasan* did not develop a philosophical synthesis because of the Japanese character—not the character of the Japanese elite—which prefers emotional joy rather than philosophical and theoretical thinking. Because of this character, *wasan* spread its popularity beyond the elite strata, becoming a national hobby. In this tautological circle, anything could be a reflection of a predetermined Japanese character, and Japanese character could be used to explain any historical phenomenon. Assumed in this logic is the unchanging, permanent nature of the Japanese character, and lost is the consideration of how social and economic factors might have contributed to the history of *wasan*. In addition, if the problem of mathematics resulted from an unchanging national character, there would be no possibility for improvement.

Ogura, in contrast, provided an analysis that presumed the possibility for change. Since, in his view, the problem of Japanese mathematics and science was due to specific social and economic conditions, it would be possible to reform. Japan would and should be able to embrace the critical scientific spirit and full modernity. Japan would be able to become a scientific Japan where science exists for the masses and scientists are actively engaged with social issues.

Ogura's vision of a scientific Japan was very different from that of the technocrats we examined in Part 1. To Miyamoto Takenosuke and his technocrat colleagues, Japan was unscientific not because it was semifeudal and lacked the scientific spirit but because it did not let technocrats run the nation and the empire. The Kōjin technocrats advocated their technocracy as the "scientific" way of solving the labor problem, with engineers acting as mediators between capitalists and workers, and of maintaining the colonial hierarchy, with engineers acting as mediators between Japan and its colonies. Ogura and the technocrats did share one criticism—that the lack of communication and collaboration among Japanese scientists had a deleterious effect on the development of science and technology in Japan. But their analyses of and solutions to this problem differed significantly. The technocrats defined the "scientific" as rational, in the sense of the rational management of the nation and the empire through technological and scientific expertise. The establishment of the Technology Agency and the Science Council staffed by technocrats was meant to overcome the problem, and social sciences and other sciences that would not immediately contribute to defense and industrial technology were considered to be unnecessary. In contrast, Ogura's vision of a scientific Japan rested on the promotion of the ideal of the universal, systematic, and critical scientific spirit, which he came to believe needed to be fostered in both social and natural sciences. Toward this goal, he found it necessary to develop a correct understanding of the problems of Japanese science based on Marxist analysis. Marxism provided Ogura with the universal standard against which he, together with Kōza-faction theorists, could measure the status and problems of Japanese science and modernity.

Ogura Kinnosuke's class analysis of science, Mikami's liberalist cultural history, and the technology-bureaucrats' technocracy all criticized the status quo of science in Japan differently. Their critiques, which pointed to similar problems, such as the lack of productive collaboration among researchers and the separation of scholarly research and society, came from their differing political positions, agendas, and visions for a scientific Japan. This politics of the scientific intensified in the 1930s, as the next chapter illustrates, with other Marxist intellectuals further developing the class analysis of science that Ogura initiated.

CHAPTER 4

Mapping Marxism onto the Politics of the Scientific

THE POPULARITY OF MARXISM among Japanese intellectuals reached its apex in the early 1930s. State suppression of Marxism and proletarian politics, however, became increasingly severe thereafter. While major Marxist works were being published at the culmination of the Rōnō and Kōza debate (*Nihon shihonshugi hattatsushi kōza* [The History of the Development of Japanese Capitalism], 1932–33; *Nihon shihonshugi bunseki* [The Analysis of Japanese Capitalism], 1933),[1] the murder of major Marxist activists such as Yamamoto Senji in 1929 and Kobayashi Takiji in 1933, as well as the arrest of leading Marxist scholars such as Kawakami Hajime and Noro Eitarō in 1933, made it clear that writing was a life-risking enterprise for Marxists. *Under the Banner of the New Science*, a Marxist magazine that nurtured Ogura Kinnosuke's class analysis in 1929, lasted only two years (October 1928–December 1929). The major proletarian cultural journals, *Bungei sensen* (Literary Battlefront, 1924–30) and *Senki* (Battle Flag, 1929–31), ceased to exist by the beginning of the decade, together with the once-active proletarian culture movement by the All-Japan Federation of Proletarian Arts (NAPF, or *Zennihon musansha geijutsu renmei*, 1928–31) and its successor, the Japan Proletarian Culture Federation (KOPF, or *Nihon puroretaria bunka renmei*, 1931–34).

This did not mean that the Marxist discourse of science disappeared. On the contrary, when the proletarian cultural movement and party politics were being crushed, science became a major battlefront for Marxist intellectuals. In the midst of this state suppression of Marxism, one group was newly organized and survived until as late as 1938, developing the theoretical elaboration of the relationship between science and society. This was Yuibutsuron Kenkyūkai, or Yuiken, which Ogura helped to organize in 1932, along with its leader Tosaka Jun and their fellow Marxist intellectuals Saigusa Hiroto, Oka Kunio, Nagata Hiroshi, Hattori Shisō, and Honda Kenzō. Yuiken played a central role in developing the Marxist politics of the scientific in Japan through its monthly journal, *Yuibutsuron kenkyū* (Study of Materialism). The journal discussed materialism from various angles, such as philosophy, history, literature, laws, and, most important, science, until Yuiken disbanded in 1938. This chapter examines the Yuiken discourse of science, or what I call the Yuiken project, and how it contributed to Marxist politics in Japan in the 1930s.

Yuiken leader Tosaka identified three dominant intellectual currents in Japan in the 1930s: liberalism, Marxism, and fascism. According to Tosaka, fascism took the form of "Japanism," the ideology that emphasized the uniqueness and superiority of Japan based on the imperial mythology and that also legitimized the military state acquiring power to mobilize the nation. He did not perceive the conflict among these three ideologies in Japan in isolation from the world. He saw them as coexisting and correspondent to the ideological struggle in Europe that Frankfurt school scholars observed and European historians have well documented.[2] To demonstrate the contested, political nature of the discourse of science, and to better locate the Yuiken project in the politics of the scientific, my analysis contextualizes three different definitions of science in the larger intellectual and political milieu of the 1930s in Japan. It will do so through two maps of the politics of the scientific, one for 1932 and the other for 1936. The 1930s was the most contested decade for the politics of the scientific, as these three dominant intellectual currents competed over the definition of science and for their own legitimacy.

The 1932 map of the politics of the scientific illustrates how liberalism, Marxism, and Japanism defined science and competed over the legitimizing power of science. The terrain of the politics of the scientific was not constant but changed as new historical events took place and new key words emerged in society. For example, the rise of a conservative, antiscience trend in the mid-1930s that emphasized the "Japanese spirit" in opposition to scientific knowledge forced the promoters of science to address the relationship between the Japanese spirit and the scientific spirit. The 1936 map will show how liberal, Japanist, and Marxist discourses dealt with this question.

The 1932 Map

In November 1932, the Tokyo Science Museum (*Tokyo kagaku hakubutsukan*) held a special exhibition, Science of Edo (*Edo no kagaku*), to celebrate its first anniversary. About a week prior to the Science of Edo exhibit, Marxist intellectuals launched the Yuiken study group and began publishing *Yuibutsuron kenkyū* monthly. In August of the same year, the government established the Institute for the Study of National Spiritual Culture (*kokumin seishin bunka kenkyūjo*) for the purpose of thought control. The Edo exhibit, the materialism study group, and the state mobilization of Japanese "spiritual culture" may seem completely unrelated on the surface, but these three events in fact marked the variations of the "scientific" on the 1932 political map.

The Tokyo Science Museum was opened as a national museum in 1931 in Ueno Park to disseminate scientific knowledge to the general public and to encourage invention and discoveries. The museum was conceived and established as part of the promotion of domestic science and science education during and immediately after World War I, though it did not open its doors until 1931. The Science of Edo exhibit displayed various Tokugawa materials, such as texts in herbology and Japanese mathematics; tools for agriculture and gold mining; and devices like the telescope and *erekiteru* machine, the first electric generator manufactured in Japan by eighteenth-century intellectual Hiraga Gennai. The purpose of this exhibit was to demonstrate the existence of sophisticated science in Japan prior to the Meiji period to correct a common assumption that science came from the West only after the Meiji Restoration.[3] The content of the display, however, partially betrayed this aim since most of the materials exhibited were from the late Tokugawa period, when Dutch learning had been introduced to Japan. Therefore, it may have dissipated the common assumption that Tokugawa Japan did not have science, but it did not deny that science came from the West.

Nonetheless, the exhibit was a great success. On November 3, the museum's anniversary holiday, thirteen thousand people visited the museum.[4] Wide advertisement in newspapers helped, but it was the newness of the theme that attracted so many visitors. As the museum newsletter emphasized, this was the first historical exhibit of science in Japan. Thanks to this success, many history-of-science exhibitions were held in the nation afterward. But there were also complaints from those who had visited the exhibit. In the visitors' book and letters to the museum, some visitors commented that the space was too small and cramped, the materials were displayed without any themes or categorization, and the catalog listed materials by the lender's name rather than by field or industry. One visitor even said: "The herbology section looked almost like a used bookstore. Important books like Siebold's were just piled up on top of each other, and we couldn't see the inside of the books."[5] These visitors' descriptions remind the reader of fair expositions popular in Japan from the end of the nineteenth century: a display of various materials, side by side, out of context of their production. The exhibit displayed historical materials but told no story. Science was, in other words, decontextualized.

Although the exhibit did not have an explicit political agenda, it was not politically neutral. Yoshimi Shun'ya, in his historical study of world expositions and fairs, argues that "the expositions were not neutral spaces . . . of industrial technology or craft design. Expositions, by nature, were the strategic space of culture that was quite political and ideological."[6] Likewise, in 1934 Ogura pointed out the political and ideological nature of science exhibits.

Ogura found historical science exhibits like the Science of Edo to be "ahistorical and unscientific."[7] As we saw in the previous chapter, Ogura had begun developing his class analysis of science from the viewpoint of historical materialism. He believed that the history of science had to be scientific itself. Ogura's definition of "scientific" history, based on Marxism, examined science as part of the superstructure: "The history of science becomes a scientific history of science only when it is sought as the history of the superstructure and examines its relationship to the base economic relations and various ideologies."[8] For him, a history that ignored the relationship between science and the social and economic conditions for the production of science was ahistorical and unscientific. Although pleased that numerous history-of-science exhibits were being held by the "liberal science education reform" educators, Ogura was highly critical of their methodology and implicit politics at the same time.

It was against this kind of "unscientific" understanding of science that Yuiken was launched on October 23, 1932. Ogura visited and critiqued the science history exhibits as one of the seven original organizers of Yuiken. The declared purpose of Yuiken was to study the relationships among science, society, and philosophy from a perspective of materialism. The next section will discuss Yuiken in detail, but here a brief summary of its arguments about science will suffice as the second marker of the 1932 map of the politics of the scientific.

To Ogura and many other Yuiken members, to regard science as independent of its social, economic, and political environments was to ignore its class character. Tosaka Jun, for example, argued in 1932: "The natural sciences are the product of a historical society. In reality, various conditions in society restrict the freedom of research that the natural sciences seek."[9] To Yuiken Marxists, assuming the independence of science from society meant ignoring the political aspect of science. As another writer put it, "[T]he equation 'two plus two equals four' is just one law in mathematical science. . . . However, if this law . . . is abused by mathematicians who belong to a certain group in the class society, then it becomes a totally different matter."[10] Yuiken Marxists believed that to idealize the science of the ivory tower as objective, that is, independent of social and economic factors, was to blind people to the external factors that influenced and constituted science. Tosaka contended: "Modern capitalism used to be a good mother for the natural sciences but not anymore; it has become the prison guard who should not be trusted."[11] In other words, Yuiken's class analysis of science asserted that, by decontextualizing science, bourgeois science pretended to be objective and thus capable of providing the sole truth when in fact it reflected the interest of the bourgeois class.[12]

To Yuiken Marxists, Marxism was the only scientific social theory that could offer a unified and systematic understanding of nature and society. To them, a social theory should be as scientific as theories that explain the natural world, and, as Tosaka argued, "the only social science that shares the conceptual system with the natural sciences . . . is Marxist materialism. It is the only *scientific* social theory."[13] The scientific nature of a theory, they believed, also rested on its universality. In Tosaka's words, "every science, every theory, needs to be *international* in terms of its cash value as an intellectual system. Even philosophical theory, which is fundamentally restricted by the national language because it cannot use equations, needs to be able to be translated."[14] To be scientific, to these Marxists, was to present a universal, systematic, and critical science that could explain the laws of the world—both of nature and society—as a whole.

To challenge this Marxist view of the "scientific," Sakuta Shōichi presented his *kokumin* science, that is, national science. Sakuta, an economics professor at Kyoto Imperial University who later became the vice president of Manchuria National University, was also a researcher at the Institute for the Study of National Spiritual Culture. This institute—the third marker of the 1932 map—was established in 1932 under the Ministry of Education as part of a state propaganda program that was later to be called the "complete reform of education" (*kyōgaku sasshin*).[15] With twenty-four researchers and staff members (increasing to forty-eight in 1942), the institute trained middle and high school teachers, ran a lecture series, and published books on topics such as classic Japanese literature, economics, and Russian studies. Its ultimate purpose was to dispel leftist thought and to clarify the Japanese national polity.[16] The institute played a significant role in state ideology construction. For example, *Kokutai no hongi* (Cardinal Principles of National Polity), a pivotal text that taught Japanese schoolchildren the major tenets of the national polity—the central place of the emperor in Japanese history and the loyalty of his subjects toward the emperor—was drafted by institute researchers along with Tokyo Imperial University professors. The Ministry of Education published and distributed the text to schools beginning in 1937 and all schoolchildren in Japan memorized it.[17]

The institute attempted to undermine Marxism by presenting its own version of the "scientific" through Sakuta's *kokumin kagaku*. Sakuta, who would later become one of the drafters of *Kokutai no hongi*, published *Kokumin kagaku no seiritsu* (Establishment of National Science) in 1934.[18] Although I translated *kokumin* in Mikami Yoshio's cultural history as "the people," Sakuta's *kokumin* should be more appropriately translated as "national." Sakuta's *kokumin* did not refer to the people as a counterconcept to the state and the elite, as Mikami's *kokumin* did. Sakuta's *kokumin* meant the subjects of Imperial Japan, the people defined solely by and part of the state.

According to Sakuta, his "national science" was a new science to study the national life in areas such as politics, law, ethics, economy, and hygiene. He claimed that "*kokumin kagaku* inherits nationalism [*kokumin shugi*] from the beginning of the Meiji period, restoring the most straightforward spirit of the establishment of our nation-state," but unlike "prescientific Meiji nationalism," his national science was "scientific." The national science was the merger of Meiji nationalism and the latest science: "It is the most recent development and is worth the name of 'new science'" (*shinkō kagaku*).[19] His reference to "new science" was a deliberate, direct challenge to Marxism. As seen in the case of the journal *Under the Banner of the New Science*, discussed in the previous chapter, Marxists had conventionally used the expression to describe their theory and politics.

Sakuta's *kokumin* science aimed at overcoming Marxist science from the perspective of the nation. According to Sakuta, science developed through three stages. The first stage was individualistic and bourgeois science. The second was Marxist "class science," which he acknowledged as having succeeded in unmasking the false myth of free will assumed in bourgeois science.[20] But the third stage, *kokumin kagaku*, was to go beyond Marxist science:

Class is a social reality. It goes without saying that, when class consciousness emerged, it was possible and necessary to study the reality from the perspective of that consciousness, and it is natural that such studies have been done. Thus, I do not deny the initial legitimacy of class science that examines class reality from the perspective of class consciousness. . . . However, that is the best [Marxist science] can do. . . . National life is something that transcends class. It is impossible to see something above from something below.[21]

If bourgeois science is thesis, Sakuta declared, then proletarian science is antithesis, and national science is the necessary synthesis. *Kokumin* science would produce "systematic and empirical knowledge" about Japanese national life from the Japanese nationals' standpoint.[22]

I call Sakuta a "Japanist" (*Nihon shugisha*). The term was used by critics and advocates alike in the 1930s for those who believed in the uniqueness and superiority of Japan. As we shall see, Tosaka was one of the most relentless critics of Japanism and identified Japanism as a Japanese version of fascism. On his list of Japanists were such intellectuals as philosophers Kihira Tadayoshi and Kanokogi Kazunobu and historian Hiraizumi Kiyoshi.[23] Some right-wing nationalists proudly identified themselves with "Japanism"; for example, poet Kageyama Masaharu named his right-wing organization the National Japanist Association (*zenkoku Nihon shugi dōmei*) in 1931. The

*Marxists + Japanists come to opp.
sides of politics in regards
to science*

100   Marxism

belief in the absoluteness of the national polity, the uniqueness and superi-ority of Japan, and Japan's leadership mission in Asia characterized Japanism. Japanism has rarely been discussed in terms of its discussion of science, as its main tenet was mostly antiscientific. However, there were some Japanists who developed a Japanist version of the "scientific."[24] Sakuta was one of them. Later in this chapter, we will see another Japanist theorist of science, Hashida Kunihiko.

One distinct difference between Marxist science and Japanist science concerned epistemology. Japanist science theorists emphasized that nation-ality informed epistemology. Sakuta, for example, contended that only the Japanese could understand Japan and Japanese national life because "only those who belong to the Japanese nation can have the will of the Japa-nese nation."[25] Theories developed by non-Japanese, therefore, would not help understand Japan. According to Sakuta, Kant and Marx knew nothing about Japan, and thus their theories on national questions should produce no understanding of the Japanese nation. Such a claim was a direct challenge to the premise on which Marxism was based—that is, that being scientific meant being universal, transcendent of spatial specificity. As Tosaka's state-ment above explains, a scientific theory needed to have international "cash value" to gain legitimacy. The scientific nature of Marxism was based on its epistemological universality, and it was precisely the universality of its scientific nature that appealed to Japanese Marxists. In contrast, for Japanist science theorists, science was not, or rather should not be, universal.

Using Tosaka's insight, I have chosen three 1932 phenomena—the Edo science exhibit, Yuiken, and the Institute for the Study in National Spiritual Culture—to map out the field of the "scientific" onto liberal, Marxist, and Japanist sciences in order to show the contested nature of the politics of the scientific in the 1930s. Liberal science based its objectivity on its indepen-dence from social and political concerns. To Marxists, however, the auton-omy of science was, like the independence of the will, an illusion. It was also propaganda of the bourgeois ideology, as it helped to affirm the status quo and deny the truly scientific, Marxist understanding of social development. For Japanists, the "scientific" needed to go hand in hand with the national. They claimed that ignoring national differences and assuming the universal-ity of the "scientific prediction" as Marxists did was itself unscientific.

Tosaka and other Marxists argued that Marxism was the only truly scien-tific philosophy and thus the only one capable of challenging irrational Japa-nese fascism.[26] Yet, as we saw, Japanist theorists also claimed their version of science as truly scientific, with which they would overcome the focus of the Marxist scientific on class. The 1930s was the most contested decade for the politics of the scientific precisely because each of these contesting ideologies made the scientific the terrain on which they competed with each other. Science became the major battlefield for these competing ideologies.

The Yuiken Project

Yuiken provided the space for Marxist intellectuals to engage in this new battlefield. Yuiken strove to understand the relationship between historical materialism as a theory of social development and the dialectics of nature as a philosophy of science while applying the relationship to an analysis of Japanese society. What distinguished Yuiken from other Marxist groups was its extensive discussion of science and the large number of natural scientists among its members. Yuiken also differed from other leftist groups because it was able to continue its activity and publication of *Yuibutsuron kenkyū* through 1938, whereas most Marxist organizations had been dissolved by the early to mid-1930s as a result of the state's severe suppression. Until its strategic dissolution in February 1938, Yuiken had maintained its activities in a "flea-infested" small office in an old wooden building in Uchisaiwaichō, Tokyo, where the group edited *Yuibutsuron kenkyū* and gathered for numerous weekly (later monthly) study groups in addition to almost nightly lectures, with a Special Higher Police officer listening to the discussions and business meetings.[27] The number of subscribers was not large; according to the report made by the Ministry of Justice, it started out at around four thousand and then decreased to somewhere between twenty-five hundred and three thousand toward the end, and most readers were from the educated class in Tokyo and Osaka metropolitan areas.[28] However, *Yuibutsuron kenkyū* did reach places farther away: Hokkaido, Kagoshima, Manchuria, Moscow, Berlin, New York, and Amsterdam. For non-Japanese readers, every issue printed a table of contents in Esperanto on the back cover.[29] Yuiken also published a series of works under the title *Yuibutsuron zensho* (Encyclopedia of Materialism) between 1935 and 1938.[30] This was an impressive achievement, considering how oppressive the state had become toward Marxism by the mid-1930s.

Three factors made this achievement possible. First, Yuiken made a conscious effort to identify itself as a scholarly forum. Although all the original organizers were Marxists, members also included renowned non-Marxist natural scientists such as physicist Terada Torahiko and parasitologist Koizumi Makoto. Their presence was a result of a deliberate effort on the part of the organizers. In the hot summer of 1932, the founding members personally appealed to natural scientists by visiting them on foot in their drenched summer kimonos.[31] They also assigned the first chief secretary of the group to Hasegawa Nyozekan, a Kyoto Imperial University philosopher, a liberal who never associated himself with Marxism. Many of these members joined Yuiken because they were interested in materialism as a

theory. It is, however, possible to suspect that, despite their claimed apolitical interest in the study of materialism, a number of these non-Marxist
members were in fact drawn to materialism as a political countertheory
to the state ideology of imperial mythology. Oka Kunio recalled that seeing the audience of more than fifty people at the inaugural assembly on
October 23, 1932, convinced him that "there were, among the intellectuals,
quite a number of hidden supporters of *our* movement."[32] The inaugural
manifesto delivered by Hasegawa, however, cautiously emphasized Yuiken's
strictly apolitical focus on the scholarly exploration of materialism:

> [T]his group can be defined only with respect to its subject of materialism; there is
> no other restriction or territoriality. Needless to say, we have to be an organization
> for the purpose of purely scholarly cooperation. For Yuiken, there would be noth-
> ing more fatally contradictory than falling into the feudalistic clique system that
> is prevalent in academia. The priority should be to make the forum open and its
> content broad, so that we can ensure the independence, collaboration, and unity of
> research.[33]

This intention to focus on materialism in general, but not exclusively historical materialism (which Japanese intellectuals considered to be the core of
Marxism), attracted scientists and liberals who did not agree with Marxism.
As Hasegawa's manifesto carefully emphasized, Yuiken was to establish purely
scholarly collaboration among scholars without any political affiliation.

Nonetheless, from the beginning, the political orientation of Yuiken
seemed clear to the authorities. The Special Higher Police regarded Yuiken
as a "dangerous thought group." Yuiken held its second public lecture in
April 1933, but the police interrupted the meeting as soon as Hasegawa announced the opening and immediately arrested several attendees. When the
newspapers reported this incident on the following day, many non-Marxist
members, including Hasegawa, left Yuiken in fear of the Special Higher Police.[34] Thus, by late 1933, most Yuiken writers were self-identified Marxists
and sympathizers, though I suspect that subscribers of its journal continued to include non-Marxists. Since discussing Marxism as a theory for a
revolution was illegal under the Peace Preservation Law, Yuiken Marxists
discussed Marxism from philosophical and scientific perspectives. For this
reason, Yuiken decided not to pay the special fees that the Newspaper Law
required of the print media to be permitted to cover current political issues.
This strategy forced the discussions of the group's Marxist politics to be
rather vague and abstract but allowed the group to continue its activities.[35]
By 1936 the Special Higher Police had removed Yuiken from the category of
"dangerous thought group": in July 1936, its secret report, while character-
izing Yuiken as a "liberal study group" that was "in effect centered on the
study of historical materialism and aimed to establish proletarian theory,"

affirmed that "this group at this point will not move on to revolutionary activities as an illegal group."[36]

The second reason for Yuiken's survival was its members' cohesion and devotion to the group. The staff who managed finance, printing, and other chores were paid very little—around fifteen yen a month, if at all, when the average salary for a white-collar job was from thirty to seventy yen—and the "secretaries" (the core members such as the editor) were never paid.[37] Those involved in Yuiken regarded Tosaka as the real backbone and energizer of the group. Tosaka, "a gentleman who always looked neat and tidy" but "could really drink," was always extremely optimistic and energetic, even in the last few years of Yuiken, when the authorities banned him and many other members from writing.[38] Despite this stressful environment, Yuiken members laughed together, went out drinking with each other in Shinjuku, and enjoyed picnics with their families along the River Nikotama.[39] At the same time, they were very aware of the potential for arrest. Becoming a Yuiken member required introduction by two existing members for identity clearance.[40] After joining the group, they frequently used pen names. Ishihara Tatsurō recalled later that "the editors did not try to find out the real identity of the writers. We were afraid that if we knew, we might reveal their real names when we got arrested and tortured. . . . Moreover, we had an unwritten code that said we would not inquire into anyone's life outside of Yuiken."[41]

Third, and most important, Yuiken was able to continue its activities until February 1938 because of its continuing and extensive discussion of the sciences. Even though *Yuibutsuron kenkyū* covered a wide array of topics such as philosophy, literature, and religion, as historian Nakayama Shigeru has argued, science functioned as a cover under which Japanese Marxists could discuss Marxism despite the state's increasing suppression in the 1930s.[42] Science, indeed, was not merely their "cover." It was also an essential element of Yuiken's intellectual challenge against what they saw as irrational and unscientific ideologies. Tosaka maintained that Yuiken regarded Marxism as the only truly scientific thought capable of critiquing Japanism and liberalism. Thus, to sharpen the scientificity of Marxism was a crucial part of Yuiken's politics. As we will see, this effort to articulate the "scientific" of scientific socialism involved two aims: one to establish the "correct" science vis-à-vis science under the current capitalist system, and the other to apply the Marxist "scientific" to the critical studies of what Yuiken identified as bourgeois and fascist currents in Japan. In other words, science not only functioned as a cover to disguise Marxist politics but was also chosen as a new battlefront of Marxist politics against what the group regarded as irrational bourgeois and fascist ideologies.

Although lumping all the Yuiken writers together does not do full justice to the diversity and disagreements among them, it is possible to summarize their shared goals and critiques and call their project a "Yuiken project." The purpose of the Yuiken project was, in the words of Kozai Yui, "nothing but a struggle against the various faces of the ideology of the ruling class."[43] Establishing its own definition and theory of science was a crucial part of this project. One of the major themes of the Yuiken project was to identify and examine the class nature of science, a theme that was discussed from the very beginning and established the foundation of the Yuiken view of science. Echoing Ogura Kinnosuke's "Arithmetic in Class Society," the Yuiken project defined science as part of the superstructure whose forms and contents were shaped by the base structure. According to Yuiken Marxist writers, science under the capitalist system was bourgeois science, just as the dominant philosophy under the capitalist system was bourgeois idealism, whereas science under the socialist system was proletarian science.

The problems of bourgeois science were most clearly articulated by Ishii Tomoyuki, a biologist, who wrote on this subject extensively under different pen names in the journal. Ishii's basic understanding of science was that it was a part of the superstructure, and thus "various contradictions in science need to be understood as a result of contradictions in the base structure."[44] According to Ishii, science under the capitalist system was science for the sake of science; that is, it was science of the "ivory tower"—though another member found this phrase too amicable for the "iron-concrete tower"[45]— which had little to do with the concerns of society or people. Moreover, it was "individualistic" and "anarchistic" because researchers rarely cooperated, much less communicated, with each other. As Ishii observed, early twentieth-century science underwent escalating division and specialization, which made it increasingly difficult for a scientist to know what was occurring in other fields of science. Ishii explained this trend in science also as a reflection of the capitalist system, which was based on the specialization and alienation of various kinds of labor. These characterizations and criticisms of bourgeois science appeared repeatedly in many other writings in *Yuibutsuron kenkyū*.[46] To Yuiken Marxists, science under the capitalist system was a bourgeois science because it served the interests of the bourgeoisie and because its research institutions belonged to them rather than to the people.

In contrast, according to Yuiken members, proletarian science was science for the masses. The Yuiken project understood Soviet science as the materialization of proletarian science. The discussions and reports on Soviet science in *Yuibutsuron kenkyū* emphasized that in the Soviet Union, science and technology were ideally united because scientists and engineers worked together under national plans to fulfill the practical needs of the nation and the people; various fields of science were connected to help develop each other dialectically, aware of where each field was located in the larger scheme of science, unlike the bourgeois science whose specialization had isolated the sciences from each other. Natural sciences were advancing by leaps and bounds because "for the first time, science [was] being developed under the most rational social system."[47] In addition, proletarian science enlightened the proletariat about the natural sciences.[48]

In addition to promoting the unity of science and technology and that of science and society, Yuiken Marxists advocated one more kind of unity—the unity of science and philosophy. This was equally important for their politics of the "scientific" because, to Yuiken Marxists, the only valid philosophy was scientific philosophy, and the only valid science was the one based on a scientific worldview. Thus, to them, the bourgeois and proletarian sciences differed both in function and purpose and in their philosophical orientation. Tosaka, one of the most relentless Yuiken critics of science, whose view of science had an immense impact on other Yuiken writers, charted the class analysis of science in 1933 as follows:

	Marxism	Bourgeois thought
philosophy	materialism	idealism
social sciences	historical materialism	idealist historicism
natural sciences	dialectics of nature	mechanism[49]

According to this chart, Marxist philosophy was based on materialism, Marxist social sciences on historical materialism, and Marxist natural sciences on the dialectics of nature (*shizen benshōhō*).[50] In contrast, in the capitalist society, bourgeois philosophy was based on idealism, bourgeois social sciences on idealist historicism, and bourgeois natural sciences on mechanism. Using this diagram, Tosaka argued that the problem with bourgeois thought was that it did not contribute to the unity of philosophy, the social sciences, and the natural sciences, for idealistic philosophy did not acknowledge the material concerns of society, its social sciences did not recognize the class reality of society, and its natural sciences were those of the ivory tower and thus detached from the needs of the proletariat and separated from industrial technology. "Philosophy, the natural sciences, and the social sciences need to have a shared system of logic, . . . a unity in their worldviews," demanded Tosaka.[51] For him, "the only social science that shares a system of categorization with natural science is Marxist historical materialism. It is the only *scientific* social theory."[52] In other words, Marxism was the only scientific social theory that would allow for the unity of the natural and social sciences, of science and technology, and of the sciences and philosophy.

Tosaka's scheme also showed that studies of nature as well as society could not avoid the influence of the class system. Yuiken's emphasis on the class character of natural science, in fact, received the most criticism from non-Marxist scientists, both inside and outside Yuiken. Ishihara Jun, a non-Marxist physicist and early Yuiken member, wrote in *Yuibutsuron kenkyū* that he did not believe class influenced natural sciences.[53] *Kagaku* (Science), a scholarly journal edited by Ishihara and other natural scientists, for example, argued that as long as nature was observed and understood correctly, then understanding should be the same no matter to which class the observer belonged.[54] Such an argument, to Yuiken Marxists, was based on the assumption that scientists could be independent of society, further proof that bourgeois society regarded scientists as part of the ivory tower. Yuiken writer Ishii Tomoyuki argued that the class character of science should not be denied in the natural sciences just because it was the study of nature, since "scientists are social beings and ideologues who breathe the air colored by society" like everyone else. Ishii also objected to the hierarchical view of the natural and social sciences that regarded the study of society as less scientific than the study of nature: "Society is also a material existence that develops according to a certain scientific law, not according to human will."[55]

Tosaka had explained this point more effectively, bringing in the ideal of the unity of the sciences and philosophy: "Concepts such as matter and energy in a physical sense are, needless to say, specific to natural sciences. It is wrong to unconditionally apply these basic concepts to other areas of science. However, the system of logical categories, or the tools of logic, that create these various basic concepts is not specific to natural sciences. . . . 'Logic' has to be true in all sciences."[56] As this quotation shows, Tosaka was not interested in drawing analogies between nature and society by mechanistically applying concepts used in the natural sciences to the study of society. His argument, which was shared by other Yuiken writers, was that what was important was the logic underlying the concepts created to understand nature and society. For Yuiken Marxists, the logic of capitalism lay in bourgeois philosophy and sciences, which contributed to their ever-increasing specialization and resulting alienation from social needs. In contrast, they argued, the logic of scientific socialism would unite them for the purpose of the welfare of the proletariat.

Yet the categorization of the bourgeois and proletarian sciences according to concepts such as mechanism and idealism caused confusion among scholars as much as it simplified the Marxist politics of the scientific. Consider positivism as an example. To Ishihara Jun, who did not believe that class analysis could be applied to the natural sciences, materialism in natural science should be understood to mean positivism; positivism accepted only objective reality that could be experienced through the physical senses and thus rid itself of any kind of speculation.[57] To Yuiken Marxists, however, positivism was a bourgeois epistemology precisely because it refused to acknowledge the influence of any kind of worldview.[58] Materialism, to Yuiken members, meant not just any materialism but the historical materialism presented by Marx and Engels. Yuiken Marxists criticized a bourgeois ideology behind science, and their goal was to unite science with one worldview, Marxism.

Yuiken biologists' discussions of eugenics in 1933 and 1934 show how they applied the class analysis of science to an analysis of a specific field of science. Eugenics was, to Yuiken biologists like Ishihara Tatsurō, "nothing but the out-dated concept of status from the feudal era wearing the jacket of science."[59] Ishihara argued that the error of eugenics resulted from the fact that it was based on Mendelist genetics, which Ishihara identified as mechanistic. To Ishi-hara, the assumption that the character of living things was fixed in the genes and independent of its social environment was as mechanistic as the function-alism of bourgeois sociology, which broke society into parts and examined those parts independently without looking at the dialectical relationship be-tween the parts and the whole.[60] Another Yuiken philosopher and biologist, Amakasu Sekisuke (Segi Ken), elaborated on Ishihara's point and criticized eugenics as "biologism" (*seibutsugaku shugi*) that regarded biology as the cause of social problems. It was clear to Amakasu that such biologism served the interest of the bourgeoisie both because it prevented people from criticizing the social system and because it provided the illusion that the upper class had always carried, and would always carry, desirable traits. Using the acquired characteristics thesis of Darwinism, Amakasu argued that the class status of intellectuals and nobles—those with "good genes"—was something acquired, not inherited.[61] Ishii Tomoyuki's articles on the theory of evolution, which appeared in *Yuibutsuron kenkyū* soon after Amakasu's discussion on eugenics in 1934, further elaborated on this point. Although some biologists had claimed genetics to be neo-Darwinism, Ishii argued, genetics was in fact an erroneous application of Darwin's theory, since it ignored Darwin's emphasis on ac-quired characteristics. As Ishii saw it, what modern biology was witnessing in genetics and eugenics was "a class struggle over the usage of Darwinism."[62]

Yuiken's discussion of science overall, however, remained abstract. What precisely differentiates an idealistic extrapolation from the Marxist world-view was never explained in *Yuibutsuron kenkyū*. Moreover, the discussion focused on criticizing what they identified as bourgeois science rather than proposing a new science in a concrete manner. Terms such as "mechanistic" and "idealistic" were sometimes exploited to make polemical accusations. When, in 1935, a question of how exactly to apply Marxism to the study of nature arose, Yuiken had a hard time reaching any concrete answers.[63] Could Marxism lead to different and better theories of nature than bourgeois sci-ence had? How should the philosophy of historical materialism be applied to the study of nature? Yuiken members were by then familiar with the Soviet debate on this very question, which was intensified by Stalin's 1934 thesis that emphasized the unity of historical materialism and the dialectics of nature as both epistemology and logic. The Soviet debate ended with the

defeat of the Deborinite faction, which had supported new physics and genetic biology, and as a result Soviet science rejected quantum mechanics, the
relativity theory, and genetics as idealistic and bourgeois, that is, unscientific.
Soviet physicists managed to escape total control by the government, but
biologists could not, as the infamous Lysenko affair demonstrates. Trofim
Lysenko, using his political connection with Communist Party leaders, per-
secuted genetic researchers and completely shut out genetics from Soviet
biology and agricultural studies.[64] Yuiken members were familiar with the
Soviet criticism of Mendelism but did not know about the terror of the Lysenko affair.[65] In addition, although Yuiken Marxists were influenced by the
Soviet debate, they did not simply duplicate it on the pages of *Yuibutsuron
kenkyū*. Amakasu Sekisuke, for example, while labeling eugenics "biologism," did not reject genetics altogether but instead proposed to develop genetics in a dialectical way, that is, to examine the complex interrelationships
among genes.[66] Like Soviet Marxists, Yuiken Marxists discussed the question of whether the dialectics of nature and historical materialism should
constitute epistemology in studying nature. However, they did not reach a
concrete answer. Even Ishii's June 1935 article subtitled "How Can We Make
the Dialectics of Nature Concrete?" remained abstract, offering no definite
way of applying the dialectics of nature to scientific research projects.[67] The
main reason for this vagueness, I believe, was the fact that natural scientists
in Yuiken, unlike Soviet scientists, did not have access to laboratories where
they could practice their science, for by the mid-1930s the state's suppression of Marxism made it almost impossible for them to keep research positions. Without being able to actively engage in laboratory research, the best
these Marxists could do was what Ishii reached as the conclusion in "How
Can We Make the Dialectics of Nature Concrete?": "to examine bourgeois
science as it is practiced and criticize it concretely."[68] By 1935 Yuiken discussion on how to apply Marxism to the practice of science had gradually
disappeared without providing any answers.

Meanwhile in Japan, the military gradually expanded its power over politics, and the state suppression of leftist thought intensified. Not only Marxists
but also liberal intellectuals were being questioned and arrested. In 1935 the
so-called organ theory of Tokyo Imperial University constitutional scholar
Minobe Tatsukichi, which defined the emperor as the highest functionary of
the national political system, was contested as too liberal by the military, even
though it had been the established interpretation of the Japanese constitutional monarchy, and was replaced by a theory that defined the emperor as
the sovereign, who transcended the constitution. In 1936 there was another
mass arrest of Marxist and leftist intellectuals. It is time to put the Yuiken
project back onto the map of the politics of the scientific and situate Marxist
intellectuals' critique of Japan and science in this changing political milieu.

Western Science Plus Japanese Spirit Equals Japanese Science?

Kanbe Isaburō (1884–1963), education reformer, described the mid-1930s as the worst time for Japanese science educators. In 1938 Kanbe wrote:

Our nation's science education developed rapidly after the Great European War [World War I] ... but our science education experienced the greatest ups and downs unseen in other areas. The highest point was around 1919 and the lowest point was around 1935, when the call for the Japanese spirit reached its apex. . . . As the cry for the Japanese spirit became louder, science education was increasingly regarded as education that overly emphasized knowledge.[69]

This observation is important for three reasons. First, it confirms that the promotion of science and technology during and immediately after World War I positively affected science education. Second, it tells us that the Japanese spirit and science education were perceived to be incompatible in the mid-1930s. And finally, according to Kanbe's observation, the worst point was around 1935, not 1938, when he was making this observation. As we examined in Chapter 2, the war with China in 1937 reinvigorated the promotion of science and technology. How exactly the tension between the "Japanese spirit" and science came to be reconciled will be discussed in Chapters 5 and 6. For now, we will focus on the perceived incompatibility of the Japanese spirit and science in the mid-1930s.

As Kanbe observed, the promotion of science and technology in Japan, especially in the area of education, faced resistance in the mid-1930s from those who regarded science as incompatible with the "Japanese spirit." What was also questioned then was the universalization of science and technology, the idea that science and technology were not Western things for Japan to borrow and copy but things that the Japanese themselves could and should produce. The disassociation of science and the West in the 1910s was at the core of the government's promotion of research and development. It also empowered technocrats to envision themselves as the creators of new technology, a new culture, and a new social order, while inspiring Ogura Kinnosuke and Tanakadade Aikitsu to promote the "scientific spirit" that would transcend the simplistic dichotomy of the Meiji slogan "Western science and technology, and Eastern ethics." Yet, as the concept of the Japanese spirit gained more currency and political power in the mid-1930s, those engaged in the politics of the scientific needed to find a way to deal with the question of whether science was compatible with the Japanese spirit and, if so, how.

The debate between the "overlearning" argument (*chishiki henchō ron*) and the scientific spirit in the mid-1930s shows how liberal, Marxist, and Japanist promoters of science dealt with this question. The so-called overlearning argument emerged around 1934 among conservative politicians and right-wing intellectuals who held an antiscience stance. One of the most visible spokesmen of the overlearning argument was Matsuda Genji (1875–1936), the minister of education under the Okada cabinet (July 1934–March 1936). In August 1934, Matsuda—who was launching his campaign to abolish Japanized foreign words such as *papa* and *mama*—told newspaper reporters that he disagreed with the current education curriculum because it crammed students with useless knowledge such as calculus that they would never use in their lives. Matsuda believed that ethics classes instead should be emphasized, that the compulsory school years should be shortened, and that sports should be encouraged more; according to him, those who practiced Japanese martial arts did not become leftists. In fact, he was on his way to a *kendō* competition when the interview was conducted.[70]

The discourse on the scientific spirit appeared in 1936 as a reaction to this overlearning argument. The debate began soon after the 2.26 Incident, an attempted coup d'état in 1936 by young army officers who belonged to the Imperial Way faction (*kōdō-ha*), the radical right wing of the army. Within the military, the Imperial Way faction had been competing with the Control faction (*tōsei-ha*), the rising faction led by Tōjō Hideki and his cohorts, who preferred to expand military power by using the framework of laws and regulations rather than that of radical, direct actions that the Imperial Way romanticized. Inspired by a right-wing ideologue, Kita Ikki, the Imperial Way men—mainly junior officers—demanded the "Shōwa Restoration": the overthrow of the government and direct rule by the emperor. On a snowy day, February 26, they took over the army headquarters, the prime minister's house, and other buildings in Tokyo and assassinated the minister of finance, Takahashi Korekiyo, and two other governmental officials. The Shōwa emperor, to whom these factions claimed devotion, was enraged by their terrorism, and their attempted coup d'état was suppressed within four days. Four years previously, those involved in the 5.15 Incident had gained sympathy from the public and were pardoned by the emperor.[71] This time, however, the culprits were severely punished, many of them facing execution, including indirectly involved civilians such as Kita Ikki.[72] Afterward, the Control faction became the dominant faction in the military, establishing the foundation for total war mobilization during World War II. The impact of the 2.26 Incident, however, reached much farther—it changed the terrain of the politics of the "scientific."

Diet members and the Ministry of Education reacted to the radicalism of the 2.26 Incident by resorting to the overlearning argument. They reasoned that an excess of knowledge and the lack of ethical training must have led to such radicalism.[73] Until the 2.26 Incident, the overlearning argument had been used to blame the school curriculum for the radicalism of leftist students. For example, when Minister of Education Matsuda Genji made his overlearning comment in 1934, his grudge was targeted at leftist students. But now, after the 2.26 Incident, it was used to explain the radical right as well. The advocates of the overlearning argument believed that radicalism of both the left and the right resulted from a lack of ethical education.

Those involved in the 2.26 Incident, however, did not seem to share this view. Waiting for his execution in prison, Isobe Asaichi, an army officer and one of the instigators of the incident, wrote that as a most loyal servant to the emperor, he did the best he could to save Japan. He was disturbed by the poverty in agrarian Japan and was convinced that such a deplorable state of Japan was brought about by the military, the bureaucracy, the Diet, and the capitalists who abused the emperor's authority for their own selfish pursuits of money and power. Facing his execution on August 19, 1937, Isobe never questioned his resolution to save Japan and the emperor:

My belief is to materialize [Kita Ikki's *Plan for the Reorganization of Japan*] without compromising any part of it. . . . It speaks truth with every single word. . . . [It is] the real expression of the Japanese national polity. Oh, the emperor! What misgovernment this has been. Why are you putting us away, preventing the most loyal and the bravest ones from serving you? Eight million gods of Japan, why are you not doing anything? Why are you not protecting the tragic emperor?[74]

As these passages from Isobe's prison diary show, what stood out in his thinking was loyalty to the emperor and a desperate sense of mission to protect the nation, which was what ethics education aimed to foster. From this perspective, the 2.26 Incident did not seem to be about a lack of ethical education or an excess of mathematics, as the government made it appear.

Tanabe Hajime (1885–1962), philosopher and Kyoto Imperial University professor, articulated what the overlearning argument was really about in a critical essay, "A Contradiction in Science Policies," published in October 1936 in the liberal magazine *Kaizō*. Tanabe argued that the problem of education was not that of quantity, but of quality.[75] According to him, the incident clearly resulted from "irrationalism that slighted knowledge, despised careful and meticulous thinking, and fancied that the mere purity of the motive would justify an action that was a result of the momentary rise of emotion." This, to Tanabe, was the real problem of education. Tanabe continued: "According to our common sense, knowledge is something that reveals the objective truth. . . . There should be only one truth to one reality. If education brings out two opposite understandings—left and right—of national reality, that is not overlearning; on the contrary, that means that learning has not achieved its real objective, that is, to pursue the scientific spirit."[76] The problem was not that school was teaching too much knowledge or not enough ethics but that school was not fostering the scientific spirit.

Tanabe also forcefully argued that it was contradictory for the government to promote natural sciences while suppressing cultural and social sciences. He pointed out the "well-known fact" that the Japan Society for the Promotion of Sciences (*Nihon gakujutsu shinkōkai*), a science society established by the state, privileged natural sciences over the human sciences and that the only human sciences projects that would receive support from the society were those that helped the state promote the Japanese spirit and Asian thought, not those that might result in a critical view of society. He argued that the government's putting forth the overlearning argument was

nothing but the state's effort to blind people's cognizance of reality and avert criticism in order to suppress the revolutionary will . . . and to force them to accept the status quo. This is a clear manifestation of the state's antipopulism [*han minshū shisō*] that attempts to keep people ignorant and dependent. This is why the state is deliberately being contradictory without any reservation. The state seeks to cultivate moral sentiments and faith [among students] by limiting knowledge in cultural and social sciences, while making every effort to promote natural sciences for the purpose of national defense.[77]

As many readers noted at the time, this was a bold criticism of the state to publish in 1936. Less than a year before, Minobe Tatsukichi had been purged from his position at Tokyo Imperial University for his "too liberal" interpretation of the Japanese constitutional monarchy. Tanabe, considered to be a liberal, had reason to worry about his career. He had earlier protested the state's intervening in academic freedom in 1933 and also publicly engaged in a debate against Minoda Muneki, an ultrarightist who accused Tanabe of being too liberal. It is also remarkable that the state allowed this publication without deleting a word. It demonstrates that the topic of science did provide a space for critics to raise issues, just as it allowed Yuiken to continue its publication (though *Yuibutsuron kenkyū* pages were filled with deleted words toward the end of its publication).

To Tanabe, the scientific spirit was about the epistemology essential for the validation of truth, a "synthesis of an empirical spirit, that is, an appreciation of facts, and a rational spirit, that is, a belief in systematic rules that govern things."[78] Although Tanabe is often associated with the Kyoto school of philosophy identified with his former mentor Nishida Kitarō's rejection of the subject-object dichotomy, Tanabe's definition of the scientific spirit is very much Cartesian. Defining science as the pursuit of truth, he emphasized that the "scientific nature" (*kagakusei*) of science was possible only when reason and empiricism were dialectically synthesized. His logic was as follows: The rational spirit observes phenomena and discerns universal rules in them. For this purpose, one has to step back from what is being observed and use intellect to go beyond immediate phenomena. Rationality requires a temporary denial of nature to get at the ideal nature of nature, that is, to re-create nature. Then, through empirical experiments, it brings nature back to reality, testing the plausibility of a rational and abstract re-creation of nature. Thus, the rational spirit that seeks abstraction and the empirical spirit that seeks embodiment are two opposite spirits, but only through their dialectical synthesis can the scientific nature of science be achieved.[79] Such truth rejected the kind of "truth" that propelled Isobe and other army officers to a coup d'état. Tanabe considered this "scientific spirit" necessary for both natural and social sciences and demanded that students learn all the sciences to nurture this spirit. To him, promoting science without promoting the scientific spirit was as ridiculous as "promoting sports while suppressing sportsmanship."[80]

Tanabe's essay inspired a discussion of the scientific spirit that flourished through the early 1940s. Historians such as Itakura Kiyonobu view this discourse as the "protest by liberal and socialist" scholars against fascism. They regard Tanabe's article as a heroic attempt to challenge the "fascist trend" despite the state's increasingly severe censorship and suppression of Marxists and liberals.[81] However, a closer look reveals the need for a more complex reading of Tanabe's critique as well as his discourse on the scientific spirit. What scholars do not usually discuss is the concluding part of Tanabe's "Contradiction in Science Policy," where Tanabe lavishly elaborated on the "Japanese spirit."

The last four pages of Tanabe's fifteen-page article argued that the ideal way to exercise the scientific spirit was to acknowledge "Eastern thought" and the "Japanese spirit." As we saw, Tanabe defined the scientific spirit as the synthesis of the "rational spirit" that induced the general law and the "empirical spirit" that tested such laws in a specific reality. Based on this definition, Tanabe argued that to teach the truth of Japanese reality required the knowledge of the "universal, scientific laws of society" (rationality) as well as the "particularity of the nation" (empiricism). To ignore the latter, he declared, was nothing but "ahistorical, abstract rationalism," something he identified as the mistake that Meiji Japan made by blindly following the Western model. This mistake had led to the "reactionary nationalism" (*handō kokumin shugi*) in today's Japan. Nonetheless, he explained, such sentiment should not be ignored as merely reactionary because "only a faith in the dignity of *kokutai* as well as the *minzoku* sentiment expressed in the mythology becomes the basis for the people's will to act; moreover, only when that will is solidified by our sense of mission in the world could scientific knowledge be actually materialized." This was necessary, Tanabe continued, "for I believe our nation's historical mission is to reach a synthesis of the Eastern idea of negation and the Western idea of affirmation, that is, the synthesis of the immediacy [*chokusetsusei*] of Japanese spirit and the logical nature [*rironsei*] of Western scientific spirit."[82] According to him, Japan should be able to "create a new culture" from such a synthesis because the nation had historically proven its significance by "synthesizing the mythological and religious ideas of India and the political and ethical practice of China and creating a totally unique unity of religion and politics."[83] He concluded the essay with a rather pragmatic suggestion: "Japanese politicians today should master science, rather than reject it, to be able to use it at their will."[84]

Tanabe's discussion of the Japanese spirit could have been his strategy to prevent censors from banning the article. At the same time, as many scholars have noted, his writings began to change just around this time to reflect positively on the authoritarian state, even endorsing a fascistic elevation of ethnic nationhood to the absolute ideal. Tanabe himself later claimed that his writings did not intend to support fascism.[85] Regardless of his intention, however, from the perspective of a critical discourse analysis, what was actually said in public is more important than what he could have meant, because the discourse of the scientific spirit continued to develop from his printed words. What is important for us is the way Tanabe incorporated the language and concept of the Japanese spirit into a protest against the state suppression of social sciences. Censorship produces new rules of discourse. If one decides to challenge authorities by participating in a discourse under politically restrictive conditions, one needs to play the game, so to speak, by using and manipulating the rules set by those conditions. Tanabe was able to publish an essay that straightforwardly accused the state of manipulating the people's minds, but he did so by promoting the uniquely Japanese science that would rest on the merger of the scientific spirit and the Japanese spirit.

A month after the publication of Tanabe's essay, Hashida Kunihiko, a renowned physiologist and professor of medicine at Tokyo Imperial University, gave a lecture titled "Science as Practice" (*Gyō toshite no kagaku*). Hashida was one of the intellectuals Tosaka identified as a Japanist and would soon become principal of the First Higher School and in 1940 the minister of education. A comparison of the two 1936 instances of the discourse of science—Tanabe's essay and Hashida's lecture—demonstrates the proximity of Tanabe's "liberal" critique to the Japanist discourse.

Hashida delivered his talk "Science as Practice" in November 1936 for a lecture series on Japanese culture sponsored by the Ministry of Education.[86] In it, he argued that Eastern culture provided a unique philosophy that promised a new, uniquely Japanese science. His theory used Nishida Kitarō's aesthetics explored in *The Study of Goodness* (*Zen no kenkyū*), a philosophical treatise hailed in Japan since its publication in 1911 as the first successful synthesis between Western philosophy (Kant) and Eastern tradition (Zen Buddhism). "Pure experience" in Nishida's influential philosophy argued against the separation of the subject and the object and instead emphasized the Buddhist unity of the two.

Whereas Tanabe's "scientific spirit" was based on the Cartesian separation of the subject and the object, Hashida's theory of science was based on the denial of such a split. Hashida maintained that Western natural sciences, like other branches of Western learning, were based on the assumed split between the subject and the object, but Eastern thought had as its ideal the union of the subject and the object. Moreover, in Eastern thought, according to Hashida, the human being was always inside nature, not outside it as Western science had assumed. Such differences meant to Hashida that the Japanese could practice science and know nature differently than Western scientists did at even so basic a level as observation.

Observation was central to Hashida's "science as practice." Believing that observation was the basis of science, Hashida argued that observation should not be done by simply seeing things with the eyes but should be about "seeing with the mind's eyes" (he used the German term *auffassen*).[87] To Hashida, the "mind" did not mean "subjectivity" as opposed to objectivity; it meant the observers themselves who were observing. He asserted that the Western assumption of the subject-object split was useless because it would lead to an epistemological dead end: "Even the criteria to determine what is objective involve subjectivity. If we suppose that objectivity resides outside subjectivity and determines what is correct, then we would have to keep searching for ultimate objectivity endlessly to assure that this decision [to determine what is objective] is really correct."[88] How, then, can we know that we observe correctly? Hashida's answer was the Eastern way of seeing. Echoing Nishida, he referred to the thirteenth-century Zen monk Dōgen's master work, *Shōbō genzō*, and the Buddhist concept that Dōgen explored, "things and the mind are one" (*busshin ichinyo*); that is, nature in the natural sciences could exist only as scientists see it.[89] According to Hashida, the "object," that which was objectified and observed, was the subject's observation itself and thus the object and the subject were one and the same. According to this understanding, the natural sciences were not nature itself but the materialization of the act called observation.[90] This was a radical denial of materialism but done with reference to Buddhist thought, not to Western idealist philosophers such as Kant.

Tanabe would have disagreed with Hashida's rejection of the subject-object split, for Tanabe's "scientific spirit" required the observer to be detached from nature to exercise the rational spirit. However, Hashida's science as practice was in fact similar to what Tanabe abstractly proposed as the "immediacy of the Japanese spirit." To Hashida, the "immediacy" that Tanabe (and Nishida) had identified as the character of Eastern philosophy meant the immediacy in observation that denied the split between the observer and the observed. While Tanabe discussed the synthesis of the West and the East and the creation of a new science in an extremely abstract manner,

Hashida theorized what the Japanese way of doing science would be like in a laboratory. This brings us back to Tosaka Jun's critique that liberalism and Japanism were only one step apart.

Yuiken Marxists did not agree with either Tanabe or Hashida. They refused to discuss the scientific spirit in terms of the synthesis of the East and the West altogether. Although historians have ignored the concluding part of Tanabe's "Contradiction of Science Policy," Yuiken Marxists in 1936 did not. In fact, they saw it as part of the alarming "fascist trend" that was emerging even among liberals. While praising Tanabe's timely refutation of the "overlearning" thesis and courageous criticism of the state, Yuiken member Imano Takeo nonetheless pointed out that Tanabe's advocacy of the fusion of the West and Japan dulled his otherwise sharp criticism. Imano warned that Tanabe's idealization of the fusion of the "practice-oriented nature of Eastern philosophy" and the "scientific nature of Western philosophy" would be a mismatch, like "grafting bamboo onto a tree," an endeavor sure to fail. To Imano, such an attempt to relate the Eastern spirit to the discussion on science was a sign of the rising reactionary conservatism among conscientious intellectuals like Tanabe. "I hope it won't thwart progressive scholars," Imano forewarned.[91]

Ogura Kinnosuke also joined the discussion on the scientific spirit, with an article, "The Duty of Natural Scientists," in December 1936. This article started with a warning that it was written "under various restrictions," asking for the reader to be aware of censorship. Nonetheless, it bluntly criticized the way science had been taught and practiced in Japan since the Meiji period.[92] Ogura fully agreed with Tanabe that government suppression of the human and social sciences was utterly contradictory to the recent popular cry for a "scientific Japan." Like Tanabe, he also ridiculed the overlearning argument as simplistic, antiscience nonsense.[93] However, Ogura ultimately remained critical of Tanabe's idealization of the synthesis of the Japanese spirit and the scientific spirit.

In this article, Ogura defined the scientific spirit as the "spirit that humbly learns the scientific legacy from the past and at the same time examines such a legacy to discover newer and more exact facts and to create more perfect theories."[94] Whereas Tanabe lamented the lack of the scientific spirit in Japanese education specifically because it would prevent the development of science in Japan, to Ogura, Japan's lack of scientific spirit meant more than a lack of such development. In the essay "The Significance of Mathematics Education" that Ogura originally published in 1923 but chose to reprint in his 1937 book, *The Scientific Spirit and Mathematical Education*, he argued that "the scientific spirit respects and promotes freedom of thought. The modern scientific spirit was born with an attempt to break down and overcome the old, fixed forms of religion, the nation-state, and ethics." The scientific spirit, according to him, was the core of modernity, and the real scientific spirit could only develop with the freedom of thought, not through a mere importation of institutions and textbooks. In other words, to him, the scientific spirit was the modern spirit, neither Western nor Eastern.[95]

Tosaka Jun made this point even more explicitly. Also refusing to discuss the scientific spirit in the East-versus-West paradigm, Tosaka defined the scientific spirit in his 1937 article "What Is the Scientific Spirit?" as follows: "The scientific spirit is . . . a universal spirit. It is not the European spirit or the Greek spirit. It is neither the Japanese spirit nor the Eastern spirit. It is not something that can be compared to such things. . . . We can call it the spirit of reality. . . . If Japan is the issue, the reality of Japan can be comprehended only with the scientific spirit."[96] As this passage shows, Tosaka's refusal to categorize the scientific spirit as either Western or Eastern was at the same time a determination to engage the "reality of Japan" in scientific analysis.

What reality was Tosaka talking about? The rest of this article discussed Japanists' usage of classic texts to explain Japan of the 1930s. He criticized their reliance on the authority of classics such as Buddhist texts in legitimizing the political and economic system of contemporary Japan—that is, an ahistorical, abusive use of Japanese history to legitimize the increasingly reactionary nationalism, the rise of the military government, and Japan's expansion into China.

Tosaka named this practice the "abuse of the spirit of citation" (*in'yō no seishin*). The practice of citation, he explained, could be scientific and meaningful only when it was used as a way of proving an argument, introducing materials, calling attention to references, or guiding the reader. But when the "spirit" of citation deviated from the practice of empirical investigation, he continued, it became abusive because it referred to the classic texts only to exploit their authority:

Originally, philologism and the spirit of citation were based on empiricism in philology. However, this spirit of philology and citation began to move away from empiricism. Constantly referring to a historical tradition of the nation [*minzoku*] eventually leads to the total annihilation of the historical facts of that nation. As the national history came to be emphasized, certain parts of the national history came to be forced into silence and certain classic texts themselves became distorted or denied.[97]

To Tosaka, to emphasize certain kinds of historical phenomena as the tradition of *minzoku* distorted not only history but also the present. Only the truly universal, scientific spirit, he argued, could understand, analyze, and guide the present-day reality of Japan.

Observing the rise of the discourse of the scientific spirit, Nagayama Yasuo, a medical doctor, has stated that it "seems strange" to see the promotion of the scientific spirit in the midst of a nationalistic, militaristic

Japan.[98] But if we look at this phenomenon as part of the politics of the "scientific," there is nothing strange about it. The discourse on the scientific spirit emerged as a critical reaction to the antiscientific overlearning argument, but it should not be regarded simply as a "protest" against the "fascist trend" in Japan. The discourse of the scientific spirit was yet another facet of the politics of the scientific, where the differing claims over the scientific clashed, with a new key term, the "Japanese spirit." Tanabe Hajime idealized the synthesis of Western and Eastern thought and declared that only the scientific spirit could achieve this historical mission of Japan. Hashida Kunihiko explored this synthesis and theorized what a Japanese way of doing science would be, using a Buddhist text, *Shōbō genzō*. To Yuiken Marxists, this was against the real scientific spirit and constituted an abuse of citation that would prevent a truly scientific understanding of Japan. Yuiken Marxists maintained that the scientific spirit was universal, neither Western nor Japanese, and that there could not be a unique, inherently Japanese science based on an erroneously selected tradition of *minzoku*.

After 1936, clarifying the relationship between *minzoku* and science became the main objective of the Yuiken project. Through this discussion, the history of science became yet again a battlefield over what should be regarded as scientific. However, this time, as we will see in the following chapter, the Marxists were claiming not only what was "scientific" but also what was "traditional" in Japan.

CHAPTER 5

Constructing the Japanese Scientific Tradition

THE DISCUSSION OF THE Japanese spirit and things "uniquely Japanese" became increasingly prevalent as the national war mobilization intensified after the wars with China in 1937 and with the United States in 1941. Since the censorship regulations made it difficult to have public discussions on the emperor and imperial authority, most contributors to this discourse engaged in literature, philosophy, language, customs, and so forth to discuss the Japanese tradition. Japanese history therefore became a rich reservoir for Japanist ideologues and the state from which Japanese "tradition" could be extracted and authenticated. History writing became politically more important in the latter half of the 1930s due to the rise of the so-called imperial historiography (*kōkoku shikan*). Advanced by Hiraizumi Kiyoshi and his colleagues at the imperial universities and endorsed by the Ministry of Education, the imperial historiography integrated Shinto mythology into the official national history in compliance with the *kokutai* ideology.

This chapter examines how, from 1936 to 1945, Yuiken Marxists critically intervened in such discourse by asserting a scientific tradition in Japanese history. Claiming the scientific and the Japanese simultaneously thus constituted the core of the new Yuiken project. This chapter focuses on writings of one Yuiken member who carried on the new Yuiken project after the group's dissolution in 1938: Saigusa Hiroto. A Marxist philosopher and historian, Saigusa carried out a search for the Japanese scientific tradition in the Tokugawa period, canonizing certain Tokugawa texts as Japanese classic scientific texts. I problematize the success of Saigusa's project in the light of the wartime state promotion of a scientific Japan. Although Saigusa's definition of science was different from that of technocrats who were behind the wartime state promotion of science-technology (see Chapter 2), his history of Japanese science and "discovery" of emerging Japanese modernity in the eighteenth century ended up providing the historical reinforcement for the "scientific Japan" that technocrats advocated. His critical intervention in the discourse of things Japanese, in other words, simultaneously incorporated his scholarship into the state's war mobilization. This process was not simple, as this chapter will demonstrate.

To understand how the Yuiken project shifted from a critique of bourgeois science to the establishment of the Japanese scientific tradition in the late 1930s, we need first to look at Yuiken Marxists' discussion of *minzoku* and how their politics of the scientific construed the meaning of the term.

Minzoku *and Science*

Minzoku first appeared as a major theme in the pages of *Yuibutsuron kenkyū* in 1936. In the September 1936 issue, the Yuiken editor—most likely Tosaka Jun—asked various Yuiken members how they defined *minzoku*. The question was posed, however, in relation to the problem of translation. "The word Nation is translated sometimes as *kokumin* and sometimes as *minzoku*. It is needless to say that *kokumin* and *minzoku* need to be distinguished, but why is Nation translated into these two words, and what is the significance of it? . . . We should have discussed this earlier, but it is still not too late to clarify the concept of *minzoku* in relation to Nation."[1]

It is significant at two levels that the Yuiken editor posed this question as a translation problem. On one level, it articulates the problem that characterized the discourse of nationalism and the nation in modern Japan, especially in the 1930s, when the word *minzoku* occupied an unprecedented space in public discourse; on a completely different level, it reminds us that, to discuss the Japanese discourse of nationalism and the nation in the English language, we are doubly challenged by the problem of translation. As the Yuiken editor's question reveals, there were many Japanese terms that were used in relation to the nation, nationality, the people, the nation-state, and so forth. The linguistic and translational confusion had already been pointed out as a serious political and intellectual problem in 1923 by Ōyama Ikuo, a socialist and political scientist.[2] To help the English reader, I might simply have supplied current dictionary definitions for these words, but such a strategy not only leads to historical inaccuracy but also ignores the complexity entailed by each of those terms, especially when the English words themselves are often ambiguous. For example, one contemporary Japanese dictionary, *Daijirin* (1995), defines *kokumin* as "members of the state [*kokka*], or those who hold citizenship of that nation [*kuni*]." Although the term *kokumin* has indeed tended to signify the legal and political membership in a country since the Meiji period, this late twentieth-century definition would ignore important historical uses, such as that of Fukuzawa Yukichi, an influential Meiji Enlightenment intellectual who used the term to refer to conscientious citizens actively involved in the making of the nation, and that of Mikami Yoshio, who used it in the populist sense of the people vis-à-vis the state in his 1923 cultural history of *wasan* (see Chapter 3). Likewise, relying on the contemporary definition of *minzoku* is also problematic. The 1995 dictionary defines *minzoku* as "a group that shares a sense of belonging, 'us.' It has conventionally referred to a group of the shared origin, language, religion, life style, habitation, and so on. *Minzoku* is shaped through politics and history, and its parameters and perceptions change. It often does not overlap with *kokumin*; it is often the case that plural *minzoku* groups coexist under a state [*kokka*]." As we will see later, this definition, too, excludes other important usages of the term that existed in interwar and wartime Japan.[3] Because even the same term would have to be translated into a different English word depending on what was meant, I translate these terms contextually. My concern as a historian, therefore, is to read each utterance of these words as accurately and carefully as possible, rather than attempt to reach a single rule of translation.

Yuiken's concern in 1936, on the other hand, lay in identifying the political significance of this problem of translation and finding what to do about it. The answers to the editor's question from eight Yuiken members appeared three months later in the November issue. They all pointed out the confusion caused by translating "nation" into *kokumin* and *minzoku* and also such different terms as "nation," "the people," "ethnicity," and the German *Volk* into the Japanese term *minzoku*. According to a brief survey of literature by Hirokawa Wataru (most likely a pen name), *Volk* was translated as *minzoku* by many but also as *kokka* (the state) and *kokumin* by some.[4] Hayakawa Jirō most succinctly articulated the political significance of the conflation: "[W]e should not forget that there is a clever 'scheme' behind the dual translations of 'nation' into *kokumin* and *minzoku*." According to him, the careless, interchangeable use of the two terms was a deliberate scheme (presumably by the bourgeois state) to confuse the political and racial membership of a nation, the two kinds of membership that did not and should not necessarily overlap in reality. Such conflation, Hayakawa added, also helped to divert critical attention away from the discourse of nationalism: "*Minzoku* art, for example, sounds like an art by the 'masses' [*taishū*], something that has nothing to do with right-wing nationalism that speaks of the purity of the national polity [*kokusui shugi*]."[5] Another contributor, Mori Kōichi, attributed the conflation more specifically to the problem of fascism.[6] However, finding exactly how to overcome this problematic conflation and ambiguity was not easy. Hayakawa, after making the previous statement, continued to argue that since it was impossible to get rid of the term *minzoku* from the Japanese language at this point, the best that conscientious scholars could do was to be aware of the danger of conflating political, cultural, and racial categories and always make clear how they used the terms by clarifying the meaning with the English or Esperanto equivalent.[7]

All the answers collected in this issue emphasized the historically constructed nature of *minzoku*, refusing any biological or racial apriority. Many of them used Joseph Stalin's definition of the nation as their anchor in the confusing deluge of "nation"-related words. Stalin's *Marxism and the National Question* (1913) emphasized the constructionist nature of a nation, defining it as "an historically evolved, stable community of language, territory, economic life, and psychological makeup manifested in a community of culture." He argued that "[n]ationality . . . is not a racial or tribal phenomenon" and that it "assumes positive political form as a nation under definite historical conditions."[8] Resonating with Stalin's definition, Kojima Hatsuo argued in *Yuibutsuron kenkyū* that "today's race [*jinshu*] is a 'historical' race. There is no such thing as a pure, biological race, as far as the definitions of *minzoku* and *kokumin* go."[9] As Stalin acknowledged the positive contribution of nationalism so long as it functioned as part of a struggle against bourgeois imperialism, the Yuiken writers did not reject the concept of *minzoku* altogether, as it was an important concept in their support for anticolonial movements in China and Korea. Many of them differentiated *kokumin* from *minzoku* by defining the former as the *minzoku* with an independent state (German: *Staat*) (e.g., Japan vis-à-vis China and Korea).[10]

The Marxist constructionist definition of *minzoku* challenged not only the *kokutai* ideology that presumed a homogeneous, unchanging nation under the emperor since mythological times but also the racialized concept of *minzoku* prevalent as part of a "scientific" discourse in the 1930s.[11] During the 1920s and 1930s, the anthropological theory of the mixed-race origin of the Japanese was well established. The mixed-race-origin theory challenged the presumption of pure Japanese blood by the Meiji *kokutai* ideology but also "scientifically" legitimized the existence of various ethnicities under the Japanese emperor and its assimilation policy. For example, when anthropologist Torii Rūzo said in 1920, "as racial studies scholars (*jinshugaku*), linguists, and historians have made clear, Koreans are the same *minzoku* as the Japanese," *minzoku* meant an ethnic group that shared the same physiological traits and linguistic history.[12] Japanese eugenicists, who began to gain institutional power in the late 1930s, especially through the newly created Ministry of Health and Welfare, regarded the Koreans and Taiwanese as a different *minzoku* from the Japanese and opposed their integration into the Japanese.[13] Whether *minzoku* was invoked for the assimilation of the colonized or for their segregation, however, these arguments were made as scientific theories in the 1930s.

The Yuiken Marxists' concept of the "scientific" rejected such a racialized view. One of the earliest, most substantive critiques of the racialized *minzoku* and its relationship with science in *Yuibutsuron kenkyū* was Ishii Tomoyuki's analysis of "*minzoku* biology," which appeared in the October 1936 issue. This field was developed by Kanazawa University biologist Koya Yoshio in the mid-1930s and became associated with the genre of racial hygiene studies (*minzoku eiseigaku*). Koya, who publicly praised Nazi eugenics policies, was a central figure in the establishment of the Association for Japanese Racial Hygiene Studies (*Nihon minzoku eiseigakkai*) and the president of this society in 1942 and 1943 and also in 1950 and 1957 (this association still exists today), while serving the Ministry of Health and Welfare.[14] More than a biological study of various ethnicities and races, Koya's *minzoku* biology research embodied his belief that ethnic differences produced different sciences. Ishii was highly critical of this field and its claims. He denied the *minzoku* character of science, arguing that a *minzoku* study of science should be different from the scientific study of *minzoku*. "German physics," which assumed that the Germans would develop a new physics just because they were German, for example, was "laughable nonsense," Ishii wrote.[15] To him, a *minzoku* study of biology developed by Koya could become as "unscientific" as this German science under Nazi fascism.[16] To Ishii, the concept of *minzoku* was problematic because of its ahistorical assumption of the fixed character of *minzoku*. One year later, Oka Kunio agreed with Ishii, arguing that "religion can be an object of scientific research but can never be a basis of science." Likewise, Oka maintained, "*minzoku* is an object of a variety of scientific research but could never define science."[17]

Against such an "unscientific" use of *minzoku*, the Yuiken discussion soon developed into a critical assessment of what was culturally regarded as characteristic of the Japanese *minzoku*, that is, the so-called things Japanese. The March 1937 issue of *Yuibutsuron kenkyū* began with Mori Kōichi's article, "What Is That Which Is Called *minzoku*-ish?" which criticized the arbitrariness of things Japanese. Mori lamented that not only those who abandoned Marxism like Kobayashi Hideo but also some Communist Party members and liberal scholars had begun to celebrate "things *minzoku*-ish and things Japanese."[18] People had pointed to the *Manyōshū*, a collection of Japanese poems from the eighth century, as a materialization of authentically Japanese feelings and thoughts, he ridiculed, but "the[se] feelings and thoughts were probably common among all the primitive peoples" in the world. Also, the Tokugawa concept of *giri ninjō* (obligation and human feelings) had been hailed as things Japanese through literary writers such as Yokomitsu Riichi, but such a concept was common among all the societies that had experienced a feudal social structure: "It has to be said that it is dogmatic to define the nature of *minzoku* by arbitrarily selecting cultural phenomena from a certain period of historical time while completely ignoring other historical developments [of the society]."[19]

This point was further discussed in a March 1937 roundtable discussion, "Various Problems of Contemporary Thought" as well as in "Commenting on Japan," the April 1937 special issue of *Yuibutsuron kenkyū*. At the roundtable discussion, Yuiken literary critic Iwakura Masaji (under the pen name Kuwaki Masaru), argued that the "'tradition' that is normally forced on us is something like a phantom that has remained sacred and unbroken since the time of gods. That's the way we are taught about tradition." In response to this comment, Hayakawa Jirō suggested that the Yuiken should "scientifically measure and examine which tradition we want to keep or destroy . . . in a scientific way."[20] A few months later, Iwakura followed up Hayakawa's point and developed his views on the "phantom" tradition in "On the Class Nature of Tradition," arguing that so-called tradition was elitist as well as unscientific. He stated:

"Tradition" was not of the masses. Moreover, it should be made clear that this "tradition" is based on an unscientific and vague notion, completely different from a tradition that scientifically makes sense. . . . "Tradition" is an arbitrary construction by those in power who have subjectively chosen from history only things that are useful for them—for example, the tolerance, innocence, and unity of the Japanese *minzoku*. If we think a bit logically, most of them are commonalities found in other *minzoku* as well.[21]

Iwakura proposed three steps to destroy this phantom tradition: first, to criticize the "tradition" of ideologues and to demonstrate the class nature of such tradition; second, "to contrast real tradition with such arbitrary constructions"; and third, to construct Japan's future culture based on the real tradition.[22] "Our tradition," according to Iwakura, was the tradition of "scientific thinking": "Scientific thinking emerged among a certain class already in the Tokugawa period and has continued to exist. Today's Japanese are trying to inherit this proud tradition, but it is being suppressed as 'Western scientism' [*seiyō kagaku shugi*]. Instead, 'Eastern intuition' [*tōyō no chokkan shugi*] is advertised as 'good tradition.'" This is a total denial of the class character of tradition, he argued.[23] According to Iwakura, the masses had created their own antireligious and antiauthoritarian tradition, seen in the history of rebellions and uprisings. What is necessary to construct a *minzoku* culture that would be respected by the world, Iwakura argued, is the "scientific spirit."[24] Here, Iwakura's use of the "scientific spirit" echoed that of Ogura Kinnosuke, who had argued that the "modern scientific spirit was born out of an attempt to break down and overcome the old, fixed forms of religion, the nation-state, and ethics."[25]

What needed to be done, then, was to present the tradition of the people against the "phantom," so-called tradition constructed by and for the elite.

The phantom could be countered only by the scientific tradition of Japan that would refute the abusive citation of tradition by reactionary nationalists. The Yuiken politics of the scientific now involved claiming both the "scientific" as well as the "traditional."

The Canonization of Japanese Science   *How?*

The Yuiken project of investigating the scientific tradition of the Japanese was put into practice by Saigusa Hiroto, one of the original seven Yuiken organizers and editor of *Yuibutsuron kenkyū* for the first few years. He was a philosopher, a historian, and an educator, remembered by those who knew him for his quiet but humorous personality, "friendly smile," and the Hiroshima accent he retained throughout his life.[26] Considering his profile as an established scholar and public figure, it is surprising how few studies have been written on him. Saigusa established a foundation of the history of technology in Japan and trained many scholars who developed the field in the postwar decades. Saigusa was elected as the third president of the largest organization of historians of science in Japan, the History of Science Society of Japan, in 1960. Saigusa also established the Kamakura Academia in 1946, a private liberal arts university that aimed to cultivate a "scientific, independent . . . and truly democratic spirit" among citizens.[27] Financial difficulties and its reputation as "too leftist" forced the Kamakura Academia to close in 1950, but the ideal of the school was inherited by the newly created Municipal University of Yokohama, which Saigusa served as president from 1961 until his death in a train accident in 1963.

Saigusa studied Western philosophy at Tokyo Imperial University between 1916 and 1922, after spending several years helping his Buddhist priest father and giving sermons. He was initially interested in phenomenology, but his interest shifted to Hegelian philosophy and Marxism after he served in the military for a year. The establishment of the Soviet Union also inspired young Saigusa. Despite his Buddhist background, he became a member of the Association of Militant Atheists (*sentōteki mushinronsha dōmei*). In the late 1920s, he devoted his energy to a reading of Hegel through Marx and attended the centennial event of Hegel's birth in Berlin during his half-year study abroad (1931–32) in Germany. Most of his writings around this time can be summed up as a philosophical exploration of materialism and a critique of bourgeois idealist philosophy, and he was a major force behind Yuiken's critique of philosophical idealism, especially neo-Kantianism, which had been popular among Japanese intellectuals since the 1920s. Together with Tosaka Jun, Saigusa directed his criticism especially toward the neo-Kantian philosopher Nishida Kitarō. Calling it the "philosophy of

worship," Saigusa criticized Nishida's philosophy as something founded neither in science nor in the reality of everyday life.[28]

Saigusa became interested in Japanese history after he was jailed for a
month in 1933 as a main organizer of the Yuiken. He was forced to resign
from his teaching positions as a result. Writing was the only means left for
him to support his family of a wife and four children. To avoid being banned
from writing, he decided to withdraw his Yuiken membership in 1933 and
continued to write for *Yuibutsuron kenkyū* only under pen names. It was
around this time that Fujikawa Yū, a historian of Japanese medicine and
mentor/friend of Saigusa from his home prefecture of Hiroshima, told him
that "it is important to study the philosophy of foreign countries, but this
is probably a good opportunity for you to learn what the Japanese have
thought."[29] Saigusa indeed began to explore this question in 1934, reading
Tokugawa texts in Fujikawa's library while helping edit Fujikawa's work.
At the same time, Saigusa stayed deeply involved with the Yuiken project
throughout its active years: he continued to write frequently for *Yuibutsuron
kenkyū* under various names and participated in its study meetings at least
until early 1937.[30]

Like other Yuiken intellectuals, Saigusa believed that presenting the scientific tradition of Japan was the most effective way to challenge the arbitrary
characterization of the Japanese *minzoku* by right-wing intellectuals and the
state. In March 1937, immediately after the *Yuibutsuron kenkyū* issue of that
month criticized the "phantom" of Japanese tradition, Saigusa wrote in a
major daily, *Tokyo Asahi shinbun*, that "intellectuals should discover our allies
in Japanese history. And by doing so, we should redefine what is Japanese."[31]
Echoing the discussion in *Yuibutsuron kenkyū*, Saigusa lamented that recent
reactionary Japanism had not looked for the right things in the Japanese past.
Instead of embracing "outmoded and irrational concepts such as *fujiyama*,
harakiri, or even *wabi* or *yūgen*," he urged an examination of the scientific
spirit in Japanese history.[32]

Saigusa's 1937 work, *Japanese Intellectual Culture*, well represents his attempt
to redefine the Japanese tradition. Declaring that it was too limiting to find
"things Japanese" in such fields as art and architecture or in such concepts as
loyalty to one's master, Saigusa urged the readers to turn their attention to Japan's intellectual history to find the "Japanese intellect" (*chisei*). The problem
with the discourse on things Japanese, Saigusa argued, was that the discussion
usually emphasized either universality or particularity. That is, the Japanist
discourse of things Japanese had insisted on the uniqueness of the Japanese
character while neglecting to see what was universal about the Japanese, and
a critique of such a discourse had emphasized universality and thus ignored
anything particular about Japan.[33] Instead, he argued, it needed to be acknowledged that although intellect was universal, the way this intellect was

manifested differed from one *minzoku* to another. The difference between Western intellect and Japanese intellect, according to Saigusa, was that the latter lacked abstraction, which to him was the reason why the Japanese did not develop a modern concept of nature as early as the West did.[34] However, this did not mean to Saigusa that no one in Japan developed the modern concept of nature: "We should look for the intellectuals in our past who are closer to our thinking, present their scholarship systematically, and demonstrate the materials that would force reactionary intellectuals to think again."[35]

To find the beginning of the modern intellect in Japan, Saigusa turned to the eighteenth-century Japanese Confucian thinker Miura Baien (1723–89). "For the concept of 'nature' to emerge in Europe, appropriate concepts of time and space needed to develop. . . . According to my research, a new concept of space as a container of things and time as a stipulator of historical time finally began with Miura Baien."[36] Baien was an important figure for Saigusa's scholarship, just as Ogyū Sorai, his contemporary Confucian scholar, was for Maruyama Masao's discussion of the (albeit unfulfilled) modernity in Japan. Unlike Ogyū, who was a scholar for the Tokugawa government involved in national affairs, Baien was a doctor in Bingo (Ōita Prefecture), away from the center of politics and intellectual circles, who rarely left his hometown throughout his life.[37] Baien nonetheless maintained intellectual and personal ties with contemporary scholars, gained knowledge of Western learning, and taught students such as Hoashi Banri. However, like Andō Shōeki, another obscure yet significant Tokugawa thinker, Baien remained little known until he was "discovered" during the Meiji period. Even then, only a few discussed Baien.[38] Saigusa was the first scholar who systematically analyzed his philosophy as explored in *Gengo* (Theory on Truth, 1775), Baien's massive and highly complex masterpiece that allegedly took twenty-three years and twenty-three drafts to complete.[39] Saigusa's study of Baien, first published in various essays in the late 1930s, culminated in *Miura Baien no tetsugaku* (Philosophy of Miura Baien, 1941) and *Baien tetsugaku nyūmon* (Introduction to the Philosophy of Baien, 1943). The former work earned Saigusa a doctoral degree a decade later.[40]

What attracted Saigusa most was the dialectical thinking he found in Baien and his view of nature. Baien described his fundamental epistemological approach as "seeing in opposite and comprehending as one" (*hankan gōitsu* 反観合一). Baien's philosophy is structured around dichotomous thinking. For example, Baien argued that something abstract (*mei* 名) assumed something concrete (*shu* 主); likewise, the sun was paired with the shadow, life with death, and so on. To Baien, the truth about the universe—both in the human and natural worlds—could only be understood as a synthesis of these dichotomous, complementary pairs. Saigusa read this as dialectics similar to Hegel's. Another important concept in Baien's philosophy is *jōri* (条理).

According to Saigusa, Baien used this term in two ways: first, as "logic," a rational analysis of the universe that Baien found Westerners excelled in; and second, as dialectical thinking.[41] The goal of Baien's work was to clarify the laws of the universe through the epistemology of dialectics, and nature was where Baien believed he would find them. Unlike his contemporaries, Baien did not attempt to find truth in great thinkers of the past. In fact, he argued that scholars did not verify great thinkers' words with nature and that people were not trained to question how natural phenomena occurred. Saigusa argued that such a view of nature could be found in a crude sense in some early Tokugawa naturalists such as Kaibara Ekken, Hiraga Gennai, and Ono Ranzan, but that Baien alone saw nature as the working of things, as something material to be observed and analyzed. It was, in Saigusa's words, the first demonstration of the "real scientific spirit" in Japanese history. To Saigusa, thus, Baien was the first truly scientific and modern intellectual in Japan: "Baien quietly accomplished a grand job of exploring scientific thinking. This helped prepare Japan for its scientific future. I believe it is our urgent task to understand Baien as a scientist who accomplished this job."[42]

Baien the scientist helped Saigusa not only find the scientific spirit in the Japanese past but also redefine the "Japanese spirit." When Saigusa was asked to write the entry on the "Japanese spirit" (*Nippon seishin*) for the 1941 *Dictionary of Contemporary Philosophy* (*Gendai tetsugaku jiten*), he defined it using Baien. Since "letting the term 'the Japanese spirit' be monopolized by a certain political movement is the main reason for the misunderstanding of the [real] Japanese spirit,"[43] this entry in the encyclopedia was Saigusa's political act of redefining the term. According to Saigusa, what contemporary Japanese called "spirit" was first explored by Baien through the concept *shin* 神, "that which creates." Baien's *shin* symbolized a sense of dynamic historical construction and human agency for that construction and was contrasted to the static concepts of *ri* 理 (logic) and *ten* 天 (nature as it is). Saigusa repeatedly argued that Baien's *shin* did not refer to a god, as the character had led people to assume; rather, "Baien's *shin* is equivalent to what we call *seishin* [spirit] as in *Nippon seishin* [the Japanese spirit]. . . . Some people say that the 'Japanese spirit' lacks any historical foundation, but [Baien's work] should correct this view."[44] By tracing the origin of the Japanese spirit in Baien, Saigusa attempted to redefine and reclaim the Japanese spirit as modern and scientific.

The above case also demonstrates that Baien was especially important for Saigusa because censorship made it impossible to use Marxism in writing to promote the scientific spirit in Japan. Saigusa explained:

There used to be a kind of scientism [*kagaku shugi*] that was based on materialism. . . . Intellectuals who lamented the emerging [Japanist] current wished that national policy would include scientism. They argued that there was a law that governed the natural and human worlds and that for the nation to develop it was necessary to cherish scientific knowledge. . . . But today even this scientism cannot be accepted without numerous restrictions. Moreover, respecting science itself can be interpreted as a lack of interest in the national crisis.[45]

Such suppression of scientism, he continued, was largely due to Japanist spiritualists who insisted that Japan's politics, economy, art, and even natural sciences needed to be based on the Japanese spirit. Under such a political atmosphere, Baien allowed Saigusa to promote the scientific spirit without contradicting the Japanese spirit.

Saigusa was aware that claiming the Japanese scientific spirit involved the issue of universality and particularity. If the scientific spirit was universal, as Yuiken Marxists claimed, it would directly contradict the Japanese spirit, which by nature was unique and particular. Saigusa maintained that "what was attractive [about European thought] to Japanese intellectuals was its universalism. . . . European thought taught them the universality of things logical and scientific. This universalism, however, does not go well with today's so-called Japanese spirit. This creates the biggest problem for us."[46] To Saigusa, this problem was not merely an issue of polemics but an intellectually and politically significant problem as well. "We were not wrong in believing that scientific thinking needed to be advocated. . . . However, we need to also respond to a challenge posed by Japanists who question universalism, that is, the question of how to deal with [each nation's unique] history."[47] Saigusa's answer was to grasp things Japanese through things universal.

Writing a history of Japanese science was Saigusa's way of understanding things Japanese through things universal. It was also Saigusa's attempt to give a concrete form to Yuiken's criticism of the "phantom" tradition. Tosaka and other Yuiken members had criticized Japanists and the authorities for the intellectual abuse of the *Manyōshū* and other Japanese "classic" texts for the arbitrary construction of things Japanese. To challenge that, during World War II Saigusa presented a different set of classics that documented a scientific tradition of Japan, the *Complete Collection of Japanese Classic Scientific Texts* (*Nihon kagaku koten zensho*).

The significance of the *Classic Scientific Texts* lay in its canonization of Japanese classics as scientific while providing a narrative that Japan witnessed the emergence of indigenous modern science during the Tokugawa period. Compiled by Saigusa with two professors in literature, Karino Ryōkichi and Niimura Izuru, and two historians of science, Kuwaki Ayao and Ogura Kinnosuke, this multivolume series designated Confucian and other Tokugawa texts as the Japanese classics of scientific texts.[48] The first volume of the collection was titled *Scientific Thought* (*Kagaku shisō*). It contained writings of Miura Bainen, Yamaga Sokō, and Hoashi Banri, who, in Saigusa's words, "believed that science or things scientific were necessary for the development of human or that of our *minzoku* life."[49] The collection—fifteen volumes planned, ten actually published—consisted of three volumes on herbology and medicine (vols. 6, 14, and 15), two on mining (vols. 9 and 10), and others on agriculture (vol. 11), water transportation (vol. 12), metalwork (vol. 13), and the study of *ri*, or reason (vol. 6).[50] The purpose of these volumes, declared Saigusa in his introduction to the series, was to demonstrate that "a modern Japanese science already existed in the Edo period. . . . Besides 'importing science' [from the West], Japan developed its own modern science and technology."[51]

The publication of *Classic Scientific Texts* marked the triumph of Saigusa's protest against the phantom tradition, but it also signified the defeat of such an attempt. While this multivolume collection successfully canonized Tokugawa Confucian scholars as modern scientific thinkers, what such a canonization meant depended on the specific wartime political map of the scientific that was shaped by the state's active mobilization of science and technology. Establishing what is scientific never occurs in a political vacuum. The shifting political map of the scientific in the early 1940s complicated and compromised Saigusa's search for a Japanese scientific past.

By 1941, the establishment of a Japanese scientific tradition no longer functioned as a radical critique of the authorities. As we saw in the previous chapter, the state itself began actively to promote science and technology for war purposes, with technocrats launching their science-technology campaign. The documentation of Japan's scientific past was welcomed by the state, which envisioned the future of a scientific Japan and empire. We know this because in 1941, to commemorate the "2600th anniversary" of the mythological foundation of Japan (1940), the state ordered Japanese scholars to compile the *History of Science in Pre-Meiji Japan*. What was planned as a multivolume history of Japanese science was not published until the 1950s, as the intensifying war with the United States made such a large-scale project difficult.[52] There is no historical record left to tell us exactly how this anthology was originally conceived and discussed, but Saigusa's *Classic Scientific Texts* allows us to see what kind of history of Japanese science was permitted and encouraged during the severely censored years of the early 1940s. Since Saigusa's collection was published by a major newspaper company, it is safe to assume that the aim and content of *Classic Scientific Texts* met the interests of the state. Moreover, Saigusa was one of the scholars asked by the state to compile the *History of Science in Pre-Meiji Japan*. In other words, Saigusa's own project to establish a scientific past of Japan was not merely tolerated but appreciated by the wartime state.

Let me elaborate further on the wartime political milieu. In September 1937, two months after the war with China began, the government launched the National People's Spiritual Mobilization Movement (*kokumin seishin sōdōin undō*), tightening its grip further via censorship of any scholarship and activities that might criticize Japan's war with China and the emperor-centered ideology that supported it. This forced the few remaining leftist groups and labor organizations to choose between arrest and survival—to survive, they would have had to support the war under the emperor ideology. At the conservative end of the leftist political spectrum, the Japanese Federation of Labor decided to abstain from striking in order to show its support of the state, and the Socialist Democratic Party (*shakai taishū tō*) publicly declared its support for Japan's war with China. Those on the far left who remained critical of Japan's imperialism and its ideology were put in jail, such as members of World Culture (*sekai bunka*), a Kyoto-based Marxist group. To avoid arrest of its members, Yuiken voluntarily dissolved itself in August 1938. Tosaka and several others immediately started a new journal, *Gakugei* (Arts and Literature),[53] but three months later, Tosaka and twelve other former Yuiken Marxists were arrested for violating the Peace Preservation Law.

For those "thought criminals" jailed in wartime Japan, death was an imminent and real possibility. The body of Kobayashi Takiji grotesquely disfigured from torture in 1933, for example, was still a vivid memory. Being jailed meant not only losing the capacity to publish but also not being able to support one's family, potentially forever. Every intellectual in wartime Japan, whether Marxist or not, was faced with a decision: finding a way to critique without being banned or arrested, going to jail, or writing in full support of the war and the wartime government. Tosaka died in jail from malnutrition in 1945, only a week before Japan's surrender. This was the reality that intellectuals who voiced criticism faced. Many of the leftist intellectuals who could afford to do so simply stopped writing.

Saigusa chose to publish. He carried on the Yuiken project of writing a history of the Japanese scientific tradition and did not criticize Japan's war with China or its claim of colonial leadership in Asia. In late 1937, when Yuiken began to discuss its dissolution, Saigusa joined the Shōwa Study Group (*Shōwa kenkyūkai*). This was a policy study group established in 1933 by elite intellectuals; by the time Saigusa joined this group, it had acquired a strong political color as a brain trust of the first and second Konoe cabinets (1937–39, 1940–41). The political goal of the study group was to provide the ideology and strategies for Japan's imperialism in Asia. Invited by Miki Kiyoshi, a philosopher whose politics also shifted from Marxism, Saigusa became a member of the culture section of the Shōwa Study Group.[54] Whether he sought to be affiliated with the state-sanctioned group as a strategy to avoid arrest or as a reflection of his full-hearted support of the wartime state does not concern our analysis here. Saigusa did not leave any account of his wartime activities; besides, we will never know the deepest inner workings of his mind, or anyone else's, especially when the circumstances were as politically convoluted as they were. What is important to our critical discourse analysis is what Saigusa published under these circumstances and how it challenged, overlapped with, and reinforced discourses that circulated in wartime Japan.

Saigusa's wartime writing ambiguously blended his earlier arguments and new assertions. In some cases, what was new after 1938 was subtle, but in other places, such as his new definition of culture (we will discuss this shortly), changes were drastic. For example, Saigusa's 1939 article "The Logic of the East Asian Cooperative Community" appeared in an opinion magazine, *Chūō kōron* (Central View), in the same month (January 1939) that the Shōwa Study Group's cultural section issued a report, *The Intellectual Logic of the New Japan.*[55] In this article, Saigusa argued that the East Asian Cooperative Community needed to offer an ideology that would make sense to the whole world. Saigusa was not unaware of the colonial reality behind the East Asian Cooperative Community, as he lamented a gap between Japanese logic and that of the colonized: "It is a positive thing for the Japanese that the Japanese write the logic of the East Asian Cooperative Community. However, that is not necessarily so for the other *minzoku* in Eastern Asia. This casts a dark light on the intellectuals." However, the essay ultimately argued for universalizing the logic of the East Asian Cooperative Community. After all, he insisted, "Truth is Truth, no matter which *minzoku* writes it."[56] This essay illuminates the ambivalent nature of Saigusa's wartime writing. On the one hand, Saigusa hoped that Japan's logic would be a universal logic, something that would make sense to the world, indirectly warning against any self-serving justification of Japan's imperialism. On the other hand, however, aspiring to make Japanese logic universal could be easily read as a demand for further extending Japan's colonial domination.

Saigusa's definition of culture in his 1943 work was the most apparent and drastic change from his earlier writings. However, upon closer look, even this example reveals that many of Saigusa's views in fact remained unchanged. When he titled his 1933 text *The Crisis of Culture*, he meant by "culture" the declining bourgeois culture of "irrational" capitalism.[57] A decade later, when he published *The Design and Reality of Japanese Culture* (*Nihon bunka no kōsō to genjitsu*) in 1943, he discussed culture approvingly as *minzoku*-based: "Culture is that by which we, *kokumin*, create lives while embodying and managing the spirit of the imperial nation."[58] According to Saigusa, this *minzoku*-specific sense of "culture," which emerged after the Manchurian Incident of 1931, gave the concept of culture a new meaning. Resembling Japanists' discourse, Saigusa argued that what Japan needed now was "the synthesis of the Japanese spirit, and the promotion of science and technology." At the same time, Saigusa explained:

After all, to think about science and technology is to think about something universal. An advance in science and technology in one nation means that that nation receives recognition in the world. . . . The world acknowledges the greatness of a certain nation only when it sees greatness in science and technology. . . . We have to reflect on this aspect of our *minzoku* spirit that has so far been ignored.[59]

While employing the Japanist language of the synthesis of science and the Japanese spirit, this statement illuminates a simultaneously subversive element of Saigusa's writing as well, because Saigusa advocated science and technology that were universal rather than a "uniquely Japanese" science-technology.

Saigusa's history writing project thus involved demonstrating the history of modern science in Japan rather than that of a uniquely Japanese science. Saigusa was well aware that as long as the definition of science was strictly based on that of the modern West, he would have to conclude that science did not exist in Japan until it was imported from the West. Thus, establishing a scientific tradition for Japan required him to redefine what was "scientific." He did this through the concepts of technology and intellect. In *Japanese Intellect and Technology* (1939), Saigusa's first work on the history of technology, he wrote that "Japan did not have a history of science in a strict sense, but it had a history of technology. Where there is technology, there is always intellect [*chisei*]."[60] In other words, for technology—"the order/law of nature that receives human spirit"—to exist, there had to be intellect— "the spirit that works on nature."[61] These definitions of technology and intellect were founded on his understanding of Engels's historical materialism formulated in the early 1930s. In the first issue of *Yuibutsuron kenkyū* (November 1932), Saigusa's manifesto, "The Position of New Materialism," quoted Engels's historical materialism to criticize a philosophy of idealism. For Saigusa, to be scientific meant to employ dialectics, and that meant, for him, following the laws of nature.[62] The history of technology thus satisfied both the historical demonstration of Japanese intellect and Saigusa's belief in dialectical materialism.

Another important concept that Saigusa used to demonstrate the dialectics of technology was *kaibutsu*. *Kaibutsu*, or "disclosure," was the central concept that bridged science and technology in Saigusa's writings. In "The History of Scientific Civilization and Thought in Japan," Saigusa defined the history of civilization as the "history of disclosure": "To civilize means to disclose what was concealed, what was buried in the soil."[63] According to Saigusa, Japanese sciences such as medicine and herbology did not develop until the early Tokugawa period because there had existed no concept of "disclosure" before. What revolutionized Japanese science was a Chinese text, *Tenkō kaibutsu* (literally, *Natural Making and Human Disclosure*), which was read in eighteenth-century Japan. Saigusa argued that with the notion of disclosure, nature came to be regarded as something that human beings could work on, a view that was necessary for the emergence of modern science.[64] Saigusa regarded mining as the best example of *kaibutsu*, which explains why *Classic Scientific Texts* included two volumes on mining. The concept of *kaibutsu* served Saigusa's purpose well not only because it supported his argument that modern science emerged in Japan in the eighteenth century but also because technology was a materialization of *kaibutsu*, an interaction between humans and nature.

Saigusa's view of technology also developed as a response to the so-called prewar technology debate (*gijutsu ronsō*) in the mid-1930s, a debate among Yuiken Marxists and other intellectuals regarding the nature of technology.[65] Despite various disagreements, the main Marxist participants, Tosaka Jun, Oka Kunio, and Aikawa Haruki, had come to agree that technology was "a system of a means of labor" by the time Saigusa joined the technology debate rather late in 1937 with his essay "Gijutsugaku to gurentsugebito" (The Borderland of Technology). He defined technology as having three essential features: "a means as a dynamic process," "a means that uses natural materials for that process," and "a means for concrete human desire."[66] His definition differed from that of his fellow Marxists, for Saigusa removed the concept of labor from the definition and emphasized its relationship with nature and human desire. His 1941 text *Ideas of Technology* argued that technology should be understood "not just as tools and machines or skills of a person but ... as something that integrates and intellectualizes natural resources and the national land."[67]

Saigusa's conception of technology here is very similar to the colonial vision of the technocrats we examined in Chapter 2. The Japanese imperialism espoused by technocrats fulfilled all three essential features of Saigusa's definition of technology: It was a process in which East Asia was rendered the "natural resources" for Japan to use in realizing its own concrete desire. Yet Saigusa never used the phrase "science-technology" in his wartime writings. Considering how widely that phrase was used in the early 1940s, not to use the phrase at all was most likely a deliberate choice that illustrates Saigusa's disagreement with the technocratic definition of science. Science to Saigusa did not refer to the knowledge produced in a laboratory to serve engineers or military technology. It referred, rather, to the universal intellect.

With his definition of technology, however, Saigusa also explicitly supported the state's war mobilization. He expanded the meaning of technology to a more abstract and symbolic level. The original essay, "Gijutsugaku to gurentsugebito," was published in Ōkōchi's journal, *Kagakushugi kōgyō* (Scientific Industry). Two years later, Saigusa rewrote this essay to include in his *Japanese Technology and Intellect*, by adding the following new section:

[Technology] is a process through which human life becomes materialized correctly and beautifully. ... Everyone knows that today the worldview is connected with politics, and politics with technology. It can be said that politics is a kind of technology. I choose to advocate the expansive definition of technology. ... Spirit has no meaning if technology is not taken into consideration. As long as spiritual mobilization [*seishin dōin*] is political, it is also technological. Spiritual mobilization gains significance only as a process that the Japanese must go through to correctly and perfectly establish a Japanese culture.[68]

To him, technology was not limited to machines and systems of production; there could also be technology in politics, science, and art. When the Japanese Marxist debate on technology came to a standstill, with too rigid a focus on technology as machines for production, Saigusa's definition provided a new perspective on the conceptualization of technology. At the same time, it also affirmed the state's Spiritual Mobilization Movement, which was aimed at expunging any leftist ideas and strengthening nationalism and militarism.

Critics have evaluated Saigusa's chimera-like writings during wartime in various ways. Three interpretations of Saigusa's scholarship, published in 1965 in two memorial issues of the journal *Kagakushi kenkyū* (Study of the History of Science), present the range of options common to interpreting writings by Saigusa and many other wartime intellectuals. First, in examining Saigusa's discussions of technology, historian Kamatani Chikayoshi argues that Saigusa denied Marxism after 1938 and that it was a clear case of political conversion, *tenkō*.[69] Also discussing Saigusa's concept of technology, the historian Sakamoto Kenzō characterizes it as a "kind of pretended *tenkō*" that Saigusa strategically adopted only to continue voicing any criticism he could insert in his writing. To prove his point, Sakamoto highlights the "distortion" that resulted from his "pretended *tenkō*," the gap between Saigusa's "resistance" and "acceptance of the national policy."[70] The third historian, Ōmori Minoru, focuses on Saigusa's history of science and its achievement, without mentioning Saigusa's political shift at all.[71]

Saigusa's ambiguous intellectual and political trajectory, however, can be better understood through the concept of participation/incorporation. Since Saigusa's definition of science and his goal to write a scientific history of Japanese science did not change before or after 1938, one may indeed agree with Ōmori in setting aside the concept of *tenkō*, but with a further examination of Saigusa's scholarship. Rather than analyze Saigusa's writings through the "gap" between Saigusa's two opposing motives, resistance to and acceptance of the national policy, it makes more sense to acknowledge that what Sakamoto calls Saigusa's "resistance" in fact became a welcome endeavor for the wartime state that aspired to promote science and technology in Japan. The discourse of science provided a space for Saigusa to continue his Yuiken project in print. By challenging the "unscientific" Japan through public discourse, however, Saigusa's promotion of a scientific Japan was incorporated into the wartime promotion of science and technology. By documenting the scientific tradition of the Japanese *minzoku*, Saigusa ended up adding a scientific past to the Japanist celebration of the nation's culture.

My point will be clearer when we place Saigusa's narrative of the history of Japanese science back into the discourse of Japanese science in the early 1940s. Numerous essays and books on the topic of Japanese science appeared after 1938, and by 1940 the history of Japanese science had become a popular subject in both scholarly and nonscholarly science magazines.[72] In fact, the History of Science Society of Japan was established in April 1941, reflecting this popularity. Despite the increasing shortage of paper in the early 1940s, the topic of science, especially Japanese science, continued to be discussed in books, journals, magazines, and newspapers. We will examine details in the next chapter, but here we focus our analysis specifically on the history of Japanese science.

Reading through numerous publications on the history of Japanese science during wartime, one notices a major characteristic in their narrative and approach: the curious combination of the Marxist externalist approach and the Taishō cultural history's emphasis on the national history but without any of the criticism that each approach had offered. As we recall, the externalist approach, developed by Marxist historians like Ogura Kinnosuke, analyzed the development of science in relation to social and economic conditions. The Taishō cultural history was developed as a challenge to the elitist historiography and attempted to write the people's history as the national history. Mikami Yoshio's *Japanese Mathematics as Seen from Cultural History*, which we examined in Chapter 3, was the first and best representative work that critically analyzed Japanese science as a reflection of the Japanese character. The curious wartime combination of the Marxist externalist approach and the liberal, anti-elitist exploration of the Japanese people's character lacked the Marxist criticism of Japan's system of political economy as well as the critique of the negative Japanese character that Mikami identified. It instead used the history of science to celebrate the scientific character of the Japanese people, the nation, and the empire.

This is evident in the collection of essays in the 1940 special New Year's "History of Japanese Science" issue of *Kagaku Pen*. *Kagaku Pen* was a monthly general magazine by Kagaku Pen Kurabu (Scientist-Writers Club) organized in 1936 by scientists Ishihara Jun, Nakatani Ukichi, and others who were interested in writing essays, commentaries, and literary works.[73] As a magazine for general readership but edited and written by scientists, it covered various topics related to science, literature, and policy. In the 1940 special issue, nine scientists and nonscientists contributed short articles whose topics ranged from the "development of the scientific spirit" to "Japanese ancient castles in architectural studies." This is a convenient place to observe the status of the field of Japanese history, since the magazine was considered politically neutral and the editors were scientists. The latter fact of course does not mean that the content of all the articles was endorsed by scientists, but it does suggest the kind of discourse that was regarded as acceptable by practicing scientists.

Yoshioka Shun'ichirō's "History of Japanese Mathematics" most clearly demonstrates what happened when the critical impulse of the externalist approach and the cultural history approach was lost. Yoshioka was a mathematician who published numerous works on mathematics, numbers, medicine, and philosophy in prewar and postwar Japan. His article closely resembled Mikami Yoshio's history of *wasan* published almost twenty years earlier and cited his work to characterize *wasan* as "hobbylike." Yoshioka's ultimate argument, however, was very different. Yoshioka wrote that during the Tokugawa period "many Japanese simply enjoyed mathematics. Back then, in fact, you could not earn a living by being a mathematician. . . . Mathematical studies were a hobby. This fact points to the wealth of the mathematical talent of the Japanese." Like most articles in this special issue, Yoshioka's treated the Tokugawa period as the pivotal era for Japanese science. He called the Tokugawa period the "Japanese renaissance," echoing Saigusa's comparison of the Western Renaissance to Japan's eighteenth century. He did recognize a shortcoming of *wasan*; he pointed out, citing Ogura Kinnosuke, that its "guildlike" sectionalism hindered the development of *wasan*. Yoshioka, however, explained that this was a result of "feudalism" and the "underdevelopment of industry." He maintained that these negative characteristics "had nothing to do with Japanese mathematical talent." In fact, according to Yoshioka, Japanese mathematical talent was further illustrated by the fact that the Japanese had the foresight to replace the impractical *wasan* with Western mathematics and excelled at it quickly.[74]

The celebration of Japanese scientific talent and tradition also dominated Haga Mayumi's essay "Japanese Nation [*minzoku*] and Science." Haga, a Japan Romantic School writer, argued that "the Japanese spirit, which has historically loved beauty and truth, and the modern scientific spirit are like close family members." Since "a search for truth has been the Japanese tradition and principle for thousands of years, . . . Japan may be the first to create a next-stage religion that affirms a new type of life based on the unity of science and principle."[75] An example Haga used to support this claim was none other than the Buddhist monk Dōgen, based on whom Japanist Hashida Kunihiko developed his theory of "science as practice" (though he did not mention Hashida). While praising Japan's successful and prompt adoption of modern science, Haga in fact acknowledged that Japan was still behind the West in terms of scientific development. He was nonetheless confident that Japan would achieve independence from Western science and technology. Mentioning Miyamoto Takenosuke's ideal of "Asia development technology," he maintained that creativity was the key for such a goal.

After all, he wrote, "Japan has imported all kinds of science and technology from the world, assimilated them, and created a unique beauty out of them through the creativity of the Japanese spirit." Whereas Western science had often been used to destroy humanity and civilization, he concluded, "Japan would elevate science to Beauty."[76]

Also included with the seven articles that lavishly celebrated the Japanese scientific talent, however, were two articles that could be easily interpreted as a critique of this discourse. "The History of Japanese Scientific Thought" by historian and former Yuiken member Kamo Giichi discussed the now-familiar figures of Miura Baien and other Tokugawa scholars whom Saigusa had been studying. But he described the Tokugawa period as the time when a "civil society" (shimin shakai) emerged along with rational, scientific thought.[77] Kamo was persistent in applying the externalist view to explain the rise of scientific thought in Japan and repeatedly emphasized that the modern, scientific thought that emerged in the eighteenth century was "the intellectual weapon of the civil class [shimin kaijyū] that represented the early stage of rational capitalism against the Confucianism of the elite class under feudalism."[78] Specifying "civil society" as a distinct, bourgeois class and emphasizing the class nature of modern scientific thought in Japan were clear critiques of the mainstream narrative by Saigusa and others who wrote the history of science as a form of minzoku history.

Nitto Shūichi, an epidemiologist at Tokyo Imperial University, offered the most clear-cut critique in his essay "On Contemporary Japanese Medicine." It started with a straightforward critique of the minzoku discourse of science: "People talk about Japanese medicine, American medicine, German medicine, French medicine, and so forth, but this is utter nonsense."[79] Asked to write on medicine in the Tokugawa period, he "deliberately decided to write a critique of contemporary medicine in Japan instead," indicating his refusal to join the discourse of Japanese scientific talent. The entire article focused on what he found to be problems of the medical and scientific fields in Japan, such as the worshiping of Western medicine, the censoring of research topics by professors in power, the lack of productive critiques among scientists, the harm caused by the academic cliques, and so on. Most of his criticisms were restatements of what Ogura Kinnosuke had pointed out more than a decade earlier but were absent in the other articles in the journal. It is likely that Nitto's piece was included—inserted, in fact, at the very end of the volume as if trying not to draw too much censorship attention—not only because he was an established scientist but also because the editors agreed with his critique.

Kagaku Pen's special issue, with contributors from various political and professional backgrounds, provides a kind of bird's-eye view of the field of the history of Japanese science during wartime. It illuminates how Saigusa's history of Japanese science, which canonized particular Tokugawa Confucian texts as scientific, had circulated among intellectuals and was used to celebrate Japanese scientific talent. Under this discourse, criticism existed. Or rather, as the *Kagaku Pen* special issue exemplified, critics were able to voice their critique of Japanese science even while celebrating Japanese culture. The critique of Japanese science, however, did not necessarily mean the critique of the wartime state or its imperial war. We have already seen that the technology-bureaucrats around this time criticized and attempted to take over the state's science policy so that they could contribute more to the state and the war.

The coexistence of the critique of Japanese science and the celebration of it characterized Ogura's wartime writing as well. As the Pacific War intensified, Ogura also began to support the state's war efforts. A comparison between his earlier writings and his 1944 book, *Mathematics in Wartime*, makes clear how his arguments changed. Ogura, who had advocated science for the masses a decade earlier, now demanded that the Japanese establish "mathematics for the imperial nation."[80] "Today's mathematics," he argued, "needs to fulfill its duty as a weapon to destroy the enemy" through the invention of military technologies and an increase in industrial production.[81] In this work, his earlier criticism of the Japanese "feudalistic" and "bureaucratic" science was completely absent, and, in turn, new concepts such as "the Japanese spirit" appeared: "Without the Japanese spirit, it is impossible to construct a Japanese mathematics. Likewise, if we fail to make a radical development of mathematics as weaponry, it means we did not fulfill our duty to our brave soldiers on the front."[82] Ogura's evaluation of *wasan* became positive, too. Although he remained critical of *wasan* for its secrecy, he no longer described is as "feudalistic." He characterized it as "art" just as Mikami had in his 1923 cultural history that Ogura had criticized. Ogura even praised *wasan* as an embodiment of "Japanese mathematical talent."[83]

As was the case with Saigusa, however, Ogura retained many of his earlier arguments as well. In fact, Ogura's earlier logic for resistance continued to support his 1944 work and in some ways led him to advocate "mathematics for the imperial nation." As we saw in his 1936 article "The Duty of Natural Scientists," one of Ogura's criticisms of Japanese scientists had been that they were selfish and had no social consciousness. Ogura did not change this opinion throughout the war years. He continued to encourage scientists to be actively involved in social needs. He also continued to demand that science be directly related to social demands. But by 1941, scientists' involvement in society meant their involvement in war efforts. In his 1941 article "The Duty of Natural Scientists during Wartime," Ogura asserted that "[j]ust as a military officer sacrifices his blood for the nation, a scientist's specialized knowledge and talent—even if his fame goes beyond the national border—

should be completely dedicated to the national cause."[84] Ogura also continued to promote the systematic and planned unity of mathematics, science,
and technology, not for the construction of proletarian science any longer
but for the mathematics of Imperial Japan. In other words, his criticism of
Japanese science and scientists did not fundamentally change. He continued to advocate science that was in touch with society, free from academic
cliques, and based on more systematic planning. His language changed, however, now fashioning his vision for a scientific Japan as the science for the
imperial nation.

Describing the history of science in the late 1930s, historian Nakayama
Shigeru has argued that "[u]nder the cover of 'science,' which could not
easily be penetrated even by fascist demagogues, the history of science provided for leftist liberals a shelter from the eyes of governmental censorship
and from the arms of police thought-control."[85] However, by 1938 the field
of the history of science had lost its critical position that required a "cover."
In fact, science became one more place from which Japanese nationalism
could draw pride. Scholars like Nakayama have considered Saigusa's and
other intellectuals' advocacy of rational thought as a form of resistance to
the wartime state, but my analysis shows that they defended rationality while
simultaneously supporting the wartime state and Japan's imperialism.

As the Yuiken discussion of tradition in 1938 concluded, the scientific
construction of the scientific tradition was crucial for Japanese Marxism.
However, when Saigusa carried out this project by canonizing certain Tokugawa texts as classic Japanese scientific texts, he contributed to the nationalist
pride in a "scientific" Japan. In other words, Saigusa's mission to redefine the
Japanese *minzoku* based on the "correct" citation of classic texts, as opposed
to the abusive citation of classics by Japanists, was co-opted by the wartime
promotion of science and technology. The difference between science as
defined by Saigusa and Ogura on the one hand and the science-technology
of the technocrats on the other continued to exist; however, by establishing
the Japanese scientific tradition, Saigusa Hiroto and Ogura Kinnosuke ironically provided a scientific past for the scientific Japan that the technocrats'
science-technology attempted to construct.

PART THREE

Popular Science

CHAPTER 6

The Mobilization of Wonder

MOST JAPANESE interested in learning science in interwar and wartime Japan were not reading the Marxist *Yuibutsuron kenkyū* or technocrats' writings. Yuiken Marxists' writings were too difficult for those readers not trained in philosophy and theory. Technology-bureaucrats also did not write for the purpose of mass consumption. Science that was consumed by the general readership in interwar and wartime Japan was that of so-called *tsūzoku kagaku zasshi*, literally, "popular science magazines," such as *Kagaku gahō* (Science Illustrated) and *Kodomo no kagaku* (Children's Science).[1] The genre of popular science magazines emerged in the early 1920s as part of both the promotion of science and technology during and after World War I and the dramatic development of print mass media in Taishō Japan. Together with such widely popular magazines as *Shōnen kurabu* (Boys' Club) and *Kingu* (King), which also began publication in the 1920s, popular science magazines occupied a smaller but nonetheless important space in Japanese interwar mass consumer culture. These magazines circulated not only in Japan proper but also throughout the Japanese Empire—Japan, Taiwan, Korea, and China. By 1940 they had even become the government's recommended magazines, and the military began to publish magazines by appropriating the techniques of these pioneering magazines.

This chapter examines popular science culture (*tsūzoku kagaku bunka*) in Japan from the 1920s to the mid-1940s, focusing on two magazines, *Science Illustrated* and *Children's Science*. The popular science magazines constituted an important site of the politics of the scientific for several reasons. The representation of science in the popular magazines was different from that of Yuiken members and that of technocrats; it was not concerned with the class nature of science or the status of engineers. Science in the magazine pages was a commodity packed with the sense of wonder—expressed mostly as *kyōi* in Japanese, which the editors considered essential to a desire to learn science. A generous number of photographs and illustrations of awe-inspiring nature and scientific enterprises were used to convey the sense of wonder to the reader. The acts of seeing and doing, such as observing, experimenting, and specimen collecting, were also emphasized.

The publication of the popular science magazines was part of the Taishō liberal education movement critical to the science curriculum established under the Ministry of Education. As we saw in Chapter 3, liberal education reformers such as Ogura Kinnosuke demanded school science education to better engage children's curiosity and to use visual and other aids to facilitate their learning process rather than focus on textbook memorization. The popular science magazines carried out this reformist mission by providing exciting, wonder-filled science as opposed to the dry, uninteresting science of the school curriculum.

As Yuiken member Tosaka Jun predicted, however, the liberalism of the popular science culture was easily co-opted by the wartime state. The world of wonders was used to provide excitement about weapons and war to the readers. The major science curriculum reform based on the 1941 National People's School Edict (*kokumin gakkō rei*) demonstrates that this world of wonder was effectively mobilized to produce the ideal imperial subject— one scientifically and technologically capable, as well as loyal to the emperor and the nation.

Packaging Wonder and Spectacle

The most widely read popular science magazines in prewar Japan were probably *Science Illustrated*, its brother magazine *Children's Science*, and *Kagaku chishiki* (Scientific Knowledge). Harada Mitsuo (1890–1977) was involved in the creation of all three. Harada studied agricultural science at Hokkaido Imperial University and received a doctorate degree in botany from Tokyo Imperial University. According to his autobiography, the genetics and embryology he learned in Tokyo greatly inspired him and made him want to "explain the wonder, mystery, and puzzle [*kyōi, shinpi, fushigi*] of nature to people, surprise them, and satisfy their desire to know."[2] During the 1910s, he launched several innovative projects toward this end—publishing a science magazine for young readers and making educational science films— but all his attempts ended in failure. He was not the most careful planner for innovative, ambitious goals like these. The largest obstacle, however, was the absence of a financial supporter who appreciated Harada's idea of pioneering the genre of popular science education.[3]

World War I brought new opportunities for him. As the national promotion of science and technology inspired the "liberal education reform movement," publishers finally became interested in the idea of science magazines and books for the popular audience. Seibundō, a Tokyo-based publisher specializing in educational texts, successfully marketed Harada's *Stories That Children Want to Hear*, a series of science-related stories for children in 1920.[4] When the Association for the Popularization of Scientific Knowledge (*kagaku chishiki fukyūkai*) asked Harada to be the editor of a magazine it was planning to launch, *Scientific Knowledge*, Harada immediately accepted, rejoicing in the great opportunity and prospect of realizing his dream. Widely advertised through full-page ads in the newspaper, the first issue of *Scientific Knowledge* (July 1921) sold very well. Harada, anxious about the sales, stood outside a bookstore near Ginza on the first day of publication and was delighted to witness at least fifty copies being sold that day.[5] Harada's involvement with *Scientific Knowledge*, however, was short. An internal conflict drove him out of the editorial position after the first issue. Two years later, he began his own magazine, *Science Illustrated*, and a year after that, *Children's Science*. Whereas *Scientific Knowledge* targeted the educated public, *Science Illustrated* and *Children's Science* aimed to reach the less educated and younger audience: *Science Illustrated* readers were in their late teens and older, and *Children's Science* was aimed at children between ten and their midteens.[6] Compared to *Scientific Knowledge*, these two magazines used simpler language with pronunciations written next to most Chinese characters and included numerous pictures and illustrations.

All three magazines presented science as a variety of knowledge that readers could and should acquire through their pages. Unlike the Marxist conception of science, science in these popular science magazines had nothing to do with class analysis or any critical examination of science and its political and economic contexts. Rather, the magazines supplied quick and easy knowledge, packaged in such ways as "the science of oceans" and "the science of the earthquake." The great Kantō earthquake of 1923 in fact dramatically increased sales of these magazines and books like *Science of the Earthquake* that marketed simplified yet up-to-date knowledge about earthquakes.[7] The popularization of science, to the promoters of popular science, meant the dissemination of the most basic and latest knowledge of science. Science promoters like Harada packaged science, wrapped it in a colorful cover, and made it available for mass consumption.

Harada believed that science needed to be explained and presented in a simple and pictorial manner to popularize it. Since scientists and scholars tended to use language that was too difficult for the popular reader, he wrote articles himself based on interviews with scholars, academic works, and reports in domestic as well as foreign science magazines such as *Scientific American*, *Popular Mechanics*, and *Science et vie*. Photos and illustrations of various subjects were also included to facilitate the reader's understanding of the material.

Simple language and illustrations alone would not be enough to popularize science. Harada believed that people needed to be excited about science as well. What was innovative about Harada's editing was his way of getting readers interested in acquiring science as knowledge. Harada used a "sense of wonder" as the gateway to science, and the mission of *Science Illustrated* was to help the reader to see and feel the wonder of nature. "Nature is full of beauty and wonder. . . . This world of beauty and wonder is something that only those who seek science can enjoy."[8] To Harada, a "sense of wonder" was most important in learning science yet was neglected in Japanese school education. He explained in the first issue of *Science Illustrated* that Western societies had progressed because many Westerners had pursued wonders abundant in nature with their eyes open as wide as possible. On the contrary, Japanese science education in elementary and middle schools bored students with the memorization of textbooks. "Just imagine," Harada exclaimed, "how fun it would be to actually see Tokyo and how boring it is to just read the tourist guidebook."[9] *Science Illustrated*, he declared, "guides you into the inner shrine of the wonder of nature."[10] The magazine introduced science as something fun and wonderful so that its readers would develop their own interest in further scientific knowledge.[11] Harada soon left the editorial position of *Science Illustrated*, but the succeeding editor, Okabe Nagasetsu, continued the same emphasis. "Scientists," Okabe explained, "are those who pursue the root of a sense of wonder, seeking to discover reasons and laws."[12] This excitement about wonder was boldly expressed in the titles of the magazine's numerous special issues, such as "The Wonder of the Sea, the Wonder of the Mountain," "The Wonder of the Body," and "The Wonder of Spiritual Phenomena."[13]

This sense of wonder was also a central concept in *Children's Science*. With a beautifully illustrated dreamy-eyed boy under the moon on the cover, the first issue (October 1924) of *Children's Science* declared the mission of the magazine as follows: "Between heaven and the Earth are things surprising, wonderful, and interesting. Only scholars know this, but they are too busy with their research to tell you all about it. . . . One job of this magazine is to introduce you to this world by selecting things that boys and girls will especially like."[14] In this statement, he also made clear that the ultimate purpose of the magazine was education: to let the reader know that "science means the clarification of the laws [of nature]. What many people regard as science is just its application. By knowing the laws, human beings can live in accordance with nature with ease and happiness, and by applying science, we can advance our society toward higher civilization."[15] Unlike school science that forced children to memorize laws of nature, *Children's Science* sought to inspire children with a sense of wonder about nature.[16]

The sense of wonder, according to Harada, could only be felt by going into and seeing nature. As Harada put it, "[T]hose who do not know the natural sciences are those who only look at the signboard in front of the peep show. Scientists actually go in and see interesting things inside."[17] Harada's association of science and the peep show was not as far-fetched as it may seem. As Ludmilla Jordanova shows in her feminist analysis of the eighteenth- to twentieth-century culture of science, "looking" and "unveiling" were a central thrust and metaphor of male scientists' inquiry into nature in Europe.[18] The significance of seeing for the learning of scientific knowledge was also emphasized in Japan by science education reformers like Tanahashi Gentarō, who choreographed many science exhibits in the late 1910s and early 1920s by paying special attention to visual entertainment.[19] The pages of *Science Illustrated* and *Children's Science* were the entry to this peep show called science, where "seeing" and a sense of wonder were intimately related.

What did the reader see in these magazines? Magazines uniquely began with a pictorial section of "extraordinary" photos of, for example, a star just being born in the universe, a large airplane flying in the two-page panoramic view of a New York skyscraper, and wild African animals.[20] In *Children's Science*, in addition to the photos, there was a two-page fold-up color illustration of the working of various machines and the diversity of living creatures. Photos and illustrations, many of which were clearly taken from foreign magazines, were inserted throughout the magazine so as not to bore the reader with text. Images of various things—such as radios, animals, urban architecture, plants, blimps, stars, and ships—were put together rather randomly. Following the several pages of the opening pictorial section were articles, subjects of which ranged as widely as the objects in the images, from how to make a radio set to how to understand sexual desire, the mechanics of an airplane to the working of the human digestive system, the latest news in astronomy to the best hiking course.[21] As random as the juxtaposition of images and topics of science, technology, and nature was, it reflected the definition of science Harada provided, that science meant the clarification of natural laws and application of these laws for higher civilization. The magazine pages presented the wonder of nature and its natural laws as well as the wonderful fruit of the application of such laws to technology.

The juxtaposition of various materials, peoples, and subjects in these popular magazines can be compared to the world's fairs and department stores. Yoshimi Shun'ya, in his study of the world's fairs and Japanese expositions, has suggested a lineage from the nineteenth-century world's fair to the early twentieth-century birth of the department store. He argues that the department store offered an experience of "seeing" inherited from the expositions: "'seeing,' that is, an experience through gaze, by walking

around, comparing products, discovering 'newness' among them, and enjoying such experience."[22] This experience of "seeing" also seems to have been
inherited by the popular science magazines. Similarities are clear: visitors
could see an array of materials from all over the world, packaged in one
location; enjoy browsing around leisurely; and consume them by way of
seeing, reading, or purchasing as they wished.[23] Moreover, even though the
Japanese science magazines did not schematically present the racialized hierarchy of civilization that physically structured the world's fairs like the one
in Chicago (1893) and Japanese fairs like the Tokyo Taishō Exhibit (1914),[24]
they nonetheless portrayed Westerners as practitioners of science, and the
non-Western "exotic" peoples as part of the natural world. A sense of wonder was invoked from looking at the unfamiliar customs and appearances of
the various peoples in "exotic" places such as Africa and the South Pacific.
These peoples never appeared as practitioners of science or inventors of
technology. They were as much a part of the wonderfully interesting natural
order as exotic flowers and animals.[25]

Yoshimi calls this aspect of visual entertainment the *misemono* spectacle.
He sees the world expositions and Japanese fairs from the three perspectives of capitalism, imperialism, and the *misemono* spectacle such as the peep
show and the freak show. *Misemono* is a Japanese term for "street shows and
performances," and Yoshimi uses it to refer to the mass entertainment aspect
of the Japanese fairs that became especially pronounced from the 1910s; the
1922 Peace Memorial Tokyo Exposition, for example, won popularity with
such tricks as the "flying beauty in the Arabian Pavilion" and a "burning
Joan of Arc on the cross [*sic*]." *Science Illustrated* and *Children's Science* emerged
also at the intersection of *misemono* entertainment, capitalism, and imperialism.[26] To entice the reader to go into the "peep show" called the wonder
of nature, the popular science magazines provided *misemono* entertainment
with extraordinary images of nature, "exotic" peoples, and technological enterprises. The world of wonder explored in the magazines could not have
existed outside the Taishō culture of consumption, where mass entertainment and mass media were established around the white-collar and working
classes in urban centers. Finally, it assumed the racial hierarchy of Western
imperialism. Moreover, as I will discuss in the next section, Japanese popular
science culture constituted a part of Japanese imperialism.

These popular science magazines, in other words, represented the science
that Japanese Marxists identified as that of bourgeois liberalism. We may
recall Marxist historian and mathematician Ogura Kinnosuke's criticism of
science history exhibits. Like the Edo science exhibit at the Tokyo Science
Museum, these magazines presented science without any reference to the
social and economic conditions of its production. Notable exceptions were
a few articles that discussed class in *Science Illustrated* in the first two years of

the 1930s, and a fictional story in *Children's Science* about a poor boy who was determined to become a biologist and study vitamins so that he could help to improve the health of his hardworking mother.[27] Besides these exceptions, references to class, proletarian science, or Marxism were absent from the magazines, even in the late 1920s and early 1930s when Marxism influenced a large number of intellectuals in Japan.

Popular science had its own antiestablishment politics, however. First, it explicitly supported nonacademic scholars. By doing so, the magazines asserted that science was something that was not and should not be exclusive to academic scientists.[28] When a nonacademic entomologist, Nawa Yasushi, died in 1926, *Science Illustrated* carried a long obituary for this scholar well known among insect lovers. He had discovered a new species of butterfly and pioneered insect education for farmers yet faced constant financial struggle to keep his research and his private insect museum running. The obituary asserted: "The nation's history really belongs to the ordinary people who would not be recorded in history. Likewise, the real progress of the nation's scientific culture can be only measured by how unknown specialists toil for their research in the mountains away from Tokyo." To rely on the government for budget and facilities was a slave mentality, the author Okabe wrote with anger: "Even though there are those rich people who celebrate their eighty-eighth birthday by stupidly spending money on actresses' naked dances, there is not a single entrepreneur who is willing to create an insect museum. . . . How could we hope for the nation's future?"[29] *Science Illustrated* also made efforts to introduce nonacademic scientists like botanist Makino Tomitarō and marine biologist Aoki Kumakichi.[30] Harada, in fact, had to leave the editorial position of *Science Illustrated* because of his harsh criticism of academic scientists who had no interest in popularizing science.

The magazine's antiestablishment stance could also be discerned in its transgression of the boundary that academic science built, by covering such topics as spiritual science (*shinrei kagaku*), a study of the psyche and of ghosts that academic scholars had dismissed as unscientific by the 1920s.[31] In the 1923 issues of *Science Illustrated*, for example, one could read a series of articles introducing folktales of sex between humans and animals and learn about hypnosis.[32] The magazine sponsored a "spiritual science experiment," a public experiment with a certain spiritualist in February 1926, and published a detailed report of what had happened during the experiment.[33] The October 1927 issue, "The Wonder of Spiritual Phenomena," contained full coverage of the spirit, the psyche, and psychology; the July 1929 issue devoted almost ten pages to "The Spiritual Issues Roundtable Discussion," with specialists in spiritual science, scientists, and a psychic medium named Kasukawa Sachiko.[34] Although the main thrust in these articles and special issues was to scientifically analyze so-called spiritual phenomena so that people would not be fooled, the magazines nonetheless treated the subject as part of the body of knowledge called science.[35]

It is also undeniable that the editors, as a way of marketing the magazine, utilized these topics to stimulate a sensationalist desire to know among the consumers. In this regard, the sense of wonder in the pages of the popular science magazines, enhanced by the *misemono* spectacle, functioned as a mediator between curiosity to see something extraordinary and a desire to know something unfamiliar.

To Harada, the dissemination of scientific knowledge through the popularization of science was crucial for the progress of the nation. This was clearly stated in a manifesto he wrote in the first issue of *Science Illustrated*: "In Japan, not so many people [*kokumin*] really know what science is. They misunderstand science and . . . are indifferent to the advancement of science. Without the advancement of science, however, there is no hope for the advancement of civilization. . . . I am a true Japanese who loves Japan. This is why I criticize Japan. I want to advance the scientific civilization of our nation and make it a first-class nation."[36] Even though Harada emphasized being Japanese here, he was different from Japanist theorists like Sakuta Shōichi and Hashida Kunihiko, since he never presumed a uniquely Japanese epistemology. Rather, to Harada, science meant a universal system of knowledge, and how much the ordinary people understood scientific knowledge served as a universal measure of the progress of the nation's civilization.

For the establishment of the scientific culture of the nation, the magazines promoted more than the sense of wonder and seeing. Performing scientific activities was as important as the sense of wonder and seeing for Harada's magazines. In the next section, we will examine what the readers "did" rather than what they "saw," that is, the readers' involvement in establishing a popular science culture in Imperial Japan through *Children's Science*, moving into the 1930s.

The Modern Emperor and His Scientific Subjects

Besides the beautiful covers and exciting photos, what initially attracted readers to both *Science Illustrated* and *Children's Science* was their radio-making instructions. By the time the first issues of these magazines appeared in the early 1920s, the Japanese had heard about the radio boom in the United States, where the first radio station opened in 1920, and had been eagerly waiting for information on the new technology. Both magazines carried a series of "how to make a radio set" articles explaining that "even a child can make it" with a cost of only fifty sen. The interested reader enjoyed a home-made radio set using materials sold by the editor, Harada Mitsuo, through the publisher and communicated with fellow amateur radio fans abroad, even before Japan's first radio broadcasting began in 1925.[37]

Although the "how to make a radio set" articles were discontinued in late 1924, when the government made laws prohibiting private radio sets in order to regulate the air waves, an emphasis on "doing science" continued in the magazines, especially in *Children's Science*. A good example is the magazine's model-making contest. The contest was first held in 1927 and continued into the early 1940s. Teenage readers of *Children's Science* sent their models of airplanes, ships, and buildings; the prize-winning models chosen by the judges were displayed in the Mitsukoshi Department Store in downtown Tokyo as well as featured in the magazine. The magazine encouraged model making because it involved creativity, contrary to the common assumption that model making was a mere copying of the original. In fact, creativity was highly promoted in both *Children's Science* and *Science Illustrated*, which devoted a few pages to the "Invention Consulting Room" (*hatsumei sōdanshitsu*) in every issue, where the consultant—Harada Mitsuo and, later, patent specialists—answered questions regarding patent laws and procedures. In *Children's Science*, "doing science" was also encouraged through "Science Experiment Reports," a serialized section that showed how different schools conducted experiments in classrooms. Through these events and pages, the magazine made sure that the wonder-filled knowledge of science was to be acquired both from seeing and from doing.[38]

The readers of *Children's Science* not only enjoyed participating in the model-making and invention contests that the magazine set up for them; they also formed science study circles on their own and created their own network in the Japanese Empire. But first, I will introduce the head of this empire, the emperor, before introducing his young scientific subjects.

An episode from the opening of the Tokyo Science Museum provides an insight into how science culture stood within the framework of Imperial Japan and how the imperial family was presented to the public. While the popular science magazines such as *Children's Science* began to entertain the reader and to popularize science in the 1920s, the Diet launched its plan to establish Japan's first national science museum. Although the demand for a science museum had existed before, it took World War I to get the Diet to take the demand seriously. As part of the promotion of the domestic production of science and technology, in 1920 the Diet approved a proposal to establish a museum for the purpose of public science education; after a decade, the Tokyo Science Museum was finally opened in Ueno Park in 1931.

On November 3, the opening day, the imperial couple made an official visit to the museum to celebrate its opening. Both Japanese and European newspapers reported this event with photographs, emphasizing the image of the emperor as modern and scientific, under such headings as "Modern

Japan—the Emperor Hirohito Visits the Newly Renovated Tokyo Science Museum."[39] The French newspaper *L'illustration* captioned its article with the headline "Vision moderne d'un empereur de legende [Modern vision of the Emperor of Legend]: Regardez l'attitude du souverain. . . . Son attention n'est pas de commande, car il est lui-même un savant spécializé dans l'historie naturelle, la microbiologie et la chimie [Look at the attitude of the emperor. . . . His attention is not that of a commander. It reveals that the emperor himself is a specialist in natural history, microbiology, and chemistry]."[40] The Shōwa emperor was indeed a natural scientist, with a special interest in marine invertebrate animals.[41] Even though the most publicized image of Emperor Hirohito was that of the highest commander of the Japanese imperial military through photographs carefully selected and distributed by the government to the mass media, his image as a friend of science also circulated widely through photographs and articles such as the one just described.[42] The emperor's donation of 1.5 billion yen in 1932 for the establishment of the Japan Society for the Promotion of Sciences also contributed to his image as an earnest advocate of science.

In the popular science magazines, the emperor's family members also appeared as supporters and practitioners of science. The first page of the September 1923 issue of *Science Illustrated* featured the mountain climbing of then Crown Prince Hirohito and his brother Prince Chichibu, explaining that their excursion was not just simply hiking but also making scientific observations of nature. The same issue showed a two-page photo of the *Astra Toress*, the largest airship the Japanese navy had purchased, and told the reader that Prince Yamashina Takehiko, Hirohito's distant cousin, had sent this photo to *Science Illustrated* "to advocate the encouragement of science." Known as the "prince of the airplanes," Prince Yamashina even invited Harada and a *Scientific Knowledge* reporter to his house, where he showed a German film about the airplanes (that was not available anywhere else) and another film he himself had produced of the Japanese navy blimp, *SS3*.[43] Events like these were surely orchestrated and ordered to be publicized by the government. The government used the popular science media to cultivate the image of the imperial family as an enlightened benefactor of science. The popular science magazines, in turn, used these images to promote their status in the mass media.

If you were a fourteen-year-old reader of *Children's Science*, you might not have seen the emperor in the magazine, since *Children's Science* did not carry imperial family–related articles or photos. But you would have learned about the opening of the Tokyo Science Museum in the magazine and might have visited with your parents as one of more than thirteen thousand visitors to its first anniversary exhibit, Science of Edo, on November 3, the day designated as the Museum Foundation Day to commemorate the imperial couple's visit for the museum's opening a year before.[44] Nationally celebrated as the Meiji

Memorial Day (the late Meiji emperor's birthday), the November 3 holiday was a designated free-admission day at the museum every year. You might have gone back to the museum the next year to see the second anniversary exhibit in 1933, the Electric Communication Demonstration Fair, where fifteen thousand visitors enjoyed the demonstration of television invented by a Japanese engineer and saw the films *The Overview of Manchukuo* and *A Movie History: The Making of the U.S.A.* Since the particularly heroic portrayal of the founding of the United States was shown together with the film about Manchukuo, you would probably have thought that the establishment of Manchukuo was as gallant and inevitable as that of the United States.[45]

Not only would you have seen Manchukuo in film but you might have been exchanging letters with your friend in Manchuria whom you had met in the readers' section of *Children's Science.* The readers' section—titled "Letters from the Reader" and later "The Chatting Room"—was in fact what differentiated *Children's Science* from other popular science magazines because of the amount of space it devoted to the section and the degree of intimacy in the readers' community developed there. At the end of every issue, an average of three or four pages introduced letters from the young readers eager to report their excitement about the magazine and what they liked about it. The earlier issues in the 1920s received many letters from those excited about this first science magazine for children. "Oh, what a wonderful magazine. What a beautiful cover! . . . With my favorite *Children's Science*, I will study science very hard," one reader wrote, echoing many other such letters.[46] Often the readers told the editor how they began buying the magazine: "I have seen *Science Illustrated* in the bookstore, but it looked too difficult for me. Last September I found *Children's Science.* . . . The world became brighter after reading it." Like this boy from Tokyo, many appreciated *Children's Science* because the *Science Illustrated* that their fathers and brothers were reading was too difficult for them. There were also many letters telling the editor from which magazine they transferred their loyalty: "I used to read *Nihon shōnen* [Japanese Boy], but I am buying *Children's Science* now."[47] In fact, choosing one magazine worthy of their small monthly allowance seemed to be an issue serious enough to damage friendships. One loyal reader from Hiroshima even stopped talking to his friend who insisted on choosing *Boys' Club* for 40 sen over *Children's Science* for 50 sen.[48] So many young readers visited this space so often that the editor had to announce in the April 1925 issue that long letters, letters not written on postcards, or those without return addresses would not be included.[49]

This community of *Children's Science* readers was personal, crossed gender lines, and extended throughout the empire. Readers introduced not only themselves but also their friends who joined the community. These letters, possibly sent with photographs, often gave the names and even addresses of the newcomers. "I am introducing my friend Miyadate Shirō-san. Our friend Wakai Gorō-san says he will also buy the magazine." "Guess what. We have one more reader. Akitagawa Eisaku-kun, who lives at 1768 Shimo-Shibuya."[50] By 1930 the readers had begun exchanging letters among themselves—many letters asked for correspondence, and many youths seemed to have responded. A boy in Gunma Prefecture, for example, received eighty letters when he posted his message in 1935.[51] If they had not received letters from their pen pals, they would post a message such as this: "Iwasaki Yoshimichi-kun in Yamaguchi Prefecture, have you received my postcard yet? Please write me back."[52] The "Letters from the Reader" section was an intimate, personal space where the readers not only visited the editor but also became friends with other readers.

Although most of the letter writers were boys, girls were also part of this intimate community. When in 1925 one reader suggested that the title of *Children's Science* should be changed to *Boys' Science* because the average readers were too old to be called "children," one girl immediately responded, arguing that "I think it should remain *Children's* because girls also read the magazine." She demanded: "In fact, please illustrate boys and girls alternately on the cover." Another girl also requested that girls should appear in the cover illustrations.[53] They were not disappointed: from the April 1925 issue on, both boys and girls appeared on the cover in most of the months. Sometimes girls alone appeared on the cover, like that of the February 1927 issue where two girls—or rather two young women—are hunting in the snowy mountains. Not all the requests were answered, however: one girl demanded that the editor feature science related to homemaking, but the editor did not seem to have heard her voice.[54] Throughout the 1930s and early 1940s, girls participated in the readers' section in almost every issue. Many of them were sisters who liked science as much as their brothers, who had introduced the magazine to them; daughters given the magazine by their fathers; and high school students interested in science. In their letters, they repeatedly encouraged other girls, sometimes specifically referring to them by name, to send more letters to the editor and to each other.[55] Some boys also sent in their hurrahs for girls.[56]

These letters came from all over the empire and beyond. Increasingly in the 1930s, the readers' network expanded into Taiwan, Korea, Manchuria, China, and the Americas (Mexico and Los Angeles). Some months, as many as three or four letters from outside Japan proper appeared in the readers' section. Most of them were Japanese children, but Korean and Chinese boys also wrote.[57] It was not rare to see, for example, a boy in Niigata posting a message to his pen pals in Manchuria, inquiring, "Hatayama-kun in Manchuria, how have you been doing?"[58] This empirewide network did not exhibit a sense of hierarchy among Japan proper and its colonies. I have found

only one letter that shows explicit admiration for Japan: an indigenous Taiwanese reader expressed deep appreciation for the Japanese colonial government's science education he received to become a researcher at a chemistry
research institute in Taiwan.[59] However, besides this letter, any indication of
the center-periphery relationship between the metropole and the colonies
is absent.

As the network expanded to the empire in the 1930s, a new activity
became popular in the readers' community: trading collections of insect
and plant specimens, stamps, and postcards. The readers loved this trading
opportunity, especially with geographically remote places such as Taiwan
and Hokkaido, for it would enormously enrich their collections of insects,
plants, stamps, and postcards with depictions of local scenery. A letter from
a Japanese boy in Shanghai asking to exchange stamps in the December
1933 issue, for example, was immediately responded to in the next issue by a
boy in Shimane Prefecture who collected stamps (though the Shanghai boy
requested stamps from Manchuria!).[60] So many readers began to ask for ex-
changes that one reader in Osaka in 1934 complained that the magazine was
being abused for collecting stamps. Another reader refuted this claim right
away, arguing that stamp collection could be part of scientific research.[61] No
further discussion took place, and letters asking to trade various collections
continued throughout the 1930s.

The editor welcomed such active readership but was most delighted when
the readers began to organize their own science groups. Within three months
after the publication of the first issue, readers voluntarily organized science
study groups and began to report their activities in the "Letters from the
Reader" section. By March 1925, a group of about ten boys in Mito City
had organized a Boys' Science Group (*kagaku shōnendan*) and reported about
their weekly meetings to do experiments and readings; a boy from Kyoto
asked other readers in his city to respond to him so that he could form a
similar study group.[62] Then, letters from Fukuoka, Hiroshima, Ibaraki, and
many other places began to report the start of their own groups and their
activities.[63] Harada was thrilled to know this. "There have been study groups
for literature and the like. But science study groups never existed before the
publication of *Children's Science*," he wrote with excitement. Soon a separate
"Reports from the Children's Science Groups" section was set up adjacent to
the "Letters from the Reader" section.[64] Like the readers' section, the science
study group network also spread out beyond Japan proper as the Japanese
Empire expanded; for example, the editor received reports from Manchurian
Hobby and Science, founded in the city of Fengtian (Shenyang), and the Boys'
Science Group from the city of Taipei, which boasted fifty-eight members.[65]

As this readers' network demonstrates, the world of wonder was at the
same time the imperial world of science. The head of this world was the

emperor, a friend of science. While Kōza-faction Marxists viewed the emperor as a remnant of Japanese feudalism, in the popular science culture the emperor symbolized modernity, progress, and science. The magazine also taught the young readers about the places where their pen pals lived, through articles such as "The Mines in Taiwan" and "Minerals Found in Manchuria," while visualizing the empire with maps of natural resources and of the wireless radio network that webbed it.[66] But as Japan expanded its military in the 1930s, the readers began to see more than minerals, fish, and radios in the magazine. The next section will discuss the coverage of weapons in the popular science magazines and the utopia of "scientific" Japan that science fiction created in the late 1930s and early 1940s.

Wonder and Wartime Science Fiction

In the 1920s, both *Science Illustrated* and *Children's Science* emphasized that science contributed to world peace. Harada Mitsuo, for example, preached peace in his November 1927 mission statement, emphasizing the international nature of science: "The real scientist loves peace without exception.... There are no national borders when it comes to scientific research.... This magazine exists for science and peace."[67] However, in the 1930s, the sense of wonder was increasingly directed toward new and imaginary weapons and future wars; by the end of the 1930s, the association between science and peace had completely disappeared from the pages of the magazines.

One obvious change that took place at the very beginning of the 1930s was the appearance of military officers as writers. The first instance in *Science Illustrated* was the "Latest Weapons Special" issue of April 1929, in which army officers appeared as the authors of the lead article and participants in the roundtable discussion on future weapons and wars. A navy officer appeared for the first time in the May 1930 issue as the author of the lead article and then quite often afterward; the May 1931 issue was the navy special, and the January and June issues of the same year also specialized in navy-related topics. After the establishment of Manchukuo, the army's presence took over; the March 1933 issue carried "The National Mobilization Roundtable Discussion" with four army officers, and the April 1933 issue, with a gas mask on the cover, included an army officer's urgent call for a gas mask association and a translation of an American army general's writing on a possible Pacific Ocean war. In *Children's Science*, too, military officers began to appear as authors from the April 1930 issue on, and the February 1932 issue specialized in war-related subjects, all written by army officers. This sudden appearance and increase of military-related articles was most likely first initiated by the military. The navy at the time was launching a massive campaign against the Diet, which had accepted the London Naval Arms

Limitation Agreement in April 1930. Against the domestic and international trend toward disarmament, both the navy and army had a stake in arousing enthusiasm among the populace for weapons. In addition, the army's appearance in popular magazines was a part of the propaganda to justify its invasion of Manchuria.[68]

The increasingly belligerent content, however, was by no means something forced onto the magazines; it was a combined result of editorial positions, marketability, and readers' requests. The magazines' support for the military was made clear in the editors' afterword section. The *Children's Science* editor cheered for the Manchurian Incident, explaining to the readers that "fighting is good if it is for justice"; the *Science Illustrated* editor announced its support for Japan's withdrawal from the League of Nations.[69] Readers also welcomed the coverage of weapons and a series of military "incidents" in northern China. Already toward the end of the 1920s, the issues that specialized in the latest weapons had captured the readers' attention. The April 1927 issue of *Science Illustrated*, "Weapons Special," broke the sales record; in the questionnaires distributed to readers in January 1929, many asked for more coverage of weapons.[70] *Science Illustrated* again published "The Latest Weapons Special" in April 1929, followed by similar special issues throughout the 1930s and early 1940s.[71] In these articles, the sense of wonder no longer came from nature. The wonder was now evoked by such titles as "The Wonder of the Front Line of the Latest Scientific War."[72]

It is hard to discern such a strong preference among *Children's Science* readers, since most of their letters to the editor during the 1930s continued to be about trading stamps and exchanging letters. But younger teenagers were as exposed to weapons on the pages as their older brothers and sisters, as *Children's Science* also published many special isuess on the latest weapons and the military.[73] One illuminating indicator of younger children's excitement over military technology is the model-making contests: the fourth model-making contest of 1933 received a dramatically increased number and quality of battleship models from readers, whereas commercial ships and architecture models decreased in both quantity and quality.[74]

While articles and photos enchanted many readers with the wonder of state-of-the-art weapons and battlecraft, another segment of the magazine excited them with future wars and imaginary weapons: science fiction. Science fiction had already been an established attraction of both *Science Illustrated* and *Children's Science* since the mid-1920s, featuring detectives, mad scientists, and imaginary technology; in the 1930s—especially toward the end of the decade—and early 1940s, however, future battles with imaginary weapons became the dominant theme of science fiction in these magazines.

Science fiction was an important part of wartime Japanese culture.[75] In the late 1930s and early 1940s, science fiction stories by such writers as Unno Jūza,

Hirata Shinsaku, and Yamanaka Minetarō occupied the bookshelves of teen-age and younger readers. In a comment on his wartime memories, renowned critic Tsurumi Shunsuke specifically mentioned science fiction: "Hirata Shin-saku's *Flying Submarine Fuji*, Minami Yōichirō's *Submarine the Silver Tiger*, Unno Jūza's *Floating Airfield*, and Yamanaka Minetarō's *Invisible Airplane*. How have these wartime SF [science fictions] stayed alive in the minds of those who were children then?"[76] Saeki Shōichi, literature professor at Tokyo University, recalls that the description of future wars in Hirata Shinsaku's works attracted many boy readers in the late 1930s. When Hirata's works were serialized in the magazine *Boys' Club*, Saeki as a boy would "wait so impatiently for a new issue to come out and devour it at once."[77] These comments are testimony to what science fiction historian Yokota Jun'ya calls "a science fiction boom based on military stories of the Shōwa teens [1935–45]."[78]

Science Illustrated and *Children's Science* played a central role in the develop-ment of science fiction in the 1920s and its succeeding "boom." Unlike in the United States, where magazines such as *Amazing Stories* carved out the genre and its fan base in the market in the 1920s and 1930s,[79] there was no magazine that specialized in the genre in Japan. Rather, science fiction in Japan devel-oped in the popular science magazines and the literature magazine *Shinseinen* (New Youth) in the 1920s. Harada and other editors of these magazines actively promoted science fiction by having prize contests in the late 1920s—the very first "science fiction prize contest" in Japan was held in the pages of *Science Illustrated* in 1927—and by including science fiction in almost every issue.[80]

Science fiction provides another example of how the popular science magazines transgressed the established boundary of the "scientific." Like spiritual science, which the academic sciences considered unscientific, sci-ence fiction was an illegitimate field that neither the established literary nor scientific community in Japan regarded as literary or scientific. Although Japanese Marxists extensively discussed the relationship between science and literature in the 1920s and 1930s, they did not take science fiction seriously.[81] In *Yuibutsuron kenkyū*, they discussed topics such as realism in literature and the class nature of literature, but only one reference—and a negative one at that—was made to science fiction. In a 1934 article, Yajima Toshinori ar-gued that the fruitful interaction of science and literature should result in "science literature" (*kagaku bungaku*) such as Jean-Henri Fabre's *Souvenirs entomologiques* (*Faaburu konchūki*) or "science essays" (*kagaku zuihitsu*) written by scientists, but not "so-called science fiction [*kagaku shōsetsu*] . . . that can only entertain children and makes no sense from the perspective of science." He called science fiction "that acrobatic thing that puts two legs in the two worlds [of science and literature]," with no merit for either field.[82]

What precisely is science fiction is a question that continues to be dis-cussed even today.[83] What I treat as science fiction in this chapter is literally what was identified as *kagaku shōsetsu* by Japanese editors and authors at the time. The Japanese phrase appeared as the name of a genre slightly earlier than the English phrase "science fiction" began to be used in 1929.[84] In Japan *kagaku shōsetsu* was already frequently used by the mid-1920s in *Science Illustrated* and *Children's Science*.[85] By discussing self-identified science fiction, I do not mean to disregard earlier works—Jules Verne translations and Oshikawa Shunrō's adventure stories in Meiji Japan, for instance—that have been treated as science fiction by most critics but were not called "science fiction" at the time. My intention in focusing on self-identified science fiction is to see how the Japanese defined and discussed the genre in relation to science in the 1930s and early 1940s.[86]

Those who took science fiction more seriously considered such a low evaluation as Yajima's as evidence of the Japanese being unscientific. Unno Jūza, for example, wrote in 1937 that "in my opinion, those writers and critics who denounce science fiction as valueless for literature do so because they don't understand. They cannot handle science fiction, so they push it away."[87] Ōshita Udaru, writer of numerous science detective stories in the 1930s, also defended science fiction in his "Study of Science Fiction" (1933). Dividing the genre into "pure science fiction" and "quasi–science fiction," he asserted that "pure science fiction" was a sophisticated literature that "requires a narrative that scientifically makes perfect sense while basing it on imaginary inspiration. The skillful unity of theory and imagination, that is the life of pure science fiction." To Ōshita, the reasons why pure science fiction had not done well in the history of literature were that it was difficult to create the perfect unity of scientific theory and imagination and that Japanese writers were not scientifically capable. Ōshita also added that the Japanese media had avoided marketing science fiction because it assumed that Japanese readers were not scientific enough to understand it. On the contrary, according to him, "quasi–science fiction"—those works that overlapped with other genres such as detective and adventure stories—had done better in Japan because these genres made it easier to integrate science as "an extra bonus or a side dish."[88]

To Edogawa Ranpo, one of the most popular detective story writers in the late 1920s and early 1930s, the real scientific spirit was in fact found in detective stories (*tantei shōsetsu*), a genre Ōshita considered "quasi–science fiction." Writing in 1937, Edogawa asserted that detective stories were a material expression of the scientific spirit:

The scientific nature of detective stories is usually thought to come from their use of knowledge in physics and chemistry . . . but logic in the arrangement of a plot (the reasoning of the detective) is also a crucial factor. These two are often inseparable, but I believe the real scientific nature of detective stories lies in the latter. Needless to say, science means not only physics and chemistry but also logic, psychology, and philosophy. What goes through these natural and spiritual sciences [*seishin kagaku*] is the scientific spirit, and the scientific nature of detective stories should precisely mean such fundamental scientific spirit.[89]

Whereas Unno's and Ōshita's defense indicated that they viewed science fiction primarily as fiction that took science as its subject, Edogawa's argument here asserted that what was more important was its nature, that is, logical reasoning.

After the war with China began in 1937, however, detective stories lost their place in the media. Even in *New Youth*, the magazine responsible for developing detective stories as a genre, detective stories were rapidly replaced by memos and discussions by military officers and stories with light humor.[90] Meanwhile, science fiction embraced the boom by specializing in war stories. Science writers such as Unno Jūza, Ran Ikujirō, Minamizawa Jūshichi, Yamanaka Minetarō, and Kigi Takatarō published many works about Japan's victory in an imagined war. These works had little to do with the "scientific spirit" that Edogawa had discussed. In these stories, the reader did not find logical reasoning. Instead, the stories excited readers with the wonder of future weapons and the invincibility of Japan.

For an example of the kind of "wonder" that attracted and excited readers during wartime, let us consider Unno's *Floating Airfield*, one of the most popular science fiction works in wartime Japan. It was serialized in *Boys' Club* from January to December 1938 and published in paperback in 1944.[91] The stage of the story is an airfield island in the middle of the South China Sea that is being constructed jointly by England, France, the United States, the Netherlands, Thailand, and China. It has been announced to be an emergency airport for aircraft traveling over the South China Sea; but thanks to the hero, Kawakami, a young Japanese chief engineer, the reader soon finds out that the airfield is really a state-of-the-art battleship, whose aim is to destroy Japan with hidden bombs. The story proceeds like an adventure story, as Kawakami steals onto the airfield disguised as a Chinese laborer under a secret mission to find the true identity of the airfield and, if necessary, to destroy it before construction is complete. Many challenges interfere with his mission, as the British commander notices the presence of the Japanese intruder; Kawakami's task becomes even harder when Sugita, a sailor loyal to his superior Kawakami, becomes a captive of the British after sneaking onto the airfield in search of Kawakami. Each crisis, however, Kawakami overcomes with his intelligence and courage. At the end, the disguised battleship is destroyed by a human weapon; Sugita carries a bomb in his arms into the explosives' storage while screaming, "His Imperial Majesty, *banzai!*"

The story is full of what the Japanese technocrats defined as "science-technology," military technology developed by the latest science: the airfield that can move at a speed of thirty-five knots, the latest "Handray Page air fighter," which could carry fifteen tons of bombs, an extremely small shortwave radio that Kawakami uses to send secret code, a gun "as big as twenty inches," and so on.[92] An enormous Japanese submarine can completely submerge in less than a minute, and its hidden catapult jumps out "as if it were set by a spring" and the "nimble" air fighter flies out without wasting a moment.[93] Equally emphasized in the story is the noble and disciplined image of the imperial soldier; the imperial soldier would never take off his uniform even in the worst heat, never break any military laws, never disobey his superior's orders. Kawakami the engineer is the embodiment of the ideal imperial military man—always sharp, courageous, and calm even in the worst crisis. His thoughtful behavior toward Sugita and Sugita's sincere loyalty to Kawakami are highlighted throughout the story. The Japanese imperial soldier also knows how to pity the enemy; Kawakami would not kill the British admiral, who has no means to defend himself.[94] These images contrast sharply with the cruelty the Japanese army exhibited toward Chinese civilians in the Nanjing Massacre a month before the first segment of the story appeared in print and with the bitter memories of many former imperial military soldiers of their superiors' brutal treatment of them.[95] Unno's story also told the reader of the righteousness of Japanese colonialism, as the story ends with Kawakami's friend saying, "The airfield was finally destroyed. Britain will finally awake from a bad dream and come to realize that the Japanese Empire has a proper place in East Asia."[96] *The Floating Airfield* was fiction that fantasized the Japanese military, its technological power, and Japan's colonialism.

According to Unno, he wrote this fiction to encourage young Japanese to study science for the nation. In the afterword to the 1944 paperback edition, Unno wrote: "From now on, the Japanese people really have to study science diligently. Even if Japan can be proud of the wonderful Japanese spirit [*Yamato damashii*] and strong economy, Japan will not be able to win future wars without excellent science. I beg you, the Japanese readers. Please help produce scientific weapons that are better than the floating airfield in this story."[97] Here, the science Unno was promoting is military science, that is, the technocrats' science-technology. Unlike Edogawa, Unno was not concerned with logical reasoning. This is clear from the story; for example, Kawakami in *The Floating Airfield* was often miraculously saved in his crisis because, as the author explained, "those who mindlessly devote themselves to the nation and walk the correct path will be helped by the heavens."[98] To Unno, science meant powerful weapons and military technology for national defense, and writing science fiction like *The Floating Airfield* was his patriotic way of promoting such science.

Promoting science for the wartime nation was often described as "scientific patriotism" (*kagaku hōkoku*), which literally means "serving the nation through science." Unno was not alone in promoting scientific patriotism. Many scientists preached scientific patriotism in the popular science culture.

In the January 1938 issue of *Children's Science*, for example, Kotake Munio, renowned chemist at Osaka Imperial University, demanded that the young readers become "scientists who devote their lives to the nation" just like the imperial soldiers, while Honda Kōtarō, the inventor of KS magnetic steel and head of the Metal Materials Research Institute at the Tohoku Imperial University, told the young readers to study hard so that they would make powerful weapons in the future.[99] Their cry for scientific patriotism and for science for the sake of the nation was just like the technological patriotism that the Japanese technocrats were promoting at this time (see Chapter 2). While older teenagers were reading science fiction like *The Floating Airfield*, younger readers of *Children's Science* also enjoyed Unno's works, like *The Undersea Empire*, in which the Japanese and German protagonists work together to reveal the evils of the British.[100] Science fiction, together with special coverage of the latest weapons, provided wonders to the readers of the popular science magazines. The sense of wonder was evoked for scientific patriotism, to excite them about their contribution to a scientific Japan.

In *Children's Science*, however, science fiction was not always about new weapons and spies. *The Flag of the Green Rising Sun* (*Midori no nisshōki*) by Kigi Takatarō could get boys and girls excited about a scientific Japan in a different way. Serialized in *Children's Science* over a period of almost two years (from January 1939 to October 1940), the story is set in an underground utopian nation that is just being built somewhere in the Middle East based on the teaching of a certain deceased Japanese elder.[101] The obvious model of this utopia, introduced as "scientific and pro-Japanese," is Manchukuo.[102] In the fictional nation, whose national flag is identical to that of the Japanese Empire except for the color of the rising sun, all the ideals that technocrats had for Manchukuo are perfectly realized: everything in the nation is mechanized with technology unimaginable to outsiders, people of different races live in harmony, and the political system is completely rationalized. The protagonists, two Japanese boys who have just graduated from elementary school, decide to live in this nation because of its sophisticated science and politics, just as the other residents do, who have come from all over the world for the same reason. Non-Japanese residents all take pains to learn Japanese so that they can be part of this nation. Both racial and class conflicts are absent: the utopian nation has no classes, since the wealth is distributed equally based on the shared property system. The protagonists themselves—one from a very poor family and the other from a very wealthy family—are symbolic of class harmony; they are best friends, and they help each other to save Japan.

What is featured as scientific in this story, subtitled a "detective science fiction"? It is the wonderful science-technology invented in the utopia: the battle craft that functions as both airplane and submarine; a new chemical called "illumirie" that, once melted in water, illuminates enemy submarines;

as well as moving walkways, teleconference communication, television shopping, and so on. It is also the rationalized and systematic political economy of the nation: tasks in different segments of society, such as production, administration, and legislation, are divided and carried out by different age groups—teenagers do production and research, those in their twenties to forties are administrators, those in their forties to sixties are responsible for legislation, and the oldest ones take care of "discussion" on national matters. All the production is managed by the state so that there is no excess or shortage; in addition, no political parties exist, as party politics is deemed to be disruptive rather than cooperative. Also presented as "scientific" is the way information is handled: all the data about the production, consumption, and military power of the world are meticulously gathered, mechanically processed, and statistically presented.[103]

Kigi's story is unique among works of wartime science fiction. Science in *The Flag of the Green Rising Sun* is about mechanization, systematization, rationalization, and regulation, unlike science in Unno's and most other works of wartime science fiction, which mostly meant military science-technology to accompany the courageous and loyal Japanese. Although it was subtitled a "detective science fiction" story, Kigi's did not exhibit the same "logical reasoning" that Edogawa considered to be the core of the scientific in his detective stories. There was no "logical reasoning" in the plot development or the detectives' reasoning, since the detective in Kigi's story disappears after the first two segments. The mystery eventually revealed is the identity of the utopia, and what is claimed to be scientific about the story is the utopian ideal itself, not the way the story is put together.

Using this utopian ideal, Kigi made explicit his critique of wartime Japan. The protagonists explain the differences between the red and green rising sun flag nations through the story: unlike the government of the green rising sun flag nation, the Japanese government cannot control or collect information properly, Japanese science education is poor and not practical, and Japan does not spend enough money for natural science research.[104] In short, compared to the green rising sun flag nation, Japan is not scientific enough. At the same time, the emperor's unique significance in the Japanese national polity is dramatically explained in the story as well. Criticism and adoration were combined; the aimed effect here was a message that to maintain the Japanese national polity, Japan needed to have superior science. The ideal of scientific patriotism was to construct the imperial and scientific Japan.[105]

Even though Kigi and Unno used different kinds of science, the message of their stories was the same: science was crucial for the preservation of the Japanese national polity, and for that reason Japanese children should take science seriously. The country of the green rising sun flag was as utopian and imaginary as the invincible and heroic Japanese military in Unno's various works. Unno enlisted in 1942 as a navy reporter at the age of forty-two and was sent to the South Pacific. When he came home after his four months of service, he allegedly told his wife that "Japanese science is inferior [to that of the United States]" and stopped dreaming about Japan's victory.[106] Yet Unno continued to write, portraying the "scientific" Japan throughout the war. Most likely, he wrote because he needed to write to eat, and his science fiction not only was sanctioned by the state but also sold well. But it is also likely that, precisely because he realized the inferiority of Japanese science, he felt even more of an incentive to promote scientific patriotism among the future generations of scientists and engineers.

The young generation of scientists and engineers included girls and women. In Kigi's story, the utopia is explicitly introduced as "the nation of boys and girls," and girl residents are as intelligent and scientifically capable as boy residents.[107] The heroine, the poor boy's older sister Chizuko, is a symbol of the scientific, courageous Japanese woman. The inserted illustrations show her as a beautiful, healthy woman about sixteen years old. Described as "'the Japanese girl' who does not forget her pride as a Japanese even when captured and torn from her parents," she is brave and calm like Kawakami even when she is kidnapped by evil men who want to find the secret of the green rising sun nation.[108] Moreover, she is scientifically knowledgeable and immediately comprehends the new machines and the new political economic system she sees in the utopia. At the end of the story, Chizuko plays the role of the bridge between the two rising sun nations. The two boys decide to stay in the green flag nation, and Chizuko is the one who brings back the ideal of the utopia to Japan to make Japan scientific.[109]

One school in Shibuya, Tokyo, was educating precisely such a Japanese woman when the story was being read by *Children's Science* readers. The Girls' Science School (*joshi kagaku juku*), reported in the April 1939 issue of *Science Illustrated*, was opened by a female teacher named Matsui Kitsuko. She believed that "to become a good partner of a man who wants to develop a future life utilizing the benefit of the civilization produced by the natural sciences while cherishing spiritual culture, it is important for a woman to have acquired rich common sense and practical skills based on scientific knowledge."[110] About sixty young women of marriageable age learned home economics, mechanics, driving, and massage techniques under "expert teachers." Taking apart such mechanical devices as a fan, developing photos, and soldering were all important parts of education at this school, because "to acquire scientific knowledge, seeing is more important than hearing, and doing is even more important than seeing," Matsui explained.[111] Such scientific knowledge was necessary, the reporter agreed, to manage the family economy and to save materials for the nation at war. These young women were expected to be the "Shōwa version" of the "good wife and wise mother" who was a scientifically capable, economically wise, and spiritually good partner of the new Japanese man.

This ideal of the new Japanese womanhood was demanded widely in wartime Japan. In a science magazine, *Kokumin kagaku gurafu* (National People's Science Graph), whose first issue stated that it was a magazine for "male youth" (*seishōnen*), many articles were clearly written for the female reader.[112] Articles like "Science of the Kitchen: The Conversation between the Housewife and Her Maid" emphasized the significance of the rationalization of home management; "How Can We Make Girl Students Do Science?" discussed the urgency of girls' science education so that they could be scientifically and economically wise homemakers; and "Science of Flower Arrangement" reminded the female reader that feminine virtue should not be forgotten but be cultivated scientifically.[113] An increasing amount of the gender-specific coverage in most popular science magazines reflected the fact that, as the war dragged on, young men, mobilized to the war front, were not the majority of the readership. Women, in turn, needed to be scientifically educated so that they could contribute on the home front to the wartime nation through their scientific knowledge, rationalized home management, and scientific education of the next generation.

The magazines did not target only housewives. Although the family ideology and pro-natal policies of the Japanese state restrained the recruitment of marriageable women in factories, the Rosie the Riveter image was not uncommon in the popular media.[114] The sudden appearance of women working with machines in factories in *Science Illustrated* in the early 1940s shows that the promotion of scientific education for women was targeted both toward the middle-class housewives who could educate their maids about the rationalization of the kitchen and toward the working-class women who were recruited to work with machines just as men were.[115]

The magazine *National People's Science Graph*, published by the *Daily Industry Newspaper* (*Nikkan kōgyō hinbunsha*) by the military's order, also demonstrates how Harada Mitsuo's editing technique was utilized by the military. With more than ten thousand subscribers in southern Japan, this magazine provided knowledge about air-raid drills, fire hazards, vegetable cultivation in the yard, rationalization of the home economy, and the latest weapons.[116] The military asked Harada to be the adviser to this magazine. The influence of Harada is evident: the magazine included numerous photos and illustrations and presented science as neatly packaged knowledge under various headings like "sound," the "South Pacific," and the "North Pole." Harada also contributed articles to almost every issue of this magazine, explaining the wonders of natural phenomena such as mist, the craters of the moon, and thermodynamics.[117]

It was not just in popular science magazines that the sense of wonder, seeing, and doing were mobilized for the scientific education of the Japanese in wartime. The next section will examine the science education reform of 1941, in which the Ministry of Education mobilized these concepts for the education of the ideal Japanese citizen.

Scientific Imperial Education

In Chapter 4, we saw the rise of the "overlearning" argument and a desire of the minister of education to replace science education with ethics classes in the mid-1930s. We also heard the educator-activist Kanbe Isaburō observing that the mid-1930s was the most barren time for science education because of such opposition. During the final years of the 1930s, however, several events forced the government to reconsider such views and instead promote science education actively. As the Japanese economy had largely recovered from the Great Depression by 1938, the lack of technicians and engineers became a noticeable problem. In the Nomonhan Incident of May 1939, the Japanese army, faced with the mechanized Soviet army, suffered a loss of more than twenty thousand soldiers, revealing the weakness of the Japanese military's mechanization; in September of that year, the German blitz demonstrated the immensely fearful power of a highly mechanized military.[118] The Japanese army and navy were eager to bring the latest science and technology to the military, and by the end of the 1930s the military was more aware than ever of a need for general science education so that the next generation of imperial subjects would be scientifically and technologically capable.[119] Under the Konoe cabinet in 1940, the promotion of science and technology became the nation's top priority, and the technocrats' movement for bureaucratic power was finally beginning to see some results. The 1941 reform of elementary science education was a response to the same sense of crisis.

In March 1941, the government issued the National People's School Edict and launched a sweeping school reform. Elementary schools were renamed National People's Schools, compulsory education was extended from six to eight years (elementary for six years and higher for two), and textbooks were rewritten to display a more militaristic and nationalistic outlook.[120] Under the new system, the entire curriculum was reorganized under five categories: ethics, science, physical education, arts and crafts, and occupational learning.[121] As the Ministry of Education's *Outline for National People's School Teaching Manual* (*Kokumin gakkō kyōsokuan setsumei yōkō*) made clear, science was regarded as necessary for the imperial subject to "learn the basic knowledge of ever-progressing science, be able to manage and create life scientifically, and be capable of contributing to the development of the national power."[122] Accordingly, elementary science education went through what one historian calls "a radical and even revolutionary reform."[123]

The reform involved two major changes. First, science was introduced in the first grade as "Nature and Mathematics Studies" (*risūka*), in contrast to earlier practice when children studied science only from the fourth grade up. Nature and Mathematics Studies consisted of "Mathematics Studies" and "Nature Studies." From the first to third grades, the "Observation of Nature" (*shizen no kansatsu*) class was set up under Nature Studies. Second, instead of emphasizing the memorization of textbooks, Nature and Mathematics Studies centered on children's voluntary search for the wonders of nature through observation and experiments; the Observation of Nature class, for this reason, did not even prepare textbooks, except for the teacher's manual.

A comparison of science textbooks may help us to understand what kinds of changes took place. One chapter of the fourth-grade textbook used prior to 1941 reads as follows: "The cherry tree becomes a large tree. It does not have leaves in winter. As it gets warm in spring, young leaves will grow from young, thin branches. . . . The flower has five petals. It has many stamens. It has one pistil."[124] The sentences were descriptive and monotonous, and the tone authoritative. Let us examine the "Planting Potatoes" chapter in the new Nature Studies textbook for the fourth grade: "Let's make potatoes and sweet potatoes in the field. If you plant potatoes and sweet potatoes you harvested last year, they will grow sprouts. Observe where the sprouts emerge. Let's check if there are any thin roots."[125] The emphasis on seeing and doing is clear here. Children were expected to think, observe, and act. To facilitate this, the tone of the textbook was more inquisitive and friendly.

This inquiry-based style, however, made some government officials and teachers uneasy. When one Ministry of Education official read the manuscript, he is said to have worried that "if you keep repeating 'let's look into . . .' and 'let's think,' students will make it a habit and start questioning Japanese history. Then Japan would be over."[126] The Japanese history here specifically referred to the imperial Shinto mythology that had been integrated into the national history taught at school. In introducing this science education reform, a persistent concern indeed was how to teach children to believe in the imperial mythology while simultaneously teaching the rational, scientific spirit. While acknowledging the need for science education, some educators and politicians were concerned, just as the former minister of education Matsuda Genji had been concerned about the "overlearning" argument, that being scientific might be incompatible with the national polity. Representing such a voice, Mikunidani Sanshirō, principal of Aoyama Teachers' School, cautioned against the influence of science education on children. At an Educational Deliberative Council (*kyōiku shingikai*) meeting held in December 1938 to discuss the 1941 reform, Mikunidani stated:

Science education needs to be encouraged strongly, but at the same time I believe it is a kind of education we have to be extremely careful about. . . . The spiritual way of thinking is clearly different from seeing things as things, as lifeless skeletons, to analyze. . . . For natural scientists, the only truth is the truth proven from the perspective of the natural sciences. . . . Natural scientists have ideas such as "the natural sciences should transcend the concepts like the nation [*kokka*] and the *minzoku*" or "the natural sciences are absolute."[127]

For someone like Tokugawa Yoshichika, a biologist (and descendant of the Tokugawa shogun family), the natural sciences were not necessarily incompatible with the national polity. To Mikunidani, Tokugawa confidently replied that "natural sciences, especially biology, have progressed greatly so far. Natural sciences today . . . can provide the biological basis for the national polity without contradiction. . . . If the natural sciences in school education emphasize its spiritual aspect and even explain ethics from that perspective, I believe we have nothing to worry about."[128] Both sides agreed that elementary schools needed to strengthen the natural science curriculum and that the curriculum needed to underline the goal of imperial education (*kōmin kyōiku*), that is, to create the ideal imperial subject loyal and devoted to the cause of the nation. The question was how to do just that.

Consider how the problem was resolved in the 1941 National People's Edict. Articles 7 and 9 outlined the Nature and Mathematics Studies and Nature Studies, respectively. Article 7 explained that the aim of the Nature and Mathematics Studies was to "teach the skill of understanding and treating general phenomena correctly, to lead children to apply such skills to everyday life, to nourish their rational and creative spirit, and to enrich the basis for their contribution to the development of national power." The new curriculum would teach that "the progress of science is a contribution to the advancement of the nation and that cultural creation is an imperial mission," as "national defense relies on the progress of science," and it does so by the "nurturing of a self-motivated and continuous posture toward studying mathematics and the laws of nature" through such activities as observation, experiments, investigation, and handicrafts. Article 9 clearly stated that the Nature Studies curriculum was set up specifically to get children interested in science during the first six years and to guide their interest into specific knowledge of "industry, national defense, disaster prevention, and home management" during the last two years. It also stated the following:

The [Nature Studies] course teaches how to be friends with nature and learn from it. By raising plants and animals, children learn the love for living things. And through incessant observation and experiments, they learn the attitude of persistent research.

While emphasizing observation outside, the course also takes advantage of specimens, models, illustrations, films, and the like to facilitate children's understanding.

Regarding physiology, the course makes clear the significance of daily sanitation and national health and promotes the application of such knowledge along with physical education classes.

Together with Art and Handicraft Studies, the course familiarizes children with mechanical tools and trains their scientific skills.

The course helps children to understand the holistic working of the natural world and leads them to voluntarily appreciate the wonder [*myōshu*] and blessing [*onkei*] of nature.[129]

The ideas stipulated here are strikingly similar to what I have discussed as Harada's editing technique in his popular science magazines. The "self-motivated" and "voluntary" interest of children in science was pursued through an emphasis on seeing and doing, such as "observation," "experiments," and the usage of "specimens, models, illustrations, films, and the like." The "creative spirit" and "the desire to discover and invent," which the magazines promoted as part of their emphasis on "doing" through such activities as invention contests and model-making contests, were demanded of the imperial subject. Most of all, the sense of wonder—*myōshu* is a more sophisticated word for *kyōi*, literally meaning an "indescribable, awesome character"—was mobilized here. Through this mobilization of the sense of wonder, the National People's School was to create the ideal imperial subject, who would be rational, creative, and technologically skillful so that he or she could contribute to "national defense" and "the rise of national power."

But something that did not exist in Harada Mitsuo's magazines also connected science education and the ideal national people. *The Teacher's Manual for the Observation of Nature* provides another logic to explain why and how the "rational spirit" was compatible with the national polity. The manual explained that "the rational spirit [*gōriteki seishin*] is a humble spirit to follow reason [*dōri*],"[130] that is, "to see, think, and treat things correctly in order to live a reasonable yet creative life so that people would contribute to the rise of the nation."[131] This Japanese word, *dōri* (literally, "the way and reason"), meant something other than "reason" in the sense of the critical mind, for the manual continued to explain that "in other words, the rational spirit was an expression of the national [*kokumin*] spirit to practice the way of the imperial nation."[132] The rational spirit, thus, meant to follow the "way and reason" of the imperial nation. As Article 9 of the edict stated, the goal of nurturing "the scientific spirit" was to acquire "knowledge of industry, national defense, disaster prevention, and home management" as well as "mechanical" and "scientific" skills by the time children graduated from the National People's School. In short, the edict reconciled the potential conflict between science education and the imperial ethics by promoting this scientific spirit together with the rational spirit that was meant to follow the way of the imperial nation.

Teaching the connection between science and the nation's destiny was not the only way the problem of science and ethics was reconciled. The new curriculum's emphasis on the observation of nature itself was explained as uniquely Japanese. The Ministry of Education, led by scientist Hashida Kunihiko, explained the philosophy of Nature and Mathematics Studies as follows:

In observing, pondering, and treating nature, what characterizes the Japanese posture? In short, it is the posture to be in harmony with nature. The creation mythology of our nation, which tells us that our ancestors were created together with the mountains, rivers, plants, and trees by the Shinto gods, is still alive in our innermost heart. Moreover, surrounded by the ocean and blessed with superior mountains, clear water, and the four changing seasons, our nation enjoys the beautiful natural environment unmatched by that of any other nation. Thus, our attitude of enjoying and harmonizing with nature has defined our national character [kokuminsei] since our country began.

For Westerners, studying science seems to mean conquering nature. But for the Japanese, it means harmonizing nature with human life, something that cannot be done without the Japanese view of life and nature. Great scientists truly respect nature and comprehend its subtleties, as they merge themselves into nature to become one and the same. It is probably impossible to take the children of the National People's School to such a mental state, but it should not be difficult to teach them this Japanese attitude toward nature.[133]

From this perspective, Article 9 of the edict, which asserted that science education should teach "how to be friends with nature" and encouraged students to "learn the love for living things," was to be interpreted as the cultivation of the Japanese attitude toward nature. The influence of Hashida's "science as practice" is clear here, insofar as it explained the Japanese way of "doing" science, implying the total unity of the observer and the observed.[134] In fact, Hashida coined a new verb, "do science," to describe this Japanese mind (kagaku suru kokoro), and the expression "do science" became a catch phrase in wartime Japan.[135]

For those teenagers who were reading Children's Science, the new Nature and Mathematics Studies may not have seemed so new.[136] After all, Children's Science, together with Science Illustrated, had centered on the "appreciation of the wonder and blessing of nature," and the readers had enjoyed "observation" and "specimens, models, illustrations, and films." And "knowledge of industry, national defense, disaster prevention, and home management" had been explained with numerous photos and illustrations in the magazines. I am not insinuating that Harada or the magazines had any direct influence on the 1941 reform. Many science education reformers had advocated the sense of wonder, seeing, and doing since the 1920s, and they indeed were actively involved in the 1941 reform through the educational deliberative council.[137] What I want to point out is that the sense of wonder, seeing, and doing—things that Harada emphasized in the popularization of science in his magazines—was mobilized by the state for the wartime promotion of science. In drafting the National People's School Edict and the new textbooks, the Ministry of Education conducted its own research on how these reformers were implementing their ideas in their classrooms, and it picked what it believed to work for the total mobilization of the nation.[138]

The 1941 science education reform was well received by education activists and critics. Ogura Kinnosuke, who had been promoting a change in mathematics education since the 1910s, commented that mathematics education "dramatically improved" with this reform.[139] Oka Genjirō, one of the editors of the *Teacher's Manual for the Observation of Nature*, recalled in 1956 that "the reputation of *The Observation of Nature* [teacher's manual] was extremely positive. Even now I sometimes meet people who tell me how excited they were when they first read the text."[140] Historians have also assessed the new science curriculum positively. For example, Itakura Kiyonobu, a historian of Japanese science education, has concluded that the science curriculum reform "was not a reflection of the character of the new ultranationalist National People's Science. It was instead a fulfillment of the liberal and individualistic science education reform movement that began in the Taishō period."[141]

To characterize the 1941 science education reform as oppositional to the "ultranationalist" state, however, is to ignore the politics of the scientific. Japanist bureaucrats who blamed science education for the radicalization of leftist and rightist youth in the mid-1930s—for example, then minister of education Matsuda—were by 1940 replaced by technocrats, their Planning Agency sympathizers, and Japanist scientists like Hashida Kunihiko who actively and adamantly advocated the promotion of science-technology as part of the total mobilization of the nation. The 1941 science education reform came about not because the government finally understood the "liberalism" of the Taishō education reform movement but because it needed increased industrial production, better military technology, and the imperial subjects capable of managing a rationalized life.[142] Rather than being considered a belated success of the liberal education reform, the National People's School science education should be seen as a central part of the total war mobilization by the state. To win the wars with China and the United States, the state needed to create imperial subjects capable of doing science and technology. And for that, it mobilized the sense of wonder, seeing, and doing science.

Conclusion

Immediate Postwar Discourse of Science

On August 15, 1945, Emperor Hirohito delivered his first radio speech, informing his nation of Japan's unconditional surrender to the Allies. Later that day, Prime Minister Suzuki Kantarō also spoke on the radio: "From now on, we need to develop science-technology, because that was our weakest point during this war."[1] A month after Suzuki's radio address, the new minister of education, Maeda Tamon, broadcast a speech to the nation in which he said, "[T]o construct a Japan of culture [*bunka Nihon*], let us nurture the scientific way of thinking."[2] The science-technology and scientific spirit that had been promoted for the war were now to be encouraged for the reconstruction of a new Japan. Overnight, science was transformed from a tool for war to the key to Japan's peacetime reconstruction.

Even though Japan experienced what was arguably the most destructive creation of science in the twentieth century, the atomic bomb, few Japanese rejected science in 1945. In fact, in the immediate postwar years, the promotion of science was voiced even louder. Historian Nakayama Shigeru writes: "No one said 'we do not want science-technology anymore because we suffered greatly from the result of the development of science-technology, the atomic bomb.' Science survived the transition from wartime to peacetime unharmed, criticized by no one."[3] Very few scientists were accused of war crimes, nor were there any scientists who were publicly held to account for their wartime research. Instead, the Japanese welcomed science in the immediate postwar years, and an uncritical celebration of science and technology continued into the 1960s, when environmental problems began to raise serious concerns.

Many, like Prime Minister Suzuki on the day of surrender, argued that Japan had lost the war because of its weak science-technology and said that this proved postwar Japan's need to rigorously promote science-technology. Yagi Hidetsugu, the inventor of the Yagi antenna who led the Technology Agency during wartime, also used this logic to urge the postwar promotion of science. According to Yagi, "[S]ince Japan ha[d] just lost a science war, it . . . need[ed] to develop science to construct a peaceful nation."[4]

Others argued that Japan's decision to enter the war itself was unscientific. If Japan had been scientific enough, according to this argument, it would have made the rational observation that it would not be able to defeat the scientifically and materially superior United States. Physicist Nakatani Ukichirō, for example, contended that Japan's loss in the war was

not only because of the "feudalistic nature" of its science but also because of the irrationality of the nation itself. . . . The most outstanding fact was that the elite in Japan, such as ministers and generals, were not scientific at all. This is the biggest cause of the present misery of Japan. I do not mean that Japan would have won the war had the leaders been more scientific. No. Even if these elite people knew science well, it was not the war Japan could win. What I want to say is that if those people were more scientific, they would not have even started the hopeless war.[5]

A new magazine by scientists and engineers, titled *Science-Technology*, also argued similarly in its inaugural manifesto (December 1947) that "if the impossibility of winning is clear, no one would start a war. It is necessary to reflect on whether science-technologists who had connections to the military provided pure, objective information."[6]

Whether the lack of science led Japan to launch the war or to the surrender, the immediate postwar Japanese discourse emphasized the unscientific and irrational character of wartime Japan. There was no reflection upon the wartime promotion of science and technology.[7] Scientists hired by the Occupation authority, such as Harry Kelly, drew up science and technology policies for occupied Japan to reform the Japanese scientific community as a crucial part of the democratization of Japan. However, the association between science and democracy was neither made nor forced by the U.S. Occupation. Japanese scientists and science promoters were the ones who considered science necessary to reconstruct Japan, and they believed that Japan was to be reconstructed as a democratic nation. The discourse of science in immediate postwar Japan was intertwined with its demand for democracy.

The most active promoter of science for peace and democracy was the Association of Democratic Scientists (*minshushugi kagakusha kyōkai*, hereafter Minka), the largest organization of natural and social scientists in the immediate postwar decade. Minka was established on January 12, 1946, to promote "scientific activities for the completion of a democratic revolution."[8] Its first president was Ogura Kinnosuke, and its board of directors included many former Yuiken members. Minka declared that Japan could and should finally be scientific now that the war was over. Ogura's analysis of Japanese science, which he published in newspapers and journals shortly after he became the president of Minka, was the same as that which he developed in the early 1930s. He maintained that "Western science—both natural and social sciences—had been democratic" because its "scientific spirit" came from the struggle to destroy superstitious and religious views of the nations.[9] He argued, just as he did in his interwar writings, that the unique problem of Japanese modernity distorted science in Japan to be "feudalistic," "bureaucratic," and "territorial." His criticism of scientists' lack of social involvement in Japan also continued in a similar vein. During the interwar years, he urged them to get involved in social issues. During wartime, he told them to participate in the state's war efforts. Now, after the war, he criticized many Japanese scientists for remaining indifferent toward efforts to democratize Japan.[10] Ogura's postwar writing maintained that "to become a truly democratic scientist is the only real patriotic way."[11]

Ogura's and Minka's association of science with democracy was naive and problematic. Ogura uncritically equated the West with the modern spirit, and democracy with progressive science. His analysis of the unique problem of Japanese modernity was based on these criteria. As historian Hiroshige Tetsu has pointed out, if the qualitative and quantitative growth of scientific enterprise is explained as a result of democracy, we would not be able to explain the rise of science in militaristic Germany or in prewar Japan. Hiroshige argues that

as long as Ogura based his characterization of "uniquely Japanese" science vis-à-vis the idealized West, his historical analysis was bound to fail. The nationalization of science was a phenomenon common to all advanced industrial nations from the late nineteenth to the early twentieth centuries, an inevitable result of the economic development of society at the time. The distortions caused by the nationalization of science did not only happen in Japan.[12]

Indeed, as we saw in Part 2, this naive equation between science and progressive democracy ironically led Ogura to endorse wartime science policy. As a Marxist who participated in the Taishō liberal education movement, Ogura criticized theoretical mathematics as the science of the bourgeois ivory tower and advocated applied mathematics as the ideal proletarian science, cooperation among scientists, and scientists' involvement in society's needs. When the technocrat "science-technology" policy promoted all these, Ogura publicly celebrated such state policies. In other words, when the state offered a vision of "scientific Japan" that included criticism of feudalistic and bourgeois practices, Ogura participated in and thus was incorporated into the now state-initiated promotion of science.[13]

It is extremely important, however, to point out that the resemblance between the wartime state and the Marxist intellectuals in terms of criticism of feudalism and capitalism was only one factor that allowed this incorporation. We should not forget that in wartime Japan censorship and fear of imprisonment and abuse in prison—including death—were real. Numerous "thought criminals" had died in prison due to torture, malnutrition, and poor hygiene. Those intellectuals who chose to publish in wartime Japan did so for financial and political reasons as well as to prevent unwarranted arrest by the Special Higher Police by appealing to their political alliance with the state. The degree of fear, the reality of tipping off and backstabbing even among friends, and the desperate desire to protect one's life and family are clear from numerous memoirs and diaries. This was especially the case with Marxist and liberal intellectuals who had been blacklisted by the Special Higher Police and thus needed to "gain points" with the wartime state to protect themselves.[14] In wartime Japan, where Marxism and liberalism were the suppressed topics of discourse, science was the only venue through which Ogura Kinnosuke and Saigusa Hiroto could continue to write. Science gave them a limited space in which to continue their critique and resistance. Yet, precisely for that reason, science also functioned as the venue through which they were incorporated into the kind of nationalism that they previously had criticized. For those who refused such participation/incorporation, however, the authorities showed no mercy, as Tosaka Jun's premature death in prison demonstrates.

The postwar promotion of science by those who were part of the wartime science mobilization, then, cannot and should not be understood apart from their own wartime writings, even though none of the science promoters publicly reflected upon his wartime writings (Ogura was one of a few who did so, but his self-criticism did not come until 1953, when he began to feel his age).[15] Rather, their immediate postwar promotion of science took the form of emphasizing the unscientific and irrational character of wartime Japan that had driven them to promote science and to collaborate. The Japanese ignored the presence of science in wartime Japan, and the immediate postwar celebration of science allowed many wartime scientific patriots to erase the connection between science and war that they themselves had made.

Here is one example. Tomizuka Kiyoshi, a member of the engineering faculty at the Aeronautic Science Institute of Tokyo University, reprinted his 1940 book, *The Construction of Scientific Japan*, in 1947. In his 1947 preface, he wrote:

I erased all the militaristic and Japanistic expressions from the earlier edition. Those expressions were only meant to be a cover-up for my criticism of the state, which, I think, should be clear if one reads it. Nonetheless, I erased them all because they do not fit today's sensibility [*gendai no kankaku*]. But most parts are reprinted here without any change. The fact that my [wartime] work still makes sense today means . . . I did not follow the currents of that time and in fact said what was right and what was wrong as I believed.[16]

It is true that Tomizuka did not change much of the rest of his 1940 writing, whose basic argument was that Japan was not yet scientific enough and thus needed to promote science. To Tomizuka, to be able to say that he did not collaborate with the wartime government was important both for his own personal pride as well as for his career so that he would not be purged. For our analysis, the fact that he could and would publish virtually the same content in immediate postwar Japan is significant for an entirely different reason. Although Tomizuka did not mention this in his postwar edition, his wartime edition came out immediately after the Konoe cabinet made the promotion of science and technology the nation's top priority. Thus, it is not true that Tomizuka "did not follow the currents of that time." He was in fact writing what the state wanted to hear. After all, the wartime state endorsed his book by allowing its publication. Tokyo Imperial University's Aeronautic Science Institute, Tomizuka's laboratory, was at the center of Japanese aeronautics, a field of strategic significance that probably received much greater funding than other fields; at the same time, precisely because of that, Tomizuka witnessed inefficient bureaucratization, the military's intrusion into the content of individual research, and the frustrating quality of the field. His wartime promotion of a scientific Japan that was embellished with jingoism allowed him to be indirectly critical of the status of Japan as much as he could in the wartime context, but such criticism was completely subsumed by the state mobilization of science. What was erased in the process of postwar reprinting was not just the "expressions" that did not fit the postwar sensibility but the collaborative nature of the relationship between science promoters and war mobilization.

The naive association of science with antimilitarism also shaped the postwar evaluation of the wartime science education reform as well as the liberal education movement. For example, as we saw in Chapter 6, historians have argued that the 1941 science education reform was a belated triumph of the persistent "liberal education reform" from the Taishō period. According to these scholars, this triumph of Taishō liberalism was achieved despite the nationalistic environment, that is, despite the fact that ethics, history, and reading textbooks became firmly grounded upon the mythology of the national polity.[17] It is easy to reach this conclusion if one assumes that the promotion of science necessarily means the promotion of democracy or antimilitarism. The 1941 reform indeed seems to have greatly improved the quality of the science curriculum, but the promotion of science and "progressive" methods of science education were not necessarily contradictory to the mythological *kokutai* ideology. In fact, the progressive science education was promoted through the claim that the ideal *kokumin* was the one loyal to the emperor *and* scientifically and technologically capable. The wartime government's New Order Movement promoted and designed science and technology through the Outline for the New Order for Science-Technology and incorporated science education into its *kokutai* ideology for the purpose of total war mobilization.

The postwar positioning of science as a counterforce against wartime fascism and irrational militarism helped the Japanese to continue utilizing the wartime ideal of science-technology. Many wartime promoters of science simply reprinted their wartime writings in the immediate postwar years, with very little revision.[18] Policymakers were no exception. The 1941 Outline for the New Order for Science-Technology and the agencies created under the plan officially disappeared when the war ended, but most of their personnel stayed in the central bureaucracy. The direct connection between wartime and postwar can be seen, for example, in *Revised Edition: The Basic Problems of the Reconstruction of the Japanese Economy* (*Kaitei Nihon keizai saiken no kihon monda*), presented in September 1946 by the Ministry of Foreign Affairs. The sixth chapter, "The Promotion of Technology" (*Gijutsu no shinkō*), written by the technology-bureaucrats who remained in office, was the first technology policy of the postwar state. Among the eleven policies advocated in this chapter, nine were almost identical to the policies highlighted in the 1941 Outline, such as the utilization and creation of resources, the facilitation of Asian technological development, and state planning of the Japanese economy.[19] The only difference was the erasure of specific references to the war and the empire. Japanese technocrats, in other words, continued their science-technology policy for achieving their own vision of a scientific Japan after 1945. Moreover, during the immediate postwar years, the technocrats finally realized their dream of having their own administrative territory in the central government. The wartime Public Works Bureau (*doboku kyoku*) of the Ministry of Home Affairs—of which Miyamoto Takenosuke was a part—became an independent ministry, the Ministry of Construction, in July 1948 to manage national land planning.[20] In 1956 the government also established the Science-Technology Agency (*kagaku gijutsu shō*) as an independent agency to administer science-technology policies. These two administrative units were precisely what technocrats had dreamed of during wartime.

The Japanist discourse of the uniquely Japanese way of appreciating nature and doing science also survived the war unharmed. We learned in Chapter 6 that during the war, Minister of Education Hashida Kunihiko and the new science curriculum taught the nation that Japanese science was different from Western science because of the distinctively Japanese attitude toward nature. This discourse is still a recurring theme in contemporary Japan. For example, Watanabe Masao's work on modern Japanese science is virtually identical to Hashida's argument from fifty years ago.[21] Watanabe is an emeritus professor at the University of Tokyo, which until recently was the only place in Japan where undergraduate students could major in the history of science. Regarding "fundamental" cultural differences between the West and the East, he contends:

The students had noticed . . . something characteristic of Japan: a love of nature which has existed from very early days. This love of nature is [reflected] in, for example, landscapes, miniature gardens [*hakoniwa*], miniature trees [*bonsai*], flower arrangement [*ikebana*], the tea ceremony [*chanoyu*], short poems called haiku, and even the art of cookery. Nature for the Japanese has not traditionally been an object of man's investigation or of exploitation for human benefit, as it has been for Westerners. . . .[22]

Obviously, this kind of sentiment has been rapidly fading in Japan since the hasty introduction of modern science and technology. The traditional sentiment, however, has not been completely replaced by the idea of man and his relation to nature which underlies Western science.[23]

The evidence Watanabe provides to support this argument was highly anecdotal and sporadic, such as his personal experiences in the United States, ancient Japanese poems, fifteenth-century paintings, and an eighteenth-century Zen priest. If Tosaka Jun had read this work, he would have called it an "abuse of the spirit of citation," in the manner that he criticized Japanists in the 1930s. Although Watanabe states that he wrote this book to promote the history of science program in Japan, there is no history in his ahistorical affirmation of the "Japanese love of nature." Conveniently ignored in such authentification of "unique" Japanese science is the wartime Japanese exploitation of natural and human resources in Asia as well as various environmental problems that Japan's development has caused in Japan and Asia.

Erasing science from our memory of wartime Japan has had serious consequences. Perhaps the worst was the case of the Green Cross Corporation of Japan. In 1989, the year the Shōwa emperor died and the era changed to that of Heisei, the upscale populist magazine *Day's Japan* carried a revealing article in its June issue. The article, "Black Blood and White Genes," was an exposé of the disturbing ties between two respected postwar institutions—the Green Cross Corporation (*midori jūji*), one of Japan's most prominent blood-processing facilities, and Japan's eminent Institute for Preventive Medicine—and Unit 731, Japan's wartime biological warfare project. Unit 731 was the Japanese Imperial Army's secret project that conducted various bacteriological and chemical experiments on involuntary living Chinese people in Manchuria. The *Day's Japan* article included dozens of photographs of men related to the two institutions and showed that they were all alumni of Unit 731. The Green Cross Corporation had housed many former personnel of Unit 731; the Institute for Preventive Medicine, with all of its past nine presidents from Unit 731, had utilized the expertise gained from the latter's wartime experiments. Many former Unit 731 researchers had been hired by major pharmaceutical and medical companies as well as by prestigious universities such as the universities of Tokyo, Kyoto, and Osaka.[24] Just like the technocrats who remained in the central bureaucracy after the war, these scientists stayed in elite institutions without being accused and contributed to the reconstruction of a "peaceful, democratic, and cultured" Japan.

Or did they? The Japanese were reminded of the troubling ties between the Green Cross Corporation and wartime biological warfare once again ten years later, in 1999, when the Green Cross Corporation was found to have provided blood contaminated with the AIDS virus to hemophiliac patients in the mid-1980s as a result of the company's faulty management. Almost two hundred Japanese patients contracted HIV as a result. Those Green Cross Corporation personnel who were tried in court, however, were sentenced to fewer than three years of imprisonment or found not guilty, and the victims' protest against this verdict still continues. Many Japanese have pointed out that this company must have inherited the mentality of the wartime biological warfare project that took human life lightly. Surely the examples of Unit 731 and the Green Cross Corporation do not support the Japanist claim that the Japanese have a special appreciation for nature and life.

Those who believe in the "uniquely Japanese view" of nature may dismiss Japan's warfare project as an exceptional deed of the "crazy Imperial Army." But to consider the project as an anomaly in Japanese history would only contribute to the further erasure of the wartime discourse of science. As we saw in Chapter 6, highly respected scientists such as Honda Kōtarō told Japanese teenagers during wartime to become scientists so that they could make strong weapons and serve the nation through science. Those researchers who became involved in the horrible human experiments were in a way answering such a call to be a scientific imperial subject.

How do we resist such an erasure of the wartime discourse of science? One way to do so is to give it a name so that it can be discussed openly. Naming and theorizing will also help locate Japan vis-à-vis other countries so as not to isolate Japan as a unique case in modern history. I propose to call it "scientific nationalism."

Scientific Nationalism

The phrase "scientific nationalism" may not sound familiar to the reader, since it is my own coinage. However, this current of nationalism should be familiar to those who study the twentieth century.[25] Scientific nationalism, as I define it, assumes that science and technology are the most urgent and important assets for the integrity, survival, and progress of the nation. It calls for the development of science and technology for the sake of the nation and advocates national and cultural changes to further that goal. It demands a scientific nation and thus entails visions of what science is or should be and what the nation is or should be.

Scientific nationalism should not be thought of as a monolithic ideology, because defining science and national culture is always a contested, multifaceted endeavor. For example, although Japanese scientific nationalism shared formulaic, censor-approved expressions such as *kagaku hōkoku* (scientific patriotism; serving the nation through science) and *gijutsu hōkoku* (technological patriotism; serving the nation through technology), it consisted of various, often competing, demands and critiques that came from different visions of a scientific Japan. This book, for example, has examined three main protagonist groups that participated in this politics of the scientific.

Even though the focus of this book is on Japan, scientific nationalism should not be assumed to be unique to Japan. It is a worldwide phenomenon of the twentieth century. The topic of nationalism and science may immediately conjure up the image of Nazi science or Soviet science. Nazi physicists such as Nobel Prize laureates Philipp Lénárd and Johannes Stark promoted "Aryan physics" (*Deutsche Physik*) in the 1930s, declaring its distinctive racial/national character. They attacked Einstein's relativity theory in defense of classical physics and sought to remove all Jewish scientists from the field where Nazi physicists sought to be the "führer of physics."[26] Another infamous example of ideological science is Lysenkoism in the Soviet Union from the 1930s to the 1960s. Rejecting genetics as bourgeois pseudoscience, the Soviet leadership executed or detained geneticists and developed agricultural science based specifically on nongenetic techniques.[27] To think of these anecdotes as the only examples of scientific nationalism, however, is to assume that only "bad" science is promoted by scientific nationalism. Other nations that have not been associated with authoritarian states have also shared the belief that national character shapes science in both practice and outcome.

Consider the space race between the United States and the former Soviet Union. Landing a man on the moon was not simply a triumph of science and technology but also a highly symbolic and political act of demonstrating each nation's wealth, intelligence, and the effectiveness of its political and ideological system. The ideology of scientific progress was integral to nationalism in each country during the cold war. The cold war also shaped how science was practiced in the United States. It firmly established what Dwight Eisenhower called the "military-industrial-academic complex."[28] Non-Western nations have their own versions of scientific nationalism, often accompanied by the incorporation of "rediscovered" indigenous science into the modern national identity. In China's case, herbal and other traditional medicines have been consciously integrated into its modern identity. Similarly "Vedic science" has recently emerged among India's Hindu nationalists.[29] Thus, although Japanese scientific nationalism claimed the uniqueness of Japanese science, there is nothing unique about such a claim.

Scientific nationalism, in fact, should be understood as a phenomenon specific to time rather than space: it is a distinctively twentieth-century phenomenon. For scientific nationalism to emerge and be identified, several factors need to exist, and these factors came together in the early twentieth century: strong trust in science and technology, the supremacy of the nation-state as a political unit, the centralization and nationalization of knowledge making, and international arenas where science is showcased as national. These arenas include internationally recognized awards such as the Nobel Prize, professional societies, and conferences, as well as wars among nations. The significance of World War I to the emergence of scientific nationalism in the world was decisive. World War I demonstrated the destructive power of modern science and technology to the world, with the introduction of chemical warfare, tanks, fighter aircraft, strategic bombing, and submarines. World War I furthermore firmly tied the power of science and technology to the fate of a nation.

The concept of scientific nationalism adds a new dimension to the currently expanding study of nationalism. Since the 1980s, nationalism has become a major topic of scholarly discussion among historians, social scientists, political theorists, and philosophers. The discussion mostly centers on the definition, typology, and origins of nationalism and whether nationalism rests on a real shared history, culture, and language or is instead a constructed product of modernity.[30] But the topic of science is almost always missing from such discussions of nationalism. Just as it is problematic to understand the twentieth century without taking nationalism seriously, it is difficult, I maintain, to understand twentieth-century nationalism without taking science seriously. A study of scientific nationalism can illuminate contradictions and ambiguities inherent in nationalism. Nationalism strives to articulate and accentuate difference. It mobilizes language, history, religion, biology, geography, political values, and many other features to identify the presumed uniqueness of a people. Nationalism thrives on the idea of national uniqueness, but it is often this very idea that makes the claims of nationalism dubious and polemical. When nationalism attempts to claim science, these contradictions and ambiguities become even more profound. Modern science is not commonly thought of as something unique to a people, as it needs to draw its legitimacy from universality. For its findings to be recognized as legitimate, the result of a scientific experiment should be the same no matter who does the experiment and where (so long as the conditions hold true). Scientific claims also need to be understood by scientifically literate persons in the world for the claims to be recognized at all. Thus, equations and numbers serve as a universal language. Scientific nationalism is paradoxical because the universality of science and particularity of nationalism often conflict with each other. And because of this paradoxical nature, the examination of scientific nationalism reveals dynamics, tensions, and politics that are a crucial part of modern nationalism.

As a vision of the nation, scientific nationalism competes with and supplements other kinds of nationalism that coexist in a given society. Scientific nationalism in Imperial Japan, for example, was never the dominant kind of nationalism; it coexisted with other variants that have been named and studied, such as official, cultural, and linguistic nationalism.[31] What distinguishes scientific nationalism from other kinds of nationalism in Japan is that it was one—and could possibly be the only one—that survived World War II untainted. Not only did the discourse of scientific nationalism continue after 1945 without much revision from wartime but it also thrived. It is possible to say that scientific nationalism became the dominant current of nationalism in immediate postwar Japan.

Based on the studies of the specific technocrats, Marxist intellectuals, and popular science promoters in the previous chapters, I hypothesize that the history of scientific nationalism would be as follows. In Japan, scientific nationalism emerged in the period of post–World War I Taishō democracy and continued to grow during World War II to become a dominant ideology in postwar years. The promotion of science in Taishō Japan was not replaced by wartime "fanaticism" but instead laid the groundwork for the wartime mobilization of science. The wartime deployment of the wide and lively science culture that developed in the 1920s, through schools, official actions, journals, newspapers, museums, films, and novels, became the basis of science mobilization policy. The wartime mobilization of science and technology, in turn, laid the foundation for the postwar discourse of scientific nationalism.

A "scientific Japan" is generally considered to be a typical ideal of postwar Japan, a new slogan that emerged after ultranationalistic militarism was defeated in 1945. Historians have contributed to this view, one that ignores the presence of wartime scientific nationalism. Until the early 1980s, the dominant interpretation of modern Japan—developed by Japanese Marxist historians, modernist historians like Maruyama Masao, and Western modernization theorists—saw the 1930s and 1940s as Japan's dark age that was ultranationalistic, unscientific, and totalitarian, and the defeat in 1945 as a major turning point that put Japan on the track of "healthy" modernization, democratization, and the promotion of science.[32] Although having lost much explanatory power as more and more scholars looked at tangible and subtle connections between wartime and postwar Japan, this narrative still remains influential in popular history writing.

Yet I am not merely repeating the continuity thesis that recent scholarship has put forth.[33] The call for a scientific Japan was in fact a direct continuation of prewar scientific nationalism, not a distinctively postwar phenomenon; postwar scientific nationalism, however, erased that history, rather deliberately. It was the same scientific nationalists, those who were busy promoting science and technology for the Japanese Empire, who continued to promote their scientific nationalism for postwar democracy; to do so, they uniformly emphasized how science was supposedly neglected in wartime Japan. The characterization of wartime Japan as irrational and even antiscientific was due not only to postwar historians ignoring the existence of scientific nationalism in wartime Japan but also to science promoters who made sure their scientific nationalism appeared new and suited for the peaceful reconstruction of the nation. It was precisely because of the survival of scientific nationalism into postwar Japan that wartime scientific nationalism became invisible. Examined from this perspective, the 1945 "turn" was neither a drastic shift for the new vision of a scientific Japan nor something to be denied in favor of an emphasis on continuity; it was yet another significant occasion for the politics of the scientific, in which scientific nationalists struggled to define and claim the scientific to take control of postwar Japan.

Between the Meiji Restoration and the Heisei Restoration

Thinking about scientific nationalism is especially important in the context of contemporary Heisei Japan (1989–present), which, on the one hand, has seen the emergence of a nationalistic, uncritical narrative of the recent Japanese past and, on the other hand, vigorously promotes the revitalization of science-technology.

Since the mid-1990s, neonationalists have been launching a concentrated effort to impede a critical examination of wartime Japan. One group, led by Tokyo University professor of education Fujioka Nobukatsu, is especially active and effective. Through the organizations the group has established—the Japanese Society for History Textbook Reform (*atarashii rekishi kyōkasho o tsukuru kai*) and the Association for the Advancement of Liberal View of History (*jiyūshugi rekishikan kenkyūkai*)[34]—history textbooks for classroom usage and numerous other books for the general readership have been published. Many of these books are furnished with illustrations by a popular cartoonist, Kobayashi Yoshinori, which has helped immensely to engage the minds of young readers.

Conservative intellectuals of this group claim to hold what they call "liberalist historicism" (*jiyūshugi shikan*). They argue that two false narratives have distorted Japanese history writing in the postwar decades. One is the "Tokyo War Crimes Tribunal historicism," which, according to the neonationalist group, regards the United States as the "hero" and wartime Japan as the "villain." The other is the "Comintern historicism," which the group contends treats socialism as the hero and imperialism (i.e., the Japanese Empire) as the villain. Rejecting both as "self-abusive," the group's "liberalist historicism" presents a third narrative, one that the group claims provides the kind of national past of which the younger Japanese generation can be proud. Their history books, including textbooks that have passed Ministry of Education screening, portray the Japanese Empire as a benevolent, harmonious empire and exclude any discussion of Japanese wartime atrocities, such as the military sexual slavery system (the "comfort women" system) or the Nanjing Massacre.[35] The meaning of the "liberalist" in their name, thus, should be understood as "liberating" the Japanese from a sense of remorse and responsibility for the nation's colonial past.

Ignoring Japan's wartime past is a common strategy for those who want to see only the positive effects of nationalism in Japan's past. This strategy commonly idealizes Meiji nationalism and emphasizes the continuity from Meiji to contemporary Japan by ignoring the wartime period. This was the strategy adopted by Shiba Ryōtaro, arguably the nation's most beloved writer of historical novels since the 1960s. Literary critic Komori Yōichi explains Shiba's narrative as follows:

> Shiba wrote that "the fanatic flow of the religious anti-West ideology was carried on by a crazy group [of military men] in Shōwa, who believed in a 'Shōwa Restoration,' caused the Greater East Asia War, and plunged Japan into the miserable disaster. . . . The Greater East Asian War was the most bizarre event in the world. Why did the army clique begin this war that was commonsensically hopeless? It is because even though the Meiji Restoration leaders rejected the religious anti-West ideology . . . it was reborn in the head of ignorant military men. Surprisingly, masked as a 'revolutionary thought,' it moved the military and drove millions of *kokumin* to death." Shiba completely denied wartime Shōwa and set the "military" and *kokumin* oppositional to each other. By doing so, he attempted to construct continuity in modern Japan through *kokumin*.[36]

"Shōwa Restoration" was the slogan for the Imperial Way faction that caused the 2.26 Incident of 1936. Shiba, who could not accept these "crazy" Shōwa military men as an actual part of Japan, made his ideal *kokumin* appear in his novels as the patriotic heroes: Meiji Restoration revolutionaries and Meiji military men who brought victories in the Sino-Japanese War and Russo-Japanese War. As Komori points out in the above passage, Shiba rejected a "Japan" represented by the Shōwa Restoration military men and the "bizarre event" of the Greater East Asian War, while idealizing a "Japan" achieved through the Meiji Restorationists and Meiji military men. As schizophrenic as this may be, Shiba's novels have made ordinary Japanese readers feel they are not responsible for any heinous acts of wartime Japan by blaming "crazy" and "ignorant" Shōwa military leaders. Fujioka and his "liberalist historicism" group skillfully utilize such a sense of salvation to put forth their dissatisfaction with any critical examination of wartime Japan as being "self-abusive."

For a critical analysis of Japanese history, therefore, it is important not to ignore "Japan of the Shōwa Restoration." It is equally important to demonstrate that wartime Japan could not be simply epitomized by the "religious" and "crazy" nationalism of a few. While scientific nationalists, historians, and neonationalists emphasized such an "irrational" and "unscientific" image of prewar Japan, scientific nationalism was an important part of wartime Japan and was embraced widely by intellectuals, policymakers, the media, and the state.

The creation of a scientific Japan is an explicit national vision for present-day Japan. Since the mid-1990s, the government has called its vision, awkwardly, "Building a Science-Technological Nation" or "Building the Nation through Science-Technology" (*kagaku gijutsu sōzō rikkoku*). In this state promotion of science-technology, one can see another attempt to connect the Meiji Restoration with the Heisei period at the cost of wartime memories. On January 6, 2001, the Japanese government initiated a major reorganization of the bureaucracy, and this reform was explained on the government's Web site with the image of Sakamoto Ryōma, a Meiji restorationist figure and Shiba Ryōtarō's hero. The Sakamoto figure says in his Tosa accent: "You have to do better than the Meiji Restoration" (*Meiji ishin ni maketara ikanzeyo*).[37] This governmental reform, in which Sakamoto's image symbolizes the Heisei Restoration, both created new ministries by integrating the older ones and established new goals. One of the newly created ministries is the Ministry of Education and Science (*monbu kagakushō*),[38] a result of the merger of the Ministry of Education and the Science-Technology Agency.

The parameters and goals of the new state initiative to promote science-technology are set by the Science-Technology Basic Plan (*kagaku gijutsu kihon keikaku*), a five-year strategic plan that started in 1996.[39] With a budget of 24 trillion yen (the budget of the first plan was 17 trillion yen), the current plan (2006–10) pledges to make Japan "a nation that can contribute to the world by creating new knowledge, . . . that can sustain international competitiveness, . . . and that can provide a safe, high-quality life."[40] For these goals, two basic strategies are laid out: the strategic distribution of funding among key areas (the designated areas are life science, information technology, environmental science, and nanotechnology) and the further systematization of science-technology development.[41] To carry out this plan, the government instituted the General Science-Technology Council (*sōgō kagaku-gijutsu kaigi*) in the cabinet as well as a special-mission minister in charge of science-technology policymaking. With this plan overseen by the council, the government also hopes to "produce thirty Nobel Prizes in science within fifty years."[42]

The Science-Technology Basic Plan is essentially another step toward the further bureaucratization and centralization of science that scholars have identified in many twentieth-century industrial nations. In many ways, this plan is a continuation of the wartime technocratic efforts to regulate and manage science and technology for the sake of the nation. Comments made in a roundtable discussion by the General Science-Technology Council members are also very similar to those of the wartime technocrats. One member of the council states: "After all, the system of science-technology requires a solid commander in chief. I expect the General Science-Technology Council to play this role. We need to avoid the budget being used nonsystematically and redundantly by different governmental offices, by providing a system to manage the budget based on the perspective of the whole."[43] Another council member jokingly demands that the mass media should be taken over by scientist-journalists.[44] My point is not that these Heisei technocrats are simply copying the wartime science-technology plan. There are, indeed, differences. The strategic areas for the new plan are different, partly because Japan is not currently at war and partly because key industries have changed in the late twentieth-century world from heavy industry to information and life technology. Also, the term "science-technology" no longer exactly means the science-technology that wartime technocrats advocated. General Science-Technology Council member Kuwabara Hiroshi emphasizes in his explanation of the basic plan that "'science' and 'engineering' . . . should not be identical. 'Science' and 'technology' should be evaluated differently." However, what has not changed is the emphasis upon the national benefit in determining how to distribute the science-technology budget. "It is indispensable to reach a correct evaluation [of various areas of science and technology] for an effective development of research," Kuwabara continues to explain. "The purpose of this evaluation is to realize the science-technology policy determined by the state."[45]

Only one person in the above roundtable discussion questions this centrality of the national benefit in promoting science, as he states that "it is good for science to be led by the nation's strategy because it in a sense pushes the project and makes science a holy area. But I am also aware of its negative aspect." Although he does not explain what he regards as its negative aspect, he continues to state that "companies such as Celera Genomics and Apple Computer in the United States are active beyond the national boundaries, by even challenging the state. . . . The real purpose should be to create such an atmosphere." Yet he concludes: "But because Japan is behind, we need to mobilize the state's power."[46]

Both the Heisei era's Science-Technology Basic Plan and the "liberalist historicism" relate their claims to the Meiji Restoration. Shōwa is erased in their presentation of an ideal Japan, but both in fact strikingly resemble Shōwa's wartime discourses.

By defining the purpose of the history of science as a "critical view toward today" (*gendai eno hihan*), historian Hiroshige Tetsu argued that "the critical view toward today is that inner impulse which drives historians of science to examine the history of science." This inner impulse is "the criticism against today, that is, to see today as part of history that is currently moving and should be overcome, instead of simply accepting and affirming it."[47] Such an impulse, of course, should not only concern historians of science. By recovering the erasure of the relationship between wartime Japan and scientific nationalism, my intellectual and cultural history of the "scientific" has attempted to provide a way to exercise this critical view toward today's Japan. As long as the promotion of science continues (and it should in my opinion), there will be the politics of the "scientific." We need to continue to pay critical attention to not only what kind of science is promoted but also how, with what language, and with what politics it is promoted.

Notes

Introduction

1. These are the words of the main organizer of "Overcoming Modernity" (*kindai no chōkoku*), Kawakami Tetsutarō, a writer for *Bungakkai*, a literary journal. "Overcoming modernity" was a popular phrase among intellectuals in Japan in the early 1940s. The symposium was published in the September and October issues of *Bungakkai* in 1942. Its book form appeared the following year and was reprinted several times in the postwar period with Takeuchi Yoshimi's retrospective essay. A rereading of the "Overcoming Modernity" symposium reveals that among the participants there was no shared understanding of modernity or what it exactly meant to "overcome"; as Takeuchi emphasized, it was not a coherent movement by intellectuals. Kawakami, Takeuchi, et al., *Kindai no chōkoku*. Kawakami's statement is on p. 166.

2. Suzuki Shigetaka, "Zadankai," in *Kindai no chōkoku*, 190.

3. Kikuchi Masashi, "Zadankai," in *Kindai no chōkoku*, 195.

4. *Kokutai* literally means the "national polity" or "national essence." The 1925 Peace Preservation Law (*chian iji hō*) forbade any attempt to threaten *kokutai*. In 1937, the government elaborated on the concept in Cardinal Principle of the National Polity (*kokutai* in *Kokutai no hongi*). For the Meiji concept of *kokutai*, see Irokawa, *Culture of the Meiji Period*.

5. National seclusion (*sakoku*) (1639–1854) was the foreign relations policy adopted by the Tokugawa shogunate as a way to strengthen the shogunate authority, to control commerce between Japan and other nations, and to push Japan away from tributary relations with China. It prohibited anyone from traveling in and out of Japan (except for the Dutch, Chinese, and Koreans, who were permitted access to Japan through a designated port) and selectively imported Western knowledge by allowing only medical and technological texts in the Dutch language.

6. The merger of "Western science and technology, and Eastern ethics" was first articulated by Sakuma Shōzan, a Confucian scholar in the mid-nineteenth century, as the imperative future direction for Japan to maintain independence from the West.

7. See Sasaki and Hirakawa, *Tokubetsu kagaku gumi*. Hirakawa was himself a student in the program.

8. The absence of scholarship that raises these questions reflects the unfortunate distance between the field of Japan studies and that of science studies. Science

studies have mostly focused on Western societies; and the history of science has been generally treated as a minor subfield in Japan studies. A few scholars have published sophisticated works on the history of science in Japan, but studies of Japanese nationalism and the history of Imperial Japan have not seriously incorporated those works. See, for example, Grunden, *Secret Weapons and World War II*; Bartholomew, *Formation of Science in Japan*; Morris-Suzuki, *Technological Transformation of Japan*; and Traweek, *Beamtimes and Lifetimes*. See also Low, "Japan's Secret War?" 347–60; Dower, "'NI' and 'F,'" 55–100; Samuels, *"Rich Nation, Strong Army"*; Mimura, "Technocratic Visions of Empire," 97–116; Pauer, "Japan's Technical Mobilization," 39–64. Although not strictly histories of science, for an account of Japanese biological warfare, see Harris, *Factories of Death*; Nakayama, *Science, Technology and Society in Postwar Japan*; and Nakayama, Swain, and Yagi, *Science and Society in Modern Japan*. Among Japanese-language works in the field of the history of science and technology in Japan, Hiroshige's work *Kagaku to rekishi* was most helpful for my project. The twenty-five-volume collection of primary materials related to the history of science and technology in Japan, edited by Nihon Kagakushi Gakkai, *Nihon kagaku gijutsushi taikei* (hereafter *NKGT*), is extremely useful for anyone interested in the field.

9. This is what differentiates my work from Jeffrey Herf's important work, *Reactionary Modernism*, which asks a similar question—that is, how did Nazi Germany promote modern technology and its Aryan ideology at the same time? Herf, however, uses his own preestablished definition of what is rational and concludes that Nazi "reactionary modernists"—ideologues who promoted Nazi technology—embraced technological rationalism but failed to promote political rationalism.

10. I use "wartime" for the years between 1937 and 1945. Although I am sympathetic to the argument that periodizes the war years as the Fifteen Years' War (1931–45) to include Japan's aggression toward China in the early 1930s, starting with the Manchurian Incident of 1931, for this book I decided not to use this periodization because this specific research found more significant changes occurring after 1937 than around the time of the Manchurian Incident.

11. Bourdieu, "Peculiar History of Scientific Reason," 3.

12. These protagonists are by no means the only people who engaged in the politics of the "scientific." For example, practicing scientists had their own views of science and how it should be promoted. They appear in the pages of this book, but not as the protagonists, as most practicing scientists were not interested in articulating their definitions and visions of science in print. Nor did they organize a sustained movement like those by technocrats and Marxists that historians could systematically examine. Most rank-and-file practicing scientists were, in my view, opportunists who joined the war mobilization because it brought a budget to their laboratories. But their story requires a separate examination.

13. Bruno Latour proposed "technoscience" to call for a study of the material as well as social dimension of the practice of the sciences. Sometimes spelled "techno-science," it has been commonly used in science and technology studies, especially by postmodernist scholars such as Donna Haraway. See Latour, *Science in Action*; Ihde and Selinger, *Chasing Technoscience*; and Haraway, *Modest_Witness@ Second_Millennium*.

14. As part of the major reorganization of the central government branches in 2001, the Ministry of Construction was merged with the National Land Agency and Ministry of Transport and renamed the Ministry of Land Infrastructure and Transport. The Science-Technology Agency was merged with the Ministry of Education to become the Ministry of Education, Culture, Sports, Science, and Technology (*monbu kagaku shō*).

15. Recently a Japanese publishing house began a series titled *Adults' Science* (the title borrows from *Children's Science*) for those adults who grew up with *Children's Science* and its imitator magazines, and sales have been phenomenal.

16. See *Unno Jūza shū*, 1997; *Unno Jūza zenshū*; *Unno Jūza shū*, 2001; and *Unno Jūza sensō shōsetsu kessakushū*.

17. Fairclough, *Critical Discourse Analysis*, 2. Also see Fairclough, *Media Discourse* and *Analysing Discourse*; and Jaworski and Coupland, *The Discourse Reader*.

18. Takeuchi, "Kindai no chōkoku," 301.

19. This approach is different from that of *tenkō* studies, a field that Japanese scholars have developed to deal with the question of resistance and collaboration. The Tenkō Study Group, which pioneered the field, defined *tenkō* as "a change of thought due to forces outside of oneself." See Kagaku, *Kyōdō kenkyū*, 2:4. Many of the *tenkō* studies involve categorizing various kinds of *tenkō*. Although this itself is an important project, my goal is not to categorize my protagonists in this way but to see how resistance could be at the same time collaboration.

I find Oguma's "inclusion/exclusion" similar to my "incorporation/participation." Oguma's work on the boundaries of the "Japanese" in the Japanese Empire argues that the concept of citizenship is always inclusive and exclusive at the same time. For the colonized to claim the benefit of citizenship, such as access to education and the right to vote, they need to demand to be "included," using the symbols and values sanctioned by the state. This view provides a sophisticated analysis of what some may call collaboration in the process of colonization. See Oguma, *"Nihonjin" no kyōkai*.

20. Like Antonio Gramsci's "hegemony," my definition of ideology emphasizes consent rather than coercion as a function of ideology. I agree with Louis Althusser's theory of "interpellation" to the extent that I acknowledge the performative function of ideology to construct the subject, but I pay more attention to what the subject does with the rules of the ideological system. As Bourdieu has argued, the subjects are not simply produced by the medium of ideological apparatuses; they are also capable of using the system of and values represented by a dominant ideology to better their position or to advance their politics within the system. Gramsci normally uses the word *hegemony* to mean the ways in which a governing power wins consent to its rule from those it subjugates. Gramsci, *Selections from the Prison Notebooks* (New York: International Publishers, 1971); Eagleton, *Ideology: An Introduction*; Althusser, "Ideology and Ideological State Apparatuses"; and Bourdieu, *Logic of Practice*. Bourdieu's theory of the "logic of the field" has helped me come to focus on this function of ideology. See Bourdieu, "The Forms of Capital"; Bourdieu and Wacquant, "The Logic of Fields," 94–114; and Bourdieu, "Genesis of the Concept of Habitus and Field," 11–24.

21. Although I coined this term in writing a Japanese history, scientific nationalism is not unique to Japanese history. As I will discuss further in the concluding

chapter, it also refers to the U.S. cold war ideology, Hindu "Vedic" science, and other discourses that embrace the development and promotion of science and technology for a more scientific nation.

22. For example, capital invested in the chemical industry increased seventeen times and in the machine industry eleven times between 1914 and 1919, while in the spinning industry, only three times. Iida, *Jūkōgyōka no tenkai*, 4:235, 240–41.

23. Yamazaki Toshio, "Kōgyō chitai no keisei to shakai seisaku," in *NKGT*, 3:305–7; Iida, *Jūkōgyōka no tenkai*, 4:285. For the construction of the Inawashiro station by Hitachi, see Morris-Suzuki, *Technological Transformation of Japan*, 105–6.

24. James Bartholomew explains that "[a]ll of the Salvarsan 606 used to treat syphilis came from Germany, and most of the thirty-four million yen spent on imported pharmaceuticals also went to that country." The blockade of information and education from Germany also caused anxiety among the Japanese, since Germany was their favorite nation in which to study abroad and attend academic conferences. Bartholomew, *Formation of Science in Japan*, 199. See also chapter 3 of Hiroshige, *Kagaku no shakaishi*.

25. Quoted in Bartholomew, *Formation of Science in Japan*, 199.

26. Hiroshige, *Kagaku no shakaishi*, 101. The Japanese military had already begun discussing science mobilization and military science education to prepare for the next war. Kawahara, *Shōwa seiji shisō kenkyū*, 145–49.

27. For this reason, in historian James Bartholomew's account, *Formation of Science in Japan*, World War I marks the critical point in the establishment of the scientific research structure in Japan.

28. Hiroshige, *Kagaku no shakaishi*, 84–86.

29. Ibid., 92–96; and Bartholomew, *Formation of Science in Japan*, 212–17. The initial funding of the Riken came from the state budget as well as the pockets of wealthy businessmen such as Iwasaki Koyata of Mitsubishi and Shibusawa Eiichi of Dai'ichi Bank; in addition, the imperial family donated 1 million yen (HRH Prince Sadanaru served as the institute's director general from 1917 to 1923). For more details on the Riken, see *NKGT*, 3:157–61. For Takamine's idea of a national science research institute in 1903, see *NKGT*, 21:189–91.

30. The Riken is equivalent to national science institutions of Western nations that were created in the late nineteenth and early twentieth centuries, such as the Physikalisch Technische Reichsanstalt and the Kaiser Wilhelm Gesellschaft network of laboratories in Germany, the National Laboratory in Britain, the National Bureau of Standards in the United States, and the Institut Centrale des Arts et Manufactures in France.

31. This is especially true in the areas that proved to be important during World War I, such as the Institute for Metals Research at Tohoku Imperial University, the Institute for Aeronautics at Tokyo Imperial University, and the Institute for Research on Nitrogen Fixation. The Institute for Aeronautics was the first aeronautics research center established in Japan. See Bartholomew, *Formation of Science in Japan*, 217–23.

Wartime shortages of materials also pushed many Japanese private corporations to set up their own laboratories. These companies, such as Takeda Pharmaceutical, Mitsubishi, and Mitsui Mining, benefited from the wartime confiscation of German patents and the withdrawal of Western companies from Japanese markets. Bartholomew, *Formation of Science in Japan*, 231. Notable examples of private research institutions include the Shiomi Institute for Physics and Chemistry and the Tokugawa Institute for Biological Research. The former was established by Osaka industrialist Shiomi Seiji in 1916. It was initially affiliated with the Osaka prefectural government and later taken over by the Ministry of Education. The latter institute was founded in 1918 by Tokugawa Yoshichika, descendant of the Tokugawa shogunate family, who later also took charge of the Shōnan Natural History Museum in Malaysia. For more on Tokugawa's colorful life as a scientist, politician, and writer, see Otabe, *Tokugawa Yoshichika no jūgonen sensō*; and Aramata, *Daitōa kagaku kidan*, chap. 6.

32. The government also set up a new Science Research Grants Program (SRGP) in 1918 that provided many grants to those projects not directly connected to strategically important areas. Bartholomew, *Formation of Science in Japan*, 240–42, 247–63. As Bartholomew explains, the significance of the SRGP was large. The Imperial Academy of Science (Teikoku gakushin) started its competitive grants in 1913, but the amounts of the grants were very small (2,460 yen in 1914; 7,000 yen in 1916; and 20,000 yen in 1918), and the funds were only available to academy members until 1919. The SRGP granted about 50,000 yen and supported all science and technical fields, "not just those popular at the moment or whose leaders were politically astute." The SRGP was also open to female scientists; Yasui Kono, who did research in plant cytology, was the first woman to receive this grant, in 1919. See Bartholomew, *Formation of Science in Japan*, 247, 253. The Katsura prize was set up by the Imperial Academy of Science for innovative contributions to research; Keimeikai, a private foundation, funded research and development projects.

33. Uchida, "Gijutsu seisaku no rekishi," 223.

34. It was clear that the imperial universities were no longer capable of accommodating the increasing demand for science and engineering experts; the annual applications at Tokyo University for applied chemistry, metallurgy, and mining engineering, for example, had risen from 35 to 105 between 1914 and 1917.

Chapter 1

1. Despite the power technocrats hold in Japan now, only a handful of historical studies have focused on them. They include Ōyodo, *Gijutsu kanryō no seiji sankaku*; Nishio, *Nihon shinrin gyōseishi no kenkyū*; Mizutani, *Kanryō no fūbō*; and Morikawa, *Gijutsusha*. Chapters 1 and 2 of Shindō's *Gijutsu kanryō* also provide brief but helpful descriptions of Japanese technocrats in general and their prewar conditions. Also see chapter 4 of Bartholomew, *Formation of Science in Japan*.

2. Books and articles introducing the American technocrat movement were in print by early 1933, and imported books on technocracy sold out at once. Japanese sociologists, economists, political scientists, and engineers were among those who introduced and advocated the idea. They include well-known intellectuals such as Matsumoto Jun'ichirō, Hayase Toshio, Baba Keiji, and Rōyama Masamichi. See Kawahara, *Shōwa seiji shisō kenkyū*, 68.

3. Burris, *Technocracy at Work*, 2–3. The term "technocracy" was coined by the American economist John Clark in the mid-1920s. "Technocratic" ideals can be found in earlier thought; as Burris points out, technocracy is a product of the

Enlightenment, inheriting its emphasis on reason, science, technology, and technical rationality. The belief in science can be found as early as the seventeenth century in the writings of Francis Bacon and later in those of eighteenth-century Enlightenment thinkers and progressive thinkers. See Burris, *Technocracy at Work*, 21–24, 28.

4. There has been an intense debate over the dominant role of experts in European Union (EU) policymaking. Claudio M. Radaelli argues that technocracy indeed rules the EU. See Radaelli, *Technocracy in the European Union*. As Radaelli maintains, the earlier utopia of technocracy—envisioned as, for example, "government of scientists" and a "Soviet of Technicians"—is different from today's technocratic rule.

5. Frederick Taylor's scientific management of industry was meant to mitigate class inequality by raising productivity, lowering prices, and increasing wages. Howard Scott, arguably the most active proponent in the 1930s of technocracy in the United States, believed that it was the best way to restructure society around the ideal of abundance for all and held it up as a counter to the capitalistic pursuit of profit for profit's sake. For accounts of the technocrat movement in the United States, see Jordan, *Machine-Age Ideology*; Alchon, *Invisible Hand of Planning*; and Purcell, *Crisis of Democratic Theory*. For the history of Taylorism in Japan, see Tsutsui, *Manufacturing Ideology*.

6. *Miyamoto Takenosuke nikki*, June 27, 1909.

7. A letter to his brother-in-law, June 27, 1909, quoted in Ōyodo, *Miyamoto*, 17.

8. Ōyodo, *Miyamoto*, 27–28. *Heimin shinbun* had been published by socialists since 1903 and later became the bulletin of the Japan Socialist Party. *Yorozu chōhō* was one of the most popular Tokyo newspapers in the late Meiji and Taishō periods as a strong advocate of constitutional and party politics.

9. *Miyamoto Takenosuke nikki*, February 27, 1915.

10. Ōyodo, *Miyamoto*, 43.

11. For an excellent analysis of masculinity and engineers, see Oldenziel, *Making Technology Masculine*.

12. The Civil Servant Appointment Law was passed in 1893 (revised in 1899) to make hiring of civil servants less political and more meritocratic. However, it created the dominance of Tokyo Imperial University law graduates and thus did not necessarily establish meritocracy. According to historian Nishio Takashi, in early Meiji Japan the government appreciated technical expertise more than law degrees; as bureaucratization proceeded, however, this changed. By the mid-1900s, university students clearly saw the law degree as a sure ticket to a successful career. See Nishio, *Nihon shinrin gyōseishi no kenkyū*; and Spaulding, *Imperial Japan's Higher Civil Service Examinations*.

13. Hata Ikuhiko's encyclopedic work lists all the names and profiles of those who passed the Civil Servant Appointment Law from 1894 to 1948, and my previous statement is based on my examination of this list. See Hata, *Senzenki Nihon kanryōsei no seido, soshiki, jinji*, 447–657.

14. Tsuji Kiyoaki, *Nihon kanryōsei no kenkyū*, 52. According to 1924 information from the Ministry of Agriculture and Commerce, law-bureaucrats in this ministry reached an annual salary of forty-five hundred yen in an average of two years, and technology-bureaucrats in five years. See Nishio, *Nihon shinrin gyōseishi no kenkyū*, 206.

15. Civil engineer Furuichi Kōi is one of these rare cases. After entering the Civil Engineering Bureau of the Ministry of Home Affairs in 1880, he held various high-ranking positions and honors, such as dean of the College of Engineering at Tokyo Imperial University, the first recipient of the doctoral degree in engineering, and the chief of the Civil Engineering Bureau. For more biographical information, see Doboku Gakkai Dobokushi Kenkyū Iinkai, *Furuichi Kimitake to sono jidai.*

16. Quoted in Bartholomew, *Formation of Science in Japan*, 245–46. Also see Ōyodo, *Gijutsu kanryō no seiji sanka*, 41–44.

17. Naoki, *Gijutsu seikatsu yori.*

18. Ichinohe, "Bunkyō yatsuatari," 3:456. Ichinohe was one of the most severe critics of academia's monopoly of science in late Meiji Japan. For a biography of Ichinohe, see Nakayama, *Ichinohe Naozō.*

19. Ōyodo, *Miyamoto*, 109–12. The first secretary of the club was the later-famous Edogawa Ranpo, a pioneer writer of Japanese suspense novels. See Kaneko, "Kōjin Kurabu no omoide," 41.

20. "Nihon Kōjin Kurabu no sōritsu," 66.

21. The manifesto was written by Miyamoto and published in its entirety in the journal *Kōgaku.* "Nihon Kōjin Kurabu no sōritsu," 66–67. The process of writing this declaration is also described by Kaneko Gen'ichirō, one of the original members, in Kaneko, "Kōjin Kurabu no omoide," 40.

22. For example, the 1890 edition of *Eiwa shūchin•shinjii*, one of the most popular English-Japanese dictionaries in the Meiji era, translated "art" as *jutsu, gigei, geijutsu, giryō, jukutatsu* 術, 技芸, 芸術, 伎倆, 熟達 (technique, skills, art); "science" as *gakumon, kagaku, chishiki, kyūri, dōgaku* 学問, 科学, 知識, 窮理, 道学 (learning, science); and "technology" as *geigaku, jutsugaku, shogeigaku* 芸学, 術学, 諸芸学 (learning, technical learning, various learning). Iida, *Ichigo no jiten*, 112–13.

23. Marx, "'Technology' and Postmodern Pessimism"; Oldenziel, *Making Technology Masculine*, chap. 1; and Misa, "Compelling Tangle of Modernity and Technology," 7, 11.

24. Probably the first treatise that differentiated technology from art is Meiji philosopher Nishi Amane's *Hyakugaku renkan* (1870). A philosopher and an expert in Western learning, Nishi divided the field of learning (*gakujutsu*) into two categories—technology (*gijutsu*) and art (*geijutsu*)—and explained the former as a learning of the body and the latter as that of the mind. In 1872, the government established the Technology Agency (*gijutsu kyoku*) in the Ministry of Civil Engineering (*kōbu shō*), the first governmental office that bore the word *gijutsu.* For more examples, see Iida, *Ichigo no jiten*, 12, 93.

25. Ibid., 73.

26. Saigusa, "Gijutsugaku no gurentsugebiito," 84–85. Some dictionaries, however, continued to translate *gijutsu* as "art." One Japanese-English dictionary published in 1935 listed "art; a useful art; technique" as the translation of *gijutsu*, and *kagaku* was translated as "science." *Shin konsaisu eiwa jiten*, 172.

27. Marx, "'Technology' and Postmodern Pessimism," 245.

28. Bartholomew, *Formation of Science in Japan*, 200–201.

29. Douglas, *Inventing American Broadcasting*; and Hughes, *American Genesis.*

30. Maier, "Between Taylorism and Technocracy," 28.

31. Few proletarian posters portrayed women, who constituted more than half of the factory workers in the textile industry, though many women initiated and participated in the labor movement. The prevalent image of a worker in the prewar Japanese labor movement was that of a male worker with muscular arms and powerful fists. These male producers were often depicted with a tool or a machine symbolizing the man's power over it. Historians' emphasis on the consumption culture and women as the symbol of the Taishō period has partly prevented an examination of masculinity during this period. As we will see later, class and masculinity were central concerns for engineers' identity formation and their conception of technology in the 1920s.

32. A philosophical discussion regarding the nature of technology took place in the mid-1930s, when a group of intellectuals, predominantly Marxists, engaged in an intense debate on the precise definition of technology. See more discussion on this in Chapter 4. Nakamura Seiji's *Shinhan gijutsu ronsōshi*—an expanded edition of his *Gijutsu ronsōshi*—is the most comprehensive, detailed account of the prewar and postwar history of the technology debate. For a wartime rendition of this debate, see Iwasaki Minoru's analysis of former Marxist philosopher Miki Kiyoshi's technology theory in "Desire for a Poetic Metasubject," 159–80.

33. For example, Christian activist Kagawa Toyohiko organized the Japan Farmers Cooperative (*Nihon rōnō kumiai*) in 1921, which grew to be the major organization of tenant farmers. Feminists such as Hiratsuka Raichō and Ichikawa Fusae organized the Association of New Women (*shin fujin kyōkai*) in 1920, advocating women's suffrage and the revision of the Peace Preservation Law of 1900 (*chian keisatsu hō*), which prohibited women from meeting for political purposes. Left-wing feminists founded Japan's first socialist women's organization, Sekirankai, a year later. And in 1922, the Japan Communist Party was organized underground.

34. "Kantōgen," *Kōjin*, June 1923: n.p.

35. Ōyodo, *Miyamoto*, 90–92.

36. For more details on his visits, see ibid., 117–20; and Miyamoto's own account, "Eikoku ni okeru shokugyō kumiai," *Kōjin*, August 1925: 2–17.

37. Koike's publications include *Eikoku no rōdōtō* (Tokyo: Kurarasha, 1924); a translation of Sidney Webb, *Rōdōsha ni kawarite shihonka ni atau* (Tokyo: Kurarasha, 1924); a translation of Upton Sinclair, *Hito wa naze binbō suruka* (Tokyo: Shunjūsha, 1927); *Bōkyū seikatsusha ron* (Tokyo: Seiunkaku Shobō, 1929); and *Kaikyūron* (Tokyo: Kurarasha, 1930).

38. Ōyodo, *Miyamoto*, 139, 145, 149.

39. "Shibu no setsuritsu ni tsuite," *Kōjin*, October 1925: 9.

40. "Declaration," *Kōjin*, September 1925: n.p.

41. "Kantōgen," *Kōjin*, May 1925: n.p.

42. Kurahashi, "Fusen o maeni shite," *Kōsei*, May 1926: 1.

43. Koike, "Rōdō•shihon tairitsu no shakai ni okeru zunō rōdōsha no igi," *Kōjin*, March 1926: 23. See also Kitaoka, "Zunō rōdōsha no kumiai undō to sono hogohō," *Kōjin*, March 1927: 2–32.

44. Koyama, "Musan seitō no zen'ei to kōei," *Kōjin*, January 1926: 13.

45. Quoted in Hayashi, *"Musan kaikyū" no jidai*, 15. *Shakai undō jiten* was edited by Communist labor organizer Tadokoro Teruaki.

46. "Nyūkai no susume," *Kōjin*, March 1927: 2.

47. Koike, "Kōjin Kurabu wa sekika shitsutsu aruka?" *Kōjin*, September 1927: 8.

48. Koyama, "Ichi kōjin no kitsumon ni kotaete shoshin o nobu," *Kōjin*, May 1927: 36–37.

49. Miyamoto, "Taishō jūyonen o kaerimite," *Kōjin*, February 1926: 2–3.

50. Quoted in Koyama, "Ichi kōjin no kitsumon ni kotaete shoshin o nobu," 32.

51. Kajiura, "Shakai Minshū to shiji chūshi ni kanshite," *Kōjin*, April 1928: 37–39; May 1928: 24–25.

52. Sakata, "Danpen," *Kōjin*, May 1928: 34–35.

53. Okazaki, "Ware ware no mondai," *Kōjin*, March 1927: 35–36. Also see Sakata, "Danpen," 36.

54. Sakata, "Naniwa yoshie ni kotaete," *Kōjin*, November 1928: 29.

55. "Kantōgen," *Kōjin*, February 1929: 1.

56. "Yo no kanji shoku ni tsuite," *Kōjin*, February 1932: 39.

57. Miyamoto, "Etsuro gashin," *Kōjin*, January 1930: 6–7.

58. Takeda Harumu, "Kantōgen," *Kōjin*, August 1929: n.p.

59. Miyamoto, "Anjū no chi," *Kōjin*, June 1930: 27–28.

60. Koyama, "Seinen gijutsusha Santarō," *Kōjin*, October 1925: 34–39; November 1925: 34–39. Santarō was most likely Koyama's alter ego: just like Santarō, Koyama was an original member of the Association for Industrial Japan (*kōgyō rikkoku dōshikai*), established by a group of engineering students from Tokyo Imperial University, Waseda University, and Tokyo Higher Engineering School in 1920. The short-lived group advocated the advancement of engineers' status and welfare and the engineers' political and economic involvement in establishing Japan as an industrial nation. See Ōyodo, *Miyamoto*, 104–5.

61. Quoted in Boltanski, *Making of a Class*, 52.

62. Quoted in ibid., 39–40.

63. Ibid., 50.

64. I find Pierre Bourdieu's figurative use of the word *capital* very useful here. For different forms of capital, see Bourdieu, "The Forms of Capital."

65. Miyamoto, "Konkuriito gishi no hanashi," *Kōjin*, October 1930: 19.

66. Bourdieu, "What Makes a Social Class? 1–17.

67. According to Burris, the belief that technological considerations render politics obsolete is "the central thrust of technocratic ideology." See Burris, *Technocracy at Work*, 2–3.

68. Miyamoto, "Gikai hinin yori gikai kaizō e," *Kōjin*, February 1931: 9.

69. Sakata, "Patoron to nashionarizumu to watashi," *Kōjin*, February 1930: 24–28.

70. Miyamoto, "Konkuriito gishi no hanashi," 18.

71. Miyamoto, "Shidō seishin no kakushin," *Kōjin*, February 1934: 5.

72. *Tenkō* is a Japanese term that literally means "change of direction" and became popular in the early 1930s. Originally used by Marxist theorists to refer to the change in their political strategy, the word acquired a more specific meaning when major Marxist figures gave up Marxism and became, often by force, nationalists. See my Introduction.

73. Miyamoto, "Shidō seishin no kakushin," 4.

74. Miyamoto, "Shakai jinshin no suii o omou," *Kōjin*, August 1932: 7. Miyamoto in this essay stated that his thirteen-month stay in Europe had convinced him that class could not overcome ethnic conflict; however, his earlier writings on his study abroad did not mention such thoughts at all.

75. "Sengen," *Kōjin*, September 1925: n.p.

76. Factory workers, for example, whom historian Andrew Gordon studied, demanded respect and fair treatment on the basis of their being imperial subjects equal to anyone else. Gordon proposes to call Taishō mass politics "imperial democracy" to emphasize the connection between democratic movements and nationalism in interwar Japan. See Gordon, *Labor and Imperial Democracy*, 6.

77. William Tsutsui's work on scientific management places the industrial rationalization movement in the larger efficiency movement. See Tsutsui, *Manufacturing Ideology*.

78. For example, see Nakajima Kumakichi, "'Gōrika' wa kin kaikin no atoshimatsu ni arazu," *Sarariiman*, September 1930, in *NKGT*, 3:541–44.

79. Jiji Shinpōsha Keizaibu, *Nihon sangyō no gōrika*, 3:536. *Jiji shinpō* was a journal that specialized in economic and political topics. Its advocacy of industrial rationalization moved the Hamaguchi cabinet to adopt this policy.

80. See *NKGT*, 3:554–55.

81. Teruoka, "Sangyō gōrika no mokuteki to gijutsu," 3:555–58. The Research Institute for Science of Labor was established in 1921 by the Ōhara Shakai Kenkyūjo to study the relationship between labor and workers' health. For more information, see Sōritsu Rokujūnen Kinenkai, *Rōdō Kagaku Kenkyūjo rokujūnen shiwa*; and Miura Toyohiko, *Teruoka Gitō*.

82. Yanagi, "Sangyō gōrika to rōshi mondai," *Kōjin*, May 1930: 27–31; and Uchino, "Sangyō gōrika to ikani kaishaku subekika," *Kōjin*, May 1930: 32–36.

83. Miyamoto, "Sangyō gōrika mondai shiken," *Kōjin*, May 1930: 23–26; and Miyamoto, "Anjū no chi," 28–29. Yamato is an ancient name for Japan. The phrase *Yamato minzoku* was and still is sometimes used interchangeably with "the Japanese nation" or "the Japanese ethnic group."

84. Miyamoto, "Sangyō gōrika mondai shiken," 23–26; and Miyamoto, "Anjū no chi," 28–29.

85. For example, in 1928 Koyama declared that the three main problems for engineers were the violation of technology, the supremacy of law-bureaucrats, and academic cliques. See Koyama, "Ware ware no mondai," *Kōjin*, May 1927: 31–44.

86. Sakata, "Dansō," *Kōjin*, October 1928: 91.

87. The Kōjin Club members often mentioned Hoover as a role model. See, for example, Miyamoto, "Echigo gashin," *Kōjin*, January 1930: 5.

88. K. M., "'Kōjin' sendengō no 'kantōgen' kara shikisha wa kataru," *Kōjin*, January 1931: 17.

89. Miyamoto, "Danjo kankei no shōrai," *Kōjin*, July 1925: 10–11.

90. "Kantōgen: Nōmin Rōdō Tō no kaisan," *Kōjin*, January 1926: 1.

91. Hashimoto Tameji, "Rika kyōiku ni okeru shinriteki kenchi," in *Rika kyōiku no shinriteki kōsatsu to jissaiteki ninmu* (Tokyo: Ikubun Shoin, 1929); quoted in *NKGT*, 10:19.

92. Sakata, "Tsugumi gari," *Kōjin*, February 1931: 27.

Chapter 2

1. Tessa Morris-Suzuki also argues that the science-centered ideology of Japanese colonialism was as equally strong as the more spiritualist and racist ideology. See Morris-Suzuki, *Re-Inventing Japan*. The relationship between technocracy and wartime nationalism, however, has been studied most extensively in the context of German history. See, for example, Macrakis and Hoffman, *Science under Socialism*; Renneberg and Walker, *Science, Technology, and National Socialism*; Herf, *Reactionary Modernism*; Harwood, "German Science and Technology"; Walker, *Nazi Science*; and Beyerchen, *Scientists under Hitler*.

2. Studies on wartime science-technology policies have tended to assume that the phrase *kagaku gijutsu* had existed before, overlooking the technocrats' status and definitional politics embedded in this vision. See Pauer, "Japan's Technical Mobilization in the Second World War"; Mimura, "Technocratic Visions of Empire"; Yamazaki Masakatsu, "Mobilization of Science and Technology"; and Sawai, "Kagaku gijutsu shintaisei kōsō no tenkai to gijutsuin no tanjō."

3. Young, *Japan's Total Empire*, 33.

4. Led by a former governor of Bengal, Victor Bulwer-Lytton (Second Earl of Lytton), the Lytton Commission investigated the case from March to June 1931 and submitted the Lytton Report in September of that year. The final report supported China's claim that the Manchurian Incident could not be justified as an act of Japanese self-defense. However, it also conceded to Japan by recommending the securing of Japanese interests in Manchuria. Nonetheless, Japan found the report unsatisfactory and withdrew from the League of Nations immediately after the Lytton Report was adopted by all members except Japan and Thailand in 1933.

5. See Young, *Japan's Total Empire*, 55–154.

6. "Kantōgen," *Kōjin*, February 1930: n.p.

7. Sakata, "Kaku hōmen yori yoseraretaru manmō taisaku iken," *Kōjin*, May 1932: 47.

8. Takahashi Saburō, "Jisei to Kōjin Kurabu," *Kōjin*, August 1932: 4–5.

9. Koike, "Manmō mondai o hōnin shitatosureba," *Kōjin*, March 1932: 40.

10. For example, see Uchino, "Kaku hōmen yori yoseraretaru manmō taisaku iken," *Kōjin*, May 1932: 45.

11. As early as in 1915, Miyamoto wrote enthusiastically in his diary that "those who want to fight for substance, go west [China]." Ōyodo, *Miyamoto*, 56.

12. Miyamoto, "Manmō mondai to gijutsuka," *Kōjin*, March 1932: 30.

13. Ibid.

14. Ibid., 31. For the conventional Japanese view of China in the early twentieth century, see Tanaka, *Japan's Orient*.

15. Miyamoto, "Manmō mondai to gijutsuka," 31.

16. My research indicates that what was called the *Manmō kaihatsu* policies (development of Manchuria–Inner Mongolia)—the research and planned development of the resources in the area—later became the blueprint for *kokudo kaihatsu* (development of the national land) for Japan proper. In this sense, Japanese technocrats viewed Manchuria not only as an open space but also as a kind of experimental lab. Such a view of the colony (though Manchuria was never officially "colonized") is similar to that of Gotō Shimpei and his colleagues, who

aimed at "scientific colonialism" in Taiwan. See Peattie, "Japanese Attitudes toward Colonialism," 84–85.

17. B. S. [full name not given], "Nihon kagaku sentan jinbutsu hōmon: Katō Yogorō hakushi to shigen kagaku mondō," *Kagaku gahō* 28, no. 6 (June 1939): 89.

18. Naoki, *Kōjin*, January 1934: n.p.

19. Takahashi Saburō, "Nihon Kōjin Kurabu sōritsu tōji no omoide o kataru," *Gijutsu Nihon*, April–May 1936: 30.

20. *Kōjin*, April 1932: 12.

21. Tsuge, "Kenkyūshitsu gaikan, shanhai shizen kagaku kenkyūjo," *Kagaku*, November 1937: 565.

22. *NKGT*, 4:323. For more on the establishment of the Continental Science Institute, see Kawahara, *Shōwa seiji shisō kenkyū*, 81–90.

23. "Tokyo-shi gijutsusha busoku ni nayamu," *Tokyo Asahi shinbun*, April 7, 1938. See *Gijutsu Nihon*, April 1938: 19–20.

24. The large budget was partly due to its strong connection to companies such as Nissan Heavy Industry in Manchuria; Nissan moved its headquarters to Manchuria in 1937. See Kawahara, *Shōwa seiji shisō kenkyū*, 88. For Nissan's involvement with Manchuria, see Kobayashi, *Mantetsu*, 143–47.

25. Express Train Asia (*Tokkyū Ajia-gō*) opened in November 1934. The express train in Japan proper, *Swallow* (*Tsubame-gō*), at the time ran at a speed of sixty-seven kilometers per hour. See Kobayashi, *Mantetsu*, 14; and Satō, *Tokkyū Ajia-gō no aikan*, 57–58.

26. Suzuki, "Tairiku hatten to kagaku," February 16, 1938, in *NKGT*, 4:324.

27. Ibid., 4:324. This statement was broadcast on radio on February 16, 1938, and was later published as part of his book *Kenkyū no kaiko* (Tokyo: Kōbundō Shobō, 1943). *Gozoku kyōwa* was one of the slogans of Manchukuo. The five ethnicities were the Japanese, Manchus, Chinese, Koreans, and Mongolians.

28. For more on Japanese farmers' immigration to Manchuria, see Yamamuro, *Manchuria under Japanese Dominion*; and Tamanoi, *Under the Shadow of Nationalism*.

29. For example, Mantetsu began to recruit engineers from Tokyo Imperial University during World War I. See Kobayashi, *Mantetsu*, 72.

30. Manshū Gijutsu Kyōkai, "Manmō zadankai," *Kōjin*, May 1932: 4–16.

31. Ikejima, "Tairiku kagaku to kenkoku daigaku," *Bungei shunjū*, June 1939: 184–89; quoted in Kawahara, *Shōwa seiji shisō kenkyū*, 88.

32. Manshū Gijutsu Kyōkai, "Manmō zadankai," *Kōjin*, May 1932: 5–7, 9, 12. Manchuria, however, did not seem to be a popular place for young engineers. When Mantetsu announced a recruitment of three hundred young engineers from Japan in 1933, only senior engineers with degrees from technical colleges applied for the job. According to documents prepared by the Mantetsu Industrial Section, one of the problems Mantetsu faced in the 1930s was the lack of talented young engineers. Japanese engineers in Manchuria could not expect any sort of pension system and needed to be prepared for a monthly salary of 25 to 30 percent less than what they would receive in Japan proper. Engineering positions in Manchuria were considered low profile by those who expected a promising career in the metropole. Miyamoto, "Manshūkoku o kataru," *Kōjin*, October 1933: 18–19; and Nakamura Takafusa, *Shōwashi*, 1:157–58.

33. Miyamoto, "Gijutsuka no shakaiteki danketsu," *Gijutsu Nihon*, June 1936: 2. For the meaning of *tenkō*, see my Introduction and Chapter 1.

34. In 1926, the Kōjin Club had as many as fifty-five hundred members. See Ōyodo, *Miyamoto*, 268.

35. "Zadankai gijutsusha no shakaiteki chii•ninmu ni tsuite," *Gijutsu Nihon*, November–December 1936: 24–46, 48.

36. Ueda Shigeru, "Nihon Gijutsu Kyōkai ni tsuite," *Gijutsu Nihon*, November–December 1936: 18–19.

37. "Zadankai gijutsusha no shakaiteki chii•ninmu ni tsuite," 24–46. The statement regarding resignation was made by Aya Kameichi from the Ministry of Railway on p. 36.

38. Kawahara, *Shōwa seiji shisō kenkyū*, 58; see also Iida, *Jūkōgyōka no tenkai*, 220–26.

39. The trend for the separation of capital from management escalated with the right-wingers' increasingly violent hostility during the Depression toward such established capitalists as Dan Takuma, head of the Mitsui zaibatsu, who was assassinated in 1932. Kawahara, *Shōwa seiji shisō kenkyū*, 59.

40. Okada, "Gijutsukan yūgū to hōka bannō haigeki," *Gijutsu Nihon*, October 1937: 12.

41. See "Kenji," *Gijutsu Nihon*, December 1937: 2–3.

42. The phrase *gijutsu hōkoku* was used by many engineer-writers at the time. Similar terms appeared in various areas, such as serving the nation through science (*kagaku hōkoku*) and industry (*sangyō hōkoku*).

43. Miyamoto, "Gijutsuka danketsu no shidō genri," *Gijutsu Nihon*, July 1937: 1.

44. From June to September 1938, for example, *Gijutsu Nihon* featured a series titled "Taishi seisaku zadankai" (Roundtable Discussions on the China Policy).

45. Miyamoto, "Bunkan seido kaikaku to gijutsukan yūgū," *Gijutsu Nihon*, February 1938: 4–6.

46. Kamei Kojirō, "Seiji, gijutsu, hōkoku," *Gijutsu Nihon*, September 1937: 10–11.

47. Quoted in *Gijutsu Nihon*, April 1938: 11 (originally in *Osaka Asahi shinbun*, March 16, 1938). Ishihara (1881–1947) was formerly a professor of physics at Tohoku Imperial University but left the university after a romantic scandal with a poet, Hara Asao. He studied under Albert Einstein in Europe and was his interpreter when Einstein visited Japan in 1922. In 1931 Ishihara became the first editor of *Kagaku* (Science), a scholarly science journal published by Iwanami Shoten.

48. Matsuoka, "Gijutsu jidai no tenkai to waga kuni gijutsusha," *Gijutsu hyōron*, March 1940: 5–6.

49. Ibid., 8.

50. Kikuchi, "Kinrō shintaisei to gijutsusha," *Gijutsu hyōron*, January 1941: 20.

51. The journal, which originally began in 1937 as a means of communication among various branches of the ever-expanding Riken Zaibatsu, soon became one of the major technocratic journals, in which various topics of technology, science, industry, and economy were discussed. The journal provided a space where activists and scholars of various politics, including Marxists, could engage in the discourse on science and technology.

52. For Ōkōchi's "scientific industry," see *Shihonshugi kōgyō to kagakushugi kōgyō*, which is a collection of the essays he wrote for the journal *Kagakushugi kōgyō*. Also

see his book *Moterukuni Nihon*. He also frequently wrote about the problems of the agricultural areas, which he attempted to solve by using his "scientific industry" and providing off-season factory employment to farmers. See, for example, *Nōson no kikai kōgyō*; and *Nōson no kōgyō*.

53. Nakamura, *Shōwashi*, 203–8, 214–15.

54. On Konoe Fumimaro's political career, see Yoshitake, *Konoe Fumimaro*.

55. Quoted in Hiroshige, *Kagaku no shakaishi*, 164. The Engineer Leadership Group was organized in 1918 by engineers in the private sector and universities. Established two years before the Kōjin Club, it was the first organization formed voluntarily by engineers. The China Technology Federation was established in 1938 by industrial engineers in support of war mobilization.

56. Ishikawa, "Kanjikai seido kaishi ni tsuite," *Gijutsu Nihon*, March 1937: 15.

57. "Miyamoto Takenosuke tsuitō zadankai," *Gijutsu hyōron*, April 1942: 55.

58. Scientists and engineers in business and academia joined the state science and technology policymaking as advisers. The Science Council was created for this purpose in 1938. The members included Ōkōchi Masatoshi; Honda Kōtarō, president of Tohoku Imperial University; Wada Koroku, director of the Aviation Research Center at Tokyo Imperial University; and Shibusawa Motoji, a professor at Tokyo Imperial University and former engineer in the Ministry of Communications.

59. Yata, "Jikyoku to gijutsu," *Gijutsu Nihon*, December 1937: 26. The opening speech of the conference, delivered by Sano Toshikata, director of the NGK, was broadcast on radio.

60. Quoted from an interview with Katō. B. S., "Nihon kagaku sentan jinbutsu hōmon," 89–90.

61. Miyamoto, "Kōa gijutsu no mittsu no seikaku," *Tairiku kensetsu no kadai* (Tokyo: Iwanami Shoten, 1941), 177–83 (originally appeared in *Teishin kyōkai zasshi*, March 1940).

62. Ibid., 179.

63. Ibid., 181.

64. After 1942 this came to be identified as the "open-information issue." It was a major national problem and caused much discussion among industrialists, policymakers, engineers, scientists, and intellectuals.

65. Takahashi Shin'ichi, "Kagakusha no ninmu," *Kagaku Pen* 5, no. 10 (October 1940): 61.

66. Nishina, "Nihon kagaku no kensetsu," *Gijutsu hyōron*, June 1942: 3.

67. Ibid., 2.

68. Morris-Suzuki, *Technological Transformation of Japan*, 152.

69. See above, n. 1; see also Morris-Suzuki, *Re-Inventing Japan*. The Japanese technocrats' claims are similar to those of Western colonizers who appear in Michael Adas's work. Adas, in *Machines as the Measure of Men*, emphasizes the significance of science as a criterion to measure the advancement of civilization and inherent human talent, which replaced the older criterion of religiosity, as a driving force as well as a justification of Western colonization of Africa and Asia.

70. For more information, see Sawai, "Kagaku gijutsu shintaisei kōsō no tenkai to gijutsuin no tanjō," 367.

71. The first one was Kikuchi Dairoku, who became the eighteenth minister of

education in 1901. Some viewed Hashida's appointment with pessimism, however. The September 1940 issue of *Kagaku Pen* featured a special section, "Shin bunsō ni nozomu" (What We Hope For from the New Minister of Education). Among five scientists who wrote in this section, there are both positive and critical views—some of them quite sarcastic—on Hashida's appointment. For example, one Tokyo Imperial University professor in engineering, Tomizuka Kiyoshi, stated that Hashida alone would not be able to bring about much change. He made a prophetic statement: "I want to express my opinion . . . [not because Hashida may be able to do something radical about the promotion of science but] only because a minister of education generations later may listen to me when Tokyo gets bombed and the Japanese nation finally awakens." Tomizuka, "Kagakuteki ni," *Kagaku Pen* 5, no. 9 (September 1940): 181.

72. The earliest mention of the term "science-technology" found in *Kōjin* is by Sunouchi Fumio, an engineer of the Tokyo subway, in the November 1939 issue, though Sunouchi did not develop any discussion regarding the term. See Sunouchi, "Kagaku gijutsu no sekai," *Gijutsu hyōron*, November 1939: 12–17.

73. Fujisawa, "Kagaku gijutsu shintaisei o kataru," *Nihon kōgyō shinbun*, September 19–October 1, 1940, quoted in Ōyodo, *Miyamoto*, 384.

74. Mōri, "Seiji ishiki to kagaku gijutsu suijun," *Gijutsu hyōron*, January 1940: 24–26. For more discussion on Mōri, see Itō, "Mōri Hideoto ron oboegaki"; and Mimura, "Technocratic Visions of Empire." However, neither Itō nor Mimura discusses Mōri's ideas about the term "science-technology."

75. Mōri, "Seiji ishiki to kagaku gijutsu suijun," 26.

76. Shinohara, "Kagaku gijutsuron," *Kagaku Pen* 5, no. 2 (February 1940): 6–15.

77. Ibid., 13.

78. Ibid., 14.

79. Ibid., 8.

80. See Aikawa, "Shintaisei to gijutsu no soshikika," *Gijutsu hyōron*, January 1941: 13–18, esp. 16. Aikawa became involved in NGK in 1940.

81. Ibid., 16–18. *Tōchika* is a Japanized Russian word, точка (a bunker or a blockhouse in English). It was and still is a common Japanese term that refers to a defensive military fortification.

82. Aida, "Gijutsu jaanarizumu jihyō," *Gijutsu hyōron*, January 1940: 61.

83. Wada, "Sōkan ni saishite goaisatsu," *Kagaku gijutsu*, January 1942: 132.

84. Since I could not find the results of this call, it is not clear what exactly *Kaizō* editors meant by "science-technology literature." Nonetheless, the important point is that a leading magazine announced the establishment of a new genre that bore the phrase "science-technology."

85. Miyamoto originally proposed the plan for a Unified Science Research Institution in May 1940. Following Miyamoto's proposal, the Defense Technology Committee, the Ministry of Commerce and Industry, and the Planning Agency submitted their drafts to the Diet. There was no standard name for the plan until August 1940, when the Planning Agency drafted the Outline for the New Order for Science-Technology. For more details of this process, see Sawai, "Kagaku gijutsu shintaisei kōsō no tenkai to gijutsuin no tanjō."

86. Ōyodo, *Miyamoto*, 426–27.

87. Ibid., 427–29.

88. Zen Nihon Kagaku Gijutsu Dantai Rengōkai, "Kagaku gijutsu shintaisei ni kansuru seimei," *Kagakushugi kōgyō,* July 1941: 2–5.

89. Ibid., 4–5.

90. The technocrats' advocacy of "science-technology" was not welcomed by every scientist. At a 1940 roundtable discussion on the New Order for Science-Technology, for example, some scientists complained about science-technology's—especially Fujisawa Takeo's—exclusive emphasis on technological, practical sciences. Scholars in social sciences did not like the term either. Fujisawa reported that he had received criticism that science should not be limited to natural sciences. "Zadankai kagaku gijutsu shintaisei to kokka kanri," in *Kagakushugi kōgyō,* December 1940: 142.

91. For example, at Tokyo Imperial University in August 1944, more than 70 percent of students in economics and almost 70 percent of students in law were drafted into the military, whereas only 1 to 2 percent of students in engineering, physics, and medicine were drafted. See Tokyo Daigakushi Shiryōshitsu, *Tokyo Daigaku no gakuto dōin•gakuto shutsujin.*

92. The strongest opposition came in its drafting stage, especially in the fall of 1940. For a detailed description of the process of the establishment of the Outline, see Sawai, "Kagaku gijutsu shintaisei kōsō no tenkai to gijutsuin no tanjō," 373–74.

93. *Haihan chiken* is a term for the abolishment of Tokugawa domains and the deployment of new prefectures in 1871. Quoted in Sawai, "Kagaku gijutsu shintaisei kōsō no tenkai to gijutsuin no tanjō," 372.

94. Hiroshige, *Kagaku no shakaishi,* 153–55.

95. Matsuoka, "Tōgi," *Gijutsu hyōron,* October 1942: 41–42. Also see Matsuoka, "Kagaku gijutsu to iu kotoba," *Gijutsu hyōron,* February 1942: 45.

96. Walter Grunden's work also demonstrates this point. See Grunden, *Secret Weapons and World War II.*

97. Sawai, "Kagaku gijutsu shintaisei kōsō no tenkai to gijutsuin no tanjō," 390.

98. Ibid., 384–88.

99. Yamazaki, "Mobilization of Science and Technology," 169.

100. Ōyodo, *Miyamoto,* 430–32.

101. Miyazaki, *Kagaku gijutsu nenkan-shōwa jūhachinenban,* 3.

102. Miyamoto died in 1941 at the age of forty-nine without seeing the establishment of the Science-Technology Council.

Chapter 3

1. Ogura, "Kaikyū shakai no sanjutsu: Bungei fukkō jidai no sanjutsu ni kansuru ichi kōsatsu," *Shisō,* August 1929: 1–19.

2. Ishihara, "Senkyūhyaku sanjūnen eno taibō: Kagakukai (1)," *Tokyo Asahi shinbun,* December 25, 1929, 5.

3. Bynum, Browne, and Porter, *Dictionary of the History of Science,* 145, 211.

4. Ibid., 211.

5. These are the words of Arnold Thackray, a leading historian of science, quoted in Graham, *Science in Russia and the Soviet Union,* 144.

6. Hessen, "Social and Economic Roots of Newton's 'Principia,'" 182.

7. Ibid.

8. For Hessen and the Deborinites-Mechanists debate, see Graham, *Science in Russia and the Soviet Union*, 92–93, 143–51; and Josephson, *Physics and Politics in Revolutionary Russia*, chap. 7.

9. Graham, *Science in Russia and the Soviet Union*, 147. Hessen was purged and died in prison in 1938.

10. Ogura, *Sūgakusha no kaisō*, 191. This autobiographical book describes Ogura's life from childhood to the end of World War II.

11. Established in 1881, this was a predecessor of the present-day Tokyo University of Science (*Tokyo rika daigaku*).

12. For Hayashi's activities as a specialist in the pedagogy of mathematics, see *NKGT*, 12:144–48, 151–55.

13. Okabe, "Kagakushi nyūmon: Sūgakusha Ogura Kinnosuke to genzai," *Kagakushi kenkyū* 34, no. 194 (Summer 1995): 140.

14. Ibid., 141. Hayashi's mentor, Fujisawa Rikitarō, was probably the first Japanese mathematician who encouraged statistics as useful learning for the nation. Although Ogura had no direct connection with Fujisawa, Fujisawa's influence via Hayashi should not be entirely dismissed. Fujisawa was the first Japanese who learned Western mathematics in Europe, when statistics was attaining its academic respect there. For the history of statistics as a social science in Europe, see Porter, *Rise of Statistical Thinking*.

15. Ogura, "Sūgaku kyōiku no igi," in *Kagakuteki seishin to sūgaku kyōiku*, 69.

16. Ibid., 69, 74.

17. Ibid., 67.

18. Quoted in *NKGT*, 6:286.

19. Ibid.

20. Matsubara, *Kyōdo chūshin teigakunen no shizen kenkyū*, 3.

21. *Rika kyōiku* 2, no. 8 (1919); partially reproduced in *NKGT*, 9:400–403.

22. Ogura's *Fundamental Problems in Mathematics Education* (*Sūgaku kyōiku no konpon mondai*, 1924) had a significant impact on this new trend in Japan. Another influential work was Mori Sotosaburō's *New Mathematics* (*Shin shugi sūgaku*, 1914), a translation of *Lehrbuch der Mathematik nach modernen Grundsätzen* by Götting Behrendsen.

23. By the late 1920s, this English-language book underwent numerous reprints and revised editions. It is not clear which edition Ogura read at the time. Cajori (1859–1930), a Swiss-born U.S. historian of mathematics, is also famous for his *History of Mathematical Notations* (1928–29).

24. Plekhanov, *Kaikyū shakai no geijutsu*.

25. Ogura, "Kaikyū shakai no sanjutsu," 1–19.

26. The earlier works on Marxism in Japan also include Nishikawa Kōjirō's *Warrior of Humanism, Father of Socialism, Karl Marx* (*Jindō no senshi shakai shugi no chichi Kaaru Marukusu*, 1902), and the translation of *Communist Manifesto* (*Kyōsantō sengen*, 1904) by Sakai and Kōtoku.

27. Hoston, *Marxism and the Crisis of Development*, 44.

28. Hirabayashi Hatsunosuke, a Marxist literature critic, emphasized that he felt "closer to Marxism than any other social theories" not because the Communist

Party endorsed it but "because Marxism is a scientific socialism." See Hirabayashi, "Kongo no bungaku riron," *Yomiuri shinbun*, January 31, 1927, quoted in Hamil, "Nihonteki modanizumu no shishō," 95–96.

29. Ishida, *Nihon no shakaigaku*, 109–11; and Hoston, *Marxism and the Crisis of Development*, 140–41, 146. Marxism also attracted many students concerned with "social problems." In the early 1920s, numerous Marxism study groups were established on campuses, including Tokyo Imperial University, Kyoto Imperial University, and Waseda University. In 1924, these study groups established a national organization, the Student Association of Social Sciences (*gakusei shakai kagaku rengōkai*). The growing presence of these leftist students gained much media attention, earning them the nicknames "Marx Boys" and "Marx Girls."

30. This Arusu series contained Paul Lafargue, *The Evolution of Private Ownership* (*Shiyū zaisan no shinka*, 1921), trans. Arahata Kanson; Harry Wellington Laidler, *The Current Situations of the International Socialist Movement* (*Sekai shakai shugi undō no gensei*, 1922), trans. Sakai Toshihiko; Louis Budin, *The Theory of Marxism* (*Marukusu gakusetsu taikei*, 1924), trans. Yamakawa Hitoshi; and V. I. Lenin, *The Study of Proletarian and Agrarian Russia* (*Rōnō Roshia no kenkyū*, 1921), trans. Yamakawa Hitoshi and Yamakawa Kikue.

31. Ishida, *Nihon no shakaigaku*, 106. This is the stage Andrew Barshay describes as "moment three," the moment of Marxism shaping the field of economics and other social sciences and leaving a decisive influence on post–World War II social sciences. See Barshay, *Social Sciences in Modern Japan*, 53–59, chaps. 3–5. For another detailed study of the history of Marxian economics in Japan, see Hein, *Reasonable Men, Powerful Words*. A broader history of economic thought in Japan is analyzed in Sugihara and Tanaka, "Introduction"; Morris-Suzuki, *History of Japanese Economic Thought*; and Takanoi, *Nihon no keizaigaku*.

32. Quoted in Ishida, *Nihon no shakaigaku*, 112 (emphasis added).

33. Ibid.

34. See Hoston, *Marxism and the Crisis of Development*, 44. Hoston explains that "Plekhanov's influence may be partly attributed to the fact that Japanese socialists had had prior contact with him (the historic hand-shake between Katayama [Sen] and Plekhanov) at the Sixth Congress of the Second International in Amsterdam in 1904." See Hoston, *Marxism and the Crisis of Development*, 305. Although Hoston states that Plekhanov's *Fundamental Problems of Marxism* was translated into Japanese before 1921 (Hoston, *Marxism and the Crisis of Development*, 44), I have found only the 1921 translation of this work, which was a translation from the German translation, *Die Grundprobleme des Marxismus*. Lenin's works were for the first time introduced as separate volumes in 1921 by Yamakawa Hitoshi and Yamakawa Kikue. See Lenin, *Shakai shugi kakumei no kensetsuteki tōmen, Rōnō kakumei no kensetsuteki hōmen,* and *Rōnō roshia no kenkyū.*

35. For Nakano's "Geijutsuron" (later retitled "Geijutsu ni tsuite") published in *Marukusushugi kōza* (October 1928), see Silverberg, *Changing Song*, 168–71. Kurahara published his translation of Plekhanov's *Art in Class Society* the same month, as part of the series Marxist Theories on Art (1928–31): Plekhanov, *Kaikyūshakai no geijutsu.*

36. Ogura, *Ichi sūgakusha no kaisō*, 101.

37. Doak, "*Under the Banner of the New Science,*" 235.

38. Hiroshige, *Kagaku to rekishi*, 63.

39. Ogura, "Sanjutsu no shakaisei," 1:286–97.

40. Ogura, "Kaikyū shakai no sanjutsu," *Shisō*, December 1929: 1–36; "Kaikyū shakai no sūgaku," *Shisō*, March 1930: 1–35; "Kaikyū shakai no sūgaku," *Shisō*, May 1930: 25–43; and "Kaikyū shakai no sūgaku," *Shisō*, June 1930: 1–21.

41. Ogura, *Kagakuteki seishin to sūgaku kyōiku*, 70.

42. Ibid., 73.

43. See Ogura, "Ideorogii no hassei: Sūgaku," 1:3.

44. Ibid., 1:6–8, 23–32, 34–40. A similar narrative was developed by Alfred Sohn-Rethel, a Marxist historian of science who began a Marxist examination of the emergence of bourgeois science in the 1930s, but his work *Geistige und körperliche Arbeit: Zur Theorie der gesellschaftlichen Synthesis* was not completed until 1972. Like Ogura, he attempts to locate science in "the ideological superstructure or the social base," the endeavor that Sohn-Rethel regards as lacking in Marxist scholarship. Sohn-Rethel defines bourgeois science as "a product of intellectual labour divided from manual labour" and traces the initial stage of this separation to Greek geometry. In his narrative, the decisive moment for the separation of intellectual and manual labor was the Renaissance, in which "the personal unity of head and hand" manifested in knowledge making in artisanship was taken over by newly emerging natural sciences and, more specifically, exact sciences—"knowledge of nature from sources other than manual labour." Like Ogura, Sohn-Rethel emphasizes the Renaissance as the beginning of bourgeois science and argues that socialism would and should realize the ideal unity of intellectual and manual labor. However, Sohn-Rethel's work is little concerned with the issue of academism that Ogura focused on. See Sohn-Rethel, *Intellectual and Manual Labour*, 2, 111, 133, 123.

45. See, for example, Ogura, "Riron sūgaku to jitsuyō sūgaku tono kōshō," in *Kagakuteki seishin to sūgaku kyōiku*, 41.

46. Ogura, "Kagakushi no igi," in *Kagakuteki seishin to sūgaku kyōiku*, 182–83.

47. Ogura, "Kindai Nihon sūgakushi gaikan," in *Nihon shihonshugi hattatsuhi kōza* (1932), reprinted in Ogura, *Sūgakushi kenkyū*, 1:256.

48. Ogura, "Nihon sūgaku kyōiku no seikishisei," in *Sūgakushi kyōiku*, 1:272.

49. Ogura, "Shizen kagakusha no ninmu," *Chūō kōron*, December 1936: 312–15.

50. Ogura, *Kagakuteki seishin to sūgaku kyōiku*, 320–26.

51. Ibid., 328.

52. Ibid., 74.

53. For examples of *wasan* problems and solutions, see Okumura, "Japanese Mathematics," *Symmetry: Culture and Science* 12, nos. 1–2 (2001): 79–86; and Fukagawa and Pedoe, *Japanese Temple Geometry Problems*.

54. For example, see Ogura, "Kindai Nihon sūgakushi gaikan."

55. Mikami's *Bunkashijō yori mitaru Nihon no sūgaku* was written in 1921 and first published in the scholarly journal *Tetsugaku zasshi* (Journal of Philosophy) from March to August 1922 (vol. 37, nos. 421–26) before it was published as a paperback in 1922. It was reprinted in 1947 (Sōgensha), 1984 (Kōseisha Kōseikaku), and 1999 (Iwanami) under the same title. I am working from the 1999 Iwanami edition, which is based on the 1947 edition that Mikami himself edited. I have compared the *Tetsugaku zasshi* version and the Iwanami edition and have found

no difference. Mikami, *Bunkashijō yori*. Whereas earlier histories of Japanese mathematics such as Ōtsuki Nyoden's *Nihon yōgaku nenpyō* (1877) and Endō Toshisada's *Dainihon sūgakushi* (1896) focused on the chronological accounts of the internal development of science, Mikami's work was the first analytical and narrative history of Japanese mathematics. Despite its significance, there are only a few commentaries published on his work. See Ōya, "Genban kaidai," 275–76, and "Kaidai," 285–341.

56. Mikami also discusses *sangaku* and *idai* and describes how *wasan* practitioners competed with each other and among different schools in *wasan* meets. See *Bunkashijō yori*, 48–51.

57. Ibid., 47.

58. Ibid., 129.

59. Ibid., 57. Mikami also included chess, martial arts, the tea ceremony, and music in the category of national hobby (*kokuminteki shumi*).

60. Ibid., 97–99.

61. Ibid., 116.

62. Ibid., 119.

63. Mikami, "Nihon sūgakusha no seikaku to kokuminsei," *Shinri kenkyū* 125 (May 1922): 326–27.

64. Ogura, "Kindai Nihon sūgakushi gaikan," 235.

65. Ibid.

66. Sasaki also emphasizes this view in "Kaisetsu," 337–38.

67. Ōkubo, *Nihon kindai shigaku no seiritsu*, 59.

68. Mikami, *Bunkashijō yori*, 27.

69. Sasaki also explains that a negative review of Mikami's introduction of *wasan* to the West, *Mathematical Papers from the Far East*, published in 1910 in English by G. E. Stechert (New York), was another factor in why Mikami could not gain support in academia. See Sasaki, "Kaisetsu," 317.

Mikami devoted considerable time to introducing the history of Japanese mathematics to the Western world. He published some works in English when virtually no history of Japanese mathematics existed in foreign languages. His *Development of Mathematics in China and Japan*, published in 1913, was the first analytical history of Chinese and Japanese mathematics in English. One chapter of Needham's *Science and Civilization of China* relied heavily on this text, and it is still read by specialists today. *A History of Japanese Mathematics*, written for the general readership by Mikami and David Eugene Smith, professor at Columbia University, achieved wide circulation. Mikami was the only Japanese member of the Internationalist Scientiarum Historia Comitatus, and he also developed a friendship with George Sarton, the founder of *Isis*, the oldest and still one of the most distinguished journals of the history of science in English. It is probably not an exaggeration when Sasaki states that Mikami "is the most well-known prewar Japanese historian of science in the world." Considering his efforts to publish the history of Japanese mathematics in English and forge an intellectual tie with Europeans and Americans, the Imperial Academy's decision to fire him seems inexplicable.

70. Tosaka, *Nippon ideorogii ron*, 39–47.

Chapter 4

1. See my discussion in Chapter 3.

2. See, for example, Mazower, *Dark Continent*.

3. Tokyo Kagaku Hakubutsukan, *Shizen kagaku to hakubutsukan* (Tokyo Science Museum's monthly newsletter), November 1932, 4. The opening day of the exhibit, November 2, also featured films and lectures delivered by ethnologist Yanagita Kunio ("On Independent Scholars in the Edo Period") and medical doctor Fujinami Gōichi ("The Hardships of Edo Scientists").

4. Tokyo Kagaku Hakubutsukan, *Shizen kagaku to hakubutsukan*, November 1932, 13.

5. Those who made this comment included scientist Tanizu Naohide, the Imperial librarian Takahashi Yoshizō, historian of science Mikami Yoshio, Imperial Museum curator Irita Seizō, Army Academy teacher Akioka Takejirō, and Tokyo Imperial University librarian Hatakeyama Genzō. The quotation is a remark by Mikami Yoshio, whose cultural history was discussed in Chapter 3. Tokyo Kagaku Hakubutsukan, *Shizen kagaku to hakubutsukan*, December 1932, 6–9.

6. For more information on Japanese fairs, see Yoshimi, *Hakurankai no seijigaku*, 262–63.

7. Ogura, "Kagakushi no igi," in *Kagakuteki seishin to sūgaku kyōiku*, 183 (originally published in *Tōkyō teikoku shinbun*, March 12, 1934).

8. Ibid., 182–83.

9. Tosaka, "Shakai ni okeru shizen kagaku no yakuwari," *Yuibutsuron kenkyū* 1 (November 1932): 45.

10. "Yuibutsuronsha XYZ," *Yuibutsuron kenkyū* 2 (December 1932): 122.

11. Tosaka, "Shakai ni okeru shizen kagaku no yakuwari," 45.

12. For example, see Amakasu [Segi Ken], "Yūseigaku ni tsuite," *Yuibutsuron kenkyū* 20 (June 1934): 55–71.

13. Tosaka, "Shakai ni okeru shizen kagaku no yakuwari," 42–43 (emphasis in original).

14. Ibid., 47 (emphasis in original).

15. Monbushō, *Gakusei 120 nenshi*, 61–62.

16. Such publications by the institute as *Kokumin seishin bunka kenkyūjo shuppan tosho mokuroku* give useful information about the institute's research interests. For more information regarding the role of this institution in Japanese wartime education, see Kubo, *Shōwa kyōikushi*, 1:344–55.

17. By November 1943 more than 1,730,000 copies of *Kokutai no hongi* had been printed. A researcher at the Institute for the Study in National Spiritual Culture, Shida Nobuyoshi, drafted and revised the text by adopting opinions from committee members such as Watsuji Tetsurō, a renowned Kyoto Imperial University professor. See Abe, *Taiheiyō sensō to rekishigaku*, 27–28.

18. Sakuta, *Kokumin kagaku no seiritsu*.

19. Ibid., 4.

20. Ibid., 11.

21. Ibid., 14.

22. Ibid., 18–20. A well-known publisher of educational books published a series of books under the title *Kokumin Kagaku* between 1941 and 1944. It included

works on resources, medicines, home economics, and transportation. It is not clear if this series had anything to do with Sakuta's *kokumin kagaku,* but the stated purpose of this publication was very similar to Sakuta's argument. See "'Kokumin kagaku' kankō no shushi." There was another series by Sankaidō Shuppanbu—*Kokumin Kagaku Bunko*—published in 1943. The three books that I have found so far in this series are on electricity, the rubber industry, and electric resources.

23. See Tosaka, *Nippon ideorogii ron.* Kanokogi Kazunobu's works include *Kanji to shinri no haji* and *Kōkoku shugi.* Kihira Tadayoshi's works include *Shinri towa nanzoya* and *Koshintō.*

24. Tsuji Tetsuo's work is one of the few studies by historians that discuss, though not critically, Japanist theorists of science such as Hashida Kunihiko. See Tsuji, *Nihon no kagaku shisō.*

25. Sakuta, *Kokumin kagaku no seiritsu,* 24.

26. Tosaka, *Nippon ideorogii ron,* 28, 32.

27. See, for example, Hirata, "Uchisaiwaichō no jimusho," *Yuibutsuron kenkyū fukkokuban geppō,* no. 1:5; and Kozai, "Senzen ni okeru yuibutsuronsha no teikō," *Bunka hyōron* 111 (December 1970): 80. The meeting to discuss the group's disbanding took place outside their office to avoid the eyes and ears of the police. *Yuibutsuron kenkyū fukkokuban geppō* by Aoki Shoten (1972–1975); the *geppō* number refers to the volume number of the reprinted edition. In this 1970s edition, the original sixty-five issues of *Yuibutsuron kenkyū* as well as eight issues of its successor, *Bungei* (Literature), were reprinted in eighteen volumes.

The Yuiken office moved from the wooden Tōhoku Building in Uchisaiwaichō to the Ichiba Building in Kanda Iwamotochō in 1937, and again to Manseibashi in 1938 after the journal changed its name to *Bungei.* Mori Kōichi later recalled that in this Manseibashi office, a Special Higher Police officer had frequented the office, sometimes killing time on duty by playing Japanese chess with the Yuiken members. Mori, "Dai jūnanakan Kaidai," *Yuibutsuron kenkyū fukkokuban geppō,* no. 17:3.

28. Kozai, "Senzen ni okeru yuibutsuronsha no teikō," 78.

29. According to Karita Shinshichi, who took care of the office chores of Yuiken from its establishment to the end, *Yuibutsuron kenkyū* was sent to Manchuria, China, Moscow, Berlin, and Amsterdam every month. Sometimes it was ordered from New York and the South Pacific islands. Karita, "Mō hitotsu no sokumen," *Yuibutsuron kenkyū* 50 (December 1936): 155. Yuiken's existence was introduced in *Pravda,* a leading Soviet newspaper. Ara, "'Purauda' ni shōkaisareta Yuibutsuron Kenkyūkai," *Yuibutsuron kenkyū fukkokuban geppō,* no. 14:5. However, it is difficult to tell exactly how widely *Yuibutsuron kenkyū* and Yuiken members' books were read in the 1930s. The Special Higher Police accused Yuiken members of having strongly influenced Japanese youth, and there is also testimony that the journal was hardly available in the countryside. See Honma, "Inaka deno 'Yuiken' kan," *Yuibutsuron kenkyū* 50 (December 1936): 151–52.

30. The original series was published by Mikasa Shobō, a publisher sympathetic to leftist publications. Date Kimio mentions strategies of Yuiken and Mikasa Shobō in publishing this series, such as using non-Marxist scholars to introduce the works

and publishing the volume on the military before the other volumes. See Date, "Dai jūgokan kaidai," *Yuibutsuron kenkyū fukkokuban geppō,* no. 15:4. The partial reprint of this series was made available by Kyūzansha in 1990 and 1991.

31. Oka, "Society for the Study of Materialism," 152. This was originally published in *Nihon no kagakusha* 5, nos. 1–2 (1970): 31–36, 4–9.

32. Ibid. (emphasis added). Also see Mori, "Dai ikkan kaidai," *Yuibutsuron kenkyū fukkokuban geppō,* no. 1:1.

33. Hasegawa, "Yuibutsuron Kenkyūkai no sōritsu ni tsuite," *Yuibutsuron kenkyū* 1 (November 1932): 7.

34. Original members Hattori and Saigusa also left the organization, though Saigusa continued to write in the journal under various pen names and later worked as its editor, as Chapter 5 discusses in detail.

35. Readers must have complained about this vagueness, for in 1936 Tosaka made a point of explaining that it was not easy to be "concrete" in discussing social sciences because "this journal was not established based on the Newspaper Law, nor has it paid any permission fees." See Tosaka, "Kikanshi gojūgo kinen no tameni," *Yuibutsuron kenkyū* 50 (December 1936): 130.

36. Shihōshō Keijikyoku, *Shisō geppō* 1 (July 1936): 5–6.

37. Ishihara Tatsurō, "Yuiken no shoki no koro no koto," *Yuibutsuron kenkyū fukkokuban geppō,* no. 8:7–8.

38. Mashita, "Tosaka Jun no omoide," *Yuibutsuron kenkyū fukkokuban geppō,* no. 2:5; Hasebe Ishirō, "Yuiken hassoku no koro," *Yuibutsuron kenkyū fukkokuban geppō,* no. 2:7; and Kamo, "Tosaka Jun no omoide," *Yuibutsuron kenkyū fukkokuban geppō,* no. 5:7.

39. Miyamoto Shinobu, "Watashi no seishun to kenkyū," *Yuibutsuron kenkyū fukkokuban geppō,* no. 11:5–6; Mori Kōichi, "Dai jūnikan kaidai," *Yuibutsuron kenkyū fukkokuban geppō,* no. 12:2; and Date, "Dai jūyonkan kaidai," *Yuibutsuron kenkyū fukkokuban geppō,* no. 14:2.

40. Yoshino, "Yuiken no yane no shitani," *Yuibutsuron kenkyū fukkokuban geppō,* no. 7:6.

41. Ishihara, "Pen neemu ni tsuite," *Yuibutsuron kenkyū fukkokuban geppō,* no. 1:8.

42. Nakayama, "History of Science," 10.

43. Kozai, "Zadankai: Teikō no kiroku—'Yuibutsuron Kenkyukai' no katsudō," *Jidai to Shisō* 3 (1971): 125–26.

44. Ishii [Ōkawa], "Shihonshigikoku no shizen kagaku (oboegaki)," *Yuibutsuron kenkyū* 9 (July 1933): 62.

45. Oka, "Genzai ni okeru kagakusha no tachiba," *Yuibutsuron kenkyū* 12 (October 1933): 147.

46. For example, see Ishii [Ōkawa], "Shizen kagaku kenkyū ni okeru futatsu no taido," *Yuibutsuron kenkyū* 13 (November 1933): 57–62.

47. For example, see Yamamoto, "Soveeto dōmei no shizen kagaku," *Yuibutsuron kenkyū* 12 (October 1933): 166. Also see Ishii [Ōkawa], "Shihonshugikoku no shizen kagaku (oboegaki)," *Yuibutsuron kenkyū* 9 (July 1933): 63–64.

48. Ishii [Ōkawa], "Shizen kagaku kenkyū ni okeru futatsu no taido," 57–62.

49. Tosaka Jun, "Shakai ni okeru shizen kagaku no yakuwari," *Yuibutsuron kenkyū* 1 (November 1932): 44. Also see Ishii [Ōkawa], "Shizen kagaku no tōhasei ni tsuite," *Yuibutsuron kenkyū* 11 (September 1933): 46–49.

50. *Shizen benshōhō*, among the Japanese Marxist intellectuals in the 1930s, referred to the dialectics of nature developed by Engels, who argued that the same
dialectical laws governed nature and history. However, how exactly to apply the
dialectics of nature to natural sciences was one of the most challenging questions
for Japanese Marxists, as I will discuss shortly. For useful explanations of these terms
in Western Marxism, see Bottomore, *Dictionary of Marxist Thought*, s.vv. "dialectical
materialism," "dialectics of nature," and "historical materialism."

51. Tosaka, "Shakai ni okeru shizen kagaku no yakuwari," 35.

52. Ibid., 42 (emphasis in original).

53. Ishihara, "Butsurigaku jō no gainen ni taisuru yuibutsusei no imi ni tsuite,"
Yuibutsuron kenkyū 12 (October 1933): 5–11.

54. Takahashi, "Shizen kagaku to shakai kagaku no kaikyūsei no mondai ni
tsukite," *Kagaku* 3, no. 11 (November 1933): 460–61.

55. Ishii [H. K.], "Kyakkanteki shizen hōsoku no tankyū to shizen kagaku no
kaikyūsei," *Yuibutsuron kenkyū* 15 (January 1934): 105.

56. Tosaka, "Shakai ni okeru shizen kagaku no yakuwari," 30.

57. Ishihara, "Butsurigaku jō no gainen ni taisuru yuibutsusei no imi ni tsuite,"
5–11.

58. For example, see Ishihara [Nakajima], "'Shizen benshōhō no gutaika' ni taisuru kengi," *Yuibutsuron kenkyū* 29 (March 1935): 90–108.

59. Ishihara, "Idengaku to Yuibutsuron," *Yuibutsuron kenkyū* 4 (February 1933):
105.

60. Ishihara, "Menderizumu ichi hihan," *Yuibutsuron kenkyū* 3 (January 1933):
71–77; and Ishihara, "Idengaku to yuibutsuron," *Yuibutsuron kenkyū* 3 (January 1933):
95–105.

61. Amakasu, "Yūseigaku ni tsuite," 55–71.

62. Ishii, "Shinkaron no hanashi (4)," *Yuibutsuron kenkyū* 23 (September 1934):
134. An essay a year earlier also declared that "the definite heir of Darwinism must
be the proletariat." See "Yuibutsuronsha XYZ," *Yuibutsuron kenkyū* 12 (October
1933): 163.

63. Yuiken sent questionnaires to scientists and philosophers, "What Does a Natural Scientist Demand from Philosophy?" and "What Does a Philosopher Demand
from Natural Sciences and Scientists?" in 1934 and 1935. Respondents included
non-Yuiken intellectuals and even those criticized in the journal, such as Shinohara
Takeshi and Kihira Tadayoshi (who returned lengthy comments). See "Shizen kagakusha wa tetsugaku ni taishite nanio yōkyū suruka," *Yuibutsuron kenkyū* 22 (August
1934): 65–70; and "Tetsugakusha wa shizenkagaku naishi shizenkagakusha ni nanio
yōkyū suruka," *Yuibutsuron kenkyū* 30 (April 1935): 76–91.

64. See Josephson, *Totalitarian Science and Technology*, 15–38; and Graham, *Science
in Russia and the Soviet Union*, 121–34. Most Yuiken natural scientists also exclusively
discussed biology and physics, but a notable exception was Miyamoto Shinobu, who
wrote on the class character of medicine. See Miyamoto, "Shakaiteki ningen no
bunseki," *Yuibutsuron kenkyū* 37 (November 1935): 5–24; and Miyamoto, "Igaku no
kagakusei yōgo no tameni—Ōta Takeo shi ni kotaeru," *Yuibutsuron kenkyū* 39 (November 1936): 156–69.

65. For example, introducing Soviet biology, Ishii Tomoyuki described it as biol-

ogy based on an accurate evaluation of Darwinism. See Ishii [Ōkawa], "Matsumoto Shigeru yaku, Daawin shugi to marukusu shugi," *Yuibutsuron kenkyū* 20 (June 1934): 118. However, no Yuiken writers mentioned Lysenko's name anywhere in *Yuibutsuron kenkyū*. Moreover, ten pages after Ishii's article, there is an ad for the Japanese translation of *Science at the Cross Roads*, in which Hessen's history of science essay discussed in Chapter 3 criticized the "Mechanists." The Japanese version of the Lysenko debate only occurred in the immediate postwar period. See Nakamura Teiri, *Nihon no ruisenko ronsō*.

66. Amakasu, "Yūseigaku ni tsuite," 57.

67. Ishii [Ōkawa], "Sōgō kagaku no kiso jōken?" *Yuibutsuron kenkyū* 32 (June 1935): 48–57.

68. Ibid., 56.

69. Kanbe, *Nihon rika kyōiku hattatsushi*, 270–71, quoted in *NKGT*, 3:17.

70. Matsuda, "Monbu daijin no chiiku henchōron," in *NKGT*, 4:171 (originally published in *Osaka Asahi shinbun*, evening ed., August 21, 1934).

71. The 5.15 Incident refers to another failed coup d'état in 1932 by navy officers, who assassinated Prime Minister Inukai Tsuyoshi.

72. Kita's *Nihon kaizō hōan taikō* (Plan for the Reorganization of Japan, 1926) greatly inspired members of the Imperial Way faction. The work was first privately published in 1920 under a different title, *Kokka kaizōan genri taikō*, and was banned immediately. The 1926 publication revised the original manuscript to avoid censorship. Kita, who was not directly involved in the coup attempt, received the death sentence; Masaki Jinzaburō, an Imperial Way faction leader who had actively supported the coup, was judged not guilty. For more details on the 2.26 Incident and the internal conflicts in the military, see Nakamura Takafusa, *Shōwashi*, 1:chap. 2.

73. Tanabe, "Kagaku seisaku no mujun," *Kaizō*, October 1936: 18.

74. Isobe, "Niiniiroku jiken gokuchū nikki," 168, 178.

75. Tanabe, "Kagaku seisaku no mujun," 18–34. For more on Tanabe, see Makoto, *Individuum, Society, Humankind*; Heisig, *Philosophers of Nothingness*; and Unno and Heisig, *Religious Philosophy of Tanabe Hajime*. For one of the most sophisticated Japanese-language discussions on Tanabe's scholarship, see Ienaga, *Tanabe Hajime no shisōshiteki kenkyū*.

76. Tanabe, "Kagaku seisaku no mujun," 19.

77. Ibid., 20.

78. Ibid., 23.

79. Tanabe, "Kagakusei no seiritsu," *Bungei shunjū*, September 1937: 50–61.

80. Tanabe, "Kagaku seisaku no mujun," 24.

81. Itakura, "Kyōgaku sasshin undōka no kagaku kyōiku," in *NKGT*, 3:19, 30.

82. Tanabe, "Kagaku seisaku no mujun," 30.

83. Ibid., 32.

84. Ibid., 33.

85. For example, see Heisig, *Philosophers of Nothingness*, 134–38. Tanabe's political stance during wartime is a subject of debate among scholars, as is that of the Kyoto school of philosophy. Tanabe is considered to be part of the Kyoto school of philosophy, but he and Nishida did not communicate with each other for the latter half of his life due to major intellectual and political disagreements. If the reader is

interested in understanding Tanabe's wartime philosophy better, I recommend reading his theory of species (*shu no ronri*) together with his articles discussed in this chapter.

86. The lecture was published later as a chapter of his book. See Hashida, *Gyō to shite no kagaku*.

87. Ibid., 25.

88. Ibid., 27.

89. Like Nishida, Hashida was a serious reader of the thirteenth-century Zen monk Dōgen's master work and Ming China scholar Wan Yang-ming's *Chuan xi lu*. Hashida, "*Seibō genzō* no sokumenkan." Tanabe also studied *Shōbō genzō*; however, his work on Dōgen, "*Shōbō genzō*" *no tetsugaku shikan*, does not contain any discussion of science.

90. Hashida, *Gyō to shite no kagaku*, 29–30, 43. To validate this view, Hashida also referred to Nishida's concept of "action without the actor" (*hataraku mono naki hataraki*) in explaining the practice of observation through the unity of subject and object. See *Gyō to shite no kagaku*, 32.

91. Imano, "Kagaku seisaku no konpon mondai," *Yuibutsuron kenkyū* 49 (November 1936): 31.

92. Ogura, "Shizen kagakusha no ninmu," 305–28 (originally published in *Chūō kōron* in December 1936).

93. Ogura had in fact already written an article in 1934 that rebuked Minister of Education Matsuda's "overlearning" comment on the way to a *kendō* competition and compared Matsuda's plan to shorten the school year and increase ethics classes with the "reactionary education" of fascist Italy. Ogura, "Sūgaku kyōiku no kaizō mondai—Matsuda bunsō no danwa ni kanshite," in *Kagakuteki seishin to sūgaku kyōiku*, 188–220 (originally published in *Chūō kōron* in October 1934).

94. Ogura, "Shizen kagakusha no ninmu," 327.

95. Ogura, "Sūgaku kyōiku no igi," in *Kagakuteki seishin to sūgaku kyōiku* (1937), 69 (originally published in *Nihon chūtō kyōiku sugakkai zasshi* 5, nos. 4–5 [1923]: 74).

96. Tosaka, "Kagakuteki seishin towa nanika," *Yuibutsuron kenkyū* 54 (April 1937): 32.

97. Ibid., 30.

98. Nagayama, "Kaisetsu: Kagaku to sensō to Unno Jūza," 270.

Chapter 5

1. Kikanshi henshūbu, "Shoka no iken o shirusu," *Yuibutsuron kenkyū* 47 (September 1936): 45.

2. Doak, "What Is a Nation and Who Belongs?" 292.

3. *Daijirin*.

4. Hirokawa, "Minzoku ni tsuite," *Yuibutsuron kenkyū* 49 (November 1936): 38–40.

5. Hayakawa, "'Kokumin' to 'minzoku,'" *Yuibutsuron kenkyū* 49 (November 1936): 49.

6. Mori, "Minzoku to kokumin oyobi Nation," *Yuibutsuron kenkyū* 49 (November 1936): 52.

7. Hayakawa, "'Kokumin' to 'minzoku,'" 50.

8. Stalin, quoted in Davis, *Nationalism and Socialism*, 163; Stalin, *Marxism and the National Question*, in Bottomore, *A Dictionary of Marxist Thought*, 344. Earlier, to prepare for the Yuiken-wide discussion on *minzoku*, Matsuoka Hiroshi published an outline of Stalin's definition of the nation in the April 1935 issue, and Mori Kōichi presented his paper on *minzoku* at a Yuiken study group in May 1936, using Stalin's definition and raising his concern about the Nazilike, biological thinking of *minzoku* prevalent in Japan. "Hōkoku kakubu kenkyūkai, minzokuron to sekaikan," *Yuibutsuron kenkyū* 44 (June 1936): 966.

9. Kojima, "Minzoku naru gainen ni tsuite," *Yuibutsuron kenkyū* 49 (November 1936): 51.

10. See, for example, Tosaka Jun, "Minzoku to kokumin: Minshū•jinmin oyobi kokka" and Ōta Takeo [Ōta Tenrei], "Minzoku to kokumin," *Yuibutsuron kenkyū* 49 (November 1936): 43, 37.

11. For an excellent study of the genealogy of the anthropological and nationalist discourse of the Japanese *minzoku*, including the *kokutai* ideology, see Oguma, *Tan'itsu minzoku shinwa no kigen*.

12. Quoted in ibid., 154.

13. For more on prewar and wartime eugenics in Japan, see Ōtsubo Sitcawich, "Eugenics in Imperial Japan."

14. Koya also published a book under the same title. His publications on this subject include *Minzoku seibutsugaku gairon* (Introduction to *minzoku* Biology, 1933) and *Minzoku seibutsugaku* (*Minzoku* Biology, 1938).

15. Ishii, "Minzoku seibutsugaku ni tsuite," *Yuibutsuron kenkyū* 48 (October 1936): 100–101.

16. Ibid., 103–5.

17. Oka, "Torusutoi no kagakuron," *Yuibutsuron kenkyū* 59 (September 1937): 17.

18. Mori, "Minzoku teki narumono towa nanzoya?" *Yuibutsuron kenkyū* 53 (March 1937): 7, 9.

19. Ibid., 13–14.

20. "Gendai shichō no shomondai," *Yuibutsuron kenkyū* 53 (March 1937): 69–71.

21. Kuwaki Masaru [Iwakura Masaji], "Dentō no kōsatsu—dentō no kaikyūsei ni tsuite," *Yuibutsuron kenkyū* 57 (July 1937): 12.

22. Ibid., 13.

23. Ibid.

24. Ibid., 15–17.

25. Ogura, "Sūgaku kyōiku no igi," in *Kagakuteki seishin to sūgaku kyōiku*, 69.

26. For example, see Hasegawa Ichirō, "Yuiken hassoku no koro," in *Yuibutsuron kenkyū fukkokuban geppō*, no. 2:7. For his biography, see Iida, *Kaisō no Saigusa Hiroto*. Iida was a student of Saigusa and a historian of Japanese science and technology himself.

27. Saigusa, "Kamakura Daigaku haikō shimatsuki," *Chūō kōron*, February 1951, quoted in Iida, *Kaisō no Saigusa Hiroto*, 148. For more about the Kamakura Academia, see *Asahi Jaanaru*, October 1969; Takase, *Kamakura Akademia danshō*; and Maekawa, *Kamakura Akademia*.

28. Saigusa, "Nishida tetsugaku no konpon mondai," *Yuibutsuron kenkyū* 18 (April 1934): 5–27. Other writings by Saigusa in *Yuibutsuron kenkyū* on the neo-Kantian philosophy include "Yuibutsuronsha ha Kanto wo ikani yomuka," *Yuibutsuron kenkyū* 3 (January 1933): 12–33; "'Shihonron' no yuibutsuronteki kiso," *Yuibutsuron kenkyū* 8 (June 1933): 21–34; and "Nihon ni okeru ishoku kannenron no tokushoku," *Yuibutsuron kenkyū* 11 (September 1933): 5–25.

29. Saigusa, "Fujikawa Yū sensei nit tsuite—botsugo nijūichi nen kinen," in *Saigusa Hiroto chosakushū*, 4:342.

30. The last available account of Saigusa's participation in the Yuiken study groups was his presentation on the concept of nature in Japanese history on February 6, 1937, which attracted fifteen people, an attendance greater than that of any other study groups. See "Kagaku kenkyūkai hōkoku," *Yuibutsuron kenkyū* 53 (March 1937): 174–75.

31. Saigusa, "Nihon shisōka sai," *Tokyo Asahi shinbun*, March 18, 1937, 14.

32. Ibid. *Fujiyama* is Mt. Fuji. *Hara-kiri* is a ritual suicide. *Wabi* and *yūgen* are widely considered to represent Japanese aesthetics by Japanese and Westerners. *Wabi* is often used with *sabi*; *Wabi-sabi* is a concept derived from the Buddhist assertion of impermanence. *Yūgen* refers to a beauty behind seeable things; it is often used to describe the depth and beauty of Noh theater, for example.

33. Saigusa, *Nihon no shisō bunka*, 1–15.

34. Ibid., 8:260–64.

35. Ibid., 408.

36. Ibid., 133.

37. Maruyama excluded Baien from his discussion of Tokugawa Confucianism in his famous 1952 work because of this nonmainstream status of Baien. See Maruyama, *Studies in the Intellectual History of Tokugawa Japan*, 178. Rosemary Mercer argues against such characterization of Baien. See Mercer, "Picturing the Universe," *Philosophy East and West* 48, no. 3 (July 1998): 478–503.

38. The earliest works on Baien include Nishimura, "Miura Baien"; Tsuchiya, "Miura Baien no gengaku"; and Oyanagi, "Miura Baien." The first collected works of Baien, *Baien zenshū*, was published in 1912. Saigusa's works were the first book-length titles devoted to the study of Baien.

39. The term *gen* is very difficult to translate into English. My translation here is based on Saigusa's understanding of the term; he interpreted *gen* as the Hegelian *Idee*, "completely fulfilled truth" or "the self of the universe." See Saigusa, *Baien tetsugaku nyūmon*, 214. Others, such as Mercer in "Picturing the Universe," have translated the title of Baien's masterpiece as "Deep Words."

40. These two works are included in volume 5 of *Collected Works of Saigusa Hiroto* (*Saigusa Hiroto chosakushū*). The following references, unless otherwise noted, are based on the page numbers of *Collected Works*.

41. Saigusa explained Baien's *jōri* in various places. See, for example, Saigusa, *Baien tetsugaku nyūmon*, 174, for Baien's dual usage of the term.

42. Ibid., 206.

43. Miki, *Gendai tetsugaku jiten*, 395, s.v. "Nippon shugi" (Saigusa).

44. Ibid., 394, s.v. "Nippon seishin" (Saigusa).

45. Saigusa, *Baien tetsugaku nyūmon*, 219. This quotation is part of a chapter titled

"Baien no riko no tetsugaku." It was originally published in the June 1938 issue of *Chūō kōron*, reprinted in his book *Nihon no chisei to gijutsu* (Tokyo: Daiichi Shobō, 1939) under "Miura Baien no seishinron," and reprinted again in *Baien tetsugaku nyūmon*.

46. Saigusa, *Baien tetsugaku nyūmon*, 222.

47. Ibid., 224.

48. The original plan was to publish "twelve volumes, plus a supplemented volume for the index, references, and a chronological table. However, as the research proceeded, we planned to add two more volumes, that is, fifteen books for fifteen volumes." In the end, though, only ten volumes were published between 1942 and 1949, even though more manuscripts were prepared. Saigusa, "Nihon kagaku koten zensho no hensan nii tsuite," in *Nihon kagaku koten zensho*, 1:3.

49. These Tokugawa Confucian scholars were later analyzed as Japanese materialists in Saigusa's 1956 work. Included are Kaibara Ekken, Ogyū Sorai, Dazai Shuntai, Tominaga Chūki, Miura Baien, Minakawa Kien, Kamada Ryūō, Yamagata Bantō, and Andō Shōeki. See Saigusa, *Nihon no yuibutsuronsha*.

50. Among these, vols. 8, 13, 14, and 15 were published after 1945.

51. Saigusa, *Nihon kagaku koten zensho*, 1:1–2.

52. The project was completed with the publication of the twenty-eight-volume *History of Science in Pre-Meiji Japan* between 1954 and 1973. For a brief, postwar account of the project, see Ogata, "Fukkokuban no kankō ni attatte," i–iii.

53. For the accounts of Yuiken's strategic dissolution and arrest, see *Yuibutsuron kenkyū fukkokuban geppō*, nos. 17, 18.

54. This study group had three other sections: foreign policies, politics, and the economy. It dissolved in November 1940 when many of its core members moved to Taisei Yokusankai. For the ideology of the group, see Ishida, *Nihon no shakaikagaku*, 136–48. For an insider account, see Sakai, *Shōwa kenkyūkai*; Saigusa's activity is mentioned on pp. 154–57. For an analysis of Miki Kiyoshi's wartime writings, see Iwasaki, "Desire for a Poetic Metasubject," 159–80; and Harootunian, "History's Actuality," in *Overcome by Modernity*, 358–414.

55. This report was published as *Shinnihon no shisō genri* by Shōwa Kenkyūkai in 1940. See Sakai, *Shōwa kenkyūkai*, 157.

56. Saigusa, "Tōa Kyōdōtai no ronri," *Chūō kōron* 616 (January 1939): 118.

57. Saigusa, *Bunka no kiki*, in *Saigusa Hiroto chosakushū*, 7:17–21 (originally published in 1933).

58. Saigusa, "Hensha no kotoba," 2.

59. Ibid., 16.

60. Saigusa, *Nihon no chisei to gijutsu*, in *Saigusa Hiroto chosakushū*, 10:291.

61. Ibid., 294.

62. Saigusa, "Shin yuibutsuron no tachiba," *Yuibutsuron kenkyū* 1 (1932): 8–27. Also see Saigusa, "Shizen ni tsuite," *Osaka gakuhō* (July 1933), in *Saigusa Hiroto chosakushū*, 1:397.

63. Saigusa, "Nihon kagaku bunmei shisōshi," *Nihon hyōron*, 2600th year special ed. (January 1940): 271. The year 1940 was said to be the year 2600 in Japanese mythological history.

64. *Natural Making and Human Disclosure* is my translation of *Tenkō kaibutsu*, or

T'ien kung k'ai wu. For scholarship on the encyclopedia in China, see Sung, *Chinese Technology in the Seventeenth Century.*

65. For a detailed study of this debate, see Nakamura Seiji, *Shinhan gijutsu ronsōshi.*

66. Saigusa, "Gijutsugaku no gurentsugebiito," 89.

67. Saigusa, *Gijutsu no shisō,* 119.

68. Saigusa, *Nihon no gijutsu to chisei,* 10:404.

69. Kamatani, "Saigusa Hiroto to gijutsu no kenkyū—tokuni 1937–1945 senjiki ni okeru," *Kagakushi kenkyū,* no. 75 (July–September 1965): 101–13.

70. Sakamoto, "Saigusa Hiroto shi no gijutsushi hōron," *Kagakushi kenkyū,* no. 74 (April–June 1965): 59–71.

71. Ōmori, "Saigusa Hiroto no Nihon kagaku gijutsushi kenkyū," *Kagakushi kenkyū,* no. 74 (April–June 1965): 49–58.

72. Nakayama, "History of Science," 10.

73. The club began with 180 members in 1936. According to the editor of the first issue, the magazine aimed to "develop its unique character as a general magazine [*sōgō zasshi*] entirely by scientists," to "be a magazine that is sophisticated and scientific to enrich the lives of the masses as well as scholarly significant enough for specialists to keep in their offices," and "to explore and popularize the scientific spirit." Nagata Tsuneo, "Henshū kōki," *Kagaku Pen* 1, no. 1 (October 1936): 132.

74. Yoshioka, "Nihon sūgakushi," *Kagaku Pen* 5, no. 1 (January 1940): 28–36, esp. 30–32.

75. Haga, "Nihon minzoku to kagaku," *Kagaku Pen* 5, no. 1 (January 1940): 73.

76. Ibid., 80.

77. Kamo, "Nihon kagaku shisō chōshi," *Kagaku Pen* 5, no. 1 (January 1940): 81–88.

78. Ibid., 85.

79. Nitto, "Gendai Nihon igakuron: Kinsei Nihon igakushi josetsu," *Kagaku Pen* 5, no. 1 (January 1940): 89. Nitto is best known for his wartime research that opposed the isolation of leprosy patients.

80. Ogura, *Senjika no sūgaku,* 120.

81. Ibid., 112.

82. Ibid., 2.

83. Ibid., 89–94. The obfuscation of social and military needs in Ogura's thinking was present already in the early 1930s. For example, in his 1933 article on the early Meiji period, Ogura portrayed the navy mathematicians Arakawa Shigehira and Nakagawa Masayuki positively as the opposite of the bureaucratic mathematicians at Tokyo Imperial University, for they promoted practical mathematics, the systematic translation of mathematical terms, and horizontal writing (as opposed to the traditional vertical writing) earlier than anyone else. In this analysis, the distinction between the needs of society and those of the military was blurred by the concept of applied mathematics. See Ogura, "Meiji jūnendai no sūgakkai to kaigun," *Sūgakushi kenkyū,* 1:301–9 (originally published in *Yuibutsuron kenkyū* in December 1933).

84. Ogura, "Gen jikyokuka ni okeru kagakusha no sekimu," *Chūō kōron,* April 1941 (included in Ogura, *Senjika no sūgaku*). Ogura was to lament his own wartime writings after the war: "We were being cowards, having no strong independent

mind, and yielded to power." See Ogura, "Ware kagakusha taru o hazu," *Kaizō*, January 1953, in *NKGT*, 6:462–65.

85. Nakayama, "History of Science," 10.

Chapter 6

1. The term *tsūzoku*, often combined with "education" and/or "science," was used to mean "nonacademic" or "popular" in prewar Japan. For example, when the Ministry of Education established a research committee for public education on topics such as hygiene, disaster prevention, and garbage in 1911, it was named Tsūzoku Kyōiku Chōsakai. The *Tsūzoku Kagaku* series published by Iwanami Shoten in 1921 consisted of ten introductory volumes on the relativity theory, airplanes, meteorites, and so on, for the general readership.

2. Harada, *Omoide no nanajūnen*, 150–51.

3. Ibid., 152–205.

4. The first edition of the nine-volume series of *Kodomo no kikitagaru hanashi* was published between 1920 and 1922. The popularity of the series resulted in multiple editions of many of the volumes through the 1920s. For Harada's recollection of how this series was published, see *Omoide no nanajūnen*, 177, 205.

5. Ibid., 223. As is the case with most popular magazines in prewar Japan, the actual number of sales is impossible to determine.

6. Harada wrote in his autobiography that he marketed *Children's Science* to those between eleven and fourteen years old, but the letters from the readers indicate that the readership included those up to seventeen years old. See ibid., 300.

7. See ibid., 261. Harada, *Jishin no kagaku* (Tokyo: Shinkōsha, 1923). He also published a number of books that packaged science in a compact, simplified manner for popular consumption under similar titles from the same publisher, such as *Hoshi no kagaku* (Science of Stars, 1922); *Yama no kagaku* (Science of Mountains, 1922); and *Umi no kagaku* (Science of Oceans, 1922).

8. Harada, *Kagaku gahō* 1, no. 4 (July 1923): 295.

9. Harada, "Kodomo ni kikaseru hanashidane," *Kagaku gahō* 1, no. 1 (April 1923): 53. Also see Harada, "Rika kyōiku," *Kagaku gahō* 2, no. 4 (April 1924): 320.

10. Harada, "Kodomo ni kikaseru hanashidane," 54.

11. See Harada, "Shin no zasshi," *Kagaku gahō* 1, no. 1 (April 1923): 95.

12. Okabe, "Mono ni odoroku kokoro," *Kagaku gahō* 3, no. 5 (November 1924): 496.

13. These are examples of many other issues that were titled "The Wonder of...": "Umi no kyōi, yama no kyōi" (July 1923), "Jintai kyōi gō" (November 1924), and "Seishin genshō no kyōi gō" (October 1927).

14. Harada, "Kono zasshi no yakume," *Kodomo no kagaku* 1, no. 1 (October 1924): 2.

15. Ibid.

16. Like *Science Illustrated*, many special issues of *Children's Science* included *wonder* in the title. See, for example, the October 1932 special issue, "Saishin denki no kyōi-gō" (The Wonder of the Latest Electricity), and the January 1928 special issue, "Mirai bunmei no kyōi-go" (The Wonder of Future Civilization).

17. Harada, "Umi no kyōi, yama no kyōi," *Kagaku gahō* 1, no. 4 (July 1923): 296.

18. Jordanova, *Sexual Visions*, esp. chap. 5.

19. These include the Cholera Prevention Exhibit (*korera byō yobō tsūzoku tenrankai*) of 1916, the Food Hygiene and Economy Exhibit (*shokubutsu eisei keizai tenrankai*) of 1918, and the Physical Education Exhibit (*undō taiiku tenrankai*) of 1922. Historian Tanaka Satoshi also emphasizes the entertainment spectacle in his study of Taishō and early Shōwa hygienic exhibitions in Japan. See Tanaka, *Eisei hakurankai no yokubō*.

20. These are the examples from the first issue of *Science Illustrated*, but the other issues have photos of this nature: "Tenkai no daishōtotsu—shinsei no shutsugen," "Nyūyōku no matenrō wo kasumete jūō ni tobichigau ōgata noriai hikōki," and "Afurika no yajū seikatsu wo totta mezurashiki shashin," all in *Kagaku gahō* 1, no. 1 (April 1923): 3–9.

21. See, for example, "Kodomo nimo dekiru musen denwa no juwa sōchi," *Kagaku gahō* 1, no. 3 (June 1923): 260–61; Hiroyama Matajirō, "Natsuno ryokō ni koredake wa kansatsu subeshi," *Kagaku gahō* 1, no. 4 (July 1924); "Kōkūkai no otona to kodomo," *Kagaku gahō* 2, no. 5 (May 1924); *Jintai kyōi-gō* (special issue), *Kagaku gahō* 3, no. 5 (November 1924); Okabe, "Iwayuru sei no nayami," *Kagaku gahō* 5, no. 5 (December 1925): 468–78; and Yamamoto Issei, "Saikin tenmongaku ni okeru chinbun," *Kagaku gahō* 11, no. 3 (September 1928).

22. Yoshimi, *Hakurankai no seijigaku*, 141.

23. These science magazines were in the category called "integrated magazines" (*sōgō zasshi*), which usually refers to such monthly journals and magazines as *Kaizō*, *Chūō kōron*, and *Shufu no tomo* because they covered a variety of topics that included social issues, literature, films, and human interest stories. It is beyond my current project to examine these "integrated magazines," but a future study on this genre may find the same lineage that I discern between the world's fair and the popular science magazines.

24. One of the attractions of the Columbus World Exposition in Chicago was its anthropology villages, where the villages of American Indians, African tribes, Asian and Middle Eastern tribes, and the German and Celt villages were physically arranged so that the most "advanced" German and Celt villages were closest to the White City, a symbol of civilization. Visitors were encouraged to start the tour of these villages from the point farthest from the White City to appreciate the progress of civilization. The succeeding world's fairs as well as Japanese domestic exhibitions copied this style in their colonial displays. See Rydell, *All the World's a Fair*. For the colonial display of the Tokyo Taishō Exhibit (*Tokyo Taishō hakurankai*) and other Japanese domestic exhibitions, see Yoshimi, *Hakurankai no seijigaku*, 212–14.

25. A comparison of three consecutive cover illustrations of *Science Illustrated* in 1928 provides one example for this. The cover of the July 1928 issue illustrated a group of goose barnacles (a kind of seashell), whose name comes from their unique shape; on the following month's cover was a group of New Guinean natives with unique and colorful ceremonial costumes; and the September cover was an illustration of Saturn as seen from Mars. New Guinean natives appeared, in other words, as just as much a part of nature as goose barnacles and Saturn.

26. Yoshimi, *Hakurankai no seijigaku*, 146–52. Regarding the Arabian Pavilion and Joan of Arc, see ibid., 150.

27. These exceptions include Maedagawa Kōichirō, "Puroretariaato to kagaku—bungakuteki ni mite," *Kagaku gahō* 14, no. 6 (June 1930): 1115–20, which argued that the lack of scientific nature in Japanese literature was a reflection of the legacy of Tokugawa feudalism in Japanese society and demanded opening up science to the proletariat; and Asō Hiroshi, "Shizen kagaku to shakai kagaku—shakaijin no mita kagakukan," *Kagaku gahō* 15, no. 5 (November 1930): 827, which contended that the most urgent task for today's human beings was to promote the development of social sciences so that the fruits of natural sciences could be used for the happiness of all humans in a most rational manner. These articles, however, were published together with anti-Marxist or anti-Soviet arguments. Asō's article, for example, was in the same issue that carried Akagaki Yoshiaki's "Atheist Museum," which criticized the Soviet Union for idolizing Lenin while suppressing religions. See Akagaki, "Mushinron hakubutsukan," *Kagaku gahō* 15, no. 5 (November 1930): 1027–30. The story about a poor boy who became a vitamin specialist is in Nojima Ryōichi, "Kagaku shōsetsu shokubutsu no hakken," *Kodomo no kagaku* 15, no. 1 (January 1932): 126–29; and Nojima, "Kagaku shōsetsu shokubutsu no hakken," *Kodomo no kagaku* 15, no. 3 (March 1932): 66–70.

28. See, for example, Harada, "Waraubeki gakusha no taido," *Kagaku gahō* 2, no. 3 (March 1924): 222.

29. Okabe, "Minkan no gakusha," *Kagaku gahō* 7, no. 4 (October 1926): 471.

30. "Kokuhōteki misaki no kuma-san ni kaitei no shinpi wo kiku," *Kagaku gahō* 20, no. 3 (March 1933): 441–49.

31. For how supernatural phenomena, which captured the attention of many academics and intellectuals in mid-Meiji Japan, came to be regarded as an illegitimate field of modern science by the end of the Meiji period, see Figal, *Civilization and Monsters*; Kawamura Kunimitsu, *Genshi suru kindai kūkan*; and Ichiyanagi, *Saiminjutsu no Nihon kindai*.

32. Fujisawa Eihiko's "Bakeru kemono: Densetsujō no jinjū konkō" was serialized in *Kagaku gahō* 1, nos. 4–6 (July–September 1923). Also see Furukawa Kojō, "Yūrei no mieru wake," *Kagaku gahō* 2, no. 6 (June 1924): 598–600.

33. This experiment, *shinrei kagaku jikken*, was held jointly with *Scientific Knowledge* and *Shufu no tomo* (Friends of Housewives), the most popular magazine for housewives in Taishō Japan. The process and result of this experiment, which ended in failure, were reported in Okabe, "Honshi kōen shinrei kagaku jikkenkai," *Kagaku gahō* 6, no. 3 (March 1926): 352–53.

34. Asano Wasaburō et al., "Shinrei mondai zadankai," *Kagaku gahō* 20, no. 6 (June 1929): 896–904. The photographs of ghosts and spirits were another popular topic; most articles were intended to prove the falseness of these photos, but some, like Fukurai Tomokichi's, argued they were real. See, for example, Fukurai, "Futatabi jintsūriki no sonzai ni tsuite—Nagao fujin no tameni kabuto o nugu," *Kagaku gahō* 10, no. 2 (February 1928): 322–27, 366.

35. See, for example, the January 1930 special issue of *Science Illustrated* titled "The Scientific Analysis of Superstitions" (*Meishin no kagakuteki kaibō*).

36. Harada, "Hyōron mochiya wa mochiya," *Kagaku gahō* 1, no. 1 (April 1923): 2.

37. For example, see "Kodomo nimo dekiru musen denwa no juwa sōchi," 260–61. For these amateur radio fans, see Yoshimi, *"Koe" no shihonshugi*.

38. *Children's Science* also held a "Science Experiment Report Contest." See "Sōkan goshūnen kinen daikenshō, kagaku jikken kiji nyūsen happyō," *Kodomo no kagaku* 11, no. 1 (January 1930): 126–27. The Invention Consulting Room was in every issue of both magazines. For the model-making contests, see, for example, "Mokei no kuni tenrankai," *Kodomo no kagaku* 6, no. 6 (December 1927): 34–60; "Kodomo no kagaku seisakuten," *Kodomo no kagaku* 10, no. 5 (November 1929): 25–50; "Dai sankai kodomo no kagaku seisakuhinten," *Kodomo no kagaku* 14, no. 5 (November 1931): 7–18; and "Dan yonkai mokei no kuni taikai," *Kodomo no kagaku* 18, no. 5 (November 1933): 9–48.

39. *Illustrated London News* (December 19, 1931), quoted in the museum newsletter, Tokyo Kagaku Hakubutsukan, *Shizen kagaku to hakubutsukan*, March 1932: 4. "Renovated" here is clearly a mistake by the London newspaper reporter.

40. Quoted in Tokyo Kagaku Hakubutsukan, *Shizen kagaku to hakubutsukan*, March 1932: 4–5.

41. Aramata Hiroshi introduced an episode about the Shōwa emperor's biological research and the military. Some in the military were not too happy that the Shōwa emperor, the nation's top commander, spent his time on biological research. One day, around the time of the 2.26 Incident of 1936, the emperor collected plankton on the way from maneuvers in Hokkaido and asked the navy if the current had changed because the plankton he collected were different from the usual. Unable to answer his question, the navy dispatched a research group and found that the current had indeed changed. Aramata states that since this incident, the military stopped complaining about the emperor's research. See Aramata, *Daitōa kagaku kidan*, 377.

42. For the photo of the telescope Hirohito "loved to use," see "Sesshō no miya denka goaiyō no tentai bōenkyō," *Kagaku gahō* 7, no. 3 (September 1926): 205.

43. Harada, "*Kagaku gahō* no kōei," *Kagaku gahō* 2, no. 3 (March 1924): n.p.

44. The reader learned about the exhibit in detail in articles like "Ueno kōen ni shinchiku ni natta Tokyo Kagaku Hakubutsukan," *Kodomo no kagaku* 15, no. 1 (January 1932): 71–73. For the Museum Foundation Day and the Edo Science Exhibit, see Tokyo Kagaku Hakubutsukan, *Shizen kagaku to hakubutsukan*, November 1932: 13.

45. Tokyo Kagaku Hakubutsukan, *Shizen kagaku to hakubutsukan*, November 1933: 4–5; December 1933: 21. Several of the multivolume series of *Eiga Amerika kenkokushi* (the original title, *Chronicles of America*, by Yale University Press in 1923) were shown every day during the ten-day exhibit. The five volumes of *Manshūkoku no zenbō*, produced by the Manchuria Railway's public relations bureau, were shown only on November 3, but another film, *Kagaku no senshi* (Warriors of Science), about a group of scientists going on a research trip to Manchuria, was shown on November 12, the last day of the exhibit.

Although the museum newsletter did not provide any information about the "first Japanese television," this was probably televised broadcasting demonstrated by Takayanagi Kenjirō (1899–1990), the first Japanese to successfully transmit visual images in 1926.

46. "Aidokusha kara," *Kodomo no kagaku* 1, no. 3 (December 1924): 77.

47. Ibid. 2, no. 1 (January 1925): 88, 89.

48. Ibid. 2, no. 4 (April 1925): 78. *Nihon shōnen*, published by Jitsugyō no Nihon since 1906, and *Shōnen kurabu*, published by Kōdansha since 1914, were two of the

most popular magazines for boys during the 1920s and 1930s. These magazines attracted readers with serialized fiction and covers illustrated by popular illustrators; they did not carry articles about science. It seems that many *Children's Science* readers felt a sense of competition toward these magazines. One reader asked the editor to publish *Children's Science* earlier in the month, around the tenth, when *Boys' Club* and *The Japanese Boy* came out so that he would not be empty-handed while his friends were reading these magazines. "Danwashitsu," *Kodomo no kagaku* 3, no. 2 (February 1926): 83.

49. Harada recalls that as the magazine became popular, he received more than one hundred letters a day. This may be his own exaggeration; however, considering that the magazine eventually hired a person specifically to sort out the readers' letters, the number of letters sent every month must have been enormous. See Harada, *Omoide no nanajūnen*, 301.

50. "Aidokusha kara," *Kodomo no kagaku* 4, no. 2 (April 1925): 334–35.

51. "Danwashitsu," *Kodomo no kagaku* 21, no. 1 (January 1935): 114.

52. Ibid. 19, no. 2 (February 1934): 131.

53. "Aidokusha kara," *Kodomo no kagaku* 2, no. 1 (January 1925): 89; "Honshi ni taisuru kibō to chūmon," *Kodomo no kagaku* 2, no. 3 (March 1925): 82; and "Honshi ni taisuru kibō to chūmon," *Kodomo no kagaku* 2, no. 4 (April 1925): 82.

54. "Danwashitsu," *Kodomo no kagaku* 19, no. 6 (June 1934): 118.

55. See, for example, ibid. 14, no. 3 (September 1931): 135; and ibid. 19, no. 3 (March 1934): 130.

56. See, for example, a letter from a boy stating, "People wrongly think that *Children's Science* is a magazine for boys. Girls, hang in there!" in ibid. 19, no. 2 (February 1934): 131.

57. For example, see ibid. 20, no. 2 (August 1934): 122–23; and *Kodomo no kagaku* 20, no. 6 (December 1934): 114–15.

58. "Danwashitsu," *Kodomo no kagaku* 20, no. 4 (October 1934): 118.

59. Ibid. 21, no. 9 (September 1935): 114.

60. Ibid. 18, no. 6 (December 1933): 129; and ibid. 19, no. 1 (January 1934): 135.

61. Ibid. 20, no. 2 (August 1934): 122; and ibid. 20, no. 4 (October 1934): 119.

62. "Aidokusha kara," *Kodomo no kagaku* 2, no. 3 (March 1925): 78–79.

63. See, for example, "Kodomo no kagakukai—chihōbukai hōkoku," *Kodomo no kagaku* 2, no. 8 (August 1925): 84.

64. Harada, "Dokusha shokun e!!" *Kodomo no kagaku* 2, no. 6 (June 1925): 83. The "Reports from Children's Science Groups" section began in the August 1925 issue.

65. "Danwashitsu," *Kodomo no kagaku* 19, no. 5 (May 1934); and ibid. 20, no. 5 (November 1934): 111.

66. "Nihon chiri shashin (3) Taiwan no fūbutsu," *Kodomo no kagaku* 3, no. 1 (January 1926): 40–41; "Manshū de hakkutsu sareru kōbutsu," *Kodomo no kagaku* 15, no. 6 (June 1932): 35–39; "Taiwan no konseiki kōzan," *Kodomo no kagaku* 18, no. 6 (December 1933): 98–101; "Nihon san gyorui no bunpuzu," *Kodomo no kagaku* 16, no. 2 (August 1932): 3; and "Nihon kakushu musenkyoku bunpuzu," *Kodomo no kagaku* 16, no. 4 (October 1932): 6.

67. Harada, "'Kodomo no kagaku' no yakume," *Kodomo no kagaku* 6, no. 5 (November 1927): 2.

68. The London Naval Arms Limitation Agreement, like the Washington Naval Arms Limitation Agreement of 1922, put Japan's Imperial Navy in a subordinate position vis-à-vis Britain and the United States. For the domestic effects of these agreements, see Samuels, *"Rich Nation, Strong Army,"* 96–97, 113–15.

69. "Henshūkyoku dayori," *Kodomo no kagaku* 15, no. 2 (February 1932): 134; and "Nishikichō yori," *Kagaku gahō* 20, no. 4 (April 1933): 700.

70. "Saishin heiki to shōraisen zadankai," *Kagaku gahō* 12, no. 4 (April 1929): 584–96.

71. "Saishin heiki tokubetsu-gō" (special issue on the latest weaponry), *Kagaku gahō* 12, no. 4 (April 1929).

72. Iwasaki Tamio, "Saishin kagakusensenjō no kyōi," *Kagaku gahō* 16, no. 5 (May 1931): 788–810.

73. For example, the February 1932 issue was titled "Saishin kagaku heiki-gō" (The Latest Scientific Weapons); the May 1935 issue, "Sekai rekkyō kūgun-gō" (The World Powers' Air Forces); the October 1935 issue, "Rikugun saikin heiki-gō" (The Army's Latest Weapons); and the June 1937 issue, "Ōru kaigun-gō" (All about the Navy). The April 1936 issue came with a separate photo book on the Imperial Navy.

74. Hayakawa Seiji, "Gunkan mokei shinsa no kansō," *Kodomo no kagaku* 18, no. 5 (November 1933): 10–11; Sekitani Ken'ya, "Shōsen shinsa no kansō," *Kodomo no kagaku* 18, no. 5 (November 1933): 12–13; and "Henshūkyoku dayori," *Kodomo no kagaku* 18, no. 5 (November 1933): 124.

75. Prewar Japanese science fiction has mostly been studied by nonacademic scholars Yokota Jun'ya and Aizu Shingo. See Yokota, *Meiji wandaa kagakukan;* Yokota, *Meiji "kūsō shōsetsu" korekushon;* and Yokota, *Nihon SF koten koten.* See also Aizu, *Nihon kagaku shōsetsu nenpyō;* and several volumes edited by Aizu and Yokota in *Shōnen shōsetsu taikei,* which contain Taishō and early Shōwa science fiction.

76. Tsurumi, "Senji ha isshoku dewa nai, soshite imamo," 4–5.

77. Saeki, "Gunji roman no kisetsu," 176.

78. According to Yokota, there were three "science fiction booms" before 1945: the 1870s–80s, of Verne's translated works; the 1900s–1910s, of science adventure fiction such as Oshikawa Shunrō; and 1935–45, of military science fiction. Yokota, *Nihon SF koten koten,* 3:208.

79. For a comprehensive history of American science fiction, see Cheng, "Amazing, Astounding, Wonder."

80. For the role *Science Illustrated* and *New Youth* played in the history of Japanese science fiction, see Yokota, " 'Shinseinen' to 'kagaku gahō,' " in *Nihon SF koten koten,* 2:121–37. Yokota quotes Harada, stating that "when I first began *Science Illustrated,* Unno Jūza asked me to develop science fiction with him. I bought Gernsback's *Amazing Stories* from the U.S. every issue, but my English was not good enough and I gave up. I gave all the copies of this magazine to my friend from junior high, Kozakai Fuboku," who became a popular science fiction writer. Quoted in Yokota, *Nihon SF koten koten,* 2:127.

The "science fiction prize contests" (*kagaku shōsetsu kenshō*) were held in 1927, 1928, and 1930 in *Science Illustrated.* See "Kenshō kagaku shōsetsu boshū," *Kagaku gahō* 9, no. 6 (December 1927): n.p.; "Sengo ni," *Kagaku gahō* 10, no. 1 (January 1928): 222; *Kagaku gahō* 11, no. 3 (September 1928): 656; and "Kenshō kagaku shōsetsu boshū, kagaku chūshin no shinbungei undō," *Kagaku gahō* 15, no. 1 (July 1930): n.p.

81. For the Japanese Marxist discussion on proletarian arts and literature, see Silverberg, *Changing Song*.

82. Yajima, "'Kagaku bungaku' sonota," *Yuibutsuron kenkyū* 23 (September 1934): 48–49, 54. Yajima wrote *Science Literature* as one volume of the Iwanami World Literature Lecture series (1932–34) in 1933.

83. Critics and scholars have reached no agreement on a definition of science fiction. Recent works that discuss its definition include Freedman, *Critical Theory and Science Fiction*; James, *Science Fiction in the Twentieth Century*; Booker, *Dystopia Literature*; Bainbridge, *Dimensions of Science Fiction*; and Barron, *Anatomy of Wonder*. For a recent Japanese-language discussion on science fiction, see Morishita, *Shikōsuru monogatari*. Morishita characterizes the essence of science fiction as "the sense of wonder" on pp. 16–17.

84. According to Edward James, the phrase first appeared in 1851 in the work of William Wilson and was also mentioned in a 1927 editorial response to a letter to *Amazing Stories*, but it was after 1929 that "science fiction" came to be used explicitly as a genre. James, *Science Fiction in the Twentieth Century*, 6.

85. From the January 1925 issue on, *Science Illustrated* carried a series of translated science fiction in the "Kagaku Shōsetsu" section, starting with Edgar Allan Poe. From the September 1927 issue on, it began to introduce Japanese science fiction; the first to appear was "Kagaku shōsetsu: Ningen no tamago" (Science Fiction: Human Eggs), a black comedy about a near future when a genius scientist makes it possible for humans to hatch eggs rather than go through the nine months of pregnancy, by a medical doctor and writer, Takada Giichirō. See *Kagaku gahō* 9, no. 1 (September 1927): 143–47.

86. One difficulty lies in the fact that the genre overlaps with many other genres, such as detective novels, fantasy stories, and time-machine travelogues, whose interactions have kept the genre dynamic and elusive. Thus, abstracting a fixed definition of science fiction from its relatively short yet dynamic history could end with the violation of historical sensitivity. For example, Ishikawa Takashi, one of the best-known scholars of science fiction in Japan, considers *Kojiki* (Record of Ancient Matters, 712), the oldest book in Japan, as the first work of science fiction, based on his definition of the genre as the literature of the "fantastic" (*fushigi*). See Ishikawa, "Nihon SF-shi no kokoromi," 120–37. I find such an approach anachronistic.

87. Unno, *Chikyū tōnan* (1937), quoted in Yokota, *Nihon SF koten koten*, 2:222.

88. Quoted in Yokota, *Nihon SF koten koten*, 2:340–41.

89. Edogawa, "Tantei shōsetsu to kagaku seishin," *Kagaku Pen* 1, no. 4 (January 1937): 19–20.

90. Nakajima, "'Shinseinen' sanjūnenshi," 5:351.

91. I rely on the 1975 reprint of the 1944 paperback, Unno, *Ukabu hikōtō*.

92. Ibid., 54, 68–69, 86, 95.

93. Ibid., 129.

94. Ibid., 35, 39, 53, 169, 268–69.

95. See, for example, Honda, *The Nanjing Massacre*; and Gibney, *Sensō*, esp. chap. 2, "Life in the Military."

96. Unno, *Ukabu hikōtō*, 281.

97. Unno, "Sakusha no kotoba," in *Ukabu hikōtō*, 284.

98. Unno, *Ukabu hikōtō*, 143.

99. Honda, "Senji ni okeru kokorogake," and Kotake, "Kuni o aisuru kagakusha," *Kodomo no kagaku* 24, no. 1 (January 1938): 14–15, 16–21.

100. Unno's "Kaitei tairiku" was serialized from April 1937 (vol. 23, no. 4) through December 1938 (vol. 24, no. 12) in *Children's Science*.

101. Kigi Takatarō was a pen name of Hayashi Takashi, a medical doctor at Keiō University. He had studied conditioned reflex under Ivan Pavlov at the Leningrad Experimental Medical Laboratory in 1932; although he was never involved in Marxist politics, his stay in the Soviet Union might explain the centralized, technocratic utopia he portrayed in *The Flag of the Green Rising Sun*. In the 1930s and early 1940s, he wrote many essays and articles on science as well as science fiction, with the encouragement of Unno, who gave him the pen name.

Kigi's *The Flag of the Green Rising Sun* was serialized first in *Children's Science*, from January 1939 to September 1940, and in *Gakusei no kagaku* (Students' Science) in October 1940. From the October 1940 issue on, the content of *Children's Science* was published under a new name, *Students' Science*, while *Children's Science* changed its content to target younger readers such as upper elementary schoolchildren. I am working from the serialized version in the magazines, but the story was also published in paperback in 1941 and is reprinted in *Kūsō kagaku shōsetsu shū*, 339–424.

102. Kigi, "Midori no nisshōki," *Kodomo no kagaku* 25, no. 10 (October 1939): 52.

103. Regarding the age-based system, see ibid., 51–52. For technologies such as the "illumirie," the moving walkway, and television shopping, see, for example, *Kodomo no kagaku* 15, no. 7 (July 1939): 48–52; ibid. 26, no. 3 (March 1940): 50–52; and ibid. 26, no. 4 (April 1940): 50–51. Regarding the political party, see ibid. 26, no. 3 (March 1940): 431. References to the "scientific" research method are in ibid. 25, no. 12 (December 1939): 49.

104. Ibid. 25, no. 12 (December 1939): 49; and ibid. 26, no. 3 (March 1940): 251.

105. Ibid. 26, no. 4 (April 1940): 52; ibid. 26, no. 6 (June 1940): 52; and ibid. 26, no. 7 (July 1940): 50–51.

106. Sano Hide, "Otto Unno Jūza no omoide," *Geppō* 4, 1.

107. Kigi, "Midori no nisshōki," 49.

108. *Kodomo no kagaku* 25, no. 7 (July 1939): 52.

109. Chizuko illustrations were inserted in almost every segment. For her role at the end of the story, see *Gakusei no kagaku*, October 1940: 48–51.

110. Ikeda Saburo, "Joshi Kagaku Juku," *Kagaku gahō* 28, no. 4 (April 1939): 89–90.

111. Ibid., 92.

112. "Kokumin gurafu o zen kokumin ni suisensuru," *Kokumin kagaku gurafu* 1, no. 1 (December 1941): n.p.

113. "Daidokoro no kagaku: Okusama to jochū-san mondō," *Kokumin kagaku gurafu* 1, no. 1 (December 1941): 6–7; "Jogakusei o dou kagaku saseru?" *Kokumin kagaku gurafu* 2, no. 9 (September 1942): 15–20; and "Josei no midashinami, ikebana no kagaku," *Kokumin kagaku gurafu* 3, no. 1 (January 1943): 22–23.

114. For the wartime mobilization of female labor, see Miyake, "Doubling Expectations."

115. For example, see "Joshi kikaikō hodōsho miru," *Kagaku gahō* 29, no. 8 (August 1940): 44–45; Hukushima Tsuyuko, "Washi suku machi," *Kagaku gahō* 29, no. 9 (September 1940); and Matsuda Keiko, "Eiyōshoku kateino naka he," *Kagaku gahō* 29, no. 11 (November 1940): 100–104.

116. Harada was asked to be the adviser in 1942 by the Science Mobilization Association (*kagaku dōinkai*), a government organization. See Harada, *Omoide no nanajūnen*, 344.

117. Harada, "Kumo, kiri, tsuyu, oyobi shimo wa doushite dekiruka," *Kokumin kagaku gurafu* 2, no. 11 (November 1942): 18–19; Harada, "Tsuki no kao," *Kokumin kagaku gurafu* 3, no. 9 (September 1943): 3; and Harada, "Netsu riyō no konjaku," *Kokumin kagaku gurafu* 4, no. 1 (January 1944): 10–11.

118. For a detailed examination of the Nomonhan Incident which took place near the northwestern border of Manchuria, see Coox, *Nomonhan*.

119. For the imperial military's efforts to develop the latest weapons and defense industry, such as the "Zero Fighter," see Samuels, *"Rich Nation, Strong Army,"* chaps. 3–4.

120. I am translating *kokumin* as "national people" here because the aim of the new *kokumin* school was to create ideal imperial subjects loyal to the emperor and devoted to the nation, that is, the people as defined by the national wartime needs and ideology.

121. For more details of the edict, see Nagahama, *Shiryō kokka to kyōiku*, 10:226–27.

122. Ethics was necessary "to learn the national spirit, to establish a belief in the national body, and to raise consciousness of the imperial nation's mission"; physical education, "to obtain active and strong minds and bodies as well as the ability to provide service to the nation"; art, "to obtain sophisticated aesthetic sensitivity and the artistic and technical ability to express"; and occupational learning, "to stay on one job and possess enthusiasm for devoting oneself to the nation through one's occupation." From *Kokumin gakkō kyōsokuan setsumei yōkō*, in Nagahama, *Shiryō kokka to kyōiku*, 174.

123. Nagahama, *Shiryō kokka to kyōiku*, 387.

124. Quoted in ibid., 392.

125. Quoted in Itakura, *Nihon rika kyōikushi*, 373. For an overview of the entire curriculum of Nature Studies, see ibid., 372.

126. Quoted in ibid., 375.

127. *Kyōiku shingikai shimon daiichigō tokubetsu iinkai kaigiroku* (1938), in *NKGT*, 10:228–29. This council was established by the Konoe cabinet in 1937 and held a series of meetings beginning on December 23, 1937, to discuss the coming education reform. See *NKGT*, 10:215–20.

128. Quoted in Itakura, *Nihon rika kyōikushi*, 352.

129. Monbushō, *Kokumin gakkōrei shikō kisoku* (1941) in *NKGT*, 10:227.

130. Monbushō, *Shizen no kansatsu*, 3.

131. Ibid., 1.

132. Ibid., 3.

133. Shimomura, "Risūka ni tsuite," in *NKGT*, 3:235.

134. For a more detailed summary of Hashida's *Gyō to shite no kagaku* (Science as Practice, 1939), see my discussion in Chapter 2.

135. See, for example, Hashida, *Kagaku suru kokoro*. The content of this work, published by the Ministry of Education, is very similar to that of his 1939 work mentioned previously. The expression "do science" has been revived in present-day Japan as part of the state promotion of science and technology.

136. The Korean children who were reading *Children's Science* also received Nature Studies education. In 1942, schools in Korea were also renamed National People's Schools, and the curriculum was reformed in accordance with the same five categories as in Japan proper. The Korean version of the *Teacher's Manual for the Observation of Nature* was the same as the *naichi* version; the only difference was that the Korean version had an extra introduction that explained the role of National People's Schools in the general education of Korea, emphasizing the slogan *naisen icchi* (unity of Japan and Korea). See Chōsen Sōtokufu, *Shizen no kansatsu*.

137. The most notable figure is Hayashi Hakutarō, one of the earliest science education reformers in Japan, who had taught at Tokyo Imperial University. The Ministry of Education appointed him chair of the council. Hayashi had been extremely critical of Sakurai Jōji, the chair of the Science Textbook Compilation Committee (*rikasho hensan iinkai*), a Ministry of Education committee that had been in charge of science curricula; after Hayashi became chair of the educational deliberative council, the committee was dissolved, and Sakurai lost his influence. See *NKGT*, 10:221. For details of the education reform movement by the Study Group of Education Science (*kyōiku kagaku kenkyūkai*), a leftist group of education reformers, in the 1930s and its involvement in the total war system since 1940, see Satō Hiromi, *Sōryokusen taisei to kyōiku kagaku*.

138. Oka Genjirō, one of the Ministry of Education officers involved in drafting Nature and Mathematics Studies, later stated that he and his colleagues especially looked at textbooks used in Nagano Prefecture, Korea, and Taiwan. Since they were outside the influence of the Ministry of Education (Nagano Prefecture had compiled its own science textbook, and Korea and Taiwan had their own textbooks published by the colonial governments), their science education had been more progressive. Oka, "Teigakunen rika seitei no ikisatsu," in *Rika no kyōiku* (February 1956), quoted in Hori, *Nihon no rika kyōikushi*, 3:932–33, 938.

139. Ogura, "Sūgaku kyōiku sasshin no tameni," in *Senjika no sūgaku*, 176.

140. From Oka, *Rika no kyōiku*, quoted in Hori, *Nihon no rika kyōikushi*, 3:938–39.

141. Itakura, *Nihon rika kyōikushi*, 368. Terakawa Tomosuke, a scholar of Japanese education, also argues that science education between 1941 and 1945, unlike other subjects that were extremely nationalistic and militaristic, was a landmark in the history of elementary science education. Terakawa identifies wartime Science and Mathematics Studies as a positive step toward postwar science education. See Terakawa, "Waga kuni ni okeru shotōka rika kyōiku no senkan," 149, 151.

142. It is ironic, however, that the worsened war situation after 1943 drove schoolchildren out to factories and fields to compensate for the lack of labor, preventing them from receiving the National People's School education that the wartime government had initiated.

Conclusion

1. Ōnuma, Fujii, and Katō, *Sengo Nihon kagakusha undōshi*, 2:16. Admiral Suzuki became prime minister in April 1945, and his cabinet dissolved on August 18, 1945.
2. Quoted in Yanabu, *Ichigo no jiten: Bunka*, 6.
3. Nakayama, *Kagaku gijutsu no sengoshi*, 9.
4. Ibid.
5. Nakatani, *Kagaku to shakai*, 5.
6. "Kagaku gijutsusha no hansei to honshi no shimei," *Kagaku gijutsu* 6, no. 3 (1947): n.p.
7. Possibly the only ones who were interested in Japan's wartime science, besides scientists themselves, were the U.S. Occupation personnel. Although their final judgment was that Japan had not made scientific and technological achievements significant enough either to launch another war against the United States soon or to attract American scientists, the Occupation authority confiscated facilities and prohibited various projects that were or could be even remotely related to war. The most famous episode was probably the destruction of the cyclotron at Riken. The cyclotron itself could not produce an atomic bomb, and Japanese scientists had already given up on making an atomic bomb before the end of the war. Despite the petition from Japanese scientists and their sympathizers abroad, the Occupation authority nonetheless destroyed the facility.
8. Watanabe Yoshimichi, "Nihon kagaku no rekishiteki kankyō to Minshushugi Kagakusha no tōmen no ninmu," in *Minshushugi kagaku*, vol. 1, quoted in Umeda, "Minshushugi Kagakusha Kyōkai sōritsu gojūnen ni yosete," *Rekishi hyōron*, no. 549 (January 1996): 74.
9. Ogura, "Minshushugi to shizen kagakusha," in *Kagaku no shihyō*, 24 (originally published in *Tokyo shinbun*, January 27 and 28, 1946).
10. Ogura, "Shizen kagakusha no hansei," in *Kagaku no shihyō*, 18 (originally published in *Sekai*, April 1946).
11. Ogura, "Minshushugi to shizen kagakusha," 25.
12. Hiroshige, *Kagaku to rekishi*, 72.
13. What was also common among all these postwar discourses of science, including Ogura's, was that the "war" meant the war with the United States. There was no reflection on Japan's war with China or the colonization of Asia. If Japan had been more scientific, according to their logic, everything would have been fine, because Japan would have either won the Pacific War or never started it in the first place—thus, by implication, would not have lost its colonies. Ogura never mentioned colonialism in his critique of Japanese science and capitalism. This is despite the fact that there were a few Minka members, such as historian Watanabe Yoshimichi (though their critique did not include any discussion of science), who did directly criticize Japanese colonialism in Asia. See Ōnuma, Fujii, and Katō, *Sengo Nihon kagakusha undōshi*, 2:17–18. Ogura's idealization of the democratic nature of Western science can also explain why he did not criticize the link between science and colonialism, because the Western powers had also been colonial powers. It is fair to point out that Western scholarship, too, did not begin the critical exploration of the connection between science and imperialism until the 1980s. Daniel Headrick's *Tools of Empire* was one of the earliest works, followed by a now-expansive scholarship that examines the

relationship between Western imperialism and the development of various fields of science and technology, especially in the nineteenth and twentieth centuries.

14. Oguma Eiji's book on the postwar discourse of nationalism details these experiences in the first chapter. I agree with Oguma that the postwar discourse should not be analyzed as simply what was said after the war but as a discourse firmly rooted in wartime experiences. Oguma, *"Minshu" to "aikoku."*

15. Ogura was to lament his own wartime writings after the war: "We were being cowards, having no strong independent mind, and yielded to power." Ogura, "Ware kagakusha taru o hazu," in *NKGT*, 6:462–65.

16. Tomizuka, *Kagaku Nihon no kōsō*, 3; and *Kagaku Nihon no kensetsu*.

17. For example, see Itakura, *Nihon rika kyōikushi*; and Terakawa, "Waga kuni ni okeru shotōka rika kyōiku no senkan," 149, 151.

18. Ogura, *Kagaku no shihyō*. Also see Yajima Toshinori, *Kagakuteki danpen*; Sugai, *Kagaku kotohajime*; and Takeuchi, *Hyakuman'nin no kagaku*.

19. Ōyodo, *Gijutsu kanryō no seiji sankaku*, 190–91.

20. The Ministry of Home Affairs was dissolved by the Occupation Army's General Headquarters (GHQ) in December 1947. For more information about the establishment of the Ministry of Construction, see Ōyodo, *Gijutsu kanryō no seiji sankaku*, 194–96.

21. Tokyo Imperial University changed its name to the University of Tokyo in 1947. The other imperial universities also dropped "imperial" from their names at the same time.

22. Watanabe, *Science and Cultural Exchange*, 344. Also see Watanabe, *Japanese and Western Science*, which is based on the same conception of "uniquely Japanese science." The latter work is a translation of Watanabe's 1976 publication in Japanese. His other major publications include *Bunka to shiteno kindai kagaku* and *Kindai kagaku to kirisuto kyō*.

23. Watanabe, *Science and Cultural Exchange*, 354.

24. Many of them received national and international recognition and became leading figures in public health, occupying such positions as chief of the Entomology Section of the Health and Welfare Ministry's Preventive Health Research Laboratories, director of the National Cancer Center, president of Japan's Medical Association, and heads of various divisions of the National Institute of Health. For Unit 731, see Harris, *Factories of Death*; and Tsuneyoshi, *Kieta saikin butai*. For the *Day's Japan* article, see Harris, *Factories of Death*, 132–33.

25. Zuoyue Wang has also independently used the term "scientific nationalism" in his historical analysis of the Science Society of China. Wang explains the concept as follows: "'scientific nationalism' here is used to describe Chinese scientists' desire to create a strong, unified, and prosperous Chinese nation, free from foreign domination, based in part on the utilization of science and technology. In this sense, Chinese scientific nationalism is slightly different from, for example, the feeling of Japanese scientists who wanted their science to excel at the international level or that of German scientists who sought to use their superior science to redeem Germany's place in the world following World War I." See Wang, "Saving China through Science," *Osiris* 17 (2002): 299.

26. "Aryan physics" was reactionary and polemical, without much substance to

offer; in fact, even the Nazi government later ceased to support Lénárd and Stark and instead employed the new "Jewish" physics for its nuclear project. See Walker, *Nazi Science*; and Beyerchen, *Scientists under Hitler*.

27. Joravsky, *The Lysenko Affair*; Graham, *Science and Philosophy in the Soviet Union*; and Graham, *What Have We Learned?*

28. For more on battles on the scientific front during the cold war, see Leslie, *Cold War and American Science*; and Wang, *American Science in an Age of Anxiety*.

29. See Brownnell, *Training the Body for China*; Hsu, *Innovation in Chinese Medicine*; and Nanda, *Prophets Facing Backward*. On how colonial India dealt with the authority of Western science, see Prakash, *Another Reason*. Another example of recent scientific nationalism is the "scientific nationalism" program that the Ukrainian government introduced to higher education in the 1990s. See Bystrytsky, "Why 'Nationalism' Cannot Be a Science," *Political Thought*, no. 2 (1994): 136–42.

30. The classic example of this debate is the one between Ernest Gellner and Anthony Smith, two major scholars of nationalism. See Gellner, *Nations and Nationalism*; and Smith, *Theories of Nationalism*. For an overview of scholarship on nationalism, see Hutchinson and Smith, *Nationalism*. For an important exception, see Crawford, *Nationalism and Internationalism in Science*.

31. For Japanese cultural nationalism, see Harootunian, *Overcome by Modernity*; Shirane and Suzuki, *Inventing the Classics*; Sakai, *Translation and Subjectivity*; Pincus, *Authenticating Culture in Imperial Japan*; and Doak, *Dreams of Difference*. For linguistic nationalism, see I, *"Kokugo" to iu shisō*; Koyasu, "'Kokugo' wa shishite 'Nihongo' wa umaretaka"; Osa, *Kindai Nihon to kokugo nashonarizumu*; Kawamura Minato, *Umi o watatta Nihongo*; and Kang, *Shokuminchi shihai to Nihongo*.

32. The modernization theorists, such as Edwin Reischauer, Marius Jansen, and John W. Hall, argued that Japan went "astray" after the failure of Taishō democracy. Reischauer, "What Went Wrong?" 489–510; Jansen, "On Studying the Modernization of Japan," *Asian Cultural Studies* 3 (1962): 1–11; and Hall, "Changing Conceptions of the Modernization of Japan," 7–41. Japanese Marxist scholars as well as modernist Maruyama Masao have argued that "Taishō democracy" was ineffective because Japan was never on the right track of modernization in the first place. Both groups, however, celebrated the beginning of the postwar era as that of a new era when real modernization of Japan could occur. Representative works for this interpretation include Ōkōchi Kazuo, "Rōdō undōshi to taishō jidai," *Tōdai shinbun*, February 7, 1962; Ogura, *Kagaku no shihyō*; Shinobu, *Taishō demokurashii shi*; and Maruyama, *Nihon seiji shisōshi kenkyū*. Despite this hope, it is also important to note that Maruyama and some Marxist intellectuals became dissatisfied with the incompleteness of postwar Japan's democratization.

33. See Yamanouchi, Koschmann, and Narita, *Total War and "Modernization."* Sheldon Garon and Andrew Gordon also examine Japan's twentieth century as one continuing process of statist development, but unlike the total war thesis their arguments maintain that this development was distinctively Japanese. See Garon, *Molding Japanese Minds*; Gordon, *Evolution of Labor Relations in Japan*; and Gordon, *Labor and Imperial Democracy*.

34. These are Fujioka and his colleagues' own English translations of their organizational names.

35. For example, see Atarashii Rekishi Kyōkasho o Tsukuru Kai, *Atarashii Nihon no rekishi ga hajimaru.* Also see a critique made by I, "Ai wa shokuminchi wo sukuuka?" 53.

36. Komori, "Bungaku to shite no rekishi / Rekishi to shite no bungaku," 8–9. Fujioka and many of his cohorts have acknowledged the strong influence of Shiba, and the so-called Shiba historicism (*Shiba shikan*) has attracted many readers to Fujioka's group.

37. See Chūō Shōchōtō Kaikaku Suishin Honbu, *Shōchō kaikaku no yonhon bashira,* an official government pamphlet, at http://www.kantei.go.jp/jp/cyuo-syocho/pamphlet/index.html (last accessed July 2008).

38. The official English translation of the name is the Ministry of Education, Culture, Sports, Science-Technology.

39. The Science-Technology Basic Law was passed in 1995 to make possible these plans and various reforms. Those who wish to learn more about the Science-Technology Basic Plans can consult the Web site of the Ministry of Education and Science at http://www.mext.go.jp/english/, or *Kagaku gijutsu kihon keikaku kaisetsu,* edited by the former Science-Technology Agency (*kagaku gijutsu shō*) (Tokyo: Ōkurashō Inshatsukyoku, 1997).

40. Naikakufu, "Kagaku Gijutsu Kihon Keikaku no gaiyō," *Toki no ugoki* 1936 (June 2001): 28–29. This monthly periodical is published by Naikakufu, the Cabinet Office.

41. Japanese scientists and scholars have criticized the top-down approach to the promotion of science. For example, see Ueda, "Shimin no tame no kagaku to kagaku gijutsu kihonhō," *Kagaku* 69 (March 1999): 273–78.

42. Omi, "Sekai saikō no kagaku gijutsu suijun no jitsugen ni mukete," *Toki no ugoki* 1936 (June 2001): 16. Omi is the current special-mission minister in charge of science-technology policy.

43. Maeda, "Zadankai," *Toki no ugoki* 1936 (June 2001).

44. Ibid., 27. The reader of this book, after reading Chapter 6 on the popular science media, might find this joke uncanny.

45. Kuwabara, "Shireitō no kinō wo ninau sōgō kagaku gijutsu kaigi," *Toki no ugoki* 1936 (June 2001): 49.

46. Maeda Katsunosuke, "Shireitō no kinō wo ninau sōgō kagaku gijutsu kaigi," *Toki no ugoki* 1936 (June 2001): 22–23.

47. Hiroshige, *Kagaku to rekishi,* 48–49.

Bibliography

Sources in English

Adas, Michael. *Machines as the Measure of Men: Science, Technology, and Ideologies of Western Dominance.* Ithaca, N.Y.: Cornell University Press, 1989.

Alchon, Guy. *The Invisible Hand of Planning: Capitalism, Social Science, and the State in the 1920s.* Princeton, N.J.: Princeton University Press, 1985.

Althusser, Louis. "Ideology and Ideological State Apparatuses." In *Lenin and Philosophy, and Other Essays*, trans. Ben Brewster, 127–87. London: Monthly Review Press, 1971.

Bainbridge, William Sims. *Dimensions of Science Fiction.* Cambridge, Mass.: Harvard University Press, 1986.

Barron, Neil, ed. *Anatomy of Wonder: A Critical Guide to Science Fiction.* New York: R. R. Bowker, 1981.

Barshay, Andrew. *The Social Sciences in Modern Japan: The Marxian and Modernist Traditions.* Berkeley: University of California Press, 2004.

Bartholomew, James R. *The Formation of Science in Japan: Building a Research Tradition.* New Haven, Conn.: Yale University Press, 1989.

Beyerchen, Alan. *Scientists under Hitler: Politics and the Physics Community in the Third Reich.* New Haven, Conn.: Yale University Press, 1977.

Biagioli, Mario, ed. *The Science Studies Reader.* New York: Routledge, 1999.

Boltanski, Luc. *The Making of a Class: Cadres in French Society.* Cambridge: Cambridge University Press, 1987.

Booker, M. Keith. *Dystopia Literature: A Theory and Research Guide.* Westport, Conn.: Greenwood Press, 1994.

Bottomore, Tom, ed. *A Dictionary of Marxist Thought.* Cambridge, Mass.: Harvard University Press, 1983.

Bourdieu, Pierre. "The Forms of Capital." In *Handbook of Theory and Research for the Sociology of Education*, ed. John Richardson, 241–58. New York: Greenwood Press, 1986.

———. "The Genesis of the Concept of Habitus and Field." *Sociocriticism* 2 (1985): 11–24.

———. *Logic of Practice.* Stanford, Calif.: Stanford University Press, 1980.

————. "The Peculiar History of Scientific Reason." *Sociologist Forum* 6, no. 1 (1991): 3–26.

————. "What Makes a Social Class? On the Theoretical and Practical Existence of Groups." *Berkeley Journal of Sociology* 32 (1987): 1–17.

Bourdieu, Pierre, and Loic J. D. Wacquant. "The Logic of Fields." In *An Invitation to Reflexive Sociology*, 94–114. Chicago: University of Chicago Press, 1992.

Brownnell, Susan. *Training the Body for China: Sports in the Moral Order of the People's Republic*. Chicago: University of Chicago Press, 1995.

Burris, Beverly H. *Technocracy at Work*. New York: State University of New York Press, 1993.

Bynum, W. F., E. J. Browne, and Roy Porter, eds. *Dictionary of the History of Science*. Princeton, N.J.: Princeton University Press, 1981.

Bystrytsky, Yevhen. "Why 'Nationalism' Cannot Be a Science." *Political Thought* 2 (1994): 136–42.

Cheng, John. "Amazing, Astounding, Wonder: Popular Science, Culture, and the Emergence of Science Fiction in the United States, 1926–1939." Ph.D. diss., University of California, Berkeley (forthcoming as *Imagining Science: Science Fiction and the Culture of Popular Science* from the University of Pennsylvania Press), 1997.

Coox, Alvin. *Nomonhan: Japan against Russia, 1939*. Stanford, Calif.: Stanford University Press, 1985.

Crawford, Elisabeth. *Nationalism and Internationalism in Science, 1880–1939: Four Studies of the Nobel Population*. Cambridge: Cambridge University Press, 1992.

Davis, Horace B. *Nationalism and Socialism: Marxist and Labor Theories of Nationalism to 1917*. New York: Monthly Review Press, 1967.

Doak, Kevin. *Dreams of Difference: The Japan Romantic School and the Crisis of Modernity*. Berkeley: University of California Press, 1994.

————. "*Under the Banner of the New Science*: History, Science, and the Problem of Particularity." *Philosophy East and West* 48, no. 2 (April 1998): 232–56.

————. "What Is a Nation and Who Belongs? National Narratives and the Ethnic Imagination in Twentieth-Century Japan." *American Historical Review* 102, no. 2 (April 1997): 283–309.

Douglas, Susan J. *Inventing American Broadcasting, 1899–1922*. Baltimore: Johns Hopkins University Press, 1987.

Dower, John. "'NI' and 'F': Japan's Wartime Atomic Bomb Research." In *Japan in War and Peace: Selected Essays*, 55–100. New York: New Press, 1993.

Eagleton, Terry. *Ideology: An Introduction*. London: Verso, 1991.

Fairclough, Norman. *Analysing Discourse: Textual Analysis for Social Research*. London: Routledge, 2003.

————. *Critical Discourse Analysis*. London: Addison Wesley, 1995.

————. *Media Discourse*. London: Edward Arnold, 1995.

Figal, Gerald. *Civilization and Monsters: Spirits of Modernity in Meiji Japan*. Durham, N.C.: Duke University Press, 1999.

Freedman, Carl. *Critical Theory and Science Fiction*. Hanover, N.H.: Wesleyan University Press, 2000.

Fukagawa, Hidetoshi, and Dan Pedoe. *Japanese Temple Geometry Problems*. Winnipeg: Charles Babbage Research Centre, 1989.

Garon, Sheldon. *Molding Japanese Minds: The State in Everyday Life.* Princeton, N.J.: Princeton University Press, 1997.

Gellner, Ernest. *Nations and Nationalism.* Ithaca, N.Y.: Cornell University Press, 1983.

Gibney, Frank, ed. *Sensō: The Japanese Remember the Pacific War.* Trans. Beth Cary. Armonk, N.Y.: M. E. Sharpe, 1995.

Gordon, Andrew. *The Evolution of Labor Relations in Japan: Heavy Industry, 1853–1955.* Cambridge, Mass.: Council on East Asian Studies, Harvard University, 1985.

———. *Labor and Imperial Democracy in Prewar Japan.* Berkeley: University of California Press, 1991.

Graham, Loren. *Science and Philosophy in the Soviet Union.* New York: Knopf, 1972.

———. *Science in Russia and the Soviet Union: A Short History.* Cambridge: Cambridge University Press, 1993.

———. *What Have We Learned about Science and Technology from the Russian Experience?* Stanford, Calif.: Stanford University Press, 1998.

Grunden, Walter. *Secret Weapons and World War II: Japan in the Shadow of Big Science.* Lawrence: University Press of Kansas, 2005.

Hall, John W. "Changing Conceptions of the Modernization of Japan." In *Changing Japanese Attitudes toward Modernization,* ed. Marius B. Jansen, 7–41. Princeton, N.J.: Princeton University Press, 1965.

Haraway, Donna. *Modest_Witness@Second_Millennium.FemaleMan_Meets_OncoMouse: Feminism and Technoscience.* New York: Routledge, 1997.

Harootunian, Harry D. "Introduction: A Sense of an Ending and the Problem of Taisho." In *Japan in Crisis: Essays on Taisho Democracy,* ed. Bernard S. Silberman and Harry D. Harootunian. Princeton, N.J.: Princeton University Press, 1974.

———. *Overcome by Modernity: History, Culture, and Community in Interwar Japan.* Princeton, N.J.: Princeton University Press, 2000.

Harris, Sheldon. *Factories of Death: Japanese Biological Warfare, 1932–1945, and the American Cover-up.* New York: Routledge, 1994.

Harwood, Jonathan. "German Science and Technology under Nationalism Socialism." *Perspectives on Science* 5, no. 1 (1997): 128–51.

Headrick, Daniel. *Tools of Empire: Technology and European Imperialism in the Nineteenth Century.* New York: Oxford University Press, 1981.

Hein, Laura. *Reasonable Men, Powerful Words: Political Culture and Expertise in Twentieth Century Japan.* Berkeley: University of California Press, 2005.

Heisig, James W. *Philosophers of Nothingness: An Essay on the Kyoto School.* Honolulu: University of Hawai'i Press, 2001.

Herf, Jeffrey. *Reactionary Modernism: Technology, Culture, and Politics in Weimar and the Third Reich.* Cambridge: Cambridge University Press, 1986.

Hessen, Boris. "The Social and Economic Roots of Newton's 'Principia.'" In *Science at the Cross Roads: Papers Presented to the International Congress of the History of Science and Technology by the Delegates of the U.S.S.R.,* ed. Nikolai Bukharin. 1931. Reprint, London: Kniga, 1971.

Honda, Katsuichi. *The Nanjing Massacre: A Japanese Journalist Confronts Japan's National Shame.* Ed. Frank Gibney, trans. Karen Sandness. Armonk, N.Y.: M. E. Sharpe, 1999.

Hoston, Germaine. *Marxism and the Crisis of Development in Prewar Japan*. Princeton, N.J.: Princeton University Press, 1986.

Hsu, Elisabeth. *Innovation in Chinese Medicine*. Cambridge: Cambridge University Press, 2001.

Hughes, Thomas P. *American Genesis: A Century of Invention and Technological Enthusiasm*. New York: Penguin Books, 1989.

Hutchinson, John, and Anthony Smith, eds. *Nationalism*. New York: Oxford University Press, 1995.

Ihde, Don, and Evan Selinger, eds. *Chasing Technoscience: Matrix for Materiality*. Bloomington: Indiana University Press, 2003.

Irokawa, Daikichi. *The Culture of the Meiji Period*. Princeton, N.J.: Princeton University Press, 1970.

Iwasaki Minoru. "Desire for a Poetic Metasubject: Miki Kiyoshi's Technology Theory." In *Total War and "Modernization,"* ed. Yasushi Yamanouchi, J. Victor Koschmann, and Ryūichi Narita, 159–80. Ithaca, N.Y.: East Asia Program, Cornell University, 1998.

James, Edward. *Science Fiction in the Twentieth Century*. Oxford: Oxford University Press, 1994.

Jansen, Marius B. "On Studying the Modernization of Japan." *Asian Cultural Studies* 3 (1962): 1–11.

Jaworski, Adam, and Nikolas Coupland, eds. *The Discourse Reader*. New York: Routledge, 2002.

Joravsky, David. *The Lysenko Affair*. Chicago: University of Chicago Press, 1970.

Jordan, John M. *Machine-Age Ideology: Social Engineering and American Liberalism, 1911–1939*. Chapel Hill: University of North Carolina Press, 1994.

Jordanova, Ludmilla. *Sexual Visions: Images of Gender in Science and Medicine between the Eighteenth and Twentieth Centuries*. Madison: University of Wisconsin Press, 1989.

Josephson, Paul R. *Physics and Politics in Revolutionary Russia*. Berkeley: University of California Press, 1991.

———. *Totalitarian Science and Technology*. Atlantic Highlands, N.J.: Humanities Press International, 1996.

Latour, Bruno. *Science in Action: How to Follow Scientists and Engineers through Society*. Cambridge, Mass.: Harvard University Press, 1987.

Leslie, Stuart. *The Cold War and American Science: The Military-Industrial-Academic Complex at MIT and Stanford*. New York: Columbia University Press, 1993.

Low, Morris. "Japan's Secret War? 'Instant' Scientific Manpower and Japan's World War II." *Annals of Science* 47 (1990): 347–60.

———. *Science and the Building of a New Japan*. New York: Palgrave Macmillan (Kindle Edition), 2005.

Macrakis, Kristie, and Dieter Hoffman. *Science under Socialism: East Germany in Comparative Perspective*. Cambridge, Mass.: Harvard University Press, 1999.

Maier, Charles S. "Between Taylorism and Technocracy: European Ideologies and the Vision of Industrial Productivity in the 1920s." *Journal of Contemporary History* 5, no. 2 (1970): 27–61.

Maruyama, Masao. *Studies in the Intellectual History of Tokugawa Japan*. Trans. Mikiso Hane. Princeton, N.J.: Princeton University Press, 1974.

Marx, Leo. "The Idea of 'Technology' and Postmodern Pessimism." In *Does Technology Drive History? The Dilemma of Technological Determinism*, ed. Merritt Roe Smith and Leo Marx, 237–58. Cambridge, Mass.: MIT Press, 1994.

Mazower, Mark. *Dark Continent: Europe's Twentieth Century*. New York: Vintage Books, 2000.

Mercer, Rosemary. "Picturing the Universe: Adventures with Miura Baien at the Borderland of Philosophy and Science." *Philosophy East and West* 48, no. 3 (July 1998): 478–503.

Mimura, Janis. "Technocratic Visions of Empire: Technology Bureaucrats and the 'New Order for Science-Technology.'" In *The Japanese Empire in East Asia and Its Postwar Legacy*, ed. Harald Feuss, 97–116. Munich: Iudicium, 1998.

Misa, Thomas J. "The Compelling Tangle of Modernity and Technology." In *Modernity and Technology*, ed. Thomas J. Misa, Philip Brey, and Andrew Feenberg, 1–31. Cambridge, Mass.: MIT Press, 2003.

Miyake, Yoshiko. "Doubling Expectations: Motherhood and Women's Factory Work under State Management in Japan in the 1930s and 1940s." In *Recreating Japanese Women*, ed. Gail Lee Bernstein, 267–95. Berkeley: University of California Press, 1999.

Morris-Suzuki, Tessa. *A History of Japanese Economic Thought*. New York: Routledge, 1989.

———. *Re-Inventing Japan: Time, Space, Nation*. Armonk, N.Y.: M. E. Sharpe, 1998.

———. *The Technological Transformation of Japan: From the Seventeenth to the Twenty-first Century*. Cambridge: Cambridge University Press, 1994.

Nakayama, Shigeru. "The History of Science: A Subject for the Frustrated." In *Science and Society in Modern Japan: Selected Historical Resources*, ed. Nakayama Shigeru, David L. Swain, and Yagi Eri, 3–16. Tokyo: University of Tokyo Press, 1974.

———. *Science, Technology and Society in Postwar Japan*. London: Kegan Paul International, 1991.

Nakayama, Shigeru, David L. Swain, and Yagi Eri, eds. *Science and Society in Modern Japan: Selected Historical Resources*. Tokyo: University of Tokyo Press, 1974.

Nanda, Neera. *Prophets Facing Backward: Postmodern Critiques of Science and Hindu Nationalism in India*. New Brunswick, N.J.: Rutgers University Press, 2003.

Needham, Joseph, ed. *Science and Civilization of China*. 7 vols. Cambridge: Cambridge University Press, 1954–.

Oka, Kunio. "Society for the Study of Materialism: Yuiken." In *Science and Society in Modern Japan: Selected Historical Resources*, ed. Nakayama Shigeru, David L. Swain, and Yagi Eri, 151–57. Tokyo: University of Tokyo Press, 1974.

Okumura, Hiroshi. "Japanese Mathematics." *Symmetry: Culture and Science* 12, nos. 1–2 (2001): 79–86.

Oldenziel, Ruth. *Making Technology Masculine: Men, Women, and Modern Machines in America, 1870–1945*. Amsterdam: Amsterdam University Press, 1999.

Osaki, Makoto. *Individuum, Society, Humankind: The Triadic Logic of Species according to Hajime Tanabe*. Leiden, The Netherlands: Brill, 2001.

Ōtsubo Sitcawich, Sumiko. "Eugenics in Imperial Japan: Some Ironies of Modernity, 1883–1945." Ph.D. diss., Ohio State University, 1998.

Pauer, Erich. "Japan's Technical Mobilization in the Second World War." In *Japan's War and Economy*, 39–64. New York: Routledge, 1999.

Peattie, Mark R. "Japanese Attitudes toward Colonialism, 1895–1945." In *The Japanese Colonial Empire, 1895–1945*, ed. Ramon H. Myers and Mark R. Peattie, 80–127. Princeton, N.J.: Princeton University Press, 1984.

Pincus, Leslie. *Authenticating Culture in Imperial Japan: Kuki Shūzō and the Rise of National Aesthetics*. Berkeley: University of California Press, 1995.

Plekhanov, Georgi V. *Kaikyū shakai no geijutsu*. Trans. Kurehara Korehito. Tokyo: Sōbunkan, 1928.

Porter, Theodore. *The Rise of Statistical Thinking, 1820–1900*. Princeton, N.J.: Princeton University Press, 1986.

Prakash, Gyan. *Another Reason: Science and the Imagination of Modern India*. Princeton, N.J.: Princeton University Press, 1999.

Purcell, Edward A., Jr. *The Crisis of Democratic Theory: Scientific Naturalism and the Problem of Value*. Lexington: University Press of Kentucky, 1973.

Radaelli, Claudio M. *Technocracy in the European Union*. New York: Longman, 1999.

Reischauer, Edwin. "What Went Wrong?" In *Dilemmas of Growth in Prewar Japan*, ed. James Morley, 489–510. Princeton, N.J.: Princeton University Press, 1971.

Renneberg, Monika, and Mark Walker, eds. *Science, Technology, and National Socialism*. Cambridge: Cambridge University Press, 1994.

Rydell, Robert. *All the World's a Fair: America's International Expositions, 1876–1916*. Chicago: University of Chicago Press, 1984.

Sakai, Naoki. *Translation and Subjectivity: On "Japan" and Cultural Nationalism*. Minneapolis: University of Minnesota Press, 1997.

Samuels, Richard J. *"Rich Nation, Strong Army": National Security and the Technological Transformation of Japan*. Ithaca, N.Y.: Cornell University Press, 1994.

Shirane, Haruo, and Tomi Suzuki. *Inventing the Classics: Modernity, National Identity, and Japanese Literature*. Stanford, Calif.: Stanford University Press, 2000.

Silverberg, Miriam. *Changing Song: The Marxist Manifestos of Nakano Shigeharu*. Princeton, N.J.: Princeton University Press, 1990.

Smith, Anthony. *Theories of Nationalism*. London: Duckworth, 1971.

Smith, David Eugene, and Mikami Yoshio. *A History of Japanese Mathematics*. Chicago: Open Court, 1914.

Sohn-Rethel, Alfred. *Intellectual and Manual Labour: A Critique of Epistemology*. Atlantic Highlands, N.J.: Humanities Press, 1978.

Spaulding, Robert M., Jr. *Imperial Japan's Higher Civil Service Examinations*. Princeton, N.J.: Princeton University Press, 1967.

Sugihara, Shirō and Toshio Tanaka. "Introduction." In *Economic Thought and Modernization in Japan*. Cheltenham, U.K.: Edward Elgar, 1998.

Sung, Ying-hsing. *Chinese Technology in the Seventeenth Century: T'ien-kung k'ai-wu*. Trans. E-tu Zen Sun and Shiou-chuan Sun. University Park: Pennsylvania State University Press, 1966; reprint, New York: Dover Publications, 1997.

Tamanoi, Mariko. *Under the Shadow of Nationalism: Politics and Poetics of Rural Japanese Women*. Honolulu: University of Hawai'i Press, 1998.

Tanaka, Stefan. *Japan's Orient: Rendering Pasts into History.* Berkeley: University of California Press, 1993.

Traweek, Sharon. *Beamtimes and Lifetimes: The World of High Energy Physicists.* Cambridge, Mass.: Harvard University Press, 1988.

Tsutsui, William. *Manufacturing Ideology: Scientific Management in Twentieth-Century Japan.* Princeton, N.J.: Princeton University Press, 1998.

Unno, Taitetsu, and James W. Heisig, eds. *The Religious Philosophy of Tanabe Hajime: The Metanoetic Imperative.* Berkeley, Calif.: Asian Humanities Press, 1990.

Walker, Mark. *Nazi Science: Myth, Truth, and the German Atomic Bomb.* New York: Plenum Press, 1995.

Wang, Jessica. *American Science in an Age of Anxiety: Scientists, Anticommunism, and the Cold War.* Chapel Hill: University of North Carolina Press, 1999.

Wang, Zuoyue. "Saving China through Science: The Science Society of China, Scientific Nationalism, and Civil Society in Republican China." *Osiris* 17 (2002): 291–322.

Watanabe, Masao. *The Japanese and Western Science.* Philadelphia: University of Pennsylvania Press, 1991.

———. *Science and Cultural Exchange in Modern History: Japan and the West.* Tokyo: Hakusen-sha, 1997.

Yamamuro, Shin'ichi. *Manchuria under Japanese Dominion.* Philadelphia: University of Pennsylvania Press, 2005.

Yamanouchi, Yasushi, J. Victor Koschmann, and Ryuichi Narita, eds. *Total War and "Modernization."* Ithaca, N.Y.: East Asia Program, Cornell University, 1998.

Yamazaki, Masakatsu. "The Mobilization of Science and Technology during the Second World War in Japan: A Historical Study of the Activities of the Technology Board Based upon the Files of Tadashiro Inoue." *Historia Scientiarum* 5, no. 2 (1995): 167–81.

Yoshitake, Oka. *Konoe Fumimaro: A Political Biography.* Trans. Shunpei Okamoto and Patricia Murray. Tokyo: University of Tokyo Press, 1983.

Young, Louise. *Japan's Total Empire: Manchuria and the Culture of Wartime Imperialism.* Berkeley: University of California Press, 1998.

Sources in Japanese

Abe Takeshi. *Taiheiyō sensō to rekishigaku.* Tokyo: Yoshikawa Kōbunkan, 1999.

Aida Gundayū. "Gijutsu jaanarizumu jihyō." *Gijutsu hyōron,* January 1940, 61.

Aikawa Haruki. "Shintaisei to gijutsu no soshikika." *Gijutsu hyōron,* January 1941, 13–18.

Aizu Shingo. *Nihon kagaku shōsetsu nenpyō.* Chiba: Risō, 1999.

Aizu Shingo and Yokota Jun'ya. *Shōnen shōsetsu taikei.* Tokyo: San'ichi Shobō, 1992.

Amakasu Sekisuke [Segi Ken]. "Yūseigaku ni tsuite." *Yuibutsuron kenkyū* 20 (June 1934): 55–71.

Ara Masahito. "'Puurauda' ni shōkaisareta Yuibutsuron Kenkyūkai." *Yuibutsuron kenkyū fukkokuban geppō,* no. 14:5.

Aramata Hiroshi. *Daitōa kagaku kidan.* Tokyo: Chikuma Shōbō, 1991.

Asahi Jaanaru. October 1969.

Atarashii Rekishi Kyōkasho o Tsukuru Kai. *Atarashii Nihon no rekishi ga hajimaru.* Tokyo: Gentōsha, 1997.

Chōsen Sōtokufu. *Shizen no kansatsu—kyōshiyō.* Seoul: Chōsen Shoseki, 1942.

Chūō Shōchōtō Kaikaku Suishin Honbu. *Shōchō kaikaku no yonhon bashira.* Available at http://www.kantei.go.jp/jp/chuo-syocho (accessed May 29, 2008).

"Daidokoro no kagaku: Okusama to jochū-san mondō." *Kokumin kagaku gurafu* 1, no. 1 (December 1941): 6–7.

Daijirin. Tokyo: Saiseidō, 1995.

Date Kimio. "Dai jūgokan kaidai." *Yuibutsuron kenkyū fukkokuban geppō,* no. 15:4.

―――. "Dai jūyonkan kaidai." *Yuibutsuron kenkyū fukkokuban geppō,* no. 14:2.

"Declaration." *Kōjin,* September 1925.

Doboku Gakkai Dobokushi Kenkyū Iinkai, ed. *Furuichi Kimitake to sono jidai.* Tokyo: Doboku Gakkai, 2004.

Edogawa Ranpo. "Tantei shōsetsu to kagaku seishin." *Kagaku Pen* 1, no. 4 (January 1937): 19–20.

Endō Toshisada. *Dainihon sūgakushi.* Tokyo, 1896.

Gakusei no kagaku. 1940–44.

Gijutsu hyōron. 1939–44.

Gijutsu Nihon. 1939.

Haga Mayumi. "Nihon minzoku to kagaku." *Kagaku Pen* 5, no. 1 (January 1940): 73–80.

Hamil, Barbara. "Nihonteki modanizumu no shishō." In *Nihon modanizumu no kenkyū,* ed. Minami Hiroshi. Tokyo: Bureen Shuppan, 1982.

Harada Mitsuo. "Dokusha shokun e!! 'Kodomo no kagakukai' kaku chihō ni setsuritsu nozomu." *Kodomo no kagaku* 2, no. 6 (June 1925): 83.

―――. *Kagaku gahō* 1, no. 4 (July 1923): 295.

―――. "Kagaku gahō no kōei." *Kagaku gahō* 2, no. 3 (March 1924): n.p.

―――. "Kodomo ni kikaseru hanashidane." *Kagaku gahō* 1, no. 1 (April 1923): 53.

―――. "'Kodomo no kagaku' no yakume." *Kodomo no kagaku* 6, no. 5 (November 1927): 2.

―――. "Kumo, kiri, tsuyu, oyobi shimo wa doushite dekiruka." *Kokumin kagaku gurafu* 2, no. 11 (November 1942): 18–19.

―――. "Netsu riyō no konjaku." *Kokumin kagaku gurafu* 4, no. 1 (January 1944): 10–11.

―――. *Omoide no nanajūnen.* Tokyo: Seibundō Shinkōsha, 1966.

―――. "Rika kyōiku." *Kagaku gahō* 2, no. 4 (April 1924): 320.

―――. "Shin no zasshi." *Kagaku gahō* 1, no. 1 (April 1923): 95.

―――. "Tsuki no kao." *Kokumin kagaku gurafu* 3, no. 9 (September 1943): 3.

―――. "Waraubeki gakusha no taido." *Kagaku gahō* 2, no. 3 (March 1924): 222.

―――. "Yama no kyōi, umi no kyōi." *Kagaku gahō* 1, no. 4 (July 1923): 296.

Hasegawa Ichirō. "Yuiken hossoku no koro." *Yuibutsuron kenkyū fukkokuban geppō,* no. 2:7.

Hasegawa Nyozekan. "Yuibutsuron Kenkyūkai no sōritsu ni tsuite." *Yuibutsuron kenkyū* 1 (November 1932): 4–7.

Hashida Kunihiko. *Gyō to shite no kagaku.* 1939. Reprint, Tokyo: Iwanami Shoten, 1942.

————. *Kagaku suru kokoro*. Tokyo: Kyōgaku Kyoku, 1940.

————. "'Kodomo no kagaku' no yakume." *Kodomo no kagaku* 6, no. 5 (November 1927): 2.

————. "*Seibō genzō* no sokumenkan." In *Shizen to hito: Hashida Kunihiko sensei kōenshū*, ed. Yamagiwa Ichizō, vol. 1. Tokyo: Jinbun Shoin, 1936.

Hata Ikuhiko. *Senzenki Nihon kanryōsei no seido, soshiki, jinji*. Ed. Senzenki Kanryōsei Kenkyūkai. Tokyo: Tokyo Daigaku Shuppankai, 1981.

Hayakawa Jirō. "'Kokumin' to 'minzoku.'" *Yuibutsuron kenkyū* 49 (November 1936): 46–50.

Hayashi Yūichi. *"Musan kaikyū" no jidai: Kindai Nihon no shakai undō*. Tokyo: Aoki Shoten, 2000.

Hirata Koroku. "Uchisaiwaichō no jimusho." *Yuibutsuron kenkyū fukkokuban geppō*, no. 1:5.

Hirokawa Wataru. "Minzoku ni tsuite." *Yuibutsuron kenkyū* 49 (November 1936): 38–40.

Hiroshige Tetsu. *Kagaku no shakaishi: Kindai Nihon no kagaku gijutsu*. 1973. Reprint, Tokyo: Chūō Kōronsha, 1979.

————. *Kagaku to rekishi*. Tokyo: Misuzu Shobō, 1965.

"Hōkoku kakubu kenkyūkai, minzokuron to sekaikan." *Yuibutsuron kenkyū* 44 (June 1936): 966.

Honma Yuiichi. "Inaka deno 'Yuiken' kan." *Yuibutsuron kenkyū* 50 (December 1936): 151–52.

Hori Shichizō. *Nihon no rika kyōikushi*. 3 vols. Tokyo: Fukumura Shoten, 1963.

I Yonsuk. "Ai wa shokuminchi wo sukuuka?" In *Nashonaru hisutorii wo koete*. Tokyo: Tokyo Daigaku Shuppankai, 1998.

————. "*Kokugo" to iu shisō: Kindai Nihon no gengo ninshiki*. Tokyo: Iwanami Shoten, 1996.

Ichinohe Naozō. "Bunkyō yatsuatari." *Gendai no kagaku* 8, no. 3 (1920). In *NKGT*, 3:456.

Ichiyanagi Hirotaka. *Saiminjutsu no Nihon kindai*. Tokyo: Aoyumisha, 1997.

Ienaga Saburō. *Tanabe Hajime no shisōshiteki kenkyū: Sensō to tetsugakusha*. 1974. Reprint, Tokyo: Hōsei Daigaku Shuppankyoku, 1988.

Iida Ken'ichi. *Ichigo no jiten: Gijutsu*. Tokyo: Sansendō, 1995.

————, ed. *Jūkōgyōka no tenkai to mujun*. Vol. 4 of *Gijutsu no shakaishi*. Tokyo: Yūhikaku, 1982.

————. *Kaisō no Saigusa Hiroto*. Tokyo: Kobushi Shobō, 1996.

Ikejima Shinpei. "Tairiku kagaku to kenkoku daigaku." *Bungei shunjū*, June 1939, 184–89.

Imano Takeshi. "Kagaku seisaku no konpon mondai—*Kaizō* oyobi *Nihon hyōron* ni okeru Tanabe shi no ronbun ni taisuru shiron." *Yuibutsuron kenkyū* 49 (November 1936): 18–32.

Ishida Takeshi. *Nihon no shakaigaku*. Tokyo: Tokyo Daigaku Shuppankai, 1984.

Ishihara Jun. "Butsurigaku jō no gainen ni taisuru yuibutsusei no imi ni tsuite." *Yuibutsuron kenkyū* 12 (October 1933): 5–11.

————. "Senkyūhyaku sanjūnen eno taibō: Kagakukai (1)." *Tokyo Asahi shinbun* (December 25, 1929): 5.

Ishihara Tatsurō. "Idengaku to yuibutsuron." *Yuibutsuron kenkyū* 4 (February 1933): 95–105.

———. "Menderizumu ichi hihan." *Yuibutsuron kenkyū* 3 (January 1933): 71–77.

———. "Pen neemu ni tsuite." *Yuibutsuron kenkyū fukkokuban geppō*, no. 1:8.

———. [Nakajima Seijosuke]. "'Shizen benshōhō no gutaika' ni taisuru kengi—futatabi shizen kagakuteki yuibutsuron no yōgo o kyōchōsu." *Yuibutsuron kenkyū* 29 (March 1935): 90–108.

———. "Yuiken no shoki no koro no koto." *Yuibutsuron kenkyū fukkokuban geppō*, no. 8:7–8.

Ishii Tomoyuki. [H. K.]. "Kyakkanteki shizen hōsoku no tankyū to shizen kagaku no kaikyūsei." *Yuibutsuron kenkyū* 15 (January 1934): 104–6.

———. "Matsumoto Shigeru yaku, Daawin shugi to marukusu shugi." *Yuibutsuron kenkyū* 20 (June 1934): 118–20.

———. "Minzoku seibutsugaku ni tsuite." *Yuibutsuron kenkyū* 48 (October 1936): 100–106.

———. [Ōkawa Ryō]. "Shihonshugikoku no shizen kagaku (oboegaki)." *Yuibutsuron kenkyū* 9 (July 1933): 62–65.

———. "Shinkaron no hanashi (4)." *Yuibutsuron kenkyū* 23 (September 1934): 129–36.

———. "Shizen kagaku kenkyū ni okeru futatsu no taido." *Yuibutsuron kenkyū* 13 (November 1933): 57–62.

———. "Shizen kagaku no tōhasei ni tsuite." *Yuibutsuron kenkyū* 11 (September 1933): 46–49.

———. "Sōgō kagaku no kiso jōken—shizen benshōhō no gutaika towa nanika?" *Yuibutsuron kenkyū* 32 (June 1935): 48–58.

Ishikawa Takashi. "Nihon SF-shi no kokoromi." In *SF no jidai: Nihon SF no taidō to tenbō*. Tokyo: Kisō Tengaisha, 1977.

Isobe Asaichi. "Niiniiroku jiken gokuchū nikki." In *Chōkokkashugi*, vol. 31 of *Gendai Nihon shisō taikei*, ed. Hashikawa Bunzō. Tokyo: Chikuma Shobō, 1964.

Itakura Kiyonobu. "Kyōgaku sasshin undōka no kagaku kyōiku." In *NKGT* 3:19, 30.

———. *Nihon rika kyōikushi*. Tokyo: Daiichi Hōki Shuppan, 1968.

Itō Takashi. "Mōri Hideoto ron oboegaki." In *Shōwaki no seiji*. Tokyo: Yamakawa Shuppankai, 1993.

Jiji Shinpōsha Keizaibu, ed. *Nihon sangyō no gōrika*. Tokyo: Tōyō Keizai Shinpōsha, 1928. In *NKGT*, 3:536.

"Jogakusei o dou kagaku saseru?" *Kokumin kagaku gurafu* 2, no. 9 (September 1942): 15–20.

"Josei no midashinami, ikebana no kagaku." *Kokumin kagaku gurafu* 3, no. 1 (January 1943): 22–23.

K. M. "'Kōjin' sendengō no 'kantōgen' kara shikisha wa kataru." *Kōjin*, January 1931: 17.

Kagaku. 1931–present.

Kagaku gahō. 1923–61.

Kagaku gijutsu. 1942–44.

Kagaku Gijutsu Shō, ed. *Kagaku gijutsu kihon keikaku kaisetsu*. Tokyo: Ōkurashō Insatsukyoku, 1997.

Kagaku Pen. 1926–41.

Kagakushugi kōgyō. 1937–45.

Kajiura Ichiman. "Shakai Minshū to shiji chūshi ni kanshite." *Kōjin*, April 1928: 37–39; May 1928: 24–25.

Kamatani Chikayoshi. "Saigusa Hiroto to gijutsu no kenkyū—tokuni 1937–1945 senjiki ni okeru." *Kagakushi kenkyū*, no. 75 (July–September 1965): 101–13.

Kamei Kojirō. "Seiji, gijutsu, hōkoku." *Gijutsu Nihon*, September 1937: 10–11.

Kamo Giichi. "Nihon kagaku shisō chōshi." *Kagaku Pen* 5, no. 1 (January 1940): 81–88.

———. "Tosaka kun no omoide." *Yuibutsuron kenkyū fukkokuban geppō*, no. 5:7.

Kanbe Isaburō. *Nihon rika kyōiku hattatsushi.* Tokyo: Keibunsha, 1938. In *NKGT*, 3:17.

Kaneko Gen'ichirō. "Kōjin Kurabu no omoide." *Gijutsu Nihon*, June 1936: 41.

Kang Shih. *Shokuminchi shihai to Nihongo: Taiwan, Manshūkoku, Tairiku senryōchi ni okeru gengo seisaku.* Tokyo: Sangensha, 1993.

Kanokogi Kazunobu. *Kanji to shinri no haji.* Tokyo: Kaizōsha, 1922.

———. *Kōkoku shugi.* Tokyo: Ōkura Seisin Bunka Kenkyūjo, 1935.

Karita Shinshichi. "Mō hitotsu no sokumen." *Yuibutsuron kenkyū* 50 (December 1936): 154–56.

Kawahara Hiroshi. *Shōwa seiji shisō kenkyū.* Tokyo: Waseda Daigaku Shuppan, 1979.

Kawakami Tetsutarō, Takeuchi Yoshimi, et al. *Kindai no chōkoku.* 1979. Reprint, Tokyo: Fuzanbō, 1994.

Kawamura Kunimitsu. *Genshi suru kindai kūkan.* Tokyo: Aoyumisha, 1989.

Kawamura Minato. *Umi o watatta Nihongo: Shokuminchi no "kokugo" no jikan.* Tokyo: Seidosha, 1994.

Kigi Takatarō [Hayashi Takashi]. "Midori no nisshōki." *Kodomo no kagaku*, October 1939–September 1940; and *Gakusei no kagaku*, October 1940.

Kihira Tadayoshi. *Koshintō.* Tokyo: Iwanami Shoten, 1932.

———. *Shinri towa nanzoya.* Tokyo: Nihon Bunka Kyōkai, 1934.

Kikanshi henshūbu. "Shoka no iken o shirusu—minzoku no gainen ni tsuite." *Yuibutsuron kenkyū* 47 (September 1936): 45.

Kikuchi Isao. "Kinrō shintaisei to gijutsusha." *Gijutsu hyōron*, January 1941: 20.

Kitaoka Sumiitsu. "Zunō rōdōsha no kumiai undō to sono hogohō." *Kōjin*, March 1927: 2–32.

Kobayashi Hideo. *Mantetsu: "Chi no shūdan" no sei to shi.* Tokyo: Yoshikawa Kōbunkan, 1996.

Kodomo no kagaku. 1924–present.

Koike Shirō. "Kōjin Kurabu wa sekika shitsutsu aruka?" *Kōjin*, September 1927: 8.

———. "Manmō mondai o hōnin shitatosureba." *Kōjin*, March 1932: 40.

———. "Rōdō shihon tairitsu no shakai ni okeru zunō rōdōsha no igi." *Kōjin*, March 1926: 23.

Kojima Hatsuo. "Minzoku naru gainen ni tsuite." *Yuibutsuron kenkyū* 49 (November 1936): 50–52.

Kōjin. 1921–39.

"Kokumin gurafu o zen kokumin ni suisensuru." *Kokumin kagaku gurafu* 1, no. 1 (December 1941): n.p.

Kokumin kagaku gurafu. 1941–44.

"'Kokumin kagaku' kankō no shushi." In Kaneko Takanosuke, *Shigen to keizai*, vol. 1 of *Kokumin kagaku sōsho*. Tokyo: Kōseikaku, 1941.

Kokumin seishin bunka kenkyūjo. *Kokumin seishin bunka kenkyūjo shuppan tosho mokuroku*. Tokyo: Kokumin Seisin Bunka Kenkyūjo, 1939.

Komori Yōichi. "Bungaku to shite no rekishi / Rekishi to shite no bungaku." In *Nashonaru hisutorii o koete*, ed. Komori Yōichi and Takahashi Tetsuya. Tokyo: Tokyo Daigaku Shuppankai, 1998.

Kōsei. 1923–38.

Koyama Toshio. "Ichi kōjin no kitsumon ni kotaete shoshin o nobu." *Kōjin*, May 1927: 36–37.

———. "Musan seitō no zen'ei to kōei." *Kōjin*, January 1926: 13.

———. "Seinen gijutsusha Santarō." *Kōjin*, October 1925: 34–39; November 1925: 34–39.

———. "Ware ware no mondai." *Kōjin*, May 1927: 31–44.

Koyasu Nobukuni. "'Kokugo' wa shishite 'Nihongo' wa umaretaka." In *Kindai chi no arukeorogii*. Tokyo: Iwanami Shoten, 1996.

Kozai Yoshishige. "Senzen ni okeru yuibutsuronsha no teikō." *Bunka hyōron* 111 (December 1970): 80.

———. "Zadankai: Teikō no kiroku—'Yuibutsuron kenkyukai' no katsudō." *Jidai to Shisō* 3 (1971): 125–26.

Kubo Yoshizō. *Shōwa kyōikushi: Tennōsei to kyōiku no shiteki tenkai*. Vol. 1. Tokyo: San'ichi Shobō, 1994.

Kurahashi Tōjirō. "Fusen o maeni shite." *Kōsei*, May 1926: 1.

Kūsō kagaku shōsetsu shū. Shōnen shōsetsu taikei, ed. Yokota Jun'ya, vol. 8. Tokyo: San'ichi Shobō, 1986.

Kuwabara Hiroshi. "Shireitō no kinō wo ninau sōgō kagaku gijutsu kaigi." *Toki no ugoki* 1036 (June 2001): 48–49.

Kuwaki Masaru [Iwakura Masaji]. "Dentō no kōsatsu—dentō no kaikyūsei nii tsuite." *Yuibutsuron kenkyū* 57 (July 1937): 6–19.

Lenin, V. I. *Rōnō kakumei no kensetsuteki hōmen*. Tokyo: Santokusha, 1921.

———. *Rōnō roshia no kenkyū*. Trans. Yamakawa Hitoshi and Yakamawa Kikue. Tokyo: Arusu, 1921.

———. *Shakai shugi kakumei no kensetsuteki tōmen: Soviet tōmen no mondai*. Tokyo: Heimin Daigaku Shuppanbu, 1921.

Maeda Katsunosuke et al. "Zadankai: Sugureta kenkyūsha ga sodatsu kenkyū kaihatsu sisutemu zukuri o." *Toki no ugoki* 1036 (June 2001): 18–27.

Maekawa Seiji. *Kamakura Akademia: Saigusa Hiroto to wakaki kamometachi*. Tokyo: Saimaru Shuppankai, 1994.

Manshū Gijutsu Kyōkai. "Manmō zadankai." *Kōjin*, May 1932: 4–16.

Maruyama Masao. *Nihon seiji shisōshi kenkyū*. Tokyo: Tokyo Daigaku Shuppankai, 1952.

Mashita Shin'ichi. "Tosaka Jun no omoide." *Yuibutsuron kenkyū fukkokuban geppō*, no. 2:5.

Matsubara Yuiichi. *Kyōdo chūshin teigakunen no shizen kenkyū*. Tokyo: Jinbun Shobō, 1931.

Matsuda Genji. "Monbu daijin no chiiku henchōron." In *NKGT*, 4:171.

Matsuoka Hisao. "Gijutsu jidai no tenkai to waga kuni gijutsusha." *Gijutsu hyōron*, March 1940: 5–6.

———. "Kagaku gijutsu to iu kotoba." *Gijutsu hyōron*, February 1942: 45.

———. "Tōgi." *Gijutsu hyōron*, October 1942: 41–42.

Mikami Yoshio. *Bunkashijō yori mitaru Nihon no sūgaku*. 1921. Reprint, Tokyo: Sōgensha, 1947.

———. *Bunkashijō yori mitaru Nihon no sūgaku*. Ed. Sasaki Chikara. Tokyo: Iwanami Shoten, 1999.

———. "Nihon sūgakusha no seikaku to kokuminsei." *Shinri kenkyū* 125 (May 1922): 311–31.

Miki Kiyoshi, ed. *Gendai tetsugaku jiten*. Tokyo: Nihon Hyōronsha, 1941.

Miura Baien. *Baien zenshū*. Tokyo: Kōdōkan, 1912.

Miura Toyohiko. *Teruoka Gitō: Rōdō kagaku o tsukutta otoko*. Tokyo: Riburo Pōto, 1991.

Miyamoto Shinobu. "Igaku no kagakusei yōgo no tameni—Ōta Takeo shi ni kotaeru." *Yuibutsuron kenkyū* 39 (November 1936): 156–69.

———. "Shakaiteki ningen no bunseki." *Yuibutsuron kenkyū* 37 (November 1935): 5–24.

———. "Watashi no seishun to kenkyū." *Yuibutsuron kenkyū fukkokuban geppō*, no. 11:5–6.

Miyamoto Takenosuke. "Anjū no chi." *Kōjin*, June 1930: 27–28.

———. "Bunkan seido kaikaku to gijutsukan yūgū." *Gijutsu Nihon*, February 1938: 4–6.

———. "Danjo kankei no shōrai." *Kōjin*, July 1925: 10–11.

———. "Eikoku ni okeru shokugyō kumiai." *Kōjin*, August 1925: 2–17.

———. "Etsuro gashin." *Kōjin*, January 1930: 6–7.

———. "Gijutsuka danketsu no shidō genri." *Gijutsu Nihon*, July 1937: 1.

———. "Gijutsuka no shakaiteki danketsu." *Gijutsu Nihon*, June 1936: 2.

———. "Gikai hinin yori gikai kaizō e." *Kōjin*, February 1931: 7–9.

———. "Konkuriito gishi no hanashi." *Kōjin*, October 1930: 17–19.

———. "Manmō mondai to gijutsuka." *Kōjin*, March 1932: 29–33.

———. "Manshūkoku to kataru." *Kōjin*, October 1933: 16–20.

———. *Miyamoto Takenosuke nikki*. Nagoya: Denki tsūshin kyōkai tōkai shibu, 1971.

———. "Sangyō gōrika mondai shaken." *Kōjin*, May 1930: 23–26.

———. "Shakai jinshin no suii o omou." *Kōjin*, August 1932: 6–8.

———. "Shidō seishin no kakushin." *Kōjin*, February 1934: 4–6.

———. *Tairiku kensetsu no kadai*. Tokyo: Iwanami Shoten, 1941.

———. "Taishō jūyonen o kaerimite." *Kōjin*, February 1926: 2–3.

"Miyamoto Takenosuke tsuitō zadankai." *Gijutsu hyōron*, April 1942: 55.

Miyazaki Tsutomu. *Kagaku gijutsu nenkan-shōwa jūhachinenban*. Ed. Kagaku Dōin Kyōkai. Tokyo: Kagaku Dōin Kyōkai, 1943.

Mizutani Mitsuhiro. *Kanryō no fūbō*. Nihon no kindai, no. 13. Tokyo: Chūō Kōronsha, 1999.

Monbushō. *Gakusei 120 nenshi*. Tokyo: Gyōsei, 1992.

———. *Kokumin gakkōrei shikō kisoku* (1941). In *NKGT*, 10:227.

————. *Shizen no kansatsu—kyōshiyō.* Tokyo: Dekohan Insatsu, 1941.

Mōri Hideoto. "Seiji ishiki to kagaku gijutsu suijun." *Gijutsu hyōron,* January 1940: 24–26.

Mori Kōichi. "Dai ikkan kaidai." *Yuibutsuron kenkyū fukkokuban geppō,* no. 1:1.

————. "Dai jūnanakan Kaidai." *Yuibutsuron kenkyū fukkokuban geppō,* no. 17:3.

————. "Dai jūnikan kaidai." *Yuibutsuron kenkyū fukkokuban geppō,* no. 12:2.

————. "Minzoku teki narumono towa nanzoya?" *Yuibutsuron kenkyū* 53 (March 1937): 6–18.

Morikawa Hidemasa, *Gijutsusha: Nihon kindaika no ninaite.* Tokyo: Nihon Keizai Shinbunsha, 1975.

Morishita Katsuhito. *Shikōsuru monogatari: SF no genri, rekishi, shudai.* Tokyo: Sōgensha, 2000.

Nagahama Isao, ed. *Shiryō kokka to kyōiku.* Tokyo: Akashi Shobō, 1994.

Nagata Tsuneo. "Henshū kōki." *Kagaku Pen* 1, no. 1 (October 1936): 132.

Nagayama Yasuo. "Kaisetsu: Kagaku to sensō to Unno Jūza." In *Unno Jūza sensō shōsetsu kessakushū,* ed. Nagayama Yasuo. Tokyo: Chūō Kōronsha, 2004.

Naikakufu. "Kagaku Gijutsu Kihon Keikaku no gaiyō." *Toki no ugoki* 1036 (June 2001): 28–29.

Nakajima Kōtarō. "'Shinseinen' sanjūnenshi." In *Shinseinen kessakusen,* ed. Nakajima Kōtarō, vol. 5. Tokyo: Rippū Shobō, 1991.

Nakajima Kumakichi. "'Gōrika' wa kin kaikin no atoshimatsu ni arazu." *Sarariiman,* September 1930. In *NKGT,* 3:541–44.

Nakamura Seiji. *Gijutsu ronsōshi.* Tokyo: Aoki Shoten, 1975.

————. *Shinhan gijutsu ronsōshi.* Tokyo: Sōfūsha, 1995.

Nakamura Takafusa. *Shōwashi.* Vol. 1. Tokyo: Tōyō keizai Shinpōsha, 1993.

Nakamura Teiri. *Nihon no ruisenko ronsō.* Tokyo: Misuzu Shobō, 1997.

Nakatani Ukichirō. *Kagaku to shakai.* Tokyo: Iwanami Shoten, 1949.

Nakayama Shigeru. *Ichinohe Naozō: Ya ni orita kokorozashi no hito.* Tokyo: Riburo Pōto, 1989.

————. *Kagaku gijutsu no sengoshi.* Tokyo: Iwanami Shoten, 1995.

Naoki Rintarō. *Gijutsu seikatsu yori.* Tokyo: Tōkyōdo, 1918.

Nihon Kagakushi Gakkai, ed. *Nihon kagaku gijutsushi taikei* [*NKGT*]. 26 vols. Tokyo: Daiichi Hōki Shuppan, 1964–72.

"Nihon Kōjin Kurabu no sōritsu." *Kōgaku* 81 (January 1921): 66.

Nishimura Tokihiko. "Miura Baien." In *Gakkai no ijin.* Tokyo: Sugimoto Ryōkōdō, 1910.

Nishina Yoshio. "Nihon kagaku no kensetsu." *Gijutsu hyōron* 3 (June 1942): 7–9.

Nishio Takashi. *Nihon shinrin gyōseishi no kenkyū.* Tokyo: Tokyo Daigaku Shuppankai, 1988.

Nitto Shūichi. "Gendai Nihon igakuron: Kinsei Nihon igakushi josetsu." *Kagaku Pen* 5, no. 1 (January 1940): 89–96.

"Nyūkai no susume." *Kōjin,* March 1927: 2.

Ogata Tomio. "Fukkokuban no kankō ni attatte." In *Meiji zen Nihon sūgakushi shinteiban,* ed. Nihon Gakushiin Nihon Kagakushi Kankōkai. Tokyo: Shuppan Kagaku Sōgō Kenkyūjo, 1979.

Oguma Eiji. *"Minshu" to "aikoku": Sengo Nihon no nashonarizumu*. Tokyo: Shin'yōsha, 2002.

——. *"Nihonjin" no kyōkai: Okinawa, Ainu, Taiwan, Chōsen shokuminchi shihai kara fukki undō made*. Tokyo: Shin'yōsha, 1998.

——. *Tan'itsu minzoku shinwa no kigen: "Nihonjin" no jigazō no keifu*. Tokyo: Shin'yōsha, 1995.

Ogura Kinnosuke. "Gen jikyokuka ni okeru kagakusha no sekimu." *Chūō kōron*, April 1941.

——. *Ichi sūgakusha no kaisō*. Tokyo: Chikuma Shobō, 1967.

——. *Kagaku no shihyō*. Tokyo: Chūō Kōronsha, 1946.

——. *Kagakuteki seishin to sūgaku kyōiku*. Tokyo: Iwanami Shoten, 1937.

——. "Kaikyū shakai no sanjutsu: Bungei fukkō jidai no sanjutsu ni kansuru ichi kōsatsu." *Shisō*, August 1929: 1–19.

——. "Kaikyū shakai no sanjutsu: Shokuminchi jidai ni okeru nanboku Amerika no sanjutsu ni kansuru ichi kōsatsu." *Shisō*, December 1929: 1–36.

——. "Kaikyū shakai no sūgaku: Furansu sūgakushi ni kansuru ichi kōsatsu." *Shisō*, March 1930: 1–35.

——. "Kaikyū shakai no sūgaku: Furansu sūgakushi ni kansuru ichi kōsatsu (2)." *Shisō*, May 1930: 25–43.

——. "Kaikyū shakai no sūgaku: Furansu sūgakushi ni kansuru ichi kōsatsu (3)." *Shisō*, June 1930: 1–21.

——. "Sanjutsu no shakaisei." *Shōwa shisōshū*. Ed. Matsuda Michio. Vol. 1. Kindai Nihon shisō taikei, no. 35. Tokyo: Chikuma Shobō, 1974.

——. *Senjika no sūgaku*. Tokyo: Sōgensha, 1944.

——. "Shizen kagakusha no ninmu." *Chūō kōron*, December 1936: 312–15.

——. *Sūgaku kyōiku no konpon mondai*. Tokyo: Tamagawa Gakuen, 1924.

——. *Sūgakusha no kaisō*. Tokyo: Kawade Shobō, 1950.

——. *Sūgakushi kenkyū*. 2 vols. Tokyo: Iwanami Shoten, 1935–48.

——. "Ware kagakusha taru o hazu." *Kaizō*, January 1953. In *NKGT*, vol. 6.

Oka Kunio. "Genzai ni okeru kagakusha no tachiba." *Yuibutsuron kenkyū* 12 (October 1933): 146–56.

——. "Torusutoi no kagakuron." *Yuibutsuron kenkyū* 59 (September 1937): 6–17.

Okabe Susumu. "Kagakushi nyūmon: Sūgakusha Ogura Kinnosuke to genzai." *Kagakushi kenkyū* 34, no. 194 (Summer 1995): 140.

Okada Doichi. "Gijutsukan yūgū to hōka bannō haigeki." *Gijutsu Nihon*, October 1937: 12.

Okazaki Naoki. "Ware ware no mondai." *Kōjin*, March 1927: 35–36.

Ōkōchi Masatoshi. *Moterukuni Nihon*. Tokyo: Kagakushugi Kōgyōsha, 1938.

——. *Nōson no kikai kōgyō*. Tokyo: Kagakushugi Kōgyōsha, 1938.

——. *Nōson no kōgyō*. Tokyo: Iwanami Shoten, 1935.

——. *Shihonshugi kyōgyō to kagakushugi kōgyō*. Tokyo: Kagakushugi Kōgyōsha, 1938.

Ōkubo Toshiaki. *Nihon kindai shigaku no seiritsu*. Tokyo: Yoshikawa Kōbunkan, 1988.

Omi Kōji. "Sekai saikō no kagaku gijutsu suijun no jitsugen ni mukete." *Toki no ugoki*, June 2001: 16.

Ōmori Minoru. "Saigusa Hiroto no Nihon kagaku gijutsushi kenkyū." *Kagakushi kenkyū* 74 (April–June 1965): 49–58.

Ōnuma Masanori, Fujii Yōichirō, and Katō Kunioki. *Sengo Nihon kagakusha undōshi.* Vol. 2. Tokyo: Aoki Gendai Sōsho, 1975.

Osa Shizue. *Kindai Nihon to kokugo nashonarizumu.* Tokyo: Yoshikawa Kōbunkan, 1998.

Ōta Takeo [Ōta Tenrei]. "Minzoku to kokumin." *Yuibutsuron kenkyū* 49 (November 1936): 37–38.

Otabe Yūji. *Tokugawa Yoshichika no jūgonen sensō.* Tokyo: Aoki Shoten, 1988.

Ōya Shin'ichi. "Genban kaidai" and "Kaidai." In *Bunkashijō yori mitaru Nihon no sūgaku.* Tokyo: Kōseisha Kōseikaku, 1974.

Oyanagi Shigeta. "Miura Baien." In *Tōyō shishō no kenkyū.* Tokyo: Seki Shoin, 1935.

Ōyodo Shōichi. *Gijutsu kanryō no seiji sankaku: Nihon no kagaku gijutsu gyōsei no makuaki.* Tokyo: Chūō Kōronsha, 1997.

———. *Miyamoto Takenosuke to kagaku gijutsu gyōsei.* Tokyo: Tōkai Daigaku Shuppankai, 1989.

Plekhanov, Georgi V. *Kaikyūshakai no geijutsu.* Trans. Kurahara Kurehito. Tokyo: Sōbunkaku, 1928.

Saeki Shōichi. "Gunji roman no kisetsu: Shōnen ni ataeta hiroikku na nagare." In *Tokkyū Ajia gō no aika,* vol. 2 of *Shōgen no shōwashi.* Tokyo: Shakai Gakushū Kenkyūsha, 1983.

Saigusa Hiroto. *Baien tetsugaku nyūmon.* Tokyo: Daiichi Shobō, 1943. Reprint, vol. 5 of *Saigusa Hiroto chosakushū.* Tokyo: Chūō kōronsha, 1982.

———. *Gijutsu no shisō.* Tokyo: Daiichi Shobō, 1941.

———. "Gijutsugaku no gurentsugebiito." *Kagakushugi kōgyō* 4 (September 1937): 89.

———. "Hensha no kotoba." In *Nihon bunka no kōsō to genjitsu.* Tokyo: Chuō Kōronsha, 1943.

———. "Nihon kagaku bunmei shisōshi." *Nihon hyōron,* January 1940 (2600th year special edition): 271.

———. *Nihon kagaku koten zensho.* 15 vols. Tokyo: Asahi Shinbunsha, 1942–49.

———. "Nihon ni okeru ishoku kannenron no tokushoku." *Yuibutsuron kenkyū* 11 (September 1933): 5–25.

———. *Nihon no shisō bunka.* Tokyo: Daiichi Shobō, 1937.

———. *Nihon no yuibutsuronsha.* Tokyo: Eihōsha, 1956.

———. "Nihon shisōka sai." *Tokyo asahi shinbun* 18 (March 1937): 14.

———. "Nippon seishin." In *Gendai tetsugaku jiten,* ed. Miki Kiyoshi. Tokyo: Nihon Hyōronsha, 1941.

———. "Nishida tetsugaku no konpon mondai." *Yuibutsuron kenkyū* 18 (April 1934): 5–27.

———. *Saigusa Hiroto chosakushū.* 12 vols. Tokyo: Chūō Kōronsha, 1972–77.

———. "'Shihonron' no yuibutsuronteki kiso." *Yuibutsuron kenkyū* 8 (June 1933): 21–34.

———. "Shin yuibutsuron no tachiba." *Yuibutsuron kenkyū* 1 (1932): 8–27.

———. "Tōa kyōdōtai no ronri." *Chūō kōron* 616 (January 1939): 114–23.

———. "Yuibutsuronsha ha Kanto wo ikani yomuka—Tanabe Hajime kyōju hihan wo fukumu." *Yuibutsuron kenkyū* 3 (January 1933): 12–33.

Sakai Saburō. *Shōwa kenkyūkai: Aru chishikijin shūdan no kiseki.* Tokyo: TBS Buritanika, 1979.

Sakamoto Kenzō. "Saigusa Hiroto shi no gijutsushi hōron." *Kagakushi kenkyū* 74 (April–June 1965): 59–71.

Sakata Tokikazu. "Danpen." *Kōjin,* May 1928: 34–35.

———. "Dansō." *Kōjin,* October 1928: 91.

———. "Kaku hōmen yori yoseraretaru manmō taisaku iken." *Kōjin,* May 1932: 47.

———. "Naniwa yoshie ni kotaete." *Kōjin,* November 1928: 29.

———. "Patoron to nashionarizumu to watashi." *Kōjin,* February 1930: 24–28.

———. "Tsugumi gari." *Kōjin,* February 1931: 27.

Sakuta Shōichi. *Kokumin kagaku no seiritsu.* 2d ed. Tokyo: Nihon Bunka Kyōkai Shuppanbu, 1934.

Sankō Bunken Kondankai, ed. *Shōwa zenki shisō shiryō.* Vol. 1. Tokyo: Bunsei Shoin, 1972.

Sano Hide. "Otto Unno Jūza no omoide." *Unno Jūza shū,* vol. 9 of *Shōnen shōsetsu taikei.* Tokyo: San'ichi Shobō, 1987.

Sasaki Chikara, ed. "Kaisetsu." In *Bunkashijō yori mitaru Nihon no sūgaku,* by Mikami Yoshio. Tokyo: Iwanami Shoten, 1999.

Sasaki Gentarō and Hirakawa Sukehiro, eds. *Tokubetsu kagaku gumi: Tokyo kōshi fuzoku chūgaku no baai.* Tokyo: Daishukan Shoten, 1995.

Satō Akira, ed. *Tokkyū Ajia-gō no aikan.* Vol. 2 of *Shōgen no shōwashi.* Tokyo: Gakushū Kenkyūsha, 1983.

Satō Hiromi. *Sōryokusen taisei to kyōiku kagaku.* Tokyo: Ōtsuki Shoten, 1997.

Sawai Minoru. "Kagaku gijutsu shintaisei kōsō no tenkai to gijutsuin no tanjō." *Osaka Daigaku keizaigaku* 41, nos. 2–3 (1991): 367–95.

Shihōshō Keijikyoku. *Shisō geppō* 1 (July 1936): 5–6. In *Shōwa zenki shisō shiryō,* ed. Sankō Bunken Kondankai, vol. 1. Tokyo: Bunsei shoin, 1972.

Shimomura Ichirō. "Risūka ni tsuite." In *Monbushō kokumin gakkō kyōsokuan setsumei yōkō oyobi kaisetsu,* ed. Nihon Hōsō Kyōkai. Tokyo: Nihon Hōsō Shuppan Kyōkai, 1940. In *NKGT,* 3:235.

Shin konsaisu eiwa jiten. 1922. Reprint, Tokyo: Sanseidō, 1935.

Shindō Muneyuki. *Gijutsu kanryō.* Tokyo: Iwanami Shoten, 2002.

Shinobu Seisaburō. *Taishō demokurashii shi.* Tokyo: Nihon Hyōronsha, 1958.

Shinohara Takeshi. "Kagaku gijutsuron." *Kagaku Pen* 5, no. 2 (February 1940): 6–15.

Shisō no Kagaku Kenkyūkai, ed. *Kyōdō kenkyū: Tenkō.* 3 vols. Reprint, Tokyo: Heibonsha, 1978.

"Shizen kagakusha wa tetsugaku ni taishite nanio yōkyū suruka." *Yuibutsuron kenkyū* 22 (August 1934): 65–70.

Sōritsu Rokujūnen Kinenkai, ed. *Rōdō Kagaku Kenkyūjo rokujūnen shiwa.* Kurashiki: Rōdō Kagaku Kenkyūjo, 1981.

Sugai Jun'ichi. *Kagaku kotohajime.* Tokyo: Ten'nensha, 1946.

Sunouchi Fumio. "Kagaku gijutsu no sekai." *Gijutsu hyōron,* November 1939: 12–17.

Suzuki Umetarō. "Tairiku hatten to kagaku." February 16, 1938. In *NKGT,* 4:324.

Takahashi Saburō. "Jisei to Kōjin Kurabu." *Kōjin,* August 1932: 4–5.

———. "Nihon Kōjin Kurabu sōritsu tōji no omoide o kataru." *Gijutsu Nihon,* April–May 1936: 30.

Takahashi Shin'ichi. "Kagakusha no ninmu." *Kagaku Pen* 5, no. 10 (October 1940): 61–65.

Takahashi Tsuneo. "Shizen kagaku to shakai kagaku no kaikyūsei no mondai ni tsukite." *Kagaku* 3, no. 11 (November 1933): 460–61.

Takanoi Yoshirō. *Nihon no keizaigaku.* Tokyo: Chūō Kōronsha, 1971.

Takase Yoshio. *Kamakura Akademia danshō.* Tokyo: Mainichi Shinbunsha, 1980.

Takeda Harumu. "Kantōgen." *Kōjin*, August 1929: n.p.

Takeuchi Tokio. *Hyakuman'nin no kagaku.* Tokyo: Momoyama Shorin, 1946.

Tanabe Hajime. "Kagaku seisaku no mujun." *Kaizō*, October 1936: 18–34.

———. "Kagakusei no seiritsu." *Bungei shunjū*, September 1937: 50–61.

———. *"Shōbō genzō" no tetsugaku shikan.* Tokyo: Iwanami Shoten, 1939.

Tanaka Satoshi. *Eisei hakurankai no yokubō.* Tokyo: Aoyumisha, 1994.

Terakawa Tomosuke. "Waga kuni ni okeru shotōka rika kyōiku no senkan." In *Rika kyōikugaku*, vol. 21 of *Kyōshoku kagaku kōza.* Tokyo: Fukunura Shuppan, 1990.

Teruoka Gitō. "Sangyō gōrika no mokuteki to gijutsu." *Economist*, April 1930. In *NKGT*, 3:555–58.

"Tetsugakusha wa shizenkagaku naishi shizenkagakusha ni nanio yōkyū suruka." *Yuibutsuron kenkyū* 30 (April 1935): 76–91.

Tokyo Daigakushi Shiryōshitsu, ed. *Tokyo Daigaku no gakuto dōin•gakuto shutsujin.* Tokyo: Tōdai Shuppankai, 1998.

Tokyo Kagaku Hakubtusukan. *Shizen kagaku to hakubutsukan*, 1932–33.

Tomizuka Kiyoshi. *Kagaku Nihon no kensetsu.* Tokyo: Bungei Shunjūsha, 1940.

———. *Kagaku Nihon no kōsō.* Reprint, Tokyo: Sekai Bunka Kyōkai, 1947.

———. "Kagakuteki ni." *Kagaku Pen* 5, no. 9 (September 1940): 181–82.

Tosaka Jun. "Kagakuteki seishin towa nanika." *Yuibutsuron kenkyū* 54 (April 1937): 23–34.

———. "Kikanshi gojūgō kinen no tameni." *Yuibutsuron kenkyū* 50 (December 1936): 128–30.

———. "Minzoku to kokumin: Minshū•jinmin oyobi kokka." *Yuibutsuron kenkyū* 49 (November 1936): 33–34.

———. *Nippon ideorogii ron.* 1935. Reprint, Tokyo: Iwanami Shoten, 1997.

———. "Shakai ni okeru shizen kagaku no yakuwari." *Yuibutsuron kenkyū* 1 (November 1932): 28–48.

Tsuchiya Gensaku. "Miura Baien no gengaku." In *Shingaku no senku.* Osaka:Tsuchiya Gensaku; Tokyo: Hatsubai Hakubunkan, 1912.

Tsuge Hidemi. "Kenkyūshitsu gaikan, shanhai shizen kagaku kenkyūjo." *Kagaku*, November 1937: 565.

Tsuji Kiyoaki. *Nihon kanryōsei no kenkyū.* 1969. Reprint, Tokyo: Tokyo Daigaku Shuppankai, 1981.

Tsuji Tetsuo. *Nihon no kagaku shisō: Sono jiritsu e no mosaku.* 1973. Reprint, Tokyo: Chūō Kōrosnsha, 1993.

Tsuneyoshi Ken'ichi. *Kieta saikin butai.* Tokyo: Kaimeisha, 1981.

Tsurumi Shunsuke. "Senji ha isshoku dewa nai, soshite imamo." In *Bessatsu Taiyō Kodomo no shōwashi.* 1986. Reprint, Tokyo: Heibonsha, 1996.

Uchida Hoshimi. "Gijutsu seisaku no rekishi." In *Kindai Nihon no gijutsu to gijutsu seisaku.* Tokyo: Tokyo Daigaku Shuppankai, 1986.

Uchino Masao. "Kaku hōmen yori yoseraretaru manmō taisaku iken." *Kōjin*, May 1932: 45.

———. "Sangyō gōrika to ikani kaishaku subekika." *Kōjin*, May 1930: 32–36.

Ueda Masafumi. "Shimin no tame no kagaku to kagaku gijutsu kihonhō." *Kagaku* 69 (March 1999): 273–78.

Ueda Shigeru. "Nihon Gijutsu Kyōkai ni tsuite." *Gijutsu Nihon*, November–December 1936: 18–19.

Umeda Kinji. "Minshushugi Kagakusha Kyōkai sōritsu gojūnen ni yosete." *Rekishi hyōron* 549 (January 1996): 74.

Unno Jūza. "Kaitei tairiku." *Kodomo no kagaku*, 1937–38.

———. *Ukabu hikōtō*. 1944. Reprint, Tokyo: Kōdansha, 1975.

Unno Jūza sensō shōsetsu kessakushū. Tokyo: Chūō Kōron Shinsha, 2004.

Unno Jūza shū. Tokyo: Riburo Shuppan, 1997.

Unno Jūza shū. Tokyo: Chikuma Shobō, 2001.

Unno Jūza zenshū. 12 vols. Tokyo: San'ichi Shobō, 1988–93.

Wada Toshihiko. "Sōkan ni saishite goaisatsu." *Kagaku gijutsu*, January 1942: 132.

Watanabe Masao. *Bunka to shiteno kindai kagaku*. Tokyo: Kōdansha, 2000.

———. *Kindai kagaku to kirisuto kyō*. Tokyo: Kōdansha, 1987.

Yajima Suketoshi. "'Kagaku bungaku' sonota." *Yuibutsuron kenkyū* 23 (September 1934): 48–62.

Yajima Toshinori. *Kagakuteki danpen*. Tokyo: Rigakusha, 1948.

Yamamoto Haruo. "Soveeto dōmei no shizen kagaku." *Yuibutsuron kenkyū* 12 (October 1933): 165–70.

Yamazaki Toshio. "Kōgyō chitai no keisei to shakai seisaku." In *NKGT*, 3:305–7.

Yanabu Akira. *Ichigo no jiten: Bunka*. Tokyo: Sanseidō, 1995.

Yanagi Sonji. "Sangyō gōrika to rōshi mondai." *Kōjin*, May 1930: 27–31.

Yata Yoshiaki. "Jikyoku to gijutsu." *Gijutsu Nihon*, December 1937: 26.

"Yo no kanji shoku ni tsuite." *Kōjin*, February 1932: 39.

Yokota Jun'ya. *Meiji "kūsō shōsetsu" korekushon*. Tokyo: PHP Kenkyūjo, 1995.

———. *Meiji wandaa kagakukan*. Tokyo: Jasuto Sisutemu, 1997.

———. *Nihon SF koten koten*. Vols. 1–3. Tokyo: Hayakawa Shobō, 1981.

Yoshimi Shun'ya. *Hakurankai no seijigaku: Manazashi no kindai*. Tokyo: Chūō Kōronsha, 1992.

———. *"Koe" no shihonshugi: Denwa, rajio, chikuonki no shakaishi*. Tokyo: Kōdansha, 1995.

Yoshino Hiroshi. "Yuiken no yane no shitani." *Yuibutsuron kenkyū fukkokuban geppō*, no. 7:6.

Yoshioka Shūichirō. "Nihon sūgakushi." *Kagaku Pen* 5, no. 1 (January 1940): 28–36.

Yuibutsuron kenkyū. 1932–38.

Yuibutsuron kenkyū fukkokuban geppō. 1972–75.

Zen Nihon Kagaku Gijutsu Dantai Rengōkai. "Kagaku gijutsu shintaisei ni kansuru seimei." *Kagakushugi kōgyō*, July 1941: 2–5.

Index

Taishō period, 3, 76, 89, 136; democracy
during, 6, 27, 28, 29, 30, 37, 90, 175, 183,
198n76, 231n32; liberal education reform
movement during, 8, 9, 71, 78–79, 144,
145, 147, 171, 177; vs. Meiji period, 15,
77–78; print mass media in, 143, 148
Taiwan, 3, 122, 154, 155, 156, 199n16,
228n138, 229n13
Takada Giichirō, 225n85
Takahashi Korekiyo, 110
Takahashi Yoshizō, 209n5
Takamine Jōkichi, 14
Takanoi Yoshirō, 206n31
Takayanagi Kenjiro, 222n45
Takeda Harumu, 35, 189n1
Takeda Pharmaceutical, 192n31
Takeuchi Yoshimi, 11, 189n1, 191n18, 230n17
Tanabe Hajime: "A Contradiction in Science
Policies," 111–14, 115, 116; vs. Hashida,
114, 115, 116, 214n89; on Japanese spirit,
113–14, 116; on overlearning argument,
111–13, 116; relationship with Nishida,
213n85; on scientific spirit, 111–13, 115,
116, 118; during wartime, 213n85
Tanahashi Gentarō, 147, 220n19
Tanakadate Aikitsu, 77–78, 109
Tanaka Satoshi, 220n19
Tanizu Naohide, 209n5
Taylor, Frederick, 194n5
*Teacher's Manual for the Observation of Nature,
The*, 169, 171, 228n136
technocracy, 197n67, 199n1; as alternative to
Marxism, 20, 28, 41–42, 92–93; defined,
20, 24, 25–27, 28, 35, 92; in European
Union, 20, 194n4; as mediation of
labor-capital conflict, 24, 25, 28, 35–36,
53–54, 68, 92; and New Order for
Science-Technology, 63, 68; and planned
economy, 53–54; in United States, 20, 35,
193nn2,3, 194n5
technocrats/technology-bureaucrats
(*gijutsu kanryō*): on basic science, 44,
54; civil engineers as, 19, 23; and class
consciousness, 6, 19–20, 24, 25, 28–42,
196n31; as creators, 24–25, 27–28, 46–47,
109; on definition of science, 5, 6–7,
11, 19, 20, 41–42, 43, 44, 60–64, 68, 71,
92, 119–20, 134, 140, 190n12, 199n2;
Diet representation for, 24, 25, 28, 34;
disillusion with party politics among,

37; on education, 41–42; as gikan, 23;
and law-bureaucrats, 6, 11, 19, 22–23,
25, 34, 40–41, 44, 47–48, 51, 52–53,
56, 60, 61, 65–66, 194nn12,14, 198n85;
and Manchurian resources, 43, 44,
45–50, 51–52, 57, 92, 162, 199nn11,16;
vs. Marxists, 11, 20, 41, 42, 61, 68, 71,
72, 92–93, 119–20, 140; and New Order
for Science-Technology, 7, 43, 44, 60,
63–68; phrase *kagaku gijutsu* coined by, 5,
6, 44, 53, 67; vs. popular science writers,
8–9, 11, 143–44; on science-technology,
5, 6–7, 19, 43–44, 53, 60–68, 119–20,
130, 134, 139, 140, 160–61, 162, 171, 175,
178, 187, 199n2, 203nn72,84; scientific
expertise of, 19–20, 36; on social sciences,
7, 44, 60–61, 72, 92; on technological
patriotism (*gitjutsu hōkoku*), 43, 52–53,
55–56, 57–59, 162, 181, 201n42, 202n69,
204n90; and trade unionism, 6–7, 13,
19–20, 24, 25, 28, 30, 33, 34–35, 36–37,
38, 41, 50; during World War I, 22, 23;
after World War II, 178, 193n1; during
World War II (after 1937), 11, 43, 52–53,
55–56, 57–68, 139, 162, 171, 178, 181, 187,
201n42, 202n69, 204n90; and zaibatsu, 51.
See also Miyamoto Takenosuke
technology: defined, 24, 25–26, 28, 78,
195n22, 196n32; Marxists on, 26–27, 28,
133–35, 196n32; relationship to art, 25–26,
195nn22,24,26
Technology Agency, 64, 67, 68, 92, 174,
195n24
tenkō, 38, 50, 135, 191n19, 197n72
Tenkō kaibatsu, 133–34
Terada Torahiko, 101
Terakawa Tomosuke, 228n141
Teruoka Gitō, 40
Thackray, Arnold, 204n5
Tōjō Hideki, 51, 110
Tokugawa Institute for Biological Research,
193n31
Tokugawa period, 2, 204n93; *giri ninjō*
during, 123; mathematics (*wasan*) during,
85, 87–93, 137, 139, 208nn56,69; Museum
of Science/Science of Edo exhibition,
95–97, 100; national seclusion policy
during, 189n5; science during, 8, 85,
87–93, 95–97, 100, 119–20, 124, 126–30,
137, 138, 139, 140, 221n27